STEPS IN COMPOSITION

STEPS IN COMPOSITION

FOURTH EDITION

LYNN QUITMAN TROYKA
JERROLD NUDELMAN

Queensborough Community College
of the City University of New York

PRENTICE-HALL, Englewood Cliffs, New Jersey 07632

Library of Congress Cataloging-in-Publication Data

Troyka, Lynn Quitman (date)
Steps in composition.

Includes index.
1. English language—Rhetoric. 2. College readers.
3. English language—Grammar—1950– I. Nudelman,
Jerrold II. Title.
PE1408.T697 1986 808′.042 85-19352
ISBN 0-13-847005-7

Editorial/production supervision: Barbara Alexander
Interior design: Rita Kaye Schwartz
Cover design: Ben Santora
Manufacturing buyer: Harry P. Baisley

Printed in the United States of America

10 9 8 7 6 5

ISBN 0-13-847005-7 01

Prentice-Hall International (UK) Limited, *London*
Prentice-Hall of Australia Pty. Limited, *Sydney*
Prentice-Hall of Canada Inc., *Toronto*
Prentice-Hall Hispanoamericana, S.A., *Mexico*
Prentice-Hall of India Private Limited, *New Delhi*
Prentice-Hall of Japan, Inc., *Tokyo*
Prentice-Hall of Southeast Asia Pte. Ltd., *Singapore*
Editora Prentice-Hall do Brasil, Ltda., *Rio de Janeiro*
Whitehall Books Limited, *Wellington, New Zealand*

To our parents

BELLE AND SIDNEY QUITMAN
FRANCES AND HENRY NUDELMAN

who taught us our first steps
and who have encouraged us ever since.

one

two

three

four

five

six

seven

eight

nine

ten

eleven

twelve

PREFACE

This Fourth Edition of *Steps in Composition*, a revision of our Alternate Second Edition, continues to reflect our conviction that writing is a lively, engaging activity. Our approach to teaching writing is practical and upbeat, with these essential elements:

- timely visuals to elicit responses as each chapter begins;
- contemporary, thought-provoking essays on the same theme as the visuals, to stimulate thinking;
- full coverage of basic grammar, rhetoric, mechanics, vocabulary building, and spelling;
- jargon-free explanations and clear examples;
- frequent "Try It Out" mini-exercises throughout the instructional material, to help students reinforce their learning as they go along;
- exercises sequenced from basic practice to participatory applications, a research-based progression that transfers well to actual writing;
- informative, entertaining exercise content, including news items with universal themes and interesting facts, to keep student interest high;
- extensive lists of topics for writing both paragraphs and essays.

As always in our successive editions of *Steps in Composition*, our revisions reflect the best new trends in our field. New features in this fourth edition include:

- "The Writing Process" to take students from planning to proofreading;
- "Prewriting Techniques" to guide students through five strategies that help writers think of ideas and get started;
- "Pronoun Choice" and "Pronoun Reference and Consistency" to expand our treatment of the pronoun, along with an updated section on "Pronoun Agreement";
- a comprehensive discussion of proofreading for the plural *-s*, to focus on this elusive skill;

- complete coverage of *a, an,* and *and,* three common words that today's students often confuse.

We retain most features added in our previous revisions, and we continue to use the same chapter organization and instructional framework, one that offers an integration of writing instruction with reading, vocabulary building, and spelling. All twelve chapters continue to feature:

Springboards to Thinking: Photographs, cartoons, and advertisements—with stimulating questions—get students' thinking started on the contemporary issue that forms each chapter's theme. In this edition, themes range from television's effects on people to the meaning of an I.Q., from problems of the elderly to troubled teenagers, from why people are rude to what is happening to honesty. Over three-quarters of the visuals are new for this fourth edition.

Essay: Lively discussions of thought-provoking topics focus on each chapter's theme. Seven of the twelve essays are new. Authors in this fourth edition include Isaac Asimov, Pete Hamill, Ruth Winter, Stacia Robbins, William Safire, Neil Postman, and Joan Libman.

Reading Survey: Questions center on main ideas, major details, inferences, and opinion. This sequence is designed to move students toward critical reading skills by leading them from literal meaning to inferential reasoning to evaluative thinking.

Vocabulary Building: Words taken from each chapter's essay are clustered around each chapter's theme. In this fourth edition, students learn and practice, for example, the vocabulary of today's fast-paced life, of growing old, of stress, of social standards. Fourteen of the lessons are new for this fourth edition. Simple, functional definitions are given within a context, and exercises encourage inductive thinking. For supplementary practice or quizzes, our *Instructor's Guide* offers additional exercises for all lessons.

Spelling: Lists of spelling demons, challenging words taken from each chapter's essay, are followed by a lesson on a spelling rule or pattern. Most exercises, new for this fourth edition, are modeled after a variety of brain teasers such as crossword, scrambled-letter, and fill-in puzzles which force students to look at each letter in a word.

Key Steps in Grammar or Rhetoric: These sections, the heart of each chapter, cover skill areas central to successful writing. For ease of reference, a gray border along the trim edge of the book sets off this material. Clear, functional explanations are used while complicated terminology and minor rules are avoided. Spaced throughout are brief "Try It Out" exercises to reinforce learning in smaller steps than the chapter's culminating exercises permit. To enhance transfer from exercise to writing, the exercise sequence provides participatory experiences. That is, never do students merely put checkmarks next to correct answers; instead, students complete, rewrite, create, or otherwise become directly involved with the skill. In this fourth edition, all but a few exercises have new content. A collection of additional exercises on all key grammar topics can be found in our *Instructor's Guide* for use as supplementary practice or quizzes. The grammatical and rhetorical skills included in this text are:

- using the writing process and prewriting strategies;
- writing effective topic sentences;
- developing paragraphs with full details and in logical order;
- writing mature, rich sentences rather than sentence fragments, comma splices, or run-ons;
- using correct verb forms;
- using pronouns correctly;
- applying paragraph principles to the expository essay—with special attention to introductory and concluding paragraphs;
- using all marks of punctuation correctly;
- writing a unified essay;
- using the right word;
- using parallelism and other techniques of sentence logic;
- writing three of the most frequently assigned types of expository essays: explaining a process, constructing a definition, and arguing an opinion.

The order in this text is flexible. Chapters can be used in whatever sequence suits personal needs and preferences. Material can be omitted, rearranged, or added without interfering with underlying pedagogical principles.

Refresher: This final exercise of the chapter, derived from the chapter's theme, invites students to apply their learning acquired in this and previous chapters. This exercise is given in a student's handwriting to symbolize the need for correction.

Springboards to Writing: This long list of suggested topics for paragraphs and essays is based on each chapter's theme. Presented in the context of the writing process, the topics offer students the opportunity to explore their thinking as well as to practice their skills.

To supplement this new edition, we have revised our comprehensive *Instructor's Guide* to include: additional exercises for all vocabulary and key grammar sections of the text; information about how teachers can best use the Reading Survey sections; a collection of recommended teaching techniques and teacher-designed classroom materials; an extensive list of audio-visual materials that can enliven a composition class; and an answer key for all exercises in the text and the *Guide*. For the first time, our *Instructor's Guide* is in an 8½″ x 11″ format so that teachers easily can photocopy material for class use.

As has been the tradition with *Steps in Composition*, another edition of the text always will be kept in print to offer instructors alternate contents but the same format and approach.

In writing the Fourth Edition, we had invaluable moral and practical support from David Troyka; and we benefited greatly from the generous help and advice of many of our colleagues, especially Emily Gordon, Alvin Schlosser, and Myra Kogen. We appreciated the pre-revision and final-manuscript reviews by Rosanna Grassi of Syracuse University, John Igo of San Antonio College, Judith Lampert of San Antonio College, and James E. O'Malley of Triton College. At Prentice-Hall, we were privileged to be associated with Phil Miller, English Editor, who was ready always to advise and assist wisely; Barbara Alexander, our Production Editor, who gave our project much patient, talented attention and Ilene McGrath, who not only copyedited our work but also advised us well. Each person has understood and facilitated our goal of creating a text that respects students and that seeks to help them fulfill their potentials as writers.

Lynn Quitman Troyka
Jerrold Nudelman

New York, 1986

STEPS IN COMPOSITION

"To start with, gentlemen, I just want to say that if at times I strike you as being strange or weird or something, or whatever, it's because I'm probably the first member of this board to grow up with television."

one

These programs are getting so ridiculous, childish and moronic! For the life of me I don't know why I enjoy them!

From The Wall Street Journal—Permission, Cartoon Features Syndicate.

SPRINGBOARDS TO THINKING

For informal, not written, response . . . to stimulate your thinking

1. Look at the cartoon on the opposite page. What reasons might the speaker have for thinking that he may seem "strange or weird" because he grew up with television?
2. Look at the cartoon above. What explanation would you give the woman to help her understand why she enjoys television shows in spite of her opinion of them?
3. Do you watch television? Why or why not? Based on your experience or on comments that you have heard about television, what is your opinion of today's television programs? Explain.
4. What effects does television watching have on today's children? On today's adults? On today's family life? Explain.
5. If television broadcasting stopped, what do you think people would do with the time that they now spend watching television? Would those activities be better or worse for the people? For society? Explain.

The Tube Syndrome

PETE HAMILL

(1) The year his son turned 14, Maguire noticed that the boy was getting dumber. This was a kid who had learned to talk at 14 months, could read when he was 4, was an A student for his first six years in school. The boy was bright, active and imaginative. And then, slowly, the boy's brain began to deteriorate. "He started to slur words," Maguire told me. "He couldn't finish sentences. He usually didn't hear me when I talked to him and couldn't answer me clearly when he did. In school, the A's became B's, and the B's became C's. I thought maybe it was something physical, and I had a doctor check him out. He was perfectly normal. Then the C's started to become D's. Finally, he started failing everything. Worse, the two younger kids were repeating the pattern. From bright to dumb in a few short years."

(2) Maguire was then an account executive in a major advertising agency; his hours were erratic, the pace of his business life often frantic. But when he would get home at night and talk to his wife about the kids, she would shake her head in a baffled way and explain that she was doing her best. Hustling from the office of one account to another, Maguire pondered the creeping stupidity of his children. Then he took an afternoon off from work and visited his oldest boy's school.

(3) "They told me he just wasn't doing much work," Maguire said. "He owed them four book reports. He never said a word in social studies. His mind wandered; he was distracted; he asked to leave the room a lot. But the teacher told me he wasn't much different from all of the other kids. In some ways, he was better. He at least did some work. Most of them, she told me, didn't do any work at all." Maguire asked the teacher if she had any theories about why the kids behaved this way. "Of course," she said. "Television."

(4) Television? Maguire was staggered. He made his living off television. Often he would sit with the kids in the TV room and point out the commercials he had helped to create. Television had paid for his house in the suburbs, for his two cars, his clothes, his food, the pictures on the walls. It even paid for the kids' schools.

"What do you mean, television?" he said.

"Television rots minds," the teacher said flatly. "But most of us figure there's nothing to be done about it anymore."

(5) At work the next day, Maguire told his secretary to do some special research for him. Within a week, he had some scary numbers on his desk.

The Scholastic Aptitude Tests (SATs) showed that the reading scores of all American high school students had fallen in every year since 1950, the year of television's great national triumph.* The math scores were even worse. The average American kid spent four to six hours a day watching television, and by age 16 had witnessed 11,000 homicides on the tube.

(6) "I came home that night, and the kids were watching television with my wife," he said. "I looked at them, glued to the set. They nodded hello to me. And suddenly I got scared. I imagined these four people, their brains rotted out, suddenly adding me to the evening's homicide count because I wanted them to talk to me. I went to the bedroom and for the first time since college, I took down *Moby Dick* and started to read."

(7) In the following week, Maguire accumulated more and more ideas about the impact of television on the lives of Americans. All classes and colors had been affected intellectually; reading requires the decoding of symbols, the transforming of a word like "cat" into a cat that lives in the imagination. Television shows the cat. No active thought is required. Television even supplies a laugh track and music to trigger the emotions the imagination will not create or release.

(8) "I read somewhere that the worst danger to kids who become TV addicts is that while they are watching TV, they're not doing anything else," Maguire said. "They're not down in the schoolyard, playing ball, or falling in love, or getting in fights, or learning to compromise. They're alone, with a box that doesn't hear them if they want to talk back. They don't have to think, because everything is done for them. They don't have to question, because what's the point if you can't challenge the guy on the set?"

(9) Television had also changed politics; Maguire's kids had political opinions based on the way candidates looked, and how they projected themselves theatrically. Politics, which should be based on the structure of analysis and thought, had become dominated by the structures of drama; that is to say, by conflict. "I knew Reagan would win in a landslide," Maguire said. "As an actor, he fit right into the mass culture formed by 30 years of television."

(10) Maguire tried to do something. He called a family conference after dinner one night, explained his discoveries, suggested a voluntary limiting of television watching, or its complete elimination for three months. "I said we could start a reading program together," he told me. "All read the same book and discuss it at night. I told them we'd come closer together, that I'd even change my job so I could be home more, and not work on television commercials any more." After ten minutes the kids began to squirm and yawn, as if expecting a commercial. Maguire's wife dazed out, her disconsolate face an unblinking mask. He gave up. Now, when he goes home, Maguire says hello, eats dinner and retreats to his bedroom. He is reading his way through Balzac.†

* Recently the SAT scores leveled off and even rose slightly; future trends are uncertain.
† Balzac was a nineteenth-century French author of short stories and novels.

(11) Lost in the 19th century, his mind teeming with unfaithful women, reckless nihilists, secret passages, voracious businessmen, Maguire is sometimes happy. Beyond the bedroom door, bathed in the cold light of the television set, are the real people in his life. Their dumbness grows, filling up the room, moving out into the quiet suburban town, joining the great gray fog that has enveloped America.

READING SURVEY

1. *Main Idea*

What is the central theme of this essay?

2. *Major Details*

a. Why did Maguire take time off from work to visit his oldest son's school?
b. What was revealed by the special research that Maguire asked his secretary to do?
c. What happened when Maguire tried to convince his family to limit their television watching so that they could spend time reading and talking about the same books?

3. *Inferences*

a. Read paragraph 4 again. Why have most teachers reached the conclusion that there is nothing to be done anymore about the problem that "television rots minds"?
b. Read paragraph 11 again. Explain Pete Hamill's comment, "Maguire is sometimes happy."

4. *Opinions*

a. Do you think television causes people's minds to become "rotted out" (paragraph 6)? Why or why not?
b. What was your experience as a child with television? How do you think television hurt you, if at all? How do you think television helped you, if at all?

VOCABULARY BUILDING

Lesson One: The Vocabulary of Today's Fast-Paced Life, Part I

The essay "The Tube Syndrome" by Pete Hamill includes words that are useful when you are discussing today's fast-paced life.

syndrome	(title)
deteriorate	(paragraph 1)
erratic	(2)
pace	(2)
frantic	(2)
baffled	(2)
hustling	(2)
distracted	(3)
staggered	(4)
impact	(7)

When people are always rushing, their behavior often reveals a **syndrome**—a collection of symptoms or characteristics that indicate a specific disease or abnormal condition—of impatience and nervousness.

When people are always rushing, the quality of their work or their personal lives can **deteriorate,** which means the quality begins to lessen or decay.

When people are always rushing, their behavior is often **erratic,** in that it varies greatly, it is irregular, and at times it may be somewhat strange.

When people are always rushing, they live at a fast **pace** in that the speed or rate at which they do things is fast.

When people are always rushing, they sometimes become **frantic** or wild with worry, anger, or fear.

When people are always rushing, they can become **baffled** easily because they can quickly become confused, bewildered, or puzzled.

When people are always rushing, they are often **hustling** or hurrying about energetically.

When people are always rushing, they can appear to be **distracted** in that their attention is drawn away from the present to other things on their mind.

When people are always rushing, they may suddenly feel **staggered,** as if hit, when they suddenly feel great surprise or shock about something important that happens.

When people are always rushing, their lifestyles have an **impact** or strong effect on everything they do.

EXERCISE 1a: Each of the vocabulary words from this lesson is shown below (in italics) as the word appeared in the essay. Write an explanation of each word within the context of the material given. Use your own paper for this assignment.

1. From title: "The Tube *Syndrome.*"
2. From paragraph 1: "And then, slowly, the boy's brain began to *deteriorate.*"
3. From paragraph 2: ". . . his hours were *erratic,* the *pace* of his business life often *frantic.*"
4. From paragraph 2: ". . . she would shake her head in a *baffled* way. . . ."
5. From paragraph 2: "*Hustling* from the office of one account to another. . . ."
6. From paragraph 3: "His mind wandered, he was *distracted.* . . ."
7. From paragraph 4: "Television? Maguire was *staggered.*"
8. From paragraph 7: ". . . Maguire accumulated more and more ideas about the *impact* of television on the lives of Americans."

Lesson Two: The Vocabulary of Today's Fast-Paced Life, Part II

Here are more words from the essay "The Tube Syndrome" by Pete Hamill that are useful when you are discussing today's fast-paced life.

trigger	(paragraph 7)	**disconsolate**	(10)
compromise	(8)	**teeming**	(11)
analysis	(9)	**reckless**	(11)
dominated	(9)	**nihilists**	(11)
conflict	(9)	**voracious**	(11)

Today's fast-paced life can **trigger** or set into motion problems that result from too much rushing.

Today's fast-paced life calls for people to **compromise** or give up some demands in order to settle their difficulties with one another.

Today's fast-paced life leaves little time for **analysis** or examining ideas by breaking them into parts for close and careful evaluation.

Today's fast-paced life can become **dominated** or controlled and overpowered by the need for haste.

Today's fast-paced life can lead to **conflict** or sharp disagreements or fights over differing interests or ideas.

Today's fast-paced life can make people **disconsolate** or so unhappy that they cannot be comforted or cheered up.

Today's fast-paced life is usually **teeming** or actively crowded with responsibilities and pressures.

Today's fast-paced life can lead to **reckless** or extremely careless behavior.

Today's fast-paced life sometimes leads people to become **nihilists** or believers in the political philosophy that the existing social system must be completely destroyed to make way for a new system.

Today's fast-paced life can make people become **voracious** or hugely greedy and unable to satisfy their desires.

EXERCISE 1b: Using the vocabulary words in this lesson, fill in the blanks.

1. Speeding, passing red lights, and tailgating are considered _________________ driving.
2. The World Series _________________ the interest of most baseball fans last week.
3. The piranha is a dangerous fresh-water fish known for its _________________ appetite for eating flesh.
4. The beaches were _________________ with bathers eager to escape the heat of the city.
5. The laboratory must make a chemical _________________ of the poisoned food.
6. In order to avoid a strike, the union and the management had to _________________ on the wage increase issue.
7. Hunger and high unemployment are all that are needed to _________________ civil disorder or rebellion.
8. A band of armed _________________ are attempting to destroy the established political system in that country.
9. A severe illness can often make a person so _________________ that he or she does not have enough will to recuperate.
10. The recent political debate was more of a personal _________________ than a discussion of the issues.

Name: ______________________ Date: ______________

SPELLING

Lesson One: Spelling Demons

These commonly used words are frequently misspelled. You should give some special attention to the Spelling Demons in this and every chapter. The Demons listed below are taken from "The Tube Syndrome."

advertising	**create**	**paid**
analysis	**describe**	**perfectly**
another	**different**	**physical**
become	**everything**	**political**
business	**finally**	**symbol**
candidate	**imagination**	**theory**
challenge	**minutes**	**thought**
commercial	**opinion**	**tried**

Lesson Two: Methods to Improve Your Spelling

Although there are no particular rules to help you learn the Demons, there are some helpful techniques for memorizing these words and any others that you find troublesome. Read each of these technique suggestions and then try each one out for yourself. Through practice, become skilled at using the techniques you favor. You will benefit greatly.

I KEEP AN INDIVIDUAL SPELLING LIST. Use either the chart in Appendix IV of this book or the last page of a notebook for your spelling list. Each time you misspell a word, add it to the list. Go back over these words in your spare time; it may be during lunch time or on the bus in the morning. The point is to make your word study a habit. After you have about fifteen words on your list, look at the types of errors you consistently make. Most people make certain kinds of spelling mistakes, and you can probably diagnose your particular kind: it could be double letters, or vowels (using an *i* for an *e* and vice versa), or vowel combinations, or confusion of *v* and *f*. If a clear pattern of kinds of mistakes is not obvious, ask your instructor to take a look. Sometimes another observer can see tendencies that you might miss.

II ENLARGE THE TROUBLE SPOT. If you forget the *d* in *knowledge,* then enlarge the *d* when you write the word on your spelling list. Do the same with the *c* in *conscious* as a reminder of your trouble spot.

knowleDge consCious

III USE THE DICTIONARY. When you write, keep a dictionary nearby so you can quickly look up any problem words that you may want to use. It is important to find the correct spelling of a word *before* you actually write it; each time that you write a word incorrectly, you reinforce the misspelling in your mind. Some students complain, "I need to know how to spell the word in order to find it in the dictionary, so what's the use?" Actually, you usually have a fairly good idea of how to spell the problem word: the confusion is centered in just one or two syllables—not the whole word. Thus, the search is not that difficult. When you look at the word, note that it is separated into syllables, so it should be easy for you to see clearly the part that was causing you trouble. After you have looked up a word often enough, you will find that you have learned to spell it and do not need to look it up again.

IV LEARN THE PROPER PRONUNCIATION. Many words are misspelled because they are pronounced incorrectly. If you omit letters from words when you say them—such as quan*t*ity and proba*b*ly—you are sure to do the same when you write them. If you add an *e* to *athletic* and *disastrous* when you speak, you will add the *e* when you write. Pronouncing *children* as *childern* will lead to writing it the same way. When you are not sure of how a word is pronounced, listen to it carefully whenever you hear it. Check the pronunciation in the dictionary or, if you are still not crystal clear on the pronunciation of certain words, ask someone you can trust.

V DIVIDE THE WORD INTO PARTS. Identify compound words, roots, suffixes, and prefixes. Then divide the word into smaller parts that are easier to spell. For example, *knowledge* could be divided into "know" and "ledge." *Considerably* can be divided into "consider" and "ably."

VI USE FLASHCARDS. Instead of using a spelling list, you may prefer to use the flashcard method. Write the troublesome word—in large letters—on one side of a 3″ × 5″ index card. Concentrate on the word for a few minutes, and then turn the card over. When you can visualize the word on the blank side of the card, you have mastered it. As an alternate method, use one side of an index card for the word and the other side for its definition. When you want to study the word, first read the definition; then spell the word that goes with it, and turn the card over to check your spelling.

VII USE MEMORY TRICKS. Sometimes it is helpful to use little memory tricks to learn a word. To memorize *business* you might remember that bu*sin*ess is no sin. You would surely remember to put the *w* in *knowledge* if you realized that a person with knowledge must kno*w* a great deal. To memorize *stationery* remember that paper is station*e*ry and that you st*a*nd still when you are station*a*ry.

EXERCISE 1c: Follow the directions for each item. Each Spelling Demon given in this chapter should be used only once.

1. In each of the following Demons, circle the letter or letters that are likely to cause you trouble. Then recopy the word in the space provided, enlarging the trouble spot so that it stands out as a reminder.

   a. paid ______________ d. thought ______________

   b. symbol ______________ e. opinion ______________

   c. tried ______________ f. physical ______________

2. Each of the following Demons contains one or more smaller words in its spelling. Using one of these smaller words and the original Demon, compose a sentence that will help you to associate the two.

   Example: *court*esy We must show *court*esy in court.

   a. everything ______________

   b. create ______________

   c. become ______________

   d. another ______________

   e. candidate ______________

   f. theory ______________

   g. minutes ______________

3. With the aid of a dictionary, divide these Demons into syllables.

   a. advertising ______________ d. describe ______________

   b. imagination ______________ e. perfectly ______________

   c. political ______________ f. analysis ______________

4. Five of the Demons in this spelling lesson have double letters in them. Write them here and either circle or enlarge any letter(s) that seem to be difficult.

   ______________ ______________

   ______________ ______________

   ____

 Name: ______________ *Date:* ______________

EXERCISE 1d: Unscramble the letters in parentheses to form the missing words in the following paragraph. If necessary, check your spelling with the list of Spelling Demons in this chapter.

Computer technology is now being used to (TEEACR) ______________ many new features that will soon be (RITED) ______________ in that (BOLYMS) ______________ of American inventiveness, the television set. As manufacturers (RIBESCED) ______________ them, these "super sets" will have a (ECTERFPLY) ______________ sharp picture. Thus, while watching (AIPD)______________ (CALITIPOL) ______________ (ISADINGVERT) ______________, the viewer will be able to see even the tiniest beads of perspiration forming on the forehead of the (DIDCANEAT) ______________ as he or she states an important (IONINOP) ______________. Then by pushing a special button, the viewer will be able to zoom in on the smallest (SIPHYCAL) ______________ details in the picture, leaving nothing to the (GINIONIMAAT) ______________. (THANERO) ______________ device will divide the screen into as many as nine (FFENTDIER) ______________ mini-screens so that the viewer can enjoy the (LLGEENCHA) ______________ of watching many channels at the same time. (LLAYFIN) ______________, a button will start a printed (SISALYAN) ______________ of the day's (ESSINBUS) ______________ news, which will run for several (NUTMIES) ______________ along the bottom of the screen. Working with the (ORTHEY) ______________ that viewers want to (BOMEEC) ______________ armchair television directors, manufacturers have (GHTOUTH) ______________ of just about (INGERYTHEV) ______________ —except a device that will automatically eliminate the (MMIALCOERCS) ______________.

Name: ______________________________ Date: ______________________

The Writing Process

You will be writing many paragraphs and essays in college, both for your English classes and for your other subjects. When you write, your goal is to get your message across to your reader as effectively as possible. To achieve this goal, you will benefit from understanding that *writing is a process.* The writing process consists of specific steps that help all writers, including professional writers, produce writing that is clear, correct, and interesting to read.

Writing involves much more then your taking a pen in hand and expecting words to flow perfectly onto paper. Most professional writers plan, write, and rewrite many drafts of a piece of writing before they can consider it finished. As a student writer, you can expect that many of your writing assignments will demand similar amounts of time and patience.

☞ *Try It Out*

Drawing upon your previous experiences in writing for class, think about the steps you usually go through from the time you are given an assignment until the time you hand it in. List your steps as completely as you can. Use your own paper for this assignment.

Experts who have studied what people do when they write have found that the writing process usually consists of five steps. Here they are, as they apply to writing assignments, whether you have chosen your own topic or the topic has been assigned.

FIVE-STEP WRITING PROCESS

STEP 1: *Prewriting.* In this step, you think and plan for your writing. To do this, you explore your ideas about your topic, gather additional information, and begin to organize your material. For help, see Prewriting Techniques, pages 15–20.

Step 2: *Drafting.* In this step, you write using the ideas and plans you developed during your prewriting. You also refine your organization into a structure suitable for a paragraph or an essay. Here you are involved with the content of your ideas, not with your grammar, punctuation, or spelling. Now you have a first draft.

Step 3: *Revising.* In this step, you read over what you have written, decide what ideas need to be improved so that you have as good a paragraph or essay as possible, and—most important—rewrite your draft to achieve the improvements you want. When rewriting, you add new points that need to be made or more specific details that better support the points you are making, or you drop some ideas that do not belong, and you rearrange the material you have. Now you have a second draft, which you should revise the same way you did your first. You should continue to revise all further drafts until you are satisfied with the outcome.

Step 4: *Editing.* In this step, you check thoroughly to make sure that your grammar, punctuation, and spelling are correct.

Step 5: *Proofreading.* In this step, you carefully reread the copy you intend to hand in. Be sure that you have no errors that you previously overlooked, and be sure that your handwriting is legible or typing is neat.

Rarely are these five steps as entirely separate from one another as this list implies. Writing moves forward, but it also sweeps backward as the writer tries to work out the best content, form, and language for fulfilling a particular assignment. For example, while prewriting, a writer might draft a few sentences or a few pages to discover fresh ideas that will help with further planning; or while drafting, a writer might go back to use some prewriting techniques for the purpose of expanding ideas and finding additional details to support key points; or while revising, a writer might edit a grammar or spelling mistake that interferes with clarity. Nevertheless, these five steps in the writing process offer a useful sequence that will help you work efficiently.

 *Try It Out*

Look back at the list of your writing steps, which you drew up for the previous "Try It Out" (page 12). Compare the similarities and differences between your list and the "Five-Step Writing Process" just described. Use your own paper for this assignment.

Generally, the writing process moves from step to step, with occasional overlapping between the final stages of one step and the beginning stages of the next. Along the way, experienced writers allow themselves time, from as little as a half hour to as much as a day or two, to put their work aside. When they come back to it, they have a fresh outlook and can make new connections and see new possibilities for improvement.

Understanding the writing process can help you in two ways. First, you will always remember that you are not finished just because your first draft is complete. Second, you will have a technique to avoid getting stuck at any step. For example, if your drafting is stalled after the first paragraph, or if you cannot think of more supporting details needed for your revision, you can use some of the prewriting techniques explained on pages 15–20 to search for new ideas.

☞ *Try It Out*

Write a brief answer to each question. Use your own paper for this assignment.

1. You have made what seem to be some good plans for your writing assignment, but you have not started writing. Is this the best time to check a point concerning punctuation? Why or why not?
2. You have reached the middle of your first draft and your plans from prewriting do not seem to be working anymore. Should you check the spelling of what you have written or should you try some more prewriting activities? Explain.
3. You have finished writing a first draft of your assignment. Is this the best time to start thinking about revising? Why or why not?
4. You have just finished checking your grammar. Is this the best time to see if your ideas are fully and clearly presented? Why or why not?

As you work with each step in the writing process, you will find that this textbook offers you much specific help. Some sections guide you in finding ideas to write about, others deal with the structure and content of paragraphs and essays, others concentrate on grammar and punctuation, and others teach about proofreading. This book gives you many opportunities to practice as you go along. Whenever you want to know where to find specific information, consult the Table of Contents in the front of this book, or for a detailed breakdown of all the subjects covered, consult the General Index in the back.

Prewriting Techniques

Prewriting techniques help you think of ideas to use in your writing. If you have trouble getting started, if you find that you run out of ideas in the middle of your writing, or if you feel that your ideas are not worthy of your reader's attention, prewriting techniques will help you. These techniques stimulate your mind to come up with good ideas. Most thinking for writing is conscious, but these techniques also draw upon your ability to "get lost in thinking" and thereby to discover new ideas and fresh insights. Here are five popular prewriting techniques:

- **I** Keeping a journal
- **II** Writing nonstop
- **III** Writing nonstop with a focus
- **IV** Brainstorming and making lists
- **V** Making a subject map

I KEEPING A JOURNAL. Keeping a journal requires you to think on paper about matters of interest to you. It means writing every day, or as many days as you can manage or as are required by your instructor. Always write for as long as possible, but consider 15 minutes a minimum for each journal session. Use a special notebook for your journal. Start each day's entry with the date. You can write about anything you wish: your reactions to what you are learning in class, your ideas about what is going on in the world, your observations about people, your feelings, or whatever else is on your mind. A journal, however, is not a diary in which you record merely what time you got up, what the weather was like, what you ate, and what you did all day. You can be personal if you wish, but you do not have to be. Your writing style can be relaxed and informal.

If at times you cannot think of anything to write in your journal, try answering any one of these questions:

> How do you feel about writing? Why? How do you feel about taking a composition class? Why?
>
> Did you ever have an unpopular opinion or belief? Explain. What made you have this opinion or belief? Do you still feel this way? Why or why not? What, if anything, happened as a result of your holding this point of view?

What are your family's attitudes concerning money? Sex? Religion? Marriage? Work? This country? Some other aspect of life? At what specific times have the members of your family displayed these attitudes? Do you agree with these attitudes? Why or why not?

What specific places make you feel happy? Sad? Lonely? Afraid? Fully alive? Depressed? What is it about each place that makes you feel as you do? Do other people react to these places in the same ways that you do? Why or why not?

What do you think your life will be like in ten years? What kind of work (if any) do you expect to be doing? What do you think your family life will be like? What particular interests might you have? What special accomplishments do you hope to achieve? What specific actions will you have to take to make these predictions come true? How would you feel if they did not come true?

You will be the main reader of your journal. It will give you a record of how your fluency in writing moves along. Also, it will be a collection of your thoughts on various subjects. If you remember to record ideas that interest you as they come to mind, your journal can be a sourcebook when you are looking for ideas for your writing assignments. Your instructor also might want to read your journal, depending upon the policy in your class.

☞ *Try It Out*

Buy a notebook to use as your journal. Start using it by writing your first day's entry. Write for at least 15 minutes.

II WRITING NONSTOP. Sometimes called *freewriting*, nonstop writing means writing without stopping for at least 10 minutes at a time. (Set a timer or alarm clock so that you do not stop even to look at the time.) Do not lift your pen from the paper. Never stop. Keep your hand moving across the page. Even if your wrist begins to hurt, do not stop; after a few sessions, your muscles will get stronger. Change nothing you have written. Do not be concerned here about grammar, punctuation, or spelling. Write about whatever is on your mind. If you cannot think of anything, write about not being able to think of anything to write about.

Nonstop writing is a warm-up activity designed to help you loosen up. Eventually your mind and body will feel at ease when your pen moves rapidly across a page, when your words flow freely, and when you become completely involved in the act of writing.

 *Try It Out*

Set a timer or alarm clock to go off in 10 minutes. Write nonstop for 10 minutes.

III WRITING NONSTOP WITH A FOCUS. To write nonstop with a focus, you choose a topic to write about before you get started, and focus on that topic only. You can use the topic of your next writing assignment or any topic that interests you. Get down whatever you know and then make mental associations, sometimes called *free associations,* to the topic. Write down whatever comes to mind without thinking about whether it relates or not.

After 10 minutes stop and read what you have written. Choose one sentence that particularly interests you from all that you have written and underline it. Now use the content of that sentence as the focus for your next 10 minutes of nonstop writing. Here is one student's focused nonstop writing on the topic of "work," with one underlined sentence that became the focus of the student's next nonstop writing.

> Work is such a bore. I hate it. I never seem to get into it. My mother says it is good experience, but I still don't like it. When I go to work, I am a teller in a bank, and sometimes it can get so boring that I go to sleep. I wish I had an exciting job to go to. I also wish when I get up to go to work that I would be happy. A job that is exciting every minute of the day. I also want to be rich and successful. I don't want to have any problems on the job. I want to be my own boss. I want to be happily married, have kids, and have a great job. <u>You have to like work.</u> It has to be something you want and like, not something boring that you cannot get into. For example, a stewardess I think would be very exciting. I think those people just love their jobs. That is what I want. This better end very soon. This better end very soon. I know someone who loves his job and would not give it up for anything. He is so happy; his family is happy too. And I think that's what counts the most, being happy with your job. Having a nice family to go home to every day would be nice too.
>
> Jean Bianchi
Student

Jean now uses the sentence "You have to like work" as the focus for her second round of nonstop writing. She writes about liking work that pays well, that keeps her mind occupied, and that gives her an opportunity to meet new people.

The second round of nonstop writing gives you the chance to focus closely on the aspect of your topic covered in the sentence you have underlined. Write nonstop again. Do not censor. Allow your mental associations to flow freely. Later, when you read back over your focused nonstop writing, you will often be pleasantly surprised to find interesting ideas and fresh perspectives. One warning: at times you will not find interesting material when you read your focused nonstop writing. Be patient with yourself. Once you get your mind into the habit of searching for ideas, the results will be more fruitful.

☞ *Try It Out*

Choose a topic to focus on. Set a timer or alarm clock to go off in 10 minutes. Write nonstop on your topic for 10 minutes. Read what you have written. Underline a sentence that particularly interests you. Again set a timer or alarm clock to go off in 10 minutes. Now write nonstop, focusing on the content of the sentence you chose.

IV BRAINSTORMING AND MAKING LISTS. When you *brainstorm,* you first jot down a list of ideas about all aspects of a topic. The ideas can be in whatever form in which they come to mind: words, phrases, questions, or sentences. After you have compiled a fairly long list of items, you group together the items that seem to belong together. Sometimes one item fits into more than one group, and sometimes an item fits into no group and has to be dropped.

On the topic "television," here is one student's record of brainstorming.

BRAINSTORMING ON "TELEVISION"

set in every house
children's cartoons
entertaining
educational
lots of violence
isn't realistic
waste of time
baseball
ads, ads, ads
news
dumb programs
love stories
football

brings people together
arguments over what to watch
soap operas
makes me lazy
great programs
watch too much
tennis
isolates people
set in every room
informative
VCR's are popular
cable TV
assumes everyone is stupid

Now the student groups items together.

GROUPING ITEMS IN THE LIST

I

assumes everyone is stupid
waste of time
dumb programs
makes me lazy
ads, ads, ads
isn't realistic

II

children's cartoons
love stories
soap operas
news
ads, ads, ads
football
baseball
tennis

III

brings people together
isolates people
arguments over what to watch

IV

set in every house
set in every room
VCR's are popular
cable TV

V

educational
relaxing
informative

Now you choose one group that particularly interests you *and* that will give you sufficient material for your assignment. Because the chances are that no one group is long enough to give you all the material you need, you now have to brainstorm to expand the list with specifics.

Using this system, the student decides that he wants to write on group I. The student then brainstorms to expand the list. By asking of the items the journalist's questions, *who, what, when, where, why, how,* the student comes up with the names of specific actors and writers, the names of specific programs and advertisements, statistics about how often advertisements are shown, descriptions of the plots of specific programs, and so on. In addition, the student relates the items to the five senses: *sight, smell, taste, hearing,* and *touch.* For example, the student mentions how laugh tracks go off when nothing is really funny, how characters wear clothing that they obviously cannot afford, and how products do not taste or smell the way they are advertised. Then the student looks over all the material and decides on a main point for the writing assignment.

☞ *Try It Out*

Brainstorm on the topic "health." First, jot down everything that comes to mind. Second, look over your jottings and group related items together. Third, choose one of the groups and expand it by asking the journalist's questions and by thinking about the five senses.Finally, decide on a tentative title suitable for the expanded list you have developed.

V MAKING A SUBJECT MAP. Making a subject map means brainstorming about your topic by drawing an informal chart that shows the connections among your ideas. Because a subject map illustrates the relationships among ideas, it organizes your material and gives you an informal outline of the points you want to make. On the topic "music," here is one student's subject map. The student started with the word *music* in the center of her map; she then branched out to her main associations with her related material.

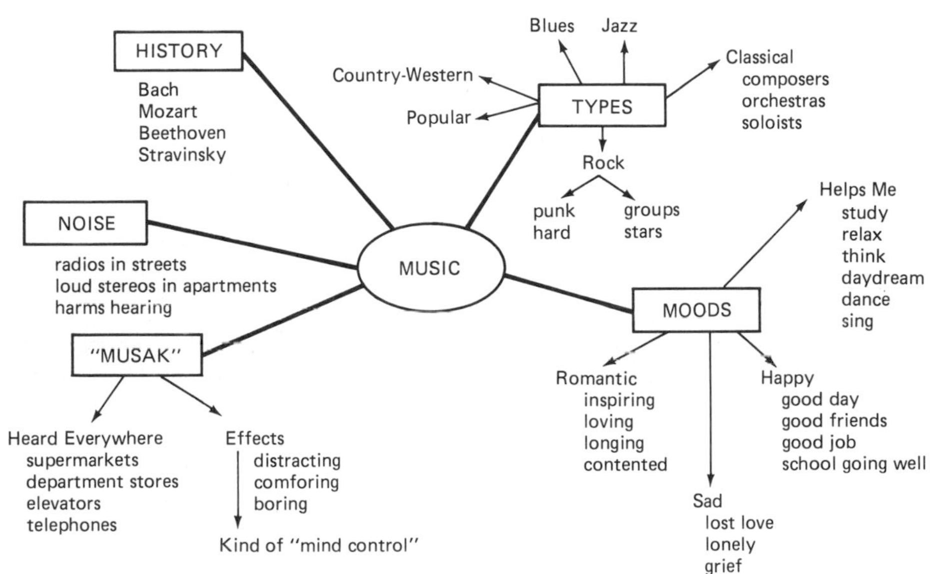

After you have drawn a subject map, look it over to see which areas seem to be fruitful for further development. For example, this student found that the area of "moods" was open to further development. She then drew a more focused subject map. Finally, after thinking about her second map, she made up this tentative title for her writing assignment: "Music Influences People's Moods."

☞ *Try It Out*

Draw a subject map on the topic of "food." Look at your map and choose one area that you think is fruitful for further development. Draw another subject map about that area. Now decide on a title suitable for a writing assignment.

The Topic Sentence

When you write paragraphs and essays, your writing will be clearer and will deliver its message more effectively if you use a topic sentence in each of your paragraphs. Here are a few basic guides for writing a topic sentence.

1. It is generally best to start each paragraph with a topic sentence, which reveals the topic of the paragraph.
2. The function of the topic sentence is to tell what the paragraph will be about. It serves as an introduction to the paragraph because it tells the reader what to expect next in the paragraph.
3. An effective topic sentence usually contains only one main idea. The paragraph that follows it develops that one main idea. Thus, an effective topic sentence makes the one main idea stand out clearly so that the paragraph has unity.

Here is an example of a paragraph that starts with a topic sentence and that contains only one main idea:

Schools should offer courses to help students deal with the problems of employment. Such a course might begin with a discussion of the job-hunting experience including how to use classified newspaper advertisements, employment agencies, and contacts with friends and relatives. This might be followed by practice sessions in writing letters of application and in filling out employment application forms. Students would then participate in job interviews staged in the classroom in order to learn the proper technique for answering questions as well as the importance of personal appearance, speech, and manners. After these essential points have been discussed, the course might even deal with the problems of job adjustment, with emphasis on how to adapt to the duties of the job and the role of being under someone's direct supervision. If schools offered such a course, students would be well prepared for the difficult task of finding a job and for the everyday pressures of keeping one.

☞ *Try It Out*

1. Underline the topic sentence in the paragraph above.
2. Is there more than one main idea in the paragraph?

Here is another example of a paragraph. As you read it, check to see if it starts with a topic sentence and if it contains only one main idea:

New cars can be purchased with a large number of rather expensive accessories. A lover of comfort and pleasure might want a stereo tape deck with front and rear speakers, air conditioning and climate control, and luxurious leather upholstery. On the other hand, a person more interested in safety would prefer to order puncture-proof tires, a rear window defroster, and chrome bumper guards. Indeed, the cost of such accessories could cause the original price of the car to double.

☞ *Try It Out*

1. Underline the topic sentence in the paragraph above.
2. Is there more than one main idea in the paragraph?

You will find additional examples of paragraphs that start with a topic sentence and contain only one main idea on pages 30, 32, and 33 in this chapter and on pages 55, 56, 57, 59, 60, and 61 in the next chapter. Read these model paragraphs carefully, with special attention to the topic sentence that starts each.

A good topic sentence always contains words that limit and control what you can discuss in the paragraph. For example, look at the topic sentence that started the sample paragraph on page 21:

> Schools should offer courses to help students deal with the problems of employment.

In the paragraph that follows this sentence, you can discuss only courses that deal with "the problems of employment." You cannot discuss the wide variety of courses that schools offer in science or in the humanities. Each of those topics would need a separate paragraph.

Name: ______________________ *Date:* ______________________

Here are other topic sentences used to start some of the sample paragraphs in this chapter. Notice that each topic sentence contains words that limit and control what can be discussed in the rest of the paragraph:

Topic Sentence	*Words that Limit and Control*
New cars can be purchased with a large number of rather expensive accessories.	rather expensive accessories
The cockroaches that inhabit many city apartments and homes are parasites that are almost impossible to exterminate completely.	impossible to exterminate completely
Some couples who are determined to reveal their individuality are getting married in unusual ceremonies.	unusual ceremonies

A good topic sentence is not too general or too narrow. A topic sentence that is too general requires much more than a paragraph to develop it. A topic sentence that is too narrow leaves little left to be said in the rest of the paragraph. For example, look at these topic sentences and the comments about them:

Topic Sentence	*Comments*
X Managing a large city is a big job.	poor: too general
X Garbage is collected in the city on Monday and Thursday.	poor: too narrow
✓ Parking regulations that ban street parking during the rush hour help keep the traffic moving in a large city.	better: not too general or too narrow—just enough to discuss in a paragraph

Once you are sure of how a topic sentence operates, you will be ready to write your own topic sentences. Before you begin, consult the list of Pointers for Writing a Topic Sentence on next page. Then continue to work through the exercises in this chapter.

POINTERS FOR WRITING A TOPIC SENTENCE

Writing is a process. When you write a topic sentence, use the "Five-Step Writing Process," which includes **prewriting, drafting, revising, editing,** and **proofreading.** (See pages 12–13.)

PREWRITING

1. Think before you write. Ask yourself: What topic am I going to write about? What do I want to say about the topic?
2. Explore ideas before you write. Read, talk with friends and family, watch documentary programs on television, look at visuals (photographs, works of art, advertisements, cartoons, posters). Use the prewriting techniques explained on pages 15–20.
3. Plan a topic sentence that is suitable for what you expect to discuss in your paragraph.

DRAFTING

4. Write the first draft of your topic sentence.

REVISING

5. Read your first draft to see if the topic sentence (a) clearly states what you will be discussing in your paragraph, (b) contains words that limit and control the content of the paragraph, and (c) is neither too narrow nor too general.
6. Rewrite to get a second draft of your topic sentence, if it is needed.

EDITING AND PROOFREADING

7. Edit to check that your grammar, punctuation, and spelling are correct.
8. Proofread to check that you have missed no errors and that your handwriting is legible or typing is neat.

A SPECIAL NOTE: After you have written your paragraph (ways to develop paragraphs are given on pages 30–33 and 55–58), check your topic sentence again. Does it clearly introduce what you discuss in your paragraph? If not, revise your topic sentence, or revise the content of your paragraph.

EXERCISE 1e: Each item in this exercise contains one main idea for a topic sentence and a list of what will be discussed in the paragraph to follow the topic sentence. You write the topic sentence for the paragraph.

Example: television sports broadcasting
... provides close-ups of the action
... provides instant replays
... provides comments of experts

Topic Sentence: Watching sports on television gives the viewer many advantages.

1. the costs of living alone
   ... rent
   ... furniture
   ... utilities
   ... food

   ____

   ____

2. regular exercise
   ... strengthens the heart muscle
   ... improves blood circulation
   ... increases the intake of oxygen

   ____

   ____

3. saving gasoline in a car
   ... make only necessary car trips
   ... have the engine tuned up
   ... check tire pressure
   ... drive within the speed limit

   ____

   ____

4. influenza
   ... high fever
   ... aches and pains
   ... stuffy nose
   ... loss of appetite

   ____

   ____

5. job interview behavior
   ... be very polite
   ... speak clearly
   ... answer questions fully
   ... ask appropriate questions

   ____

   ____

Name: ______________________ Date: ______________________

EXERCISE 1f: Follow the directions given for each item.

1. a. Jot down three points you might make in a paragraph about TV dinners.

   i. ______________________________

   ii. ______________________________

   iii. ______________________________

   b. Could any of your points be included in a paragraph that starts with this topic sentence: "Most TV dinners taste terrible"?

   i. yes __________ no __________

   ii. yes __________ no __________

   iii. yes __________ no __________

   c. Write a topic sentence that could be used for at least one of the points you jotted down about TV dinners.

   ____

   ____

2. a. Jot down three points you might make in a paragraph about weather forecasters.

   i. ______________________________

   ii. ______________________________

   iii. ______________________________

   b. Could any of your points be included in a paragraph that starts with this topic sentence: "Weather forecasters sometimes make the wrong predictions"?

   i. yes __________ no __________

   ii. yes __________ no __________

   iii. yes __________ no __________

   c. Write a topic sentence that could be used for at least one of the points you jotted down about weather forecasters.

   ____

   ____

Name: ______________________________ *Date:* ______________________________

EXERCISE 1g: In each topic sentence given, circle the words that limit and control what should be discussed in a paragraph that might follow it.

Example: A blind date can be (disastrous.)

1. Hitchhiking can be extremely dangerous.
2. Eating on an airplane is an unpleasant experience.
3. The way people dress often reveals a great deal about their personalities.
4. A flea market is a good place to find a bargain.
5. A school graduation ceremony is sometimes a boring event.
6. Personal computers are much cheaper than they used to be.
7. Jealousy is a very destructive emotion.
8. Some radio disc jockeys are known for making outrageous remarks.
9. Everyone should know how to cook a balanced meal.
10. Gossip columnists sometimes print incorrect information.

EXERCISE 1h: Revise each of the topic sentences below so that it is neither too narrow nor too general.

1. Computers have become an important part of our lives.

 ____

 ____

2. The average American drinks about thirty gallons of soda each year.

 ____

 ____

3. Shyness can make a person's life very difficult.

 ____

 ____

4. Participating in a sport provides many benefits.

 ____

 ____

Name: ________________________ *Date:* __________________

5. Alexander Graham Bell invented the telephone in 1867.

6. Most Americans are very wasteful.

7. The most popular hobby in the world is coin collecting.

8. Crime has a terrible effect on our society.

9. Life is quite a challenge for most handicapped people.

10. About half of the American population wears eyeglasses.

EXERCISE 1i: Using all of the Pointers for Writing a Topic Sentence, write a good topic sentence for each subject given below.

1. the police:

2. amusement parks:

3. unions:

Name:

Date:

4. newspapers: ______________________________

____

5. bicycles: ______________________________

____

EXERCISE 1j: ESSAY ANALYSIS Answer these questions about the essay "The Tube Syndrome."

1. a. What is the topic sentence of paragraph 1?

____

____

b. What specific word or words in the topic sentence limit what can be discussed in the paragraph?

____

c. Is there anything in the paragraph that does not belong?

____

2. a. What is the topic sentence of paragraph 7?

____

____

b. What specific word or words in the topic sentence limit what can be discussed in the paragraph?

____

c. Is there anything in the paragraph that does not belong?

____

3. a. What is the topic sentence of paragraph 9?

____

____

b. What specific word or words in the topic sentence limit what can be discussed in the paragraph?

____

c. Is there anything in the paragraph that does not belong?

____

Name: ______________________ Date: ______________________

Paragraph Development: Part 1

Once you have written your topic sentence, you are ready to write the rest of your paragraph. Paragraph development puts the "meat on the bones" of your topic sentence. Paragraph development helps you emphasize and "drive home" your main point.

This chapter shows you three methods of paragraph development:

- **I** facts
- **II** examples
- **III** incident, anecdote, or story

The next chapter shows you three more methods. Once you are somewhat familiar with these ways to develop a paragraph, you will find it easier to write. As you study and practice these methods, refer to Pointers for Writing a Paragraph on the next page.

I Here is an example of a paragraph developed with *facts:*

The cockroaches that inhabit many city apartments and homes are parasites that are almost impossible to exterminate completely. One hundred seventy million years older than the dinosaur, the cockroach, with its five eyes and six legs, can hide in the dark for weeks without food or water. Whenever a new roach poison is created, some of the insects become immune. And in one year a female can have 35,000 offspring. This, coupled with the fact that there are, at last count, 55 kinds of roaches in the United States, makes us hope only to control the pest but probably never to kill him completely.

HINT: *Facts* usually include numbers, statistics, or other things that can be proved.

Try It Out

1. Underline the topic sentence in the paragraph above.
2. Is there more than one main idea in the paragraph?
3. In your own words state two of the facts used to develop the paragraph.

Name: ______________________ *Date:* ______________________

POINTERS FOR WRITING A PARAGRAPH

Writing is a process. When you write a paragraph, use the "Five-Step Writing Process," which includes **prewriting, drafting, revising, editing,** and **proofreading.** (See pages 12–13.)

PREWRITING

1. Think before you write. Ask yourself: What subject interests me? What do I want to say about the subject?
2. Explore ideas before you write. Read, talk with friends and family, watch documentary programs on television, look at visuals (photographs, works of art, advertisements, cartoons, posters). Use the prewriting techniques explained on pages 15–20.
3. Begin to organize your material. Plan your topic sentence (for help, see Pointers, page 24), and remember that it limits and controls what you discuss in your paragraph.
4. Select the type of paragraph development that suits your topic sentence and that suits the list of ideas you have drawn up. Paragraphs can be developed in many different ways. This book shows you six of them:

   Facts . . . . page 30
   Examples . . . . page 32
   Incident, anecdote, or story . . . . page 33
   Definition . . . . page 55
   Comparison and contrast . . . . page 56
   S-N-S (statistics, names, and the senses) . . . . page 57

DRAFTING

5. Write the first draft of your paragraph.

REVISING

6. Read over your first draft to see what ideas need to be improved. Remember that the key is to *develop*—to go into detail about what you said in your topic sentence.
7. Rewrite to get a second draft and further drafts if they are needed.

EDITING AND PROOFREADING

8. Edit to check that your grammar, punctuation, and spelling are correct.
9. Proofread to check that you have missed no errors and that your handwriting is legible or typing is neat.

EXERCISE 1k: Choose one of these topic sentences and develop it into a paragraph using *facts*. Use separate paper.

1. Taking care of a dog (cat) is very time-consuming.
2. Going to college can be very expensive.
3. Some popular foods are bad for people's health.

II Here is an example of a paragraph developed with *examples:*

Some couples who are determined to reveal their individuality are getting married in unusual ceremonies. For example, a couple employed as linesmen for the Southwestern Bell Telephone Company exchanged their wedding vows clad in jeans and climbing equipment atop a brightly decorated telephone pole while the justice of the peace shouted instructions from the ground. Elsewhere, a couple dressed in swimsuits were married on the high diving board of a local swimming pool because they felt that swimming was an important part of their lives. Furthermore, one couple was wed at the firehouse where the groom was a fireman because the bride wanted to make their wedding just a little different. Another wedding was held in a 747 jet as it flew over Washington State at an altitude of 10,000 feet. Thus, the wedding ceremony has become another example of how more and more people are showing their individuality today.

Try It Out

1. Underline the topic sentence in the paragraph above.
2. Is there more than one main idea in the paragraph?
3. In your own words, state two of the examples used to develop this paragraph.

EXERCISE 1l: Choose one of these topic sentences and develop it into a paragraph using *examples.* Use separate paper.

1. The modern shopping mall has a variety of attractive stores.
2. Many television shows underestimate the intelligence of the audience.
3. My daydreams reveal a great deal about the real me.

Name: ______________________ *Date:* ______________________

III Here is an example of a paragraph developed with an *incident, anecdote, or story:*

Perhaps city residents and wild animals were never meant to go together, even in zoos. Recently a visitor to a large city zoo, ignoring all fences and warning signs, put his arm into the cage of a six-year-old polar bear. Perhaps the man wanted to feed the bear, or touch him, or even tease him. But the bear, basically a citizen of the wilds, almost instantly sprang forward and sank his teeth into the man's hand. As the man screamed for help, and the bear's keeper tried to get the bear under control, the bear sucked in more of the man's arm. Finally, a policeman had to shoot and kill the bear so that the man's arm could be released—which it was. Thus, there was the killing of a polar bear and the wounding of a city citizen, two animals who were meant to be residents of their own worlds, not each other's.

 *Try It Out*

1. Underline the topic sentence in the paragraph above.
2. Is there more than one main idea in this paragraph?
3. In your own words explain why the incident supports the topic sentence.

EXERCISE 1m: Choose one of these topic sentences and develop it into a paragraph using an *incident*. Use separate paper.

1. I vividly remember a time when I had an encounter with a very rude person.
2. I once saw a dramatic incident involving the police.
3. I recently had an experience that really taught me a lesson.

EXERCISE 1n: ESSAY ANALYSIS Answer these questions about the essay "The Tube Syndrome."

1. Is paragraph 1 developed with facts, examples, or an incident?

____

2. Is paragraph 3 developed with facts, examples, or an incident?

____

3. Is paragraph 4 developed with facts, examples, or an incident?

____

4. Is paragraph 5 developed with facts, examples, or an incident?

____

5. Is paragraph 7 developed with facts, examples, or an incident?

____

6. Is paragraph 8 developed with facts, examples, or an incident?

____

7. Is paragraph 10 developed with facts, examples, or an incident?

____

EXERCISE 1o: Write an essay on one of the five topics given below. Using the essay outline below, try to use a different type of paragraph development for each of the pressures you select. For help in planning your essay, refer to the Pointers for Writing an Essay, which appear on the next page. Use your own paper for this assignment.

The Pressures of Being Married

The Pressures of Being Single

The Pressures of Being a Student

The Pressures of Being an Employee

The Pressures of Being a Pet

I. Introduction

II. One Pressure (you select)

III. Another Pressure (you select)

IV. A Third Pressure (you select)

V. Conclusion

Name: ______________________________ *Date:* ______________________________

POINTERS FOR WRITING AN ESSAY

Writing is a process. When you write an essay, use the "Five-Step Writing Process," which includes **prewriting, drafting, revising, editing,** and **proofreading.** (See pages 12–13.) For more information on writing an essay, see Chapters Seven and Twelve.

PREWRITING

1. Think before you write. Ask yourself: What subject interests me? What do I want to say about the subject?
2. Explore ideas before you write. Read, talk with friends and family, watch documentary programs on television, look at visuals (photographs, works of art, advertisements, cartoons, posters). Use the prewriting techniques explained on pages 15–20.
3. Begin to organize your material. Look over the ideas you have compiled and see what goes together and what is best saved for another essay. Now look over your remaining ideas and divide them into three main idea groups. For help, see pages 249–252.
4. Plan your topic sentences (see Pointers, page 24) to serve as a mini-outline of your essay. Next, plan the content of your paragraphs (see Pointers on page 31, The Introductory Paragraph on pages 258–259, and The Concluding Paragraph on pages 260–261). Try this essay format:

    Introductory Paragraph
    First Main Idea Paragraph
    Second Main Idea Paragraph
    Third Main Idea Paragraph
    Concluding Paragraph

DRAFTING

5. Write the first draft of your essay.

REVISING

6. Read over your first draft. As needed, add new main ideas or better supporting details for your main ideas. Also, as needed, drop ideas that do not fit, and rearrange the material so that it is well organized.
7. Rewrite to get a second draft and further drafts if they are needed.

EDITING AND PROOFREADING

8. Edit to check that your grammar, punctuation, and spelling are correct.
9. Proofread to check that you have missed no errors and that your handwriting is legible or typing is neat.

EXERCISE 1p: REFRESHER On separate paper, rewrite the following paragraph. Remove any material that is not part of the main idea stated in the topic sentence. Add facts, examples, or incidents to develop the paragraph more fully.

Some television programs are very educational. For example, "Sesame Street" uses clever visual images to teach young children how to count and work with the alphabet. This show also acts as an excellent baby sitter, allowing parents to have some time for themselves while their children are being entertained by Big Bird and Cookie Monster. Another highly educational program is "Nova," which has already dealt with a wide variety of topics such as genetic engineering, the artificial heart, and undersea exploration. Because of educational shows like these, watching television can really be a worthwhile experience for people of all ages.

Name: ____________________ Date: ____________________

SPRINGBOARDS TO WRITING

Using your knowledge of the writing process, explained on pages 12–14, write a paragraph or essay related to this chapter's central theme, *the impact of television on people's minds,* which is introduced on pages 1–4.

PREWRITING

To think of topics to write about, look at the two cartoons, read the essay, and answer the questions that follow each. If you prefer, select one of the writing springboards below. (All paragraph numbers refer to the essay that starts on page 2.) To develop your ideas, use the prewriting techniques described on pages 15–20.

WRITING A PARAGRAPH (For help, see the Pointers on page 31.)

1. Television is (is not) good for my family life.
2. Watching television does (does not) affect my school work.
3. By the age of 16, the average American child has witnessed 11,000 homicides on television. Is such viewing harmful?
4. Watching television game shows is (is not) a waste of time.
5. The nightly television news programs do (do not) concentrate too much on tragic events involving people's personal suffering.
6. Advertisements for beer and wine should (should not) be banned from television.
7. Our political system is (is not) hurt when political candidates spend as much money as they can afford on television advertisements.

WRITING AN ESSAY (For help, see the Pointers on page 35.)

8. Paragraph 4 states: "Television rots minds." Agree or disagree.
9. Is American Culture Enveloped in a Great Gray Fog? (See ¶ 11.)
10. What Is Good (Bad) about Television?
11. Why Do People Become Addicted to Television?
12. Why Are Soap Operas Popular?
13. Should Parents Control Their Children's Television Viewing Habits?
14. Television Advertisements Insult People's Intelligence
15. Life as Shown on Television Is (Is Not) Realistic
16. Cable TV is (Is Not) a Good Alternative to Commercial TV
17. My Preferred Pleasure: Reading or Watching TV (See ¶ 11.)

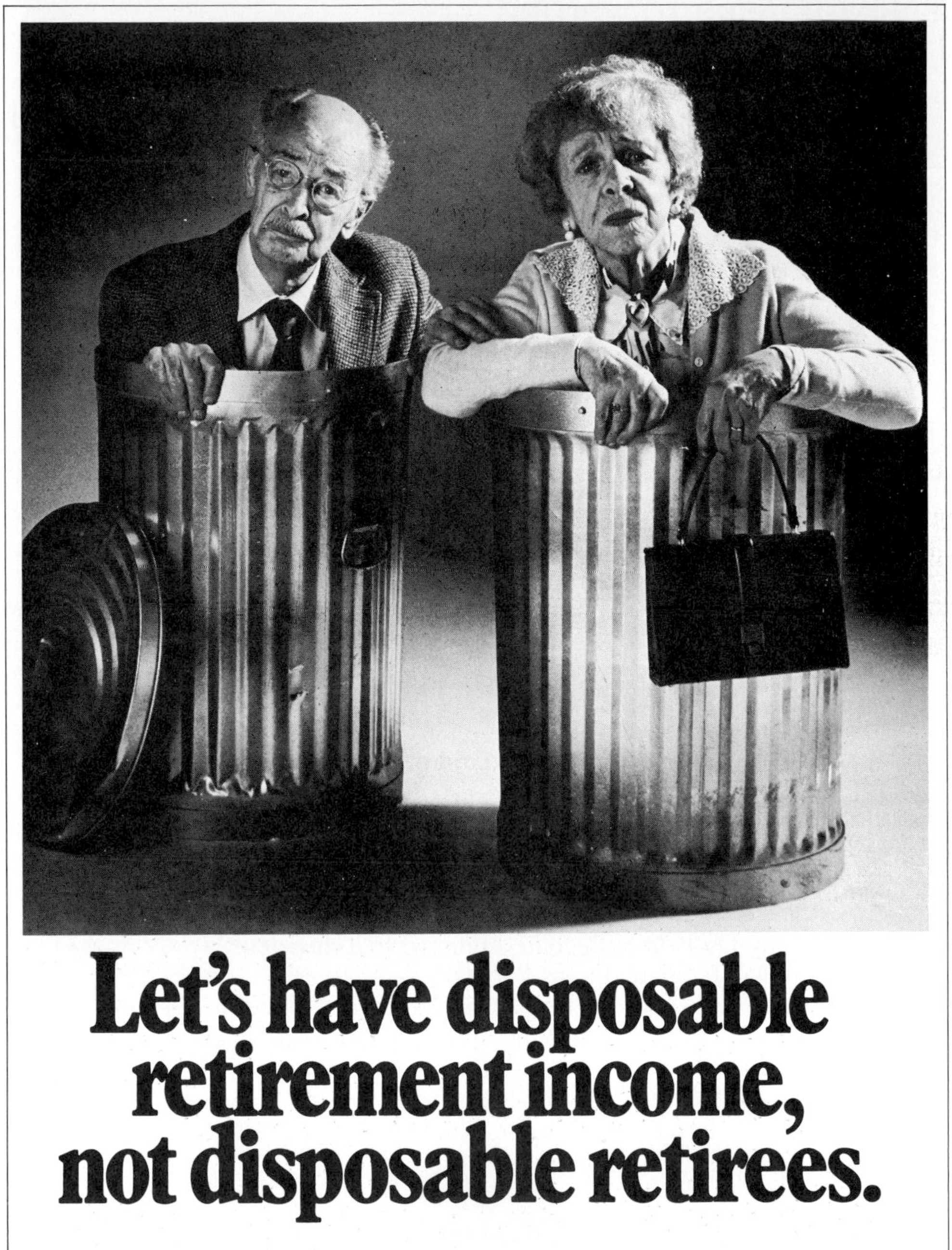

Let's have disposable retirement income, not disposable retirees.
Ætna
LIFE & CASUALTY

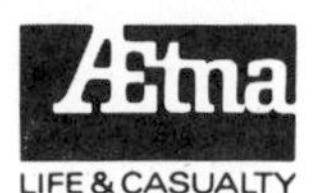

Courtesy of AEtna Life & Casualty.

two

Full-time granny, part-time cop.

My name's McGruff, the Crime Dog. And that's Mimi Marth. She and her neighbors in Hartford, Connecticut make crime prevention a part of their day. How 'bout you?
Write to: McGruff,™ Crime Prevention Coalition
Box 6600, Rockville, Maryland 20850
People working together can help.

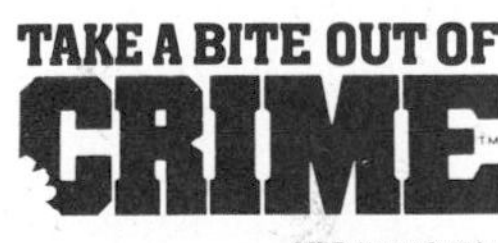

Courtesy of the Advertising Council, Inc.

SPRINGBOARDS TO THINKING

For informal, not written, response . . . to stimulate your thinking

1. In the advertisement on the opposite page, the words *disposable retirement income* mean "available income for retired people." The company being advertised offers pension plans that help people save money for their retirement. What is the message being communicated by this advertisement?
2. What are some of the reasons that many of today's senior citizens have financial problems? What is your opinion of the Social Security system in America? (Note: If you work, your salary deduction labeled "F.I.C.A." goes to Social Security.)
3. Why do many senior citizens today feel that they are being treated like "garbage"—both by the government and by younger people?
4. In the advertisement above, what is the woman doing? What is your opinion of what she is doing?
5. What nonfinancial problems do people encounter as they grow older? What can be done to make everyone more understanding of and sympathetic to senior citizens today?

Old Before Her Time

KATHERINE BARRETT

(1) This is the story of an extraordinary voyage in time, and of a young woman who devoted three years to a singular experiment. In 1979, Patty Moore—then aged twenty-six—transformed herself for the first of many times into an eighty-five-year-old woman. Her object was to discover first-hand the problems, joys and frustrations of the elderly. She wanted to know for herself what it's like to live in a culture of youth and beauty when your hair is gray, your skin is wrinkled and no men turn their heads as you pass.

(2) Her time machine was a makeup kit. Barbara Kelly, a friend and professional makeup artist, helped Patty pick out a wardrobe and showed her how to use latex to create wrinkles, and wrap Ace bandages to give the impression of stiff joints. "It was peculiar," Patty recalls, as she relaxes in her New York City apartment. "Even the first few times I went out I realized that I wouldn't have to *act* that much. The more I was perceived as elderly by others, the more 'elderly' I actually became . . . I imagine that's just what happens to people who really are old."

(3) What motivated Patty to make her strange journey? Partly her career—as an industrial designer, Patty often focuses on the needs of the elderly. But the roots of her interest are also deeply personal. Extremely close to her own grandparents—particularly her maternal grandfather, now ninety—and raised in a part of Buffalo, New York, where there was a large elderly population, Patty always drew comfort and support from the older people around her. When her own marriage ended in 1979 and her life seemed to be falling apart, she dove into her "project" with all her soul. In all, she donned her costume more than two hundred times in fourteen different states. Here is the remarkable story of what she found.

(4) **Columbus, Ohio, May 1979.** Leaning heavily on her cane, Pat Moore stood alone in the middle of a crowd of young professionals. They were all attending a gerontology conference, and the room was filled with animated chatter. But no one was talking to Pat. In a throng of men and women who devoted their working lives to the elderly, she began to feel like a total nonentity. "I'll get us all some coffee," a young man told a group of women next to her. "What about me?" thought Pat. "If I were young, they would be offering me coffee, too." It was a bitter thought at the end of a disappointing day—a day that marked Patty's first appearance as "the old woman." She had planned to attend the gerontology conference anyway, and almost as a lark decided to see how professionals would react to an old person in their midst.

(5) Now, she was angry. All day she had been ignored . . . counted out in a way she had never experienced before. She didn't understand. Why didn't people help her when they saw her struggling to open a heavy door? Why didn't they include her in conversations? Why did the other participants seem almost embarrassed by her presence at the conference—as if it were somehow inappropriate that an old person should be professionally active?

(6) And so, eighty-five-year-old Pat Moore learned her first lesson: The old are often ignored. "I discovered that people really do judge a book by its cover," Patty says today. "Just because I looked different, people either condescended or they totally dismissed me. Later, in stores, I'd get the same reaction. A clerk would turn to someone younger and wait on her first. It was as if he assumed that I—the older woman—could wait because I didn't have anything better to do."

(7) **New York City, October 1979.** Bent over her cane, Pat walked slowly toward the edge of the park. She had spent the day sitting on a bench with friends, but now dusk was falling and her friends had all gone home. She looked around nervously at the deserted area and tried to move faster, but her joints were stiff. It was then that she heard the barely audible sound of sneakered feet approaching and the kids' voices. "Grab her, man." "Get her purse." Suddenly an arm was around her throat and she was dragged back, knocked off her feet.

(8) She saw only a blur of sneakers and blue jeans, heard the sounds of mocking laughter, felt fists pummeling her—on her back, her legs, her breasts, her stomach. "Oh, God," she thought, using her arms to protect her head and curling herself into a ball. "They're going to kill me. I'm going to die. . . ."

(9) Then, as suddenly as the boys attacked, they were gone. And Patty was left alone, struggling to rise. The boys' punches had broken the latex makeup on her face, the fall had disarranged her wig, and her whole body ached. (Later she would learn that she had fractured her left wrist, an injury that took two years to heal completely.) Sobbing, she left the park and hailed a cab to return home. Again the thought struck her: What if I really lived in the gray ghetto . . . what if I couldn't escape to my nice safe home. . . ?

(10) Lesson number two: The fear of crime is paralyzing. "I really understand now why the elderly become homebound," the young woman says as she recalls her ordeal today. "When something like this happens, the fear just doesn't go away. I guess it wasn't so bad for me. I could distance myself from what happened . . . and I was strong enough to get up and walk away. But what about someone who is really too weak to run or fight back or protect herself in any way? And the elderly often can't afford to move if the area in which they live deteriorates, becomes unsafe. I met people like this and they were imprisoned by their fear. That's when the bolts go on the door. That's when people starve themselves because they're afraid to go to the grocery store."

(11) **New York City, February 1980.** It was a slushy, gray day and Pat had laboriously descended four flights of stairs from her apartment to go shopping. Once outside, she struggled to hold her threadbare coat closed with one hand and manipulate her cane with the other. Splotches of snow made the street difficult for anyone to navigate, but for someone hunched over, as she was, it was almost impossible. The curb was another obstacle. The slush looked ankle-deep—and what was she to do? Jump over it? Slowly, she worked her way around to a drier spot, but the crowds were impatient to move. A woman with packages jostled her as she rushed past, causing Pat to nearly lose her balance. If I really were old, I would have fallen, she thought. Maybe broken something. On another day, a woman had practically knocked her over by letting go of a heavy door as Pat tried to enter a coffee shop. Then there were the revolving doors. How could you push them without strength? And how could you get up and down stairs, on and off a bus, without risking a terrible fall?

(12) Lesson number three: If small, thoughtless deficiencies in design were corrected, life would be so much easier for older people. It was no surprise to Patty that the "built" environment is often inflexible. But even she didn't realize the extent of the problems, she admits. "It was a terrible feeling. I never realized how difficult it is to get off a curb if your knees don't bend easily. Or the helpless feeling you get if your upper arms aren't strong enough to open a door. You know, I just felt so vulnerable—as if I was at the mercy of every barrier or rude person I encountered."

(13) **Ft. Lauderdale, Florida, May 1980.** Pat met a new friend while shopping and they decided to continue their conversation over a sundae at a nearby coffee shop. The woman was in her late seventies, "younger" than Pat, but she was obviously reaching out for help. Slowly, her story unfolded. "My husband moved out of our bedroom," the woman said softly, fiddling with her coffee cup and fighting back tears. "He won't touch me anymore. And when he gets angry at me for being stupid, he'll even sometimes. . . ." The woman looked down, embarrassed to go on. Pat took her hand. "He hits me . . . he gets so mean." "Can't you tell anyone?" Pat asked. "Can't you tell your son?" "Oh, no!" the woman almost gasped. "I would never tell the children; they absolutely adore him."

(14) Lesson number four: Even a fifty-year-old marriage isn't necessarily a good one. While Pat met many loving and devoted elderly couples, she was stunned to find others who had stayed together unhappily—because divorce was still an anathema in their middle years. "I met women who secretly wished their husbands dead, because after so many years they just ended up full of hatred. One woman in Chicago even admitted that she deliberately angered her husband because she knew it would make his blood pressure rise. Of couse, that was pretty extreme. . . ."

(15) Patty pauses thoughtfully and continues. "I guess what really made an impression on me, the real eye-opener, was that so many of these older women had the same problems as women twenty, thirty or forty. Problems with men . . . problems with the different roles that are expected of them.

As a 'young woman' I, too, had just been through a relationship where I spent a lot of time protecting someone by covering up his problems from family and friends. Then I heard this woman in Florida saying that she wouldn't tell her children their father beat her because she didn't want to disillusion them. These issues aren't age-related. They affect everyone."

(16) **Clearwater, Florida, January 1981.** She heard the children laughing, but she didn't realize at first that they were laughing at her. On this day, as on several others, Pat had shed the clothes of a middle-income woman for the rags of a bag lady. She wanted to see the extremes of the human condition, what it was like to be old and poor, and outside traditional society as well. Now, tottering down the sidewalk, she was most concerned with the cold, since her layers of ragged clothing did little to ease the chill. She had spent the afternoon rummaging through garbage cans, loading her shopping bags with bits of debris, and she was stiff and tired. Suddenly, she saw that four little boys, five or six years old, were moving up on her. And then she felt the sting of the pebbles they were throwing. She quickened her pace to escape, but another handful of gravel hit her and the laughter continued. They're using me as a target, she thought, horror-stricken. They don't even think of me as a person.

(17) Lesson number five: Social class affects every aspect of an older person's existence. "I found out that class is a very important factor when you're old," says Patty. "It was interesting. That same day, I went back to my hotel and got dressed as a wealthy woman, another role that I occasionally took. Outside the hotel, a little boy of about seven asked if I would go shelling with him. We walked along the beach, and he reached out to hold my hand. I knew he must have a grandmother who walked with a cane, because he was so concerned about me and my footing. 'Don't put your cane there, the sand's wet,' he'd say. He really took responsibility for my welfare. The contrast between him and those children was really incredible. The little ones who were throwing pebbles at me because they didn't see me as human. And then the seven-year-old taking care of me. I think he would have responded to me the same way even if I had been dressed as the middle-income woman. There's no question that money does make life easier for older people, not only because it gives them a more comfortable life-style, but because it makes others treat them with greater respect."

(18) **New York City, May 1981.** Pat always enjoyed the time she spent sitting on the benches in Central Park. She'd let the whole day pass by, watching young children play, feeding the pigeons and chatting. One spring day she found herself sitting with three women, all widows, and the conversation turned to the few available men around. "It's been a long time since anyone hugged me," one woman complained. Another agreed. "Isn't that the truth. I need a hug, too." It was a favorite topic, Pat found—the lack of touching left in these women's lives, the lack of hugging, the lack of men.

(19) In the last two years, she had found out herself how it felt to walk

down Fifth Avenue and know that no men were turning to look after her. Or how it felt to look at models in magazines or store mannequins and *know* that those gorgeous clothes were just not made for her. She hadn't realized before just how much casual attention was paid to her because she was young and pretty. She hadn't realized it until it stopped.

(20) Lesson number six: You never grow old emotionally. You always need to feel loved. "It's not surprising that everyone needs love and touching and holding," says Patty. "But I think some people feel that you reach a point in your life when you accept that those intimate feelings are in the past. That's wrong. These women were still interested in sex. But more than that, they—like everyone—needed to be hugged and touched. I'd watch two women greeting each other on the street and just holding onto each other's hands, neither wanting to let go. Yet, I also saw that there are people who are afraid to touch an old person . . . they were afraid to touch me. It's as if they think old age is a disease and it's catching. They think that something might rub off on them."

(21) **New York City, September 1981.** He was a thin man, rather nattily dressed, with a hat that he graciously tipped at Pat as he approached the bench where she sat. "Might I join you?" he asked jauntily. Pat told him he would be welcome and he offered her one of the dietetic hard candies that he carried in a crumpled paper bag. As the afternoon passed, they got to talking . . . about the beautiful buds on the trees and the world around them and the past. "Life's for the living, my wife used to tell me," he said. "When she took sick she made me promise her that I wouldn't waste a moment. But the first year after she died, I just sat in the apartment. I didn't want to see anyone, talk to anyone or go anywhere. I missed her so much." He took a handkerchief from his pocket and wiped his eyes, and they sat in silence. Then he slapped his leg to break the mood and change the subject. He asked Pat about herself, and described his life alone. He belonged to a "senior center" now, and went on trips and had lots of friends. Life did go on. They arranged to meet again the following week on the same park bench. He brought lunch—chicken salad sandwiches and decaffeinated peppermint tea in a thermos—and wore a carnation in his lapel. It was the first date Patty had had since her marriage ended.

(22) Lesson number seven: Life does go on . . . as long as you're flexible and open to change. "That man really meant a lot to me, even though I never saw him again," says Patty, her eyes wandering toward the gray wig that now sits on a wig-stand on the top shelf of her bookcase. "He was a real old-fashioned gentleman, yet not afraid to show his feelings—as so many men my age are. It's funny, but at that point I had been through months of self-imposed seclusion. Even though I was in a different role, that encounter kind of broke the ice for getting my life together as a single woman."

(23) In fact, while Patty was living her life as the old woman, some of her young friends had been worried about her. After several years, it seemed as if the lines of identity had begun to blur. Even when she wasn't in makeup,

she was wearing unusually conservative clothing, she spent most of her time with older people and she seemed almost to revel in her role—sometimes finding it easier to be in costume than to be a single New Yorker.

(24) But as Patty continued her experiment, she was also learning a great deal from the older people she observed. Yes, society often did treat the elderly abysmally . . . they were sometimes ignored, sometimes victimized, sometimes poor and frightened, but so many of them were survivors. They had lived through two world wars, the Depression and into the computer age. "If there was one lesson to learn, one lesson that I'll take with me into *my* old age, it's that you've got to be flexible," Patty says. "I saw my friend in the park, managing after the loss of his wife, and I met countless other people who picked themselves up after something bad—or even something catastrophic—happened. I'm not worried about them. I'm worried about the others who shut themselves away. It's funny, but seeing these two extremes helped me recover from the trauma in my own life, to pull *my* life together."

(25) Today, Patty is back to living the life of a single thirty-year-old, and she rarely dons her costumes anymore. "I must admit, though, I do still think a lot about aging," she says. "I look in the mirror and I begin to see wrinkles, and then I realize that I won't be able to wash *those* wrinkles off." Is she afraid of growing older? "No. In a way, I'm kind of looking forward to it," she smiles. "I *know* it will be different from my experiment. I *know* I'll probably even look different. When they aged Orson Welles in *Citizen Kane* he didn't resemble at all the Orson Welles of today."

(26) But Patty also knows that in one way she really did manage to capture the feeling of being old. With her bandages and her stooped posture, she turned her body into a kind of prison. Yet, inside she didn't change at all. "It's funny, but that's exactly how older people always say they feel," says Patty. "Their bodies age, but inside they are really no different than when they were young."

READING SURVEY

1. Main Idea

What is the central theme of the essay?

2. Major Details

a. Why did Patty disguise herself as an 85-year-old woman?
b. What are the seven lessons Patty Moore learned?
c. What did Patty learn from the older people she observed?

3. *Inferences*

a. Read paragraph 14 again. Why should unhappily married people consider divorce "an anathema" in their middle years?
b. Read paragraph 25 again. After her many unpleasant encounters as an 85-year-old, why is Patty Moore "kind of looking forward" to growing older?

4. *Opinions*

a. Do you think that an elderly man would encounter the same types of experiences that Patty Moore did as an elderly woman? Explain.
b. What specific actions can the elderly take to avoid difficulties of the sorts that Patty Moore encountered?

VOCABULARY BUILDING

Lesson One: The Vocabulary of Growing Old, Part I

The essay "Old Before Her Time" by Katherine Barrett includes words that are useful when you are discussing the experience of growing old.

gerontology	(paragraph 4)	**paralyzing**	(10)
animated	(4)	**ordeal**	(10)
nonentity	(4)	**laboriously**	(11)
condescended	(6)	**manipulate**	(11)
audible	(7)	**jostled**	(11)

Today, growing old is better understood because of **gerontology,** the science that studies the process and problems of aging.

Today, growing old does not mean the end of being **animated**—acting in a lively, spirited, energetic manner.

Today, growing old does not mean becoming a **nonentity**—a person or thing of little or no importance.

Today, growing old does not mean that a person has to be **condescended** to—be treated graciously even though looked down upon as being inferior.

Today, growing old does not mean having the problem of being deaf, because the hard-of-hearing can wear hearing aids which make all sounds **audible** or loud enough to be heard clearly.

Today, growing old does not mean that life becomes **paralyzing**—controlled by a feeling of shocking helplessness or inability to move or escape.

Today, growing old does not mean that life becomes an **ordeal**—a difficult, painful experience.

Today, growing old does not mean that all activities are undertaken **laboriously**—in a hard, long, and slowly labored way.

Today, growing old does not mean that objects become difficult to **manipulate**—to handle with skill.

Today, growing old does not mean that the elderly are easily **jostled** or pushed around roughly or shoved in a crowd.

EXERCISE 2a: For each word in italics below, circle the definition closest in meaning.

1. *Gerontology* is a science that deals with
   a. fish.
   b. outer space.
   c. rare gems.
   d. aging.

2. To be *animated* is to
   a. act like an animal.
   b. be lively and spirited.
   c. feel depressed.
   d. be hungry and thirsty.

3. A *nonentity* can best be described as
   a. an insignificant person or thing.
   b. an incorrect answer to a question.
   c. an incomplete description.
   d. an angry editorial or essay.

4. Anyone who has been *condescended* to has been
   a. spoken to by someone descending a staircase.
   b. promoted to a higher paying job.
   c. criticized for having revealed a secret.
   d. treated graciously although considered inferior

5. When something is *audible*, it
   a. is ready to be audited.
   b. is worth little or no money.
   c. is loud enough to be clearly heard.
   d. can be seen clearly by the naked eye.

6. A *paralyzing* experience is so
   a. common that it can be predicted.
   b. pleasant that it is relaxing.
   c. shocking that it stops movement.
   d. unusual that it cannot be believed.

7. An *ordeal* is
   a. an order that cannot be carried out.
   b. a difficult and painful experience.
   c. a profitable business venture.
   d. a violent and destructive act of nature.

8. If a task was *laboriously* performed, the work was
   a. quick and easy.
   b. of poor quality.
   c. time-consuming and hard.
   d. of excellent quality.

9. To *manipulate* is to
   a. perform with skill.
   b. think through a problem.
   c. go back on a promise.
   d. do a kindly act.

10. Anyone who has been *jostled* has been
    a. accused of a crime.
    b. pushed around in a crowd.
    c. badly treated by a friend.
    d. cheered on by a crowd.

Lesson Two: The Vocabulary of Growing Old, Part II

Here are more words from the essay "Old Before Her Time" by Katherine Barrett that are useful when you are discussing the experience of growing old.

obstacle	(paragraph 11)	**tottering**	(16)
deficiencies	(12)	**seclusion**	(22)
barrier	(12)	**abysmally**	(24)
anathema	(14)	**catastrophic**	(24)
disillusion	(15)	**stooped**	(26)

In modern life, senior citizens can achieve a great deal as long as they do not consider old age an **obstacle** or **barrier**—as something that stands in their way or separates them from what they want.

In modern life, senior citizens can emphasize the positive and downplay their **deficiencies** or shortcomings.

In modern life, senior citizens have to try to ignore the fact that some younger people think that the elderly are an **anathema**—people or things that are strongly disliked or considered to be cursed.

In modern life, senior citizens can hold onto their dreams and not allow others to **disillusion** them—to destroy their false ideas leaving them disappointed or even bitter.

 Name: ______________________ Date: ______________

In modern life, senior citizens are rarely in such poor health that they are seen **tottering** as they walk—walking in an unsteady or shaky way.

In modern life, senior citizens can stay active and thereby avoid being in **seclusion**—being alone, removed from the outside world, and withdrawn from others.

In modern life, senior citizens are sometimes treated **abysmally**—in a horrible and deeply miserable way.

In modern life, senior citizens sometimes have to deal with problems that are **catastrophic**—events so bad that they end in cruel misfortune, disaster, or tragedy.

In modern life, senior citizens can exercise and seek medical help to avoid having **stooped** or bent-over posture.

EXERCISE 2b: For each word in italics below, circle the definition closest in meaning.

1. An *obstacle* is something that
   a. has little or no value.
   b. stands in the way.
   c. is considered a work of art.
   d. improves the flavor of food.

2. A person having *deficiencies* can best be described as having
   a. a series of business setbacks.
   b. a very high I.Q.
   c. more than one shortcoming.
   d. good health and appearance.

3. A *barrier* is a
   a. windmill.
   b. hurdle.
   c. musical instrument.
   d. lawyer.

4. An *anathema* is anything that is
   a. admirable.
   b. of poor quality.
   c. controversial.
   d. strongly disliked.

5. To *disillusion* someone is to
   a. disappoint a person by destroying his or her false ideas.
   b. give moral support to a person suffering from grief.
   c. falsely accuse a person of a crime or wrongdoing.
   d. compliment a person for his or her outstanding performance.

6. If you saw a *tottering* person, he or she would be
   a. looking dirty and shabby.
   b. leaning against a wall.
   c. walking in a shaky way.
   d. shouting rudely at children.

7. Being in *seclusion* means
   a. belonging to an exclusive club.
   b. living in a college dormitory.
   c. being a member of a varsity team.
   d. living apart from the outside world.

8. To be treated *abysmally* is to be treated
   a. horribly and miserably.
   b. as a young child.
   c. as an equal.
   d. with respect and dignity.

9. A *catastrophic* event is one that
   a. was predicted to happen.
   b. has obvious historical importance.
   c. is sudden and violent, causing great disaster.
   d. marks an important national holiday.

10. To be *stooped* is to
   a. be visibly drunk.
   b. have a bent-over posture.
   c. be in a deep sleep.
   d. be sitting on the steps.

SPELLING

Lesson One: Spelling Demons

Here are some more words that are frequently misspelled. Using the helpful techniques given in Chapter One, be sure to learn these new Demons, which are taken from "Old Before Her Time."

approach	**existence**	**obstacle**
available	**extremely**	**paralyze**
beautiful	**forty**	**peculiar**
completely	**forward**	**presence**
concern	**hundred**	**probably**
disappoint	**imagine**	**strength**
embarrass	**meant**	**unusually**
escape	**ninety**	**using**

 Name: ______________ Date: ______________

Lesson Two: Sound-Alikes

Many of your spelling errors may be caused by a confusion of words that have different spellings but similar pronunciations. Since the confused words sound alike, their pronunciation is no clue to their spelling. Instead you must rely on their meanings if you are to spell them correctly. Below is a list of some of these troublesome Sound-Alikes. They are words that you use frequently in your writing, so be sure to learn to spell them correctly.

1. *capital* (chief, major; leading city; money)
   Albany is the capital of New York.
   Pam invested all her capital.
   capitol (only the name of a building)
   We met on the steps of the Capitol in Washington.

2. *hear* (listen)
   We could not hear the radio because of the interference.
   here (in this place)
   The boys will wait here for their friends.

3. *its* (belongs to it)
   The dog could not wag its tail.
   it's (it is)
   It's the best of all possible worlds.

4. *passed* (went by)
   I passed your home on the way to school.
   past (a former time)
   If we are not careful, the past will catch up with us.

5. *peace* (the absence of war and strife)
   The United Nations hopes to bring peace to the world.
   piece (a portion of)
   Have a piece of cake with your coffee.

6. *principal* (most important; chief person; the original amount of a loan)
   What is the principal idea of this essay?
   Ms. Denn is the school principal.
   Sue paid the interest and fifty dollars on the principal.
   principle (a basic doctrine or rule)
   The many principles of physics are difficult to learn.

7. *then* (at that time)
   We went to an early movie, and then we went home.
   than (used to compare unequal things)
   His speech was much longer than mine.

8. *their* (belonging to them)
   It is their privilege to vote against the amendment.
   there (at that place)
   There is the oldest schoolhouse in America.
   they're (they are)
   They're the best audience one could hope for.

9. *to* (toward; part of the infinitive)
   Phyllis gave her schedule to me.
   They like to condemn all his decisions.
   too (also; more than enough)
   Judy likes Greek tragedy too.
   Peter watches too much TV.
   two (the number 2)
   We consulted two authorities.

10. *weather* (the state of the atmosphere)
    The weather was fine for a trip to the lake.
    whether (indicates a choice)
    Lynn could not decide whether to stay home or go out.

11. *who's* (who is)
    Who's against the new French government?
    whose (belonging to whom)
    Whose children are they?

12. *your* (belonging to you)
    It is your decision to make.
    you're (you are)
    You're the last obstacle to my happiness.

A SPECIAL NOTE: Memory tricks are especially helpful for learning these Sound-Alikes:

Remember that you *hear* with your *ear.*
We waited *here* and not *there.*
The princi*pal* is my *pal* and the *chief* person in a school.
The princip*le* is a ru*le.*
The capit*o*l has a d*o*me.
The w*ea*ther was cl*ea*r.
He ate a *piece* of *pie.*

EXERCISE 2c: Underline the correct word from each set of words in parentheses.

Graffiti, those scribblings and drawings on walls that you have (passed, past) just about every day of (your, you're) life, are one of the oldest methods used by people (to, too, two) communicate. In fact, such wall writings were popular over (to, too, two) thousand years before Christianity; Greek workers (who's, whose) lives were spent building the Great Pyramid at Giza left (their, there, they're) signatures on this Egyptian monument. The ancient Italian city of Pompeii had some of (its, it's) walls marked up with (peaces, pieces) of graffiti (to, too, two). (Their, There, They're) well-preserved clues to the (passed, past) because in 79 A.D. a volcano exploded and (than, then) buried the city under volcanic ash, which protected the graffiti from the (weather, whether) for many hundreds of years.

(Weather, Whether) these wall markings are found in ancient Pompeii or in modern America, they fall into three (principal, principle) categories. The (principal, principle) behind the most common type, identity graffiti, is the graffiti writer's desire to call attention (to, too, two) his or her name in a society where most people feel lost in the crowd. The example (your, you're) probably most familiar with is: "Kilroy was (hear, here)." Another reason for identity graffiti was pointed out by a high school (principal, principle) who found that a teacher (who's, whose) (to, too, two) busy to (hear, here) what students are saying encourages them to scrawl (their, there, they're) names on (their, there, they're) desk tops in revenge. The second type of graffiti offers a message or opinion. For example, the thought, "(Their, There, They're) will be (peace, piece) in 1995—with or without people," was written on a wall of the (Capital, Capitol) in Washington, D.C. (Their, There, They're), someone also wrote: "Of course I smoke. (Its, It's) safer (than, then) breathing!" The final type of graffiti is decorative and colorful artwork; it can be seen throughout New York City, often called the graffiti (capital, capitol) of the world, where several young people have formed an organization, United Graffiti Artists, to sell (their, there, they're) art. Thus, graffiti are becoming an acceptable form of communication that will likely survive periodic cleanups and paint jobs.

Name: ______________________ Date: ______________________

EXERCISE 2d: Using the Spelling Demons in this chapter, fill in the blanks with any missing letters.

1. Emba____a____ed by his lack of stre____th, the nin____ty-pound weakling started taking an unus____ly large number of vitamin pills; after f____rty days of us____ng this ap____r____ch, however, he was di____pointed to discover that he was now a one-hun____d-pound weakling.

2. Sometimes, people who are caught in an ext____m____y dangerous situation are so comple____y paral____ed with fear that they make no attempt to e____ape injury.

3. I could not im____ne what my wife m____nt when she made that pec____l____r remark about looking fo____ard to being single again.

4. Many of us are so con____rned with overcoming the obs____a____es of everyday e____ist____n____e that we prob____ly overlook the pre____en____e of the b____t__ful aspects of nature that are av____la____e for our enjoyment.

Name: ________________________ Date: ________________

Paragraph Development: Part II

In Chapter One you learned three methods of paragraph development: *facts, examples,* and *incidents.* Here are three other ways of developing a paragraph. These methods are somewhat more complicated because they use a combination of facts, examples, reasons, and incidents. As you study and practice these methods of paragraph development, refer back to Pointers for Writing a Paragraph, page 31.

I definition
II comparison and contrast
III S-N-S (*s*tatistics, *n*ames, and the *s*enses)

I Here is an example of a paragraph developed with a *definition:*

Nowadays, more and more people are enjoying the benefits of organically grown fruits and vegetables. This trend profits from our increased awareness of environmental decay, for no artificial fertilizers or insect sprays are used on the plants. Only natural, organic compounds are used to treat the soil. Some growers even go so far as to raise their crops in a greenhouse with purified, pollution-free air and water. Because of this special care, the produce is often quite expensive; a pound of tomatoes, for example, could cost as much as two dollars. But compared with ordinary fruits and vegetables, the organically grown varieties are generally larger in size, deeper in color, tastier, and above all, more nourishing. For these reasons, most health food consumers are willing to be called "health food nuts."

 *Try It Out*

1. Underline the topic sentence in the paragraph above.
2. Is there more than one main idea in the paragraph?
3. In your own words state the definition of organically grown fruits and vegetables as given in the paragraph.

Name: ______________________ Date: ______________________

EXERCISE 2e: Choose one of these topic sentences and develop it into a paragraph using a *definition*. Use separate paper.

1. Maturity means more than just physical growth.

2. A good textbook is easy to recognize.

3. ______________ is the easiest (hardest) course that I have ever taken.

II Here is an example of a paragraph developed through *comparison and contrast:*

Several drug rehabilitation centers are now using methadone, a manufactured opiate, as a replacement for heroin. Doctors have found that methadone blocks the addict's craving for heroin and the capacity to get high on it. Because methadone may be legally prescribed, it costs only twenty-five cents to one dollar a dose, compared to $60 to $200 a dose for heroin. In addition, the addict takes the artificial drug orally, avoiding the nuisance and health hazard of the needle. Whereas the effects of methadone last for anywhere between 24 and 36 hours, heroin must be taken three or four times a day. Most important of all, the methadone user does not experience the sensations of a heroin high, so that he or she is able to go to school or maintain a job. Most doctors admit that methadone may not be the best solution for addiction problems but, until something better is found, it does allow the heroin addict to function as a reasonably normal member of society.

☞ *Try It Out*

1. Underline the topic sentence in the paragraph above.
2. Is there more than one main idea in the paragraph?
3. In your own words state three of the comparisons and contrasts used to develop the paragraph.

EXERCISE 2f: Choose one of these topic sentences and develop it into a paragraph using *comparison and contrast.* Use separate paper.

1. My neighborhood has (has not) stayed the same ever since I started to live there.

2. My parents are very similar to (different from) each other.

3. Watching a movie on television is not the same as seeing a movie in a theater.

Name: ______________________ *Date:* ______________

III Here is an example of a paragraph developed with *S-N-S* (*s*tatistics, *n*ames, and the *s*enses):

Broad Street needs to be cleaned up. Empty beer cans, candy wrappers, popsicle sticks, used tissues, and torn old newspapers fill the gutters along the entire ten-mile length of the street. The walls of the buildings are covered with multi-colored, dust-covered graffiti and chalk markings. Dog droppings have made the sidewalks into an obstacle course for people and animals alike. The three blocks between Elm and Main Streets are particularly disgusting, with piles of decaying garbage and discarded furniture lining the sidewalks. Smelling like a foul garbage dump, the rotting food sickens people even if they have strong stomachs, and the sight of old broken chairs, split mattresses, and cracked mirrors depresses everyone who walks by. The worst spot of all is in front of the old Calcite Supermarket where two abandoned cars stand, their tires gone, their windshields broken, and their seats torn into pieces. These rusty tin buckets provide an ideal home for the three wild dogs that roam the street daily, looking for food and scaring passersby. Surely this filthy street deserves care from a city that can trace its beginnings to 1890, when Broad Street was the only paved street in town.

 *Try It Out*

1. Underline the topic sentence in the paragraph above.
2. Is there more than one main idea in the paragraph?
3. Identify the statistics used in the paragraph. Then identify the names used. Finally, identify the senses used.

EXERCISE 2q: Choose one of these topic sentences and develop it into a paragraph using *S-N-S*. Use separate paper.

1. When I need to be alone to think, the best place for me is ______________.

2. A visit to a zoo can awaken all the senses.

3. Watching the players is only a small part of what a fan experiences at a football (soccer, basketball, baseball) game.

EXERCISE 2h: ESSAY ANALYSIS Answer these questions about the essay "Old Before Her Time."

1. What is being defined in paragraph 1?

___

2. What is being compared in paragraph 15?

___

3. What are the S-N-S details in paragraph 16?

___

4. What is being contrasted in paragraph 17?

___

EXERCISE 2i: Write an essay on one of the six topics given below. Using the essay outline shown below, try to use a different type of paragraph development for each of the qualities you select. For help in planning your essay, refer to the Pointers for Writing an Essay on page 35. Use your own paper for this assignment.

Qualities That Make an Ideal Date

Qualities That Make an Ideal Mate

Qualities That Make an Ideal Parent

Qualities That Make an Ideal Student

Qualities That Make an Ideal Teacher

Qualities That Make an Ideal Friend

I. Introduction

II. One Quality (you select)

III. Another Quality (you select)

IV. A Third Quality (you select)

V. Conclusion

 Name: ___ *Date:* ___

Ordering of Details in a Paragraph

Now that you know the six basic methods of paragraph development, it will be helpful to plan the details of your chosen method of development. Before haphazardly throwing information into a paragraph, decide on a plan for the order and arrangement of your details. The three basic, and most useful, arrangements are:

- **I** details arranged by order of importance
- **II** details arranged by order of time
- **III** details arranged by order of location

The order you select should depend on the topic of the paragraph and the kinds of details that it will be necessary to use. The ordering of details in any of these three ways will improve the clarity and effectiveness of your writing.

I DETAILS ARRANGED BY ORDER OF IMPORTANCE. Just as an orchestra begins quietly and builds to the climactic crash of the cymbals, so you may build your paragraph the same way with the least important details first and the most important last. Notice how it is done in this paragraph:

People often complain about foolish things. Very demanding types will find fault with every little detail, like a speck of grease on a wall or someone being three minutes early or late for an appointment. Other people often feel frustrated by the weather, no matter what it happens to be, or about their health, no matter how minor the illness. Often such lack of judgment is quickly put in its place when a real trauma strikes: loss of a job, serious illness, unexpected death. Now complaining turns to worry or grief, and the petty details picked at previously seem utterly unimportant.

HINT: You may choose to give your most important details first and the least important last, but the opposite order is generally more effective.

EXERCISE 2j: Use order of importance to fill in the details for the following topic sentence.

I want the person I marry (am married to) to have a number of important qualities.

1. ______________________________

2. ______________________________

3. ______________________________

4. ______________________________

5. ______________________________

EXERCISE 2k: Choose one of these topic sentences and develop it into a paragraph that uses details arranged according to *order of importance*. Use separate paper.

1. A person should make a career choice on the basis of more than salary.
2. I wish that I could change some things about myself.
3. This year's new cars have several good features.

II DETAILS ARRANGED BY ORDER OF TIME. If you are telling how something is made, how a game is played, or how a system developed, you should use the order of happening, often called *chronological order*. You will be telling the sequence of events in the order of their occurrence. Notice how it is done in this paragraph:

Is it really possible to escape the materialism of our capitalistic society? In an attempt to do just that, many have formed communes—often with interesting results. In Indiana, for example, a group of people pooled their funds to buy a large tract of land in the wilderness. Here they would build a peaceful community free from the pressures of the machine age. But because they had no money for their living expenses, they began to chop down the trees and sell them to a local mill. Within a few months, they were chopping down large amounts of timber so that they could raise enough money to plant and harvest their own crops. Realizing that the mill was making most of the profit, a clever member of the commune eventually suggested that the group build its own mill. As a result, the commune now has machinery for cutting down the trees, a mill for

 Name: ______________________ Date: ______________________

transforming them into lumber, and a fleet of trucks for transporting the lumber to the market. What had started as a quiet agricultural community has now become the largest capitalistic business in the entire region.

EXERCISE 2l: Use chronological order to fill in the details for the following topic sentence.

It was a perfect day from beginning to end.

1. ______________________________

2. ______________________________

3. ______________________________

4. ______________________________

5. ______________________________

EXERCISE 2m: Choose one of these topic sentences and develop it into a paragraph using details arranged according to *order of time*. Use separate paper.

1. I make every minute count when I am on vacation.
2. ______________ has the silliest plot for a movie (television program) that I have seen in a long time.
3. Once while on a date I found myself in a very embarrassing situation.

III DETAILS ARRANGED BY ORDER OF LOCATION. When you describe a place or wish to take your reader from one place to another, you must do it in an orderly fashion so that the reader can picture the scene in his mind. You would use order of location to describe such things as a college campus, or your room, or even something as small as a penny. In each instance, you should give the position of one thing in relation to something you have already described. For example:

A street carnival easily draws people to its festive atmosphere and unusual attractions. With one end of the street left open for people to come and go, the rest of the space is happily jammed with people and booths. On one side of the street a ferris wheel, bordered with flashing multi-colored lights, carries delighted customers high up the circle and down. Across the way a spinning rocket fills its riders with thrills and fear. At the far end of the street a merry-go-round attracts the close interest of the younger children. Set between the rides are booths of all descriptions: a wheel of fortune that tests luck; a ball toss game that challenges skill; palm readers that tell fortunes; jars of beans that defy guessing powers; and, of course, food stands that sell ice cream, hot dogs, and other temptations. Though some of the attractions might seem unimportant separately, the carnival atmosphere encourages the enthusiastic participation of everyone who steps into the street.

EXERCISE 2n: Use order of location to fill in the details for the following topic sentence.

A well-equipped gymnasium must include a number of important facilities.

1. ______________________________

2. ______________________________

3. ______________________________

4. ______________________________

5. ______________________________

6. ______________________________

EXERCISE 2o: Choose one of these topic sentences and develop it into a paragraph using details arranged according to *order of location*. Use separate paper.

1. My bedroom is a clear expression of my personality.
2. The green side of a one-dollar bill has quite a variety of designs and drawings.
3. The layout of my favorite store makes locating various products easy.

Name: ______________________ *Date:* ______________________

EXERCISE 2p: ESSAY ANALYSIS Answer these questions about the essay "Old Before Her Time."

1. a. Are the details in paragraph 3 arranged in order of importance, time, or location?

   ____

   b. Would another arrangement of the details in paragraph 3 have been as effective? Why?

   ____

2. a. Are the details in paragraphs 7, 8, and 9 arranged in order of importance, time, or location?

   ____

   b. Would another arrangement of the details in paragraphs 7, 8, and 9 have been as effective? Why?

   ____

3. Paragraphs 6, 10, 12, 14, 17, 20, and 22 present the seven lessons that Patty Moore learned when she was disguised as an eighty-five-year-old woman. The author of the essay has arranged these lessons using time order. How would you arrange the seven lessons using order of importance? Be prepared to defend the order you select.

   ____

   ____

   ____

   ____

   ____

   ____

   ____

   ____

   ____

Name: ______________________ *Date:* ______________________

EXERCISE 2q: REFRESHER On separate paper rewrite the following paragraph. Remove any material that is not part of the main idea stated in the topic sentence. Add facts, examples, incidents, definitions, comparisons and contrasts, or S-N-S to develop the paragraph more fully.

Although loneliness is a major problem for many older Americans, they can take some steps to overcome it. First, they might start attending a local senior citizens' center if they are lucky enough to have one in their community. These centers give people the opportunity to socialize and to participate in a number of interesting activities. The federal government should really open more of these centers throughout the country. It is also a good idea for the elderly to have pets. Caring for an affectionate, playful cat or dog is an excellent way to reduce feelings of loneliness. In addition, recent studies indicate that people who have pets tend to be healthier than those who do not. By taking such steps as these, the elderly can fill their empty hours with a wealth of rewarding experiences that will bring joy and a sense of purpose to their lives.

 Name: ____________________ Date: ____________________

SPRINGBOARDS TO WRITING

Using your knowledge of the writing process, explained on pages 12–14, write a paragraph or essay related to this chapter's central theme, *problems of the elderly,* which is introduced on pages 38–45.

PREWRITING

To think of topics to write about, look at the two advertisements, read the essay, and answer the questions that follow each. If you prefer, select one of the writing springboards below. (All paragraph numbers refer to the essay that starts on page 40.) To develop your ideas, use the prewriting techniques described on pages 15–20.

WRITING A PARAGRAPH (For help, see the Pointers on page 31.)

1. My Opinion of Patty Moore's Experiment (See essay, pages 40–45.)
2. I do (do not) like being around senior citizens.
3. Companionship is (is not) enough reason for senior citizens to marry.
4. Senior citizens are often the victims of crime.
5. Agree or disagree: Retirement communities for the elderly are just high-class "gray ghettos." (See ¶ 9.)
6. I recall an incident when I saw an elderly person discriminated against.
7. Experts say that the key problems in growing old are isolation, poor health, poverty, and fear of old age. Which do you think is the worst? Why?

WRITING AN ESSAY (For help, see the Pointers on page 35.)

8. The Problems of Growing Old
9. I Am (Am Not) Worried about Growing Old
10. Why Are the Old Often Ignored? (See ¶ 6.)
11. Age Is a State of Mind
12. How We Can Make Life Easier for Senior Citizens
13. Agree or disagree: With Age Comes Wisdom
14. Elderly Parents Should (Should Not) Live with Their Children
15. People Should (Should Not) Be Required to Retire at Any Age
16. We Live in a Youth-Oriented Society
17. What Does It Take to Be a "Survivor"? (See ¶ 24.)
18. Agree or disagree: "Life goes on as long as you're flexible and open to change." (See ¶ 22.)

Wide World Photos.

three

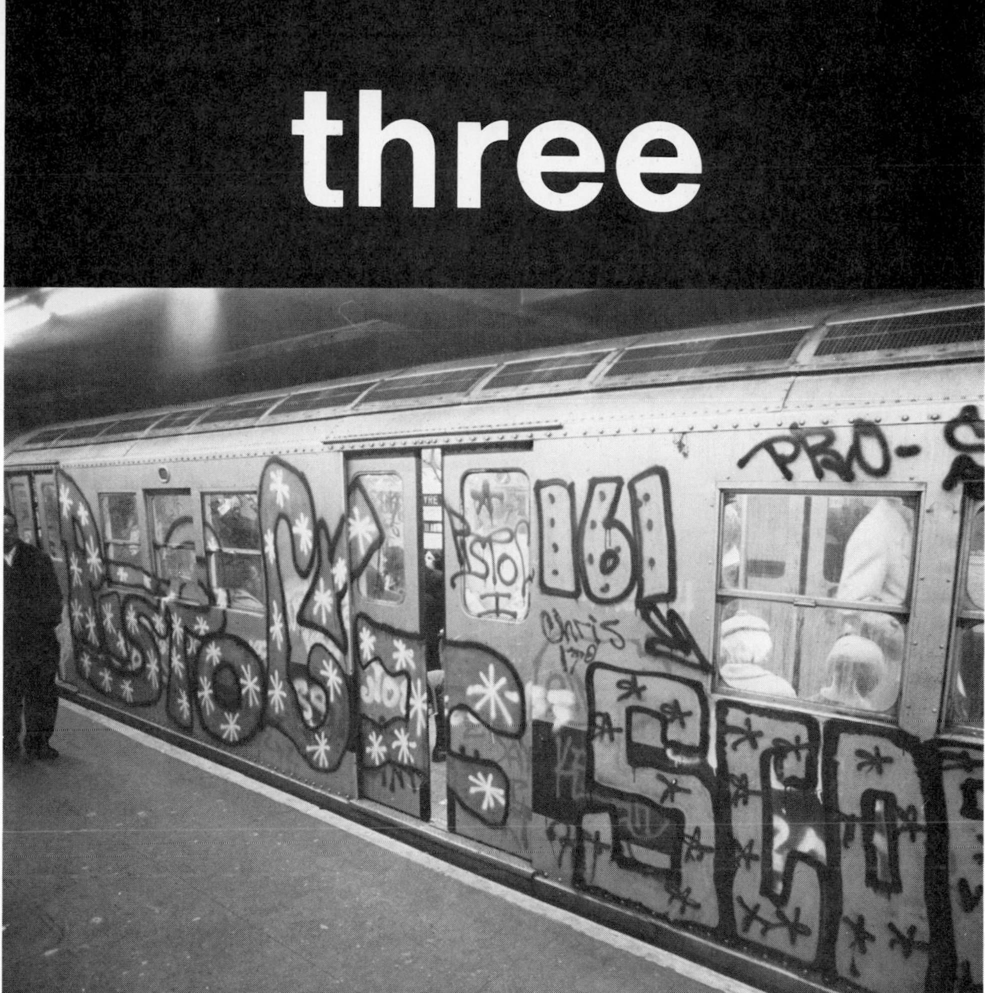

UPI/Bettmann Archive.

SPRINGBOARDS TO THINKING

For informal, not written, response . . . to stimulate your thinking

1. What is the condition of the outside of the house shown in the photograph on the opposite page? How do you think the people who live near this house feel about the way it looks? Explain.
2. What is the condition of the outside of the subway car shown in the photograph above? How do you think subway riders feel about the way the car looks? Explain.
3. Do you think that people should have the right to keep the outsides of their houses in whatever condition they want? Why or why not? What do you think should be the penalty for people who put graffiti on subway cars, buses, walls, and other public places?
4. Do you think that people have the right in their homes to play their stereos very loud or to have very noisy parties, even if the music and noise disturb their neighbors? Why or why not?
5. Why are many people today often selfish, inconsiderate, and rude? What effects does such behavior have on our society and on everyone's quality of life?

Why People Are Rude

DAVID A. WIESSLER

(1) Rudeness is becoming a common occurrence in American life. If you don't like it, lump it. Or mind your own business. Or get out of the way. That is the kind of talk and attitude that's cropping up more often in almost every public experience—on the highways, in theater lines, over the telephone, on public transit. The examples are almost endless:

• Sitting in a New York movie theater, a man refuses to turn down his radio despite requests from the usher and others watching the show.

• An Atlanta newsstand operator is unable to wait on his customers because passers-by shout at him for directions, information or change without waiting their turns.

• A woman stands in a Washington, D.C., supermarket line while her children do the shopping. When the cart is full, she has the children wheel it to the front of the line where she is standing ahead of everyone else.

(2) What's behind such incidents? Some experts say the trend began in the 1960's when traditional values and manners came under fire. Others blame the fast-paced American lifestyle for creating a society that has little time any more to be polite. This is particularly true in big cities, where people are surrounded by strangers. "In a small town, the person to whom you are rude is more likely to be someone you are going to see again tomorrow," observed psychologist Stanley Milgram at the Graduate Center of the City University of New York. "In the city, it is very unlikely you will ever again encounter someone with whom you have a minor conflict."

(3) Some call New York City the rudeness capital of the world. Stroll down its streets and you encounter taxi drivers who believe a "walk" sign at an intersection is an invitation to nudge their bumpers against pedestrians' knees. On one afternoon, an angry pedestrian reacted by kicking the cab, prompting the driver to get out and give chase. In the same city, hardly a day goes by that the average office worker doesn't ride an elevator with someone who insists on smoking—despite rules against it. "If you don't like it, get out and switch to another elevator," one smoker recently told another passenger who objected to his cigar smoke in a midtown elevator. In New York and other cities, quiet strolls are becoming a thing of the past. The culprits: pedestrians who carry powerful stereos set at full volume.

(4) Stress also plays a role in incidents of callous behavior. Cindy Kludt, a counselor who works with nurses suffering from stress, says rudeness can often be epidemic in hospitals where people are constantly working under life-and-death circumstances. "If people at the top are rude or noncaring, it rolls downhill, affecting everyone's behavior."

(5) Combine stress with anonymity—as occurs regularly on highways—and rudeness abounds. Motorists regularly force bicyclists off the road, and large trucks tailgate autos moving too slowly in front of them. Bottles and trash are thrown at road crews in Houston and elsewhere by drivers upset because lanes are restricted. Telephone conversations with strangers offer still more opportunities for incivility. A clerk at a store in Santa Barbara, California, says he is jarred by the number of people who call for information and hang up abruptly without even a "thank you."

(6) Public officials often are the target of people frustrated by bureaucracy's red tape. Staff assistants in Texas for Democratic Representative Jack Hightower tell of rude, abusive, and sometimes threatening calls and visits from people who feel government agencies are mistreating them. Rudeness in public dealings cuts both ways, however. In Miami, one county official says that members of the Dade County Commission often talk among themselves and walk around while people are testifying before that group. "I have seen people stop their testimony and ask, 'Are you going to pay attention to me?' " she says.

(7) Others observe that many men today use coarse language in front of women, which was rather rare a generation ago. "Men used to be careful not to cuss in front of women, putting on a sophisticated behavior," says psychologist Chaytor Mason of the University of Southern California. "Now, with women more competitive, men have decided to take their gloves off and show them."

(8) Sometimes, such behavior goes beyond verbal abuse. A hostess in an Atlanta area restaurant was slapped by a patron after she told him no table would be available for two hours. Daniel Radler of Cambridge, Massachusetts, recently won $3,500 in damages for injuries suffered when he chided a woman for smoking on a bus in violation of posted rules. After being told to "get lost," he was beaten with an umbrella by the woman and her male companion. Houston utility crews report increasing violence from people who have gripes with the power company. One worker was shot in the stomach with a pellet gun, and another's truck was set afire. "Our repair crews and meter readers have a rough time in some apartment houses where you have a lot of people in relatively little space," says an executive of the Houston Lighting & Power Company. "That's where you find the shortest fuses."

(9) Perpetrators—and victims—of the new crudity can be of any age, sex or income level, although experts say the country's youth may be ruder because of their immaturity. One group that seems to be on the receiving end of crude behavior more often: the handicapped. In a recent incident in Detroit, a male performer had a woman removed from a theater for alleg-

edly disrupting the performance with her high-pitched laugh. The woman, who suffers from cerebral palsy, has filed suit against the performer and the theater. "Handicapped people are facing more and more hostility," says Mark Stroh, a spokesman for a Michigan group helping the handicapped. "They were just locked away twenty years ago. Now, they're getting out, and many people aren't tolerant of them." Jane Everhart, director of the Detroit cerebral palsy association, remembers when her mother had larynx surgery and had to speak with the aid of a voice enhancer. When her mother phoned an automobile dealership, a receptionist broke into laughter upon hearing the voice and then laughed even more when told the reason for its strange sound.

(10) Whatever the cause of rudeness, people are at a loss to do much about it, although the temptation is to fight fire with fire. A man in a Detroit bank became so abusive to a teller that others in line shouted him down. Signs at Six Flags Magic Mountain, an amusement park near Los Angeles, read: "Warning. Breaking lines is cause for removal from the park. No refunds."

(11) Still, psychologists see little hope for a decline in today's rude behavior. In fact, some see a new pattern emerging in big cities—the "norm of noninvolvement" as one psychologist calls it. For example, a young man recently felt compelled to tell fellow subway travelers that the reason he gave up his seat to an elderly man was that "I was about to get off anyway." In short, in an environment where rudeness has almost become the norm, people now are making excuses for being polite and considerate.

READING SURVEY

1. *Main Idea*

What is the central theme of the essay?

2. *Major Details*

a. According to David Wiessler, what is behind the many incidents of rudeness described?
b. Why are people who live in large cities more likely to be rude than are those who live in small towns?
c. What sort of people are most likely to be the perpetrators—or the victims—of rudeness?

3. *Inferences*

a. Read paragraph 9 again. Why are the handicapped on the "receiving end" more often than are other groups?
b. Read paragraph 11 again. Why should people have to make excuses for being polite and considerate?

4. Opinions

a. Read paragraph 8 again. Do you think that smoking should be banned in public places such as restaurants and buses? Why or why not?

b. Read paragraph 9 again. Do you agree that the country's youth are ruder than others? Explain, giving specific examples to support your opinion.

VOCABULARY BUILDING

Lesson One: The Vocabulary of Rudeness

The essay "Why People Are Rude" by David A. Wiessler includes words that are useful when you are discussing rudeness.

despite	(paragraph 1)	**coarse**	(7)
culprits	(3)	**crudity**	(9) . . . **crude** (9)
callous	(4)	**disrupting**	(9)
incivility	(5)	**hostility**	(9)
abusive	(6) . . . **abuse** (8)	**tolerant**	(9)

People who behave rudely do so **despite** or in spite of the fact that the behavior is annoying and upsetting.

People who behave rudely are often the **culprits** or offenders who are guilty of creating conflicts between people.

People who behave rudely usually have attitudes that are **callous** or unfeeling and lacking in pity.

People who behave rudely are noted for the **incivility** or lack of courtesy or politeness in their behavior.

People who behave rudely are **abusive** in that they cruelly misuse or hurt others. Sometimes the **abuse** takes the form of physical harm or insulting language.

People who behave rudely are usually **coarse** in that their manners are rough or harsh, and often they offend others' sense of what is proper.

People who behave rudely often use **crudity**—remarks or acts that are **crude** or lacking in good taste, grace, or sensitivity.

People who behave rudely often are a **disrupting** influence because they are disorderly and thereby interrupt or disturb the orderly course of whatever is going on.

People who behave rudely are usually filled with **hostility** or active feelings of unfriendliness and anger toward others.

People who behave rudely are usually not **tolerant** or accepting of beliefs and practices different from their own.

EXERCISE 3a: Each of the vocabulary words from this lesson is shown below (in italics) as the word appeared in context in the essay. Write an explanation of each word within the context of the material given. Use your own paper for this assignment.

1. From paragraph 1: ". . . a man refuses to turn down his radio *despite* requests from the usher and others. . . ."
2. From paragraph 3: ". . . quiet strolls are becoming a thing of the past. The *culprits:* pedestrians who carry powerful stereos set at full volume."
3. From paragraph 4: "Stress also plays a role in incidents of *callous* behavior."
4. From paragraph 5: "Telephone conversations with strangers offer still more opportunities for *incivility.*"
5. From paragraph 6: "Staff assistants in Texas . . . tell of rude, *abusive,* and sometimes threatening calls. . . ."
6. From paragraph 7: "Others observe that many men today use *coarse* language in front of women. . . ."
7. From paragraph 8: "Sometimes, such behavior goes beyond verbal *abuse.*"
8. From paragraph 9: "Perpetrators—and victims—of the new *crudity* can be of any age, sex, or income level. . . ."
9. From paragraph 9: "One group that seems to be on the receiving end of *crude* behavior more often: the handicapped."
10. From paragraph 9: ". . . a male performer had a woman removed from a theater for allegedly *disrupting* the performance. . . ."
11. From paragraph 9: "Handicapped people are facing more and more *hostility.* . . ."
12. From paragraph 9: "Now, they're getting out, and many people aren't *tolerant* of them."

Lesson Two: The Vocabulary of Stress

The essay "Why People Are Rude" by David A. Wiessler includes words that are useful when you are discussing stress.

stress	(paragraph 4)	**chided**	(8)
epidemic	(4)	**gripes**	(8)
anonymity	(5)	**norm**	(11)
restricted	(5)	**noninvolvement**	(11)
jarred	(5)	**compelled**	(11)

When people are under pressure, they can feel **stress** because of the strain of physical and mental tensions.

When people are under pressure, stress can become **epidemic** because it spreads rapidly and affects everyone in the family or the community.

When people are under pressure, they might be driven by a fear of **anonymity** because they do not want to be anonymous or unknown to others who see them only as part of a group and not as individuals.

When people are under pressure, they can feel **restricted** because they sometimes feel limited and confined.

When people are under pressure, they can easily feel **jarred** by events that shock or jolt them.

When people are under pressure, they are sometimes **chided** or mildly scolded by their friends.

When people are under pressure, they often say that they have many **gripes,** a slang word for complaints.

When people are under pressure, the level of stress in their lives is usually above the **norm** or the average because they have a large number of problems to deal with.

When people are under pressure, they can often feel that they have no energy left "to get involved," so they prefer **noninvolvement.**

When people are under pressure, they sometimes feel forced into action or they cannot stop themselves from acting because they feel **compelled** to act.

EXERCISE 3b: Each of the vocabulary words from this lesson is shown below (in italics) as the word appeared in context in the essay. Write an explanation of each word within the context of the material given. Use your own paper for this assignment.

1. From paragraph 4: "*Stress* also plays a role. . . ."
2. From paragraph 4: ". . . rudeness can often be *epidemic* in hospitals where people are constantly working under life-and-death circumstances."
3. From paragraph 5: "Combine stress with *anonymity*—as occurs regularly on highways—and rudeness abounds."
4. From paragraph 5: "Bottles and trash are thrown at road crews in Houston and elsewhere by drivers upset because lanes are *restricted.*"
5. From paragraph 5: "A clerk at a store in Santa Barbara, California, says he is *jarred* by the number of people who call for information and hang up abruptly without even a 'thank you.' "
6. From paragraph 8: ". . . he *chided* a woman for smoking on a bus in violation of posted rules."
7. From paragraph 8: "Houston utility crews report increasing violence from people who have *gripes* with the power company."
8. From paragraph 11: "In fact, some see a new pattern emerging in big cities—the '*norm* of *noninvolvement*'. . . ."
9. From paragraph 11: "For example, a young man recently felt *compelled* to tell fellow subway travelers that the reason he gave up his seat to an elderly man was that 'I was about to get off anyway.' "

SPELLING

Lesson One: Spelling Demons

Here are more words that are frequently misspelled. Using the helpful techniques given in Chapter One, you should make it a point to learn these new Demons, which were taken from "Why People Are Rude."

among	**commission**	**operator**
association	**counselor**	**opportunity**
attitude	**decide**	**performance**
becoming	**environment**	**remember**
before	**experience**	**restaurant**
behavior	**handicapped**	**surround**
careful	**manner**	**tomorrow**
circumstance	**occurrence**	**woman**

Lesson Two: Spelling Rule–Changing *Y* to *I*

Many of the words in David A. Wiessler's essay can be learned easily with the help of this one simple spelling rule.

> Words ending in *y* preceded by a consonant change *y* to *i* before suffixes—*except* when the suffix begins with *i*.

☞ *Try It Out*

Add the suffixes indicated to the following words.

	-ed	*-ing*	-(*e*)s
try	________	________	________
pray	________	________	________
carry	________	________	________

Here are some examples:

story + es = stor*ies*
destroy + ed = destroy*ed*
family + es = famil*ies*

apply + ing = appl*ying*
classify + ed = classif*ied*
lovely + est = love*liest*

 Name: ________________ *Date:* ____________

☞ *Try It Out*

Apply the *y* to *i* rule to the following words.

supply + (e)s = ______________ satisfy + ed = ______________

merry + ly = ______________ hurry + ing = ______________

display + (e)s = ______________ crazy + est = ______________

A SPECIAL HINT: Here are four words that you see frequently which—if you look at them closely—are exceptions to the above rule.

lay + ed = laid pay + ed = paid
say + ed = said day + ly = daily

EXERCISE 3c: Apply the *y* to *i* rule to these new words.

1. diary + (e)s = ______________
2. beauty + ful = ______________
3. turkey + (e)s = ______________
4. vary + ation = ______________
5. busy + est = ______________
6. spy + ing = ______________
7. marry + ed = ______________
8. deny + al = ______________
9. twenty + th = ______________
10. happy + ness = ______________
11. delay + ed = ______________
12. multiply + cation =______________
13. category + (e)s = ______________
14. necessary + ly = ______________
15. employ + ment = ______________
16. envy + ous = ______________
17 likely + hood = ______________
18. worry + er = ______________
19. quality + (e)s = ______________
20. obey + ing = ______________

Name: ______________ Date: ______________

EXERCISE 3d: Using the definitions given as clues, fill in this puzzle. If necessary, check your spelling with the list of Demons in this chapter.

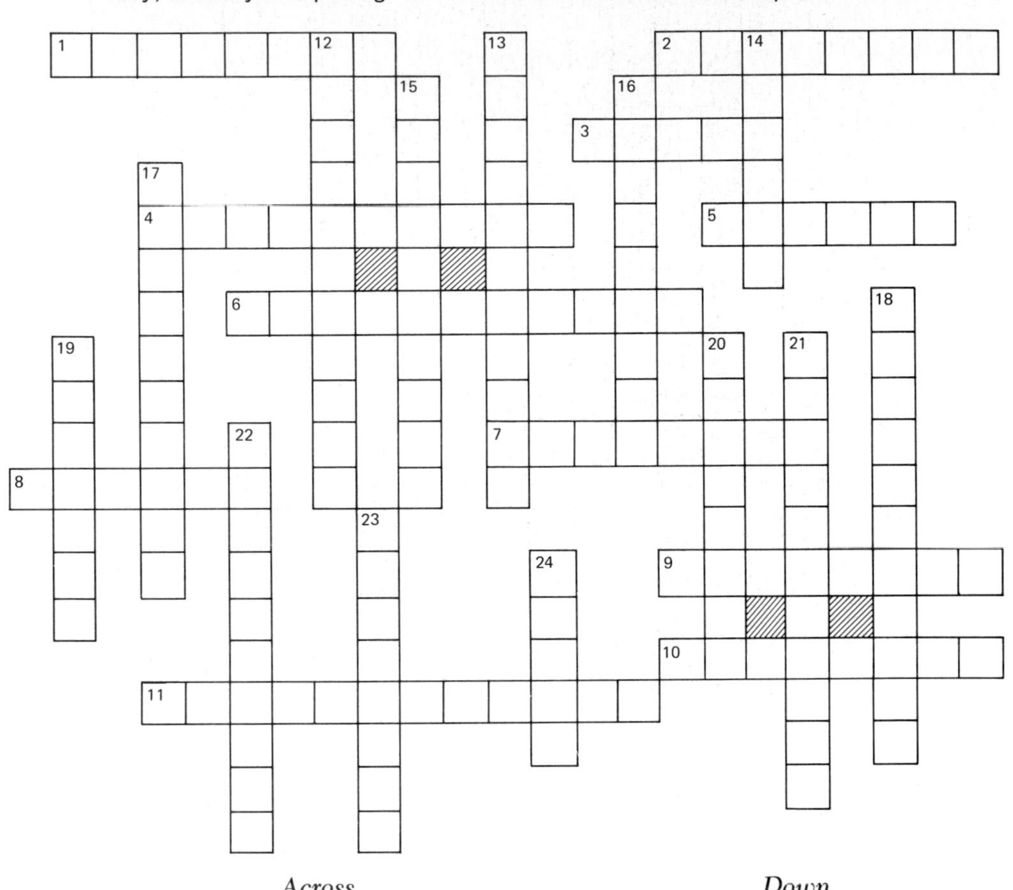

Across

1. to think of again
2. yesterday, today, ________
3. female
4. a happening or incident
5. ________, during, after
6. disabled in some way
7. A telephone ________ can help you make a call.
8. to make up one's mind
9. to encircle on all sides
10. a person's conduct
11. under the ________s

Down

12. Pollution ruins the ________.
13. A.A.A. = American Automobile ________
14. method
15. training or practice
16. He is my camp ________.
17. money that some salespeople receive for making a sale
18. chance
19. cautious
20. a point of view
21. a theatrical presentation
22. cafeteria
23. changing into
24. in the middle of

 Name: ________ Date: ________

The Sentence Fragment

A group of words set off as a sentence must be complete. This is a simple requirement and an easy one to test, but the writing of sentence fragments is a common error for the beginning writer. To avoid writing sentence fragments, you must learn this:

Three-step Test of Sentence Completeness

I Find the conjugated verb.
II Find the subject.
III Look to see if the subject and verb are introduced by a DANGER WORD. (See list on page 80.) If this is so, the sentence is not a complete thought.

I FRAGMENT CAUSED BY A MISSING CONJUGATED VERB. A VERB expresses action, existence, occurrence, etc. A word is usually a verb if it can be put into the past tense:

Today I *want.*	Yesterday I *wanted.*
Today I *am.*	Yesterday I *was.*
Today I *have.*	Yesterday I *had.*
Today I *give.*	Yesterday I *gave.*

A SPECIAL NOTE: For help in understanding the many forms of the verb *to be* (*am, is, are, was, were*), see pages 150, 164, and 174.

The verb in a sentence must be complete and conjugated. Notice that there are two ways it is not conjugated:

a. If it has an *-ing* ending without a helping verb

Fragment	*Corrected*
X Jim studying data processing	✓ Jim *is* studying data processing. OR ✓ Jim *was* studying data processing.

b. If it is an infinitive (*to* run, *to* go, *to* do, etc.)

Fragment	*Corrected*
X Jim to program a computer	✓ Jim *is* to program a computer. OR ✓ Jim programs a computer.

Each sentence must have a complete conjugated verb. The verb in one sentence cannot be thought of as part of the next sentence; the verb *must actually appear* in the sentence.

X Marie has many varied interests. Such as psychology, philosophy, and politics.

The first statement is a complete sentence; the second is a fragment because it has no verb.

Try It Out

Draw two lines under the verbs in the following word groups. Then correct any fragments so that they are complete sentences.

1. The old rusty car and stacks of oily, smelly paint cans in my neighbor's new garage.
2. The airplane trying to make a safe landing in spite of its damaged landing gear.
3. A cockroach can live for several weeks without a head.

II FRAGMENT CAUSED BY A MISSING SUBJECT. The SUBJECT is the noun or pronoun unit about which something is said. To find the subject of a sentence, first find the complete conjugated verb. Then simply ask, "*Who* or *what* is doing the action?" For example:

✓ The boy threw the ball.

The verb is *threw. Who* or *what* threw? The *boy* threw. Therefore, *boy* is the subject of the sentence.

In a command the subject is usually not given but it is implied as *you.* For example:

✓ Run for your life! Close the window before it rains!

Who should run? *You.* Who should close the window? *You.* Therefore, *you* is the subject of these and most commands.

A word group may sometimes be the subject of a sentence:

✓ Going to a movie is great fun.
✓ Whoever can pass the test will be given an "A" as a grade.

To find the subject, you just find the verb and ask the same question: Who or what is great fun? *Going to a movie.* Who or what will be given an "A" as a grade? *Whoever can pass the test.* Therefore, a word group is the subject of each sentence.

You may sometimes forget to include the subject of a sentence because you have just used it in the preceding sentence and it seems to be the subject of the fragment. However, you must always remember that the subject *must* be included in each sentence (with the exception of a command).

X The athlete felt nervous as she ran across the mat. Did a forward somersault and then finished with a back flip.

The first statement is a complete sentence; the second is a fragment because it has no subject. *Who* did a forward somersault and a back flip? The fragment does not tell us.

To correct this error:

Connect the fragment to the preceding sentence.

Examples: The athlete felt nervous as she ran across the mat, did a forward somersault, and then finished with a back flip.

OR

Put a subject into the fragment.

She did a forward somersault and then finished with a back flip.

Try It Out

Draw two lines under the verbs and one line under the subjects in the following word groups. If a subject is missing, put one in to make the fragment into a complete sentence.

1. Suddenly the jewelry maker sneezed loudly.
2. Fell to his knees and then began to hunt for the dozens of unset diamonds scattered on the floor.

III FRAGMENT CAUSED BY A DANGER WORD. If the conjugated verb and its subject are introduced by a DANGER WORD, you do not have a complete sentence; it does not express a complete thought. It is a cliff-hanger, because it begins a statement but does not finish it.

Example: If you come home . . . *what?*

The most commonly used DANGER WORDS are:

after	unless
although (though)	how
as (as if)	when
because	where
before	while
if	until
since	so that

who	whoever
whom	whomever
which	what
that	whatever

Most of the DANGER WORDS are readily noticed because they come before the expression they affect.

X Because he is such a dependent person
X After the waiter calculated the bill
X Although a family budget is important

The introductory DANGER WORD makes each of these a fragment without a complete thought. What happened because he is such a dependent person? What happened after the waiter calculated the bill? What happened although a family budget is important? The DANGER WORDS suggest that the answers to these questions must be included in the sentence.

The DANGER WORDS that are listed in the right-side box on the opposite page (especially *who*, *which*, and *that*) frequently appear between the subject and verb.

X A person who is very competitive
X The movie which won many awards
X The trash that clutters our streets

None of these incomplete sentences tells the reader what happened. What will a person who is very competitive do? What about the movie? What about the trash? The thought is not complete.

A SPECIAL NOTE: Do not avoid the DANGER WORDS completely. *When used correctly*, they are excellent tools for writing complex sentences. This use will be fully illustrated in the next chapter.

To correct the fragment caused by a DANGER WORD:

	Examples:
Attach the fragment to the previous sentence or to the one that follows, whichever is most closely connected in thought to the fragment.	Frank constantly asks for help because he is such a dependent person. After the waiter calculated the bill, he presented it to the customer.
OR	
Complete the fragment with the necessary words.	A person who is very competitive usually enjoys sports.

A PROOFREADING SUGGESTION: You may find it easier to spot a fragment in your writing if you read your paragraphs from the last sentence to the first sentence. In this way, you disconnect the fragment from the surrounding sentences, which are usually closely linked to the fragment in thought and which, therefore, might blend when you read them.

Try It Out

Draw two lines under the verbs, draw one line under the subjects, and circle any DANGER WORDS in the following word groups. Correct the fragments so that they are complete sentences.

1. You are dropped from the sixtieth to the first floor in only thirty seconds.
2. When you ride a high-speed elevator in a modern office building.
3. A sure way to feel that your stomach has jammed into your throat.

EXERCISE 3e: Rewrite any fragments so that they are complete sentences. Some of the word groups may already be complete; if the word group is complete, put a period at the end and write nothing else.

1. When the convict was released from prison

2. Misunderstanding her student's explanation

3. Salespeople who are rude to their customers

4. A magazine listing best-selling computer software

5. Before accepting the soap opera star's invitation to dinner

6. In order to make lasting friendships

7. If you ignore your teeth, they might disappear forever

8. After the shocking facts are revealed

Name: ____________ Date: ____________

9. Michael Jackson, a popular and talented entertainer

___

10. A sample of water from the polluted river

___

11. Spilling your coffee on your boss's desk

___

12. Whoever jogs at least two miles a day

___

13. The average telephone conversation lasts five minutes

___

14. The first person who landed on the moon

___

15. The sexy novel about life in a small town

___

16. A robot that can cook your dinner

___

17. Exhausted from driving all night

___

18. Because the rattlesnake was sleeping

___

19. The President's message on hunger in America

___

20. To believe that flying saucers are real

___

Name: ___ Date: ___

EXERCISE 3f: Each of the following paragraphs contains one fragment. Make it into a complete sentence, rewriting where necessary. Use the space provided.

1. At the age of 65, Harland Sanders decided to start a new business. After profits dropped off at his Corbin, Kentucky, restaurant. He sold restaurant owners across the nation the right to use his secret recipe for "Kentucky Fried Chicken." When he retired nine years later, he had earned $2 million and his face was world famous.

   ____

2. A young surgeon had to earn extra money to help repay his education loans. He took a part-time job as a butcher's assistant at a meat market. One day, a woman who was rushed to the hospital with severe appendicitis started to explain her problem to the surgeon. Then suddenly screamed in terror and shouted, "Oh, no! Help! He's my butcher!"

   ____

3. How to train your pet dog. First, let him get used to the leash by having him always wear it. Second, pull gently on the leash and speak firmly when teaching him what to do. Finally, reward him when he does well.

   ____

   ____

4. Pancho Villa, the Mexican revolutionary general, leading the last army that successfully invaded the United States in March 1916 at Columbus, New Mexico. He was chased by General Pershing and general-to-be George Patton, but he got away from them in the mountains. In fact, he had escaped capture many times during the long Mexican Revolution. After he retired to a ranch in Durango, Mexico, he was ambushed and killed in 1923.

   ____

   ____

5. In the year 996 the Persian ruler Agud made a declaration. To control mass starvation as a result of a terrible famine throughout his kingdom. He ordered that for every person who died of starvation one rich person would be executed. No one starved.

   ____

   ____

 Name: ______________________ *Date:* ______________________

6. It is not always easy to succeed. The book *M*A*S*H* was rejected by twenty-one publishers before its author, Richard Hooker, sold it in 1968. This shows that some people can make hard work pay off. Just as long as they have the confidence not to give up.

____

____

7. Mother Theresa is counted among the most famous nuns who ever lived. Born in Yugoslavia, she went to India, where she founded the Missionaries of Charity in 1948. She received many awards for her service to the human race. Including the Pope John XXIII Peace Prize in 1971 and the Nobel Peace Prize in 1979.

____

____

8. Leo Hirshfield, who introduced the first candy wrapped in paper. He was only twenty-nine at the time. It was a chewy, tube-shaped chocolate. He named it after his little girl, Clara "Tootsie" Hirshfield.

____

____

9. Between 1940 and 1973 the Central Intelligence Agency (CIA) secretly funded a nationwide series of harmful mind-control experiments. The people used in the projects were not informed of the risks they were taking. According to CIA data obtained through the Freedom of Information Act and testimony at a 1977 Senate committee hearing. The program had been meant to develop chemicals that would protect people against Communist brainwashing techniques.

____

____

10. Skylab, the U.S. space station that reentered the atmosphere in 1979, caused much worry around the world. People feared it would come down in a populated area. A terrible thing to think about while weeding the garden, walking to the store, or playing ball. Luckily, the only large piece to fall on land was a one-ton segment that did not cause any damage.

____

____

Name: ____________________ Date: ____________________

Comma Splices and Run-On Sentences

Like sentence fragments, the comma splice and the run-on sentence are serious errors which can be eliminated with the help of the three-step test of sentence completeness (see page 77). Let's use the test on the following sentences:

✓ Tony is immoral. He steals hubcaps for a living.

Both of these sentences are complete because they each have a subject and verb not introduced by a DANGER WORD. Now let's examine the same sentences which have undergone one seemingly minor change:

X Tony is immoral, he steals hubcaps for a living.

We still have the same complete sentences, but they have now been joined by a comma. Because two complete sentences cannot be joined by just a comma, the above illustration is an error. It is called a *comma splice.*

Notice how the next set of sentences makes the same mistake:

X The U.S. Post Office Department provides reliable service, however, sometimes a letter is not delivered for weeks, months, or even years.

There are two separate subjects and two separate verbs. Thus, we have two distinct sentences that should not be joined with a comma, as the corrected sentences indicate:

✓ The U.S. Post Office Department provides reliable service. However, sometimes a letter is not delivered for weeks, months, or even years.

Now use the test of sentence completeness to examine the following:

X Because Karen was very competitive, she entered a pie-eating contest, then she had to spend a week in the hospital.

Although the first possible subject and verb are cancelled out by the DANGER WORD *because,* we are still left with two subject–verb sets. Again we have two sentences that have been joined together with a comma and need to be separated.

√ Because Karen was very competitive, she entered a pie-eating contest. Then she had to spend a week in the hospital.

Compare the previous error to the one made in the next sentences:

X Sex education must certainly be a thought-provoking subject it is easy to form a discussion group for such a topic.

Here we also have two separate subject–verb sets in what should be two sentences. But unlike the comma splice, these sentences have been joined together without even a comma. This is called a *run-on sentence.*

√ Sex education must certainly be a thought-provoking subject. It is easy to form a discussion group for such a topic.

Now the sentences are written correctly. You should note that the run-on is considered a more serious error than the comma splice because it implies that the writer does not sense a pause between two distinct thoughts.

When you proofread your writing for mistakes, pay particular attention to certain words and thought relationships that frequently lead to comma splice and run-on errors.

POINTERS FOR AVOIDING COMMA SPLICES AND RUN-ONS

1. Words and expressions such as *therefore, however, then, furthermore, for example,* and *thus* (see page 324 for a complete list) help your writing to flow more smoothly. But do *not* use these words to join two complete sentences.

X Many people are lonely however, few know how to make friends.

X Many people are lonely, however, few know how to make friends.

√ Many people are lonely. However, few know how to make friends.

2. The words *I, you, he, she, we, they,* and *it* refer to someone or something already mentioned. But do *not* use these words to join two complete sentences.

X Bicycles are enjoyable to ride they give people a feeling of great freedom.

X Bicycles are enjoyable to ride, they give people a feeling of great freedom.

√ Bicycles are enjoyable to ride. They give people a feeling of great freedom.

3. A sentence sometimes explains or adds to a point made in a previous sentence. Although the two sentences are closely linked in thought, they must be punctuated as two separate sentences.

X There are many varieties of tomato beefsteak and plum are two popular ones.

X There are many varieties of tomato, beefsteak and plum are two popular ones.

√ There are many varieties of tomato. Beefsteak and plum are two popular ones.

There are several ways to correct the comma splice and run-on sentence. The method you choose will depend on the content of your sentences. To correct your error you might:

End the first sentence with a period and begin a new sentence with a capital letter.

Examples: The U.S. Post Office Department provides reliable service. However, sometimes a letter is not delivered for weeks, months, or even years.

OR

Place a semicolon between two sentences if they are closely related in idea. Do *not* begin the second sentence with a capital letter.

Because Karen was very competitive, she entered a pie-eating contest; then she had to spend a week in the hospital.

OR

If the two sentences are of equal importance, join them with one of these seven conjunctions: *and, or, nor, but, for, so, yet.* Notice that the conjunction is preceded by a comma.

Tony is immoral, for he steals hubcaps for a living.

☞ *Try It Out*

Draw two lines under the verbs, draw one line under the subjects, and circle any DANGER WORDS in the following word groups. Then correct the comma splices and run-on sentences.

1. Whenever the Australian walking fish gets tired of swimming around, it leaves the water, then it climbs a tree to enjoy a snack of insects.
2. A Norwegian named Hans Langseth grew the world's longest beard it was 17½ feet in length.
3. A common housefly has a life span of two weeks, however, people with fly swatters usually try to shorten that time considerably.

Name: ______________________ Date: ______________________

EXERCISE 3g: Identify the comma splices and run-ons and revise them in the spaces provided. Some of the sentences may be correct as they are; if they are correct, write *correct*.

1. The pilgrims in Connecticut had to be over twenty-one and licensed to smoke legally, moreover, they needed a doctor's note saying that the tobacco was necessary for their health.

   ____

   ____

2. Please pay me the money you owe me I am broke.

   ____

   ____

3. Many common North American animals that are not native to this country thrive well here today, included among those that were imported but most people think are native are sparrows and honeybees.

   ____

   ____

4. In 1921 the officials at Ellis Island decided to serve a traditional American food to all new arrivals to the country the choice, of course, was ice cream.

   ____

   ____

5. Although pigs will eat almost anything, they do not overeat the way that people do maybe we are the real pigs.

   ____

   ____

6. In today's world markets, coffee exports provide the principal income for twenty-four Third World nations, as a result, those countries often refer to their dark, rich coffee beans as "the golden."

   ____

   ____

Name: ______________________ *Date:* ______________________

7. Deborah Sampson disguised herself as a man in order to fight in the American Revolution she had to refuse medical aid for her wounds twice so that her identity could remain a secret.

8. Albert Schweitzer, the great humanitarian, had a special fondness for his cat Sizi, who often fell asleep on his writing arm instead of waking the cat Schweitzer would write with his other hand.

9. A horned toad is a frightening enemy it can squirt blood from its eyes at its victims.

10. Plain aspirin, known as acetysalicylic acid, is made from thick, black, smelly coal tar, it is the world's most frequently used medicine.

11. Because of their strict interpretation of the Bible, the American Puritans banned many things on Sundays that most people now take for granted, such as cooking food, traveling anywhere except to the place of worship, and kissing one's children.

12. Some people learn traffic rules by accident, isn't that a shame?

13. The American government uses huge quantities of paper, for example, more than one hundred tons of wastepaper, which accumulate daily at federal offices, are carted away at the end of each business day.

____

____

14. Louisa May Alcott was a nineteenth-century author of very popular and successful children's novels, one of which is the famous *Little Women*, nevertheless, it was said that she did not particularly like children.

____

____

15. In 1889 the final bare-knuckles boxing championship was fought in Richburg, Mississippi, between John L. Sullivan and Jake Kilrain those men boxed for seventy-five rounds before Sullivan won and retired from the ring holding the last of the bare-knuckles crowns.

____

____

16. Artificial insemination has been used successfully by cattle breeders for over fifty years, more than 50,000 prize offspring can be produced every year from one bull, just as long as he is a genuine champion.

____

____

17. To reduce bad breath usually associated with garlic or onions, do not eat them at the same time as fatty foods, otherwise, the fat will trap their smell and release it each time you exhale.

____

____

18. In 1881, workers at over seventy Russian factories were assigned to twenty-hour shifts, then if they made any mistakes they were fined and would often end up with no money to take home.

____

____

Name: ______________________ Date: ______________________

19. Microwaves are used for dozens of purposes such as radar and a long-distance telephone network, they are best known to the general public, however, as the amazing power source in ovens that can, for example, bake a potato in 5 minutes.

EXERCISE 3h: Follow the directions for each item. Be sure to use whatever punctuation is required. If necessary, refer back to page 88 for help.

1. Write a sentence about one of your dreams, using two complete sentences joined by one of the seven connectors: *and, but, for, nor, or, so, yet.*

2. Write two complete sentences about a used car, beginning the second sentence with the word *it.*

3. Using home computers as your subject, write two complete sentences that can be joined by a semicolon.

4. Write two complete sentences about nuclear war, beginning the second sentence with the word *therefore.*

Name: ______________________ Date: ______________________

5. Write a statement about designer jeans, using two complete sentences joined by one of the seven connectors: *and, but, for, nor, or, so, yet.*

____

____

6. Write two complete sentences describing your schedule of classes. Begin the second sentence with the word *then.*

____

____

____

7. Using a hug as your subject, write two complete sentences that can be joined by a semicolon.

____

____

8. Write two complete sentences about a soap opera, beginning the second sentence with the expression *for example.*

____

____

____

9. Write two complete sentences about one of your relatives, beginning the second sentence with the word *he* or *she.*

____

____

____

10. Write two complete sentences about doing the laundry, beginning the second sentence with the word *however.*

____

____

____

Name: ______________________ *Date:* ______________________

EXERCISE 3i: REFRESHER

1. Correct the fragments, comma splices, and run-ons in the paragraph below.
2. Answer the additional questions that follow the paragraph.

Two well-known psychologists recommend that people follow a series of specific steps when they are about to have an argument. Let's say, for example, that Linda is angry with her boyfriend, George. Because he criticizes her in front of other people. Using the psychologists' "fair fight" procedure. Linda would first tell George that she has a complaint that she would like to discuss with him at some future time, in this way, he is not caught off guard. When the two later meet to settle the problem, Linda would begin by stating her grievance, then George would repeat in his own words what Linda has just said. This "feedback" technique guarantees that he has been listening carefully and has understood Linda's point of view. Next, Linda would make her demand for change. Which is that George must not criticize her in front of others. Again, George would repeat what Linda has just said now he would have a chance to give his side of the issue, which Linda would "feed back" to prevent misunderstandings. This exchange would continue until the two finally reach an agreement and make an appointment to discuss the problem again in a few months. The second meeting will give Linda and George the opportunity to discuss how well the agreement has worked. And to make any necessary changes that will improve the situation still further. If people follow this "fair fight" procedure, then perhaps an argument can actually strengthen a relationship rather than tear it apart.

ADDITIONAL QUESTIONS FOR EXERCISE 3i:

1. What is the topic sentence of the paragraph?

____

____

2. Is there more than one main idea in the paragraph?

____

____

3. What order is used to develop the paragraph?

____

____

 Name: ______________________ Date: ______________

SPRINGBOARDS TO WRITING

Using your knowledge of the writing process, explained on pages 12–14, write a paragraph or essay related to this chapter's central theme, *rudeness,* which is introduced on pages 67–68.

PREWRITING

To think of topics to write about, look at the two photographs, read the essay, and answer the questions that follow each. If you prefer, select one of the writing springboards below. (All paragraph numbers refer to the essay that starts on page 68.) To develop your ideas, use the prewriting techniques described on pages 15–20.

WRITING A PARAGRAPH (For help, see the Pointers on page 31.)

1. Rudeness on mass transportation is (is not) very common.
2. Store customers are (are not) often rude to salespeople.
3. Smoking should (should not) be banned in indoor public places. (See ¶ 3.)
4. Drivers are (are not) often rude. (See ¶ 5.)
5. Agree or disagree: "The country's youth may be ruder because of their immaturity." (See ¶ 9.)

WRITING AN ESSAY (For help, see the Pointers on page 35.)

6. Agree or disagree: "Rudeness is becoming a common occurrence in American life." (See ¶ 1.)
7. How Rudeness Changes People's Outlooks on Life
8. Why I Am (Am Not) Frequently Rude to Others
9. Modern Life Is (Is Not) Stressful (See ¶ 4.)
10. How Stress Harms People
11. Why are the "shortest fuses" found in "some apartment houses where you have a lot of people in relatively little space"? (See ¶ 8.)
12. How I Cope with Stress in My Life
13. The American Lifestyle Is (Is Not) Too Fast Paced (See ¶ 2.)
14. Good Manners Are (Are Not) Important in Today's Society
15. How Society Discriminates Against the Handicapped (See ¶ 9.)
16. How Life Can Be Made Easier for the Handicapped
17. "Noninvolvement" Is (Is Not) the Norm in Today's Cities (See ¶ 11.)

UPI/Bettman Archive.

four

"Mom, meet Janet. She's going to be my first wife."

Courtesy of George Dole in Saturday Review.

SPRINGBOARDS TO THINKING

For informal, not written, response . . . to stimulate your thinking

1. What is unusual about the wedding ceremony on the opposite page?
2. Do you think the bride and groom are taking their marriage ceremony seriously? Why or why not? Do you think unusual wedding ceremonies indicate that people have too relaxed an attitude toward marriage? Explain. In general, do you approve of wedding ceremonies that express the individuality of the bride and groom? Explain.
3. What are the children in the cartoon showing that they have learned about adult life today? If you were the mother in the cartoon, what would you say to your son?
4. Is lack of seriousness about marriage one of the reasons the divorce rate is so high today? Explain. What other reasons might explain today's high divorce rate?
5. Should schools give courses that prepare people for marriage? Why or why not? What might such a course include? What other practical suggestions do you have for helping people prepare for successful, lasting marriages?

School for Marriage

JOAN LIBMAN

(1) Kim and Gary Humphries, both 17 and wearing blue jeans, sit in divorce court waiting for the judge to approve their property settlement. They have agreed to sell the house, pay off the debts and divide whatever cash is left. Kim will keep the car, the master-bedroom furniture and all the kitchen utensils. Gary will take the guest-room and family-room furniture. They will share custody of their five-year-old son, Lyle. The judge looks up from his desk. "Okay," he says, turning the last page of the settlement, "you guys are divorced." The spectators roar with laughter.

(2) Their reaction isn't all that inappropriate, since Kim Campbell and Gary Humphries were never really married. Their "wedding" was a mock ceremony in a class in contemporary family living at Parkrose Senior High School in Portland, Oregon. The "judge" is their teacher, Cliff Allen. The spectators are classmates. Lyle is an imaginary child.

(3) Classes in sex education, parenthood and family living aren't new, of course, but the U.S. Department of Education says the Parkrose program goes dramatically further than most: It begins by pairing off the boys and girls in the class; then the partners are stuck with each other through a term that emphasizes the economic realities of married life.

(4) During the term, which takes the pupils through a ten-year-marriage cycle, spouses must rent an apartment, prepare a budget, buy insurance, calculate the cost of having a baby, purchase a home, and file income-tax returns. They are even required to take turns spinning the "wheel of misfortune," and cope with the disasters that come up: death in the family, a home destroyed by fire, a six-month prison term, birth of triplets, or a mother-in-law moving in. Then as the course ends, each couple must face the ultimate in family trauma—divorce and dividing up the property.

(5) Students who have taken the class say its emphasis on stark economic realities helps later on, when they eventually do marry. Shannon and Brad Lusby recently sat with me in their pale gold living room, and opened the shabby notebook they had worked on four years ago when they were both students at Parkrose High. The frayed mock marriage certificate states that Brad E. Lusby and Shannon L. Jordan were joined in "lawful wedlock" in November 1971.

(6) "I was really naïve about money when we were in high school," says Brad, a solidly built young man who used to pitch for the Parkrose baseball team. "That class really made me see how important it was to have a good job and know what we were doing before we got married." Today, Brad

has completed two years of an electrician's apprenticeship program, and the couple has recently purchased a small house. "We'd already filled out mortgage forms and figured insurance in class, so I knew how to go about it," Brad adds.

(7) "A million things went wrong the first year of our marriage, but at least we *were* ready for the financial part," 21-year-old Shannon reports. She was so seriously ill she had to be hospitalized four times and was forced to give up her job; Brad was sent out of town to work, and a woman ran a stop light and wrecked the couple's car. "After seven months, I was about ready to throw in the towel," Shannon recalls. "But I went to my hope chest and got out my class notebook. I kept remembering what our teacher, Mr. Allen, used to say about the things that drive people apart. He used to say that you really have to listen and that you can't just shut someone up. Finally, Brad and I had a knock-down, drag-out fight and told each other exactly how we felt. We've been really happy ever since."

(8) The Lusbys' experience comes as heartening news to teacher Cliff Allen, who is also the school's former football coach and head of the social-studies department. Allen first got the idea for the class in the early 1960s, a time when many of his football players were plunging into early—and often disastrous—marriages. Five years ago, he decided to put together a course on family finances. "It bothered me that for their twelve school years, our system protects kids and then, suddenly throws them out on their own. No wonder they can't handle marriage. The big problem isn't sex any more. It's money."

(9) On some occasions, the dose of class-inspired reality seems too harsh. Classmates Gail Richey and Forrest Goodling spin the wheel of misfortune, and it lands on "death in the family." They decide the deceased will be their own five-year-old "son." (The choice of a make-believe child is not at all unusual for students, says Cliff Allen. It is less painful than facing the possibility of the death of a real-life loved one.) Gail and Forrest head for a local mortuary to find out about funerals. The mortician, wearing a pin-striped suit, starts the paper work, asking questions about flowers, a soloist and limousine service. Then Gail and Forrest walk down some dimly lit stairs to a room filled with display caskets. The mortician gives them a lecture on embalming ("It's more difficult with a child, because the veins are smaller") and the advantages of a sealed casket ("This one over here is guaranteed not to leak for fifty years," he says). By the time the session is over the couple knows that their son's burial will cost about $1,500, and that they will now have to go back over their finances to figure out how to pay the bill.

(10) Rochelle De Haan and her "husband" Brian Gaunt are faced with another kind of serious problem. When they spin the wheel of misfortune, it lands on "mother-in-law." "All right," says Mr. Allen, "your mother-in-law is moving in. What are you going to do with her? Where will she sleep? Will you have to add a room to your home? Can you afford to feed her?"

"She's going to get a job and work," says Rochelle.

"You'd make your aging mother-in-law work?" Allen asks.

"She's only 55," Brian answers.

"She's 55 today," says the teacher, "but remember, this happens after you've been married ten years. Now she's 65 years old."

"That's not fair," protests Rochelle.

"Life's not fair," says Mr. Allen. Rochelle and Brian will have to come up with a workable solution.

(11) For Rochelle, a blonde 17-year-old with a steady boyfriend (not Brian), the class has been a revelation. She had been thinking about getting married at 19, and starting a family that would eventually include eight children. "Then I realized that with $12,000 a year and one child, we'd only have $10 spending money a month," she says. She also found that money was what she and her "husband" kept getting into squabbles about. The experience was enough to make her change her plans. "When I marry," she now says, "I'd like to be at least 23 and finished with college. And three children will be enough. Big families are too expensive."

(12) Without exception, students are shocked when they learn how much things cost. One couple planned a first-year budget that lacked such basics as water, electricity and furniture. Kim Campbell and Gary Humphries were astonished by the tax levy on their house payment. "We fork over more than $300 a month and $75 of that goes to the government," Kim says.

(13) Even in school, financial responsibilities sometimes cause strain. Wes Johnson, a Parkrose teacher who also teaches the course, tells the story of the "couple" who almost split up in class. "She made a mistake on the adding machine, they had a big fight, and he was really rough on her. I got them back together so they could finish the term, but their relationship was never the same again."

(14) On another occasion, a couple argued about what kind of house they should buy. "Finally, she started yelling and he hit her and knocked her down," says Johnson. Then there was the member of the Parkrose football team who got so frustrated by discussions with his "wife" that at the end of the term he vowed, "I'll never get married."

(15) Some couples take the class knowing they want to marry one another. Sue and Rick Bauer, now 21, live five minutes from the Parkrose campus. They were seniors when they enrolled and had been going together for two years. The Bauers think the Parkrose experience influenced their decisions about their life together. For one thing, they postponed their wedding. And after learning how expensive house payments are, they decided "not to buy one until we really have enough money. Otherwise we'd be in hock for the rest of our lives." Now that they've been married two months, the Bauers are busily cutting corners. They do as much marketing as possible at a discount supermarket. They check ads, shop for specials and buy in bulk whenever possible. Sue plans to make her own clothes.

(16) But a high school class can't teach a couple everything. Shannon and Brad Lusby wish they had more preparation in learning how to handle in-laws. "Christmas around our house is ridiculous," they say. "Both families

expect us Christmas Eve and Christmas Day, and that's besides going to church. It can drive you crazy."

(17) The Bauers wish someone had told them how expensive their wedding would turn out to be. "My parents gave us a lovely wedding," says Susie, "but by the time I paid $150 for my dress, and took care of the pictures and contributed to our honeymoon, we had very little left in our savings account," she says. Her husband doesn't think the class was entirely realistic. "It's not like really spending your own money," he says. "When you're married and you have to work for everything you've got, somehow it's different."

(18) But many students feel the course helps them anticipate potential problems that are not just economic. Kim Campbell and Gary Humphries came to understand how difficult custody decisions are in a divorce. Even though their "son" Lyle was imaginary, he played a big part in their "marriage" and neither partner wanted to give him up.

(19) "Look," Gary was heard saying one day before the "court" appearance, "my dad was sick until I was five, and after my mother died, I didn't have anyone to talk to because Dad and I didn't really know each other. So I don't want to give up Lyle." Kim and Gary finally decided to share custody and permit liberal visitation rights.

(20) After her make-believe marriage to someone of another faith, Rochelle De Haan has changed her feeling about the role of religion. "I'm a Mormon, and I now see it's going to be important for me to marry someone of the same religion. Going to church means a lot to me and I wouldn't want to have to go alone all the time."

(21) Scott Ryan, a 22-year-old computer operator, came to the same conclusion when he finished the Parkrose course four years ago. Two years later he married Starla Welton, a girl from a different high school. "We have our religion in common, we go to church together," he says. The Ryans, who recently bought a small house in Portland, say they made good use of Scott's homeowner's expertise. "Before we signed up, Scott checked the basement and the roof and the gutters for leaks. He also called the city, to check on taxes," Starla says. "It's funny," she continues, "but when we went together, he used to talk about that course a lot. He seemed so well prepared. And when we started talking about getting married, he sat down and figured out a budget. We were still in college, and we wanted to be able to manage without either of us having to quit school."

(22) She regrets that her high school, in a nearby community, didn't offer the same kind of help. "Where I went to school, an unmarried teacher in health class talked generalizations about marriage for a few weeks, and that was that. It's really a shame. A girl friend of mine got married during her junior year and she had no idea what she was getting into. I was so naïve I might have married right after high school, too. That would really have been a mistake."

(23) Cliff Allen finds such reactions encouraging—so encouraging, in fact, that he's working up a new, more ambitious course. The subject of this one: life. It's got to start with birth—and end, of course, with death.

READING SURVEY

1. *Main Idea*

What is the central theme of this essay?

2. *Major Details*

a. At Parkrose Senior High School, what financial decisions must the students make during the ten-year mock marriage course?
b. What gave teacher Cliff Allen the idea to start a course in marriage at the school?
c. According to Cliff Allen, what is the big problem with marriage today?

3. *Inferences*

a. Read paragraph 7 again. Why did Brad and Shannon's "knock-down, drag-out fight" in which they told each other exactly how they felt help their marriage?
b. Read paragraph 17 again. Why is it "different" when you "have to work for everything you've got"?

4. *Opinions*

a. In what ways do you think school should prepare people for life?
b. What problems other than family finances do you think are responsible for the high rate of divorce in the United States?

VOCABULARY BUILDING

Lesson One: The Vocabulary of Marriage and Divorce

The essay "School for Marriage" by Joan Libman includes words that are useful when you are discussing marriage and divorce.

custody	(paragraph 1)	**trauma**	(4)
mock	(2)	**squabbles**	(11)
spouses	(4)	**frustrated**	(14)
disasters	(4) . . . **disastrous** (8)	**visitation rights**	(19)

In divorce, if there are children, one of the parents is given **custody** in that the legal responsibility for the children is given by the courts to that parent.

In marriage, **mock** love is not real affection, because it is pretended or imitation affection.

In marriage, the **spouses** are the husband and wife.

In marriage, **disasters** can put a strain on a relationship because these sudden, terrible events cause great misfortune. On the other hand, **disastrous** results of events can bring a couple closer together as they unite to face the harm and grief they have suffered.

In marriage, a **trauma** can be upsetting because this physical or psychological shock is usually long-lasting.

In marriage, frequent **squabbles** can hurt a relationship because these many minor arguments often add up to create a large problem.

In marriage, the husband and wife become **frustrated** if they are blocked from fulfilling their needs.

In divorce, the parent who did not receive custody of the children is usually given **visitation rights** that provide for that parent to visit the children from time to time.

EXERCISE 4a: Using the vocabulary words in the lesson, fill in the blanks.

1. The divorce orders gave the father weekly ____________________

   ____________________ to see both his children.

2. Frequent family ____________________ can lead to larger, more important quarrels.

3. Law students often practice with ____________________ court trials to develop their skills in courtroom techniques.

4. Both of the ________________ agreed to try to help their marriage by consulting a marriage counselor.

5. Today, it is not as unusual as it used to be for the father in a divorce to be awarded ________________ of his children.

6. The spouses were so ________________ by the constant strain of terrible ________________ which brought them great harm and sadness that their relationship began to suffer.

7. It was years before he fully recovered from the ________________ of his wife's walking out on him.

8. The divorce of the parents had a ________________ effect on the children, who were deeply hurt and frightened.

Lesson Two: The Vocabulary of Family Finances

The essay "School for Marriage" by Joan Libman includes words that are useful when you are discussing family finances. Some additional commonly used words about family finances are also given below.

settlement	(paragraph 1)	**tax levy**	(12)
budget	(4)	**credit rating**	
calculate	(4)	**liability**	
mortgage	(6)	**asset**	
finances	(8)	**installment**	

When planning a divorce, the husband and wife have to discuss how they will divide their money and property so that there is a fair **settlement.**

When planning a marriage, the couple should discuss their **budget** so that they will know the details of their expected income and expenses.

When planning a marriage, the couple should **calculate** their expected income and expenses so that they will determine mathematically how they will handle their money.

When planning to buy a home, people often get a **mortgage** by pledging the home in return for money which they pay back in regular payments over a period of time.

When planning a marriage, a couple needs to discuss **finances** carefully so that all money matters are understood from the outset.

When planning to buy a home, people should find out what their yearly **tax levy** will be so that they will know in advance the amount of taxes they will have to pay as a result of owning the property.

When planning to buy now and pay later, people should remember that paying their bills on time will give them a good **credit rating** so that their future ability to borrow money will be good.

When planning for the future, a person should consider what money is owed—that is, every **liability**—and what money or property is owned—that is, every **asset.**

When planning to buy on an **installment** plan, people should know that they will have to make regular periodic payments of money to repay the loan.

EXERCISE 4b: Using the vocabulary words in the lesson, fill in the blanks.

1. Homeowners eagerly look forward to the day when the ________________ on their home will finally be paid in full.
2. The ________________ ________________ on most homes is going up because of the huge expense of running governments today.
3. Some retired people on fixed monthly budgets have trouble handling their ________________ toward the end of each month because they do not space their purchases properly.
4. When you buy something with a credit card, you are creating a financial ________________ for yourself.
5. In setting up a household ________________, wise people set aside some money for unexpected emergencies.
6. In order to ________________ payroll taxes, a bookkeeper must know the total amount of the payroll.
7. In a divorce, a fair ________________ is one of the most important concerns that a judge has to deal with.
8. A home is a valuable ________________.
9. The ________________ ________________ of anyone who has ever borrowed money is on record with most agencies that lend money.
10. Making expensive purchases on the ________________ plan is a common American way of life.

SPELLING

Lesson One: Spelling Demons

Here are some more words that are frequently misspelled. Using the helpful techniques given in Chapter One, you should make it a point to learn these new Demons, which are taken from "School for Marriage."

ambitious	**during**	**occasion**
anticipate	**emphasize**	**planned**
appearance	**entirely**	**possible**
choice	**financial**	**prepare**
decision	**handle**	**really**
disastrous	**imaginary**	**religion**
discussion	**influence**	**responsibility**
divide	**marriage**	**ridiculous**

Lesson Two: Proofreading

When a friend or teacher points out a misspelled word in your writing, do you sometimes insist, "But I know how to spell that word"? As we search for errors in our writing, we all tend to overlook the easy words and concentrate on the difficult ones. But this leads to the painful experience of losing credit on a paper because of some careless spelling errors. Thus, one of the most important skills that a writer can learn is to proofread.

When you first learned to read, your eyes concentrated on each word and each letter within that word. But as your reading speed increased, you began to scan the sentences, paying attention only to certain key words. This is a fine technique for reading—but not for *proofreading*. To proofread your writing with success, you must slow down your reading speed in order to take in the individual letters of each word. It has been found that the most effective way to do this is to place a ruler or sheet of paper under the line you are proofreading. Your eyes are now forced to move more slowly because they cannot automatically run on to the next line.

With the sheet of paper or ruler placed under the line, begin to examine each word, allowing the tip of your pen or pencil to rest on each syllable as you read it. If necessary, pronounce each word aloud. Most important, as you proofread do not exceed your vision span; that is, do not exceed the number of letters you are able to identify clearly with a single glance. To determine your vision span, look at the top of the following triangle and then look down, reading the letters on each line *without moving your eyes*. When you can no longer identify all the letters on a line with a single glance, you have reached your limit and have determined your vision span.

e
e n
e n h
e n h s
e n h s v
e n h s v k
e n h s v k b
e n h s v k b t
e n h s v k b t m
e n h s v k b t m l
e n h s v k b t m l o

Most people are able to identify about six letters without moving their eyes. Whatever your span, do not try to exceed it when you are proofreading your writing. Now read the triangle of words given below. When you reach a group of letters that exceeds your vision span, you should divide them into smaller units that you can check more accurately.

I
a m
s a d
w h e n
b o o k s
r e v e a l
v a r i o u s
p e r s o n a l
h a r d s h i p s
c o n c e r n i n g
i l l u s t r i o u s
g o v e r n m e n t a l
a c q u a i n t a n c e s

These few simple proofreading techniques can probably help you to eliminate about half of your spelling errors. Just remember to place a sheet of paper or a ruler under the line of writing, to use a pen or pencil to mark off the syllables, and not to exceed your vision span.

Although this discussion has been limited to proofreading for spelling errors, the methods given are also useful for finding errors in grammar and punctuation. Again, it is a matter of reading slowly and with enough concentration to pick out your errors.

EXERCISE 4c: PROOFREADING Using the proofreading techniques given in this chapter, proofread the following paragraph for spelling errors. Make the needed corrections in the space directly above the misspelled words. If necessary, check your spelling against the list of Spelling Demons in this chapter.

Studies indicate that arguments about financal matters are often a major factor in a couple's desicion to get a divorce. The studies also emphasise that these money problems influnce the marrages of people from all age groups and economic levels of society. For example, a teen-age couple may not be perpared to handel the responsibity of spending money wisely. As a result, they could fail to antisipate the need for funds to deal with a posible emergency. Then when such a special ocassion arises, the financal pressures can lead to arguments that realy destroy the marrage. Such arguments can also devide a wealthy couple. In one instance, a famous comedian who earned 5 million dollars a year from television apearences planed to file for divorce because of his wife's rediculus spending habits: Durning the course of just one year, she spent $500,000 entirly on her wardrobe. Perhaps disasterous marrages such as these can be avoided if couples have honest discusions about how to handel money.

EXERCISE 4d: Follow the directions for each item. Each Spelling Demon given in this chapter should be used only once.

1. Seven of the Demons have double letters in them. Write them here and either circle or enlarge any letter(s) that seem difficult.

   ____________________ ____________________

   ____________________ ____________________

   ____________________ ____________________

   ____

2. Several of the Demons contain an equal number of vowels (*a, e, i, o, u*) and consonants. Write six of them here and either circle or enlarge any letter(s) that seem difficult.

   ____________________ ____________________

   ____________________ ____________________

   ____________________ ____________________

3. Each of the following Demons contains one or more smaller words in its spelling. Using one of these smaller words and the original Demon, compose a sentence that will help you to associate the two.

   Example: en*tire*ly The tire was en*tire*ly flat.

   a. entirely ____________________

   ____

   b. emphasize ____________________

   ____

   c. imaginary ____________________

   ____

   d. during ____________________

   ____

e. ambitious ______________________________

____

4. Using each set of Demons given below, create a complete sentence that makes sense.

   Example: *caution, disease, population, particular*
   We must *caution* the *population* against the spread of a *particular disease.*

   a. financial, disastrous, prepare ______________________________

   ____

   ____

   ____

   b. handle, responsibility, influence ______________________________

   ____

   ____

   ____

 Name: ______________________________ Date: ______________________________

Coordination

When two ideas are mentioned in a sentence, it is good to show their relationship to one another. One way to show relationship of ideas is to put them together using *coordination.* When you coordinate ideas, be sure that both ideas are related and of *equal importance.*

How to Employ Coordination

Example: His heartbeat became fainter, and soon he was dead.

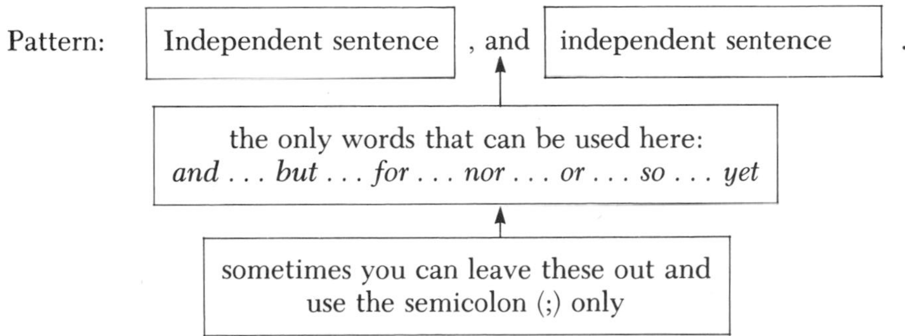

More examples:

She had prayed he would live, *but* she knew he would die.
She wept very hard, *for* now she was alone.
She would never forget his face, *nor* would she forget his warm eyes.
There was no one else in her life, *so* she missed him very much.
She knew she had to start getting over her sense of loss, *yet* she thought of him constantly.
Even months later she would listen for his heavy breathing, *or* she would expect to hear his frisky bark.
It was time to buy a new one; everyone told her that she must.

Try It Out

Practice correct coordination. Does (a) or (b) coordinate better?

1. The doctor ate more after she stopped smoking, ________.
   a. but she did not gain much weight.
   b. but she lost her briefcase at the hospital.
2. Either we balance our budget, ____________.
   a. or we will have enough money to buy a Cadillac.
   b. or we will be unable to cover our expenses.
3. The popular tennis star did not play well, _________.
   a. for he had barely recovered from a nasty cold.
   b. for his children had finished their homework.

Here is more information about coordination. First of all, notice in the preceding examples that there is always a comma between two independent sentences joined by the words *and, but, for ,nor, or, so,* and *yet.* Some professional writers have begun to leave out this comma, but you will be safer as you practice your writing skills if you continue to use it.

Also, try to avoid coordinating more than two independent sentences into one sentence. If you overuse words such as *and* and *but,* for example, your writing might become difficult to read because you might be stringing your ideas together without attention to their relationships.

Try It Out

Write the following with correct coordination.

1. A sentence about the Soviet Union: ______________________________

   ____
2. A sentence about video games: ______________________________

   ____
3. A sentence about your favorite dessert: ______________________________

   ____

 Name: ______________________ *Date:* ______________

EXERCISE 4e: Does (a) or (b) coordinate better?

1. The world's first oil well was drilled in Pennsylvania, ________.
   a. but Texas has become the leading oil-producing state.
   b. but the governor was defeated in her reelection bid.

2. A good restaurant must never compromise on food quality, ________.
   a. or the pigeons will gather outside the kitchen.
   b. or the owners will begin to lose some of their best customers.

3. The computer has streamlined business accounting, ________.
   a. yet it cannot replace bad management.
   b. yet computer science is a popular college major.

4. The actress wants to get the leading role, ________.
   a. so she spends all of her spare time studying her lines.
   b. so she goes out for lunch often.

5. The newlywed couple needed $10,500 to purchase a new car, ________.
   a. but their neighbor was injured in a boating accident.
   b. but they could raise only $6,500 by taking out a bank loan and asking their families for help.

6. The "Fasten Seat Belts" sign had just lit up, ________.
   a. and the plane began to go into a steep dive.
   b. and the pilot was 50 years old.

7. Feeding the chickens is a chore that demands daily attention, ________.
   a. yet the eggs can freeze in subzero temperatures.
   b. yet it is among the easiest chores on a small farm.

8. The weather forecaster did not predict rain for the weekend, ________.
   a. nor did he mention anything about snow.
   b. nor is Death Valley's climate comfortable during July.

9. To be the subject of gossip is unpleasant, ________.
   a. but to litter the streets is offensive.
   b. but to be embarrassed is more distressing.

10. World War II was more of a worldwide war than was World War I, ________.
    a. for many more nations participated in the combat.
    b. for the United Nations held its founding conference in San Francisco.

Name: ____________________ Date: ____________________

EXERCISE 4f: For each item, write an independent sentence that coordinates well with the sentence given. Remember that both parts must be related and of equal importance.

1. The student needed a job badly, so ______________________________

____.

2. Dancing most of the night felt wonderful, but ____________________

____.

3. The world must learn to control the spread of nuclear weapons, or

____

____.

4. The mail-order catalog offered many appealing gadgets, yet

____

____.

5. Boxing is a dangerous sport, for ______________________________

____

____.

6. Raising a child can be difficult; ______________________________

____

____.

7. The rodeo was about to start, and ______________________________

____

____.

8. Learning to play a musical instrument is not easy, nor ____________

____

____.

 Name: ______________________ *Date:* ______________

9. Videotape recorders permit people to watch their favorite programs whenever they wish, but____

____.

10. The popcorn smelled delicious but tasted like cardboard, so____________

____.

EXERCISE 4g: ESSAY ANALYSIS Find examples of coordination in the essay "School for Marriage." Give the first and last word of the entire sentence and the connector used to put the two parts together.

	first word	. . . ,	connector	. . .	last word
1. paragraph 3:	__________	. . . ,	__________	. . .	__________
2. paragraph 6:	__________	. . . ,	__________	. . .	__________
3. paragraph 6:	__________	. . . ,	__________	. . .	__________
4. paragraph 7:	__________	. . . ,	__________	. . .	__________
5. paragraph 7:	__________	. . . ,	__________	. . .	__________
6. paragraph 9:	__________	. . . ,	__________	. . .	__________
7. paragraph 13:	__________	. . . ,	__________	. . .	__________

EXERCISE 4h: On separate paper, write a sentence with correct coordination for each of the topics given below. Use each of the eight types of connectors (*and, but, for, nor, or, so, yet, ;*) at least once.

1. a spy
2. junk food
3. horror movies
4. country and western music
5. a comic strip
6. a guilty conscience
7. the United States Marines
8. red roses
9. Dolly Parton
10. a tiger

Subordination

Subordination is often used by good writers who want to communicate complex relationships between ideas. In the subordination of two related ideas, *one idea is more important than the other.* The more important idea is put into an independent sentence which could stand alone. The less important idea is put into a subordinate section that could never stand alone because it is *dependent* on the independent sentence.

How to Employ Subordination

Example: Because he got home late, he missed his dinner.

Pattern: Because ~~~~~~, | independent sentence | .

Use *any* of the following to subordinate one idea to another:

after	provided that
although	since
as	so that
as if	than
as long as	though
as though	unless
because	until
before	when
even though	whenever
how	where
if	wherever
in order that	whether
once	while

A SPECIAL NOTE: You have seen most of these words before. Many of them are the DANGER WORDS discussed in Chapter Three. Now you can see that when one of these words starts a sentence, there can be a danger if a full independent sentence does not follow the dependent section. However, if you follow the pattern of subordination shown above, these words will not be dangers. Instead, they will enhance your writing considerably.

More examples:

After its descent was completed, the UFO turned off its motors.
Although the spouses always argued, they loved each other.
As more people interact with one another, they will become acquainted.
Before the storm isolated the village, most people fled.
If peace cannot be achieved soon, many more people will die.
Since the clock is not reliable, I will return it.
Unless college students study, they will not pass their courses.
Until the economic recession is over, it will be difficult to find a job.
Where there is smoke, there is fire.

☞ *Try It Out*

Practice subordination. Make up an appropriate independent sentence.

1. Because the department store ran a gigantic sale, ______________________

   ____.

2. Until oil was discovered on her land, ______________________

   ____.

3. Although we were cheated out of our money, ______________________

   ____.

Now make up an appropriate dependent section.

4. ____, they forgot to lock their front door.

5. ____, we became good friends.

   OR

   ____, we became good friends.

   OR

   ____, we became good friends.

Name: ______________________ Date: ______________________

Here is more information about subordination. Notice on pages 118 and 121 that there is always a comma between the subordinate (dependent) section and the independent sentence—*when the subordinate section comes first.* When the subordinate section comes last, however, there is usually not a comma between the independent sentence and the subordinate section.

Example: Because he got home late, he missed his dinner.

Pattern: Because ~~~~~~, | independent sentence |.

Example: He missed his dinner because he got home late.

Pattern: | Independent sentence | because ~~~~~~.

☞ *Try It Out*

Use subordination.

1. A sentence about luxury: Although ______________________________

   ______________________________.

2. A sentence about poverty: Before ______________________________

   ______________________________.

3. A sentence about smoking: ______________________________

   until ______________________________.

Once you have learned the pattern of subordination, try to use it. The more you do, the more comfortable it will be for you. Very often a writer likes to change from using coordination to using subordination. This can be done easily, just as long as the less important idea is in the dependent section and the more important idea is in the independent section.

Example of coordination: He got home late, and he missed his dinner.

Example of subordination: Because he got home late, he missed his dinner.

 Name: ______________________ *Date:* ______________________

☞ *Try It Out*

Rewrite these sentences using subordination rather than coordination.

1. Hospital clinic patients often have to wait long hours to see a doctor, so they are wise to arrive early in the day.

____

____

____

2. The city is in the middle of a drought, and people are being asked not to wash their cars.

____

____

____

3. The actors took their bows, but the audience did not applaud.

____

____

EXERCISE 4i: Fill in the blank lines. In some sentences you will need an independent sentence while in others you will need a dependent section. Notice that a comma separates the parts.

1. Whenever people are watching television, ______________________________

____

______________________________.

2. As long as the score is tied, ______________________________

____

______________________________.

3. Because the outer space rescue mission was a failure, ____________

____

____.

4. ____, the nuclear plant had to close down permanently.

5. ____, the teacher walked out of the room suddenly.

6. ____, a stereo sound system has to be chosen carefully.

7. ____, test scores will rise and grades will improve.

8. Although many people prefer to live in large cities, ____________

____

____.

9. So that more marriages will be successful, ____________________

____

____.

10. Once you have decided to go to college, ______________________

____

____.

EXERCISE 4j: Fill in a dependent section after the independent sentences given. Notice that a comma is not used.

1. Photography can be a creative hobby __________________________

____

____.

 Name: ______________________ *Date:* ______________

2. Finding an apartment can be an exhausting process ____________

____

____.

3. The temperature had reached 100 degrees ____________

____

____.

4. The waiter ignored his customers ____________

____

____.

5. An uncomfortable pair of shoes can ruin a person's day ____________

____

____.

EXERCISE 4k: On separate paper, write a sentence using subordination for each topic below. Put the subordinate section before the independent section. Use a comma to separate the parts.

1. a magic trick
2. advertisements on television
3. a rumor
4. the space shuttle
5. credit cards
6. music videos
7. a nightmare
8. the "Walkman" cassette player
9. a cup of tea
10. grandparents

EXERCISE 4I: Here are sentences that use coordination. While a few are better in this form, most should be changed to subordination. Decide which ones would benefit from a change to subordination and rewrite them accordingly.

1. The movie had received excellent reviews, but it was a financial disaster.

    ____

    ____

2. It was a stolen car, so the police carefully examined it for fingerprints.

    ____

    ____

3. The final exam was over, and the students eagerly left the school.

    ____

    ____

4. The congresswoman could not forget that she had barely won the election, nor could she forget that the male voters had given her the most support.

    ____

    ____

    ____

5. Adults average only seven to eight hours of sleep a night, yet most newborns sleep between fourteen and eighteen hours a day.

    ____

    ____

    ____

6. Poor quality control of American products is costly, for it makes them less competitive against imports.

    ____

    ____

 Name: ________________________ *Date:* ________________

7. You overeat at every meal, and you are likely to gain weight.

____

____

8. Your alternatives are simple: Either you accept the job or you go on welfare.

____

____

9. Alma had very high grades and had experience breeding dogs, but she was not admitted to veterinary school.

____

____

10. The jails suddenly became overcrowded, so the authorities decided to release prisoners who had committed minor crimes.

____

____

____

EXERCISE 4m: ESSAY ANALYSIS In the essay "School for Marriage" find examples of subordinate sentences that start with dependent sections. Give the first and last word of the entire sentence.

	first word	...	last word
1. paragraph 10:	____________	...	____________
2. paragraph 17:	____________	...	____________
3. paragraph 18:	____________	...	____________
4. paragraph 21:	____________	...	____________
5. paragraph 22:	____________	...	____________

Name: ____________________ Date: ____________________

A Special Case of Subordination

Subordination that starts with *who* or *which* often works best in the middle of the sentence.

Example: Juan, who is worried about pollution, plans to be an ecologist.

Special Case Pattern: | Independent, who ~~~~~~~ sentence | .

More examples:

The S.S. Norway, which is docked at Pier 67, is crippled by a dock workers' strike.
Julia, who has an analytical mind, thinks carefully before she acts.

☞ *Try It Out*

Fill in an appropriate subordinate section.

1. Babe Ruth, who____,
   holds the world's record for strikeouts.

2. Coca-Cola, which ____,
   is consumed by people in 155 countries.

Here is more information about subordination: Use *who* to refer to a person, and use *which* to refer to a thing or place.

Note that in the pattern above, commas surround the subordinate section. This is because the subordination *adds information about a specific subject.* In the examples above Juan is a specific man, the S.S. Norway is a specific ship, and Julia is a specific woman. Therefore, the information given in the subordination is ADDED INFORMATION not basic for identification, and you need to ADD COMMAS. When the INFORMATION IS NEEDED for basic identification, however, NO COMMAS are used to surround the subordinate section.

 Name: ____________________ *Date:* ____________

Example: The man who is worried about pollution plans to be an ecologist.

Pattern: | Independent who ~~~~~~ sentence |.

More examples:

The ship which is docked at Pier 67 is crippled by a dock workers' strike.
The woman who has an analytical mind thinks carefully before she acts.

☞ *Try It Out*

Fill in an appropriate subordinate section. Are commas needed?

1. The athlete who ______________________________ was very sickly as a child.

2. Many old cars which ______________________________ have become very valuable.

EXERCISE 4n: Fill in an appropriate subordinate section. Surround the section with commas when necessary.

1. The air which ______________________________ is the healthiest possible for hay fever sufferers.

2. Marilyn Monroe who ______________________________ had a lonely, harsh childhood.

3. The Spanish language which ______________________________ is sometimes known as the "unofficial second language of the United States."

4. The soap opera star who ______________________________ lives alone with her pet tarantula.

5. Helen Keller who ______________________________ lectured all over America, Europe, and Japan to promote liberal social causes.

6. The land which ______________________________ contains huge amounts of crude oil.

7. The store manager who ____________________
discovered that the 80-year-old customer was a shoplifter.

8. The island of Jamaica which ____________________
covers 4,244 square miles.

9. The birthday of Martin Luther King which ____________________

____________________ is a national holiday.

10. The wedding ring which ____________________
slipped off his finger while he was swimming.

EXERCISE 4o: Combine these sentences using the words of coordination and subordination given in parentheses. Be sure to insert commas where needed. First, look at the examples given. Use your own paper if you need more space.

Examples:

A. The cactus known as Queen of the Night blooms only at midnight.

Its flower has a perfume that can be smelled half a mile away.

(and)

The cactus known as Queen of the Night blooms only a midnight, and its flower has a perfume that can be smelled half a mile away.

B. Lincoln's Gettysburg Address lasted only two minutes.

It is considered one of the greatest speeches ever made.

(although)

Although Lincoln's Gettysburg Address lasted only two minutes, it is considered one of the greatest speeches ever made.

C. Charles Felu painted several masterpieces with his foot.

Charles Felu was a famous armless artist.

(who)

Charles Felu, who was a famous armless artist, painted several masterpieces with his foot.

1. Nashville, Tennessee, is known as the music capital of the world.

   Over 52 percent of all single records are recorded in the 35 studios located there.

   (for)

   ____

2. Winds blowing 8 to 12 miles per hour are considered a gentle breeze.

   Winds blowing 74 or more miles per hour are considered a hurricane.

   (while)

   ____

3. A potato famine struck Ireland in the 1840's.

   It led many people to migrate to America.

   (which)

   ____

4. The British won the Battle of El Alamein in World War II.

   They had not won a land battle against the Germans.

   (before)

   ____

5. The planet Venus is covered with a cloudy, white atmosphere that reflects sunlight well.

   It is the third brightest object in the sky next to the sun and the moon.

   (since)

   ____

6. The insect known as the water tiger lives under water.

   It is able to breathe air through two hairy snorkels.

   (although)

   ____

Name: ______________________ Date: ______________________

7. A traveler circles the globe and thereby crosses the International Date Line.

He or she must advance the date one full day when crossing in a westerly direction.

He or she must set back the date one full day when crossing in an easterly direction.

(if, and)

____

8. King Ramses II ruled ancient Egypt.

He ruled for 67 years.

He outlived twelve of his sons.

He died at the age of 90.

(who, and)

____

9. A $25,000 pearl was ruined.

It was cooked.

It was discovered in an oyster.

(because, before)

____

10. The chicken came first.

The egg came first.

No one seems to know.

(whether, or)

____

11. A plane flies faster than sound travels.

It breaks the sound barrier.

The people in the area hear what sounds like a thunderclap.

The people on the plane do not hear it.

(whenever, and, yet)

---

12. Charles Charlesworth reached his fourth birthday.

    He began to sprout whiskers and develop white hair and wrinkled skin.

    He finally died of old age.

    He was just seven years old.

    (as, until, when)

---

13. Ulysses S. Grant was the eighteenth President of the United States.

    He died penniless.

    His autobiography earned $450,000 after it was published.

    He finished writing it four days before he died.

    (who, but, which)

---

14. Dartmouth College is in Hanover, New Hampshire.

    It was founded in the 1770's.

    It was considered a college in the wilderness.

    It charged only $13.32 a year tuition.

    (when, which, and)

---

15. The gaff topsail female catfish lays eggs.

    The male carries them in his mouth.

    They hatch 80 days later.

    The male does not eat for 80 days.

    (after, until, so)

EXERCISE 4p: Combine these sentences using words of coordination and subordination. Be sure to insert commas where needed. Use your own paper for this assignment.

1. A man and a chimpanzee have equally hairy hands.

   The hair on a man's hands is finer and shorter.

2. The corn crop gets the proper mixture of sun and water.

   The corn will be plentiful and tasty.

3. Annie Smith Peck was an active mountain climber until she was 82.

   She was the first American woman to climb the Matterhorn.

4. The Union forces won the Battle of Gettysburg.

   The defeat of the Confederate Army was assured.

5. Most Americans know Idaho best for its famous potato.

   People who live in Idaho love the state for its beautiful scenery.

6. At any one time, over 2½ billion one-dollar bills are in circulation.

   Over 21 million one-hundred-dollar bills are in use.

7. The true history of the American flag is difficult to discover.

   Historians disagree about who designed it, who made it, and whether it flew during the American Revolution.

8. A jet broke the sound barrier over a village in France.

   The force of the resulting thunderclap shattered 3,000 bottles of wine.

9. For each of her eggs, the Mason bee uses clay and sand to build an individual cell.

   Each cell is stocked with pollen and honey.

10. The average life expectancy of someone born in 1910 was 47 years.

    The average life expectancy of someone born in 1970 is 70 years.

 Name: ______________________ Date: ______________________

11. There is a Japanese symbol.

    It means "to get information."

    It is formed by putting the symbol for "mouth" inside the symbol for "gate."

12. Dr. Linus Pauling is a Nobel Prize-winning scientist.

    Dr. Pauling claims that large doses of vitamin C prevent colds.

    Many doctors disagree with his findings.

13. "Rollie" can use roller skates.

    "Rollie" is a penguin at the San Diego Zoo.

    The Roller Skating Association made him an official member.

14. Death Valley is 282 feet below sea level.

    It is the lowest altitude in the United States.

    Mount McKinley is 20,320 feet above sea level.

    It is the highest altitude in the United States.

15. In the late 1600's, a law professor taught at a university in Sweden.

    He lectured there for eighteen years.

    No one ever attended his lectures.

    He was boring.

EXERCISE 4q: REFRESHER

1. Find and correct any fragments, comma splices, and run-ons.
2. Rework the sentences so that there are at least three examples of subordination and one of coordination.

A judge in Traverse City, Michigan, has made an unusual decision in a divorce case. When Allen Church and his former wife, Cheryl, appeared before Judge Charles M. Forster. They each asked for custody of their three teenage sons. Court testimony showed that both of the Churches were good parents. Judge Forster granted them joint custody of the boys. A joint custody decision usually means that the children live with one parent for six months of the year and then with the other parent for the rest of the year. An arrangement which often prevents youngsters from gaining the sense of security that is brought about by a stable home environment. To help prevent this problem, Judge Forster ruled that the three boys would continue to occupy the family home while the parents would take monthly turns living with them. At first, the Churches were shocked by the judge's decision, however, the arrangement has worked out well so far. At the end of every month, one parent moves out of the house then the other one moves in. Each of them has a second home nearby for use during the "off months." Allen and Cheryl Church no longer live in the house on a full-time basis, they share all of the bills for its upkeep. As strange as this whole custody arrangement may seem, it does guarantee that the children will see both of their parents frequently. Without being pulled away from old friends, familiar school surroundings, and a permanent home setting.

 Name: __________ Date: __________

SPRINGBOARDS TO WRITING

Using your knowledge of the writing process, explained on pages 12–14, write a paragraph or essay related to this chapter's central theme, *marriage,* which is introduced on pages 98–103.

PREWRITING

To think of topics to write about, look at the photograph and cartoon, read the essay, and answer the questions that follow each. If you prefer, select one of the writing springboards below. (All paragraph numbers refer to the essay that starts on page 100.) To develop your ideas, use the prewriting techniques described on pages 15–20.

WRITING A PARAGRAPH (For help, see the Pointers on page 31.)

1. People should (should not) be required to take a course in marriage before they get married.
2. Agree or disagree: Our laws should make it harder to get married than to get divorced.
3. Should marriage licenses have an expiration date, just as other licenses do?
4. Read the *Refresher* on page 134. What do you think of the judge's decision?
5. An unmarried couple should not (should) have children.

WRITING AN ESSAY (For help, see the Pointers on page 35.)

6. Why Get Married?
7. Why Do People Get Divorced?
8. What I Learned about Marriage from Observing My Parents' Marriage
9. The Case for (against) Teenage Marriage (See ¶11.)
10. The Case for (against) Having a Large Family (See ¶11.)
11. Should People Live Together Before They Are Married?
12. Children Are (Are Not) the Biggest Losers in a Divorce
13. Why I Would (Would Not) Marry Someone of Another Religion
14. Why I Would (Would Not) Marry Someone of Another Race
15. Why I Would (Would Not) Marry Someone from Another Ethnic Background
16. My Idea of a Perfect Wedding
17. Suggest and discuss courses (other than the one described in the essay, pages 100–103) that schools should offer to help people learn to deal with the realities of life.

M. C. Escher, Relativity, *© M. S. Escher Heirs c/o Cordon Art—Baarn—Holland. Collection Haags Gemeentemuseum—The Hague.*

five

SPRINGBOARDS TO THINKING

For informal, not written, response . . . to stimulate your thinking

1 What does the photograph above show? Does it surprise you? Why or why not? In reality, it is a wall sculpture of a 10-foot-long hand with plastic bricks at its base anchored to the brick wall; the sculpture was designed as a landmark for a new post office building in Cologne, West Germany. What is your opinion of having such a wall sculpture on a building? Explain.

2. Study the lithograph* on the opposite page. Where do the staircases end? Where is each moving figure going? What else do you notice?

3. Why do you think the artist, M. C. Escher, titled his lithograph "Relativity"?

4. Can you always trust your eyes? Why or why not?

5. Are people always what they seem to be? Explain. What kinds of standards do you use to judge people? Are your standards always accurate? Explain.

* A lithograph is a print made on a flat stone or a metal plate using both a kind of grease that absorbs printing ink and water which does not.

What Is Intelligence, Anyway?

ISAAC ASIMOV

(1) What is intelligence, anyway? When I was in the army, I received a kind of aptitude test that all soldiers took and, against a normal of 100, scored 160. No one at the base had ever seen a figure like that, and for two hours they made a big fuss over me. (It didn't mean anything. The next day I was still a buck private with KP—kitchen police—as my highest duty.)

(2) All my life I've been registering scores like that, so that I have the complacent feeling that I'm highly intelligent, and I expect other people to think so, too. Actually, though, don't such scores simply mean that I am very good at answering the type of academic questions that are considered worthy of answers by the people who make up the intelligence tests—people with intellectual bents similar to mine?

(3) For instance, I had an auto-repair man once, who, on these intelligence tests, could not possibly have scored more than 80, by my estimate. I always took it for granted that I was far more intelligent than he was. Yet, when anything went wrong with my car I hastened to him with it, watched him anxiously as he explored its vitals, and listened to his pronouncements as though they were divine oracles—and he always fixed my car.

(4) Well, then, suppose my auto-repair man devised questions for an intelligence test. Or suppose a carpenter did, or a farmer, or, indeed, almost anyone but an academician. By every one of those tests, I'd prove myself a moron. and I'd *be* a moron, too. In a world where I could not use my academic training and my verbal talents but had to do something intricate or hard, working with my hands, I would do poorly. My intelligence, then, is not absolute but is a function of the society I live in and of the fact that a small subsection of that society has managed to foist itself on the rest as an arbiter of such matters.

(5) Consider my auto-repair man, again. He had a habit of telling me jokes whenever he saw me. One time he raised his head from under the automobile hood to say: "Doc, a deaf-and-mute guy went into a hardware store to ask for some nails. He put two fingers together on the counter and made hammering motions with the other hand. The clerk brought him a hammer. He shook his head and pointed to the two fingers he was hammering. The clerk brought him nails. He picked out the sizes he wanted, and left. Well, doc, the next guy who came in was a blind man. He wanted scissors. How do you suppose he asked for them?"

(6) Indulgently, I lifted my right hand and made scissoring motions with my first two fingers. Whereupon my auto-repair man laughed raucously

and said, "Why, you dumb jerk, he used his *voice* and asked for them." Then he said, smugly, "I've been trying that on all my customers today." "Did you catch many?" I asked. "Quite a few," he said, "but I knew for sure I'd catch *you*." "Why is that?" I asked. "Because you're so god-damned educated, doc, I *knew* you couldn't be very smart."

(7) And I have an uneasy feeling he had something there.

READING SURVEY

1. *Main idea*

What is the central theme of the essay?

2. *Major Details*

a. To what does Isaac Asimov attribute his high scores on aptitude tests?
b. What is Isaac Asimov's opinion of intelligence tests?
c. What is the joke that the auto mechanic told Isaac Asimov?

3. *Inferences*

a. Read paragraph 1 again. What is Isaac Asimov suggesting when he refers to KP as "my highest duty"?
b. Read paragraph 6 again. Why does the auto mechanic feel that educated people "couldn't be very smart"?

4. *Opinions*

a. Would you want to know what your I.Q. is? Why or why not?
b. How would you define intelligence? Explain.

VOCABULARY BUILDING

Lesson One: The Vocabulary of Intelligence

The essay "What Is Intelligence, Anyway?" by Isaac Asimov includes words that are useful when you are discussing intelligence. Some additional commonly used words about intelligence are also given below.

aptitude	(paragraph 1)	**moron**	(4)
academic	(2) . . . **academician** (4)	**verbal**	(4)
intellectual bents	(2)	**genius**	
pronouncements	(3)	**shrewd**	
divine oracles	(3)	**astute**	

Having intelligence means having a good **aptitude**—a talent, natural ability, or quickness for specific physical tasks or mental activities.

Having intelligence often means having **academic** interests—interests associated with schooling or being a scholarly person. An **academician** is a person who has such interests.

Having intelligence usually means having **intellectual bents**—leanings toward mental activities that involve an interest in and ability with advanced fields of knowledge.

Having intelligence sometimes means making statements that other people take to be **pronouncements**—formal statements based on facts or judgments stated by reliable experts.

Having intelligence sometimes means making statements that other people take to be **divine oracles**—statements of great wisdom or knowledge that are considered holy because they are inspired by or given by God (or, in ancient Greece and Rome, by "the gods").

Having intelligence means not being a **moron**—either a person with an I.Q. of 50–70 or a person of normal intelligence who does or says foolish or stupid things.

Having intelligence usually means being highly **verbal**—easily able to understand and use a large number of words.

Having intelligence sometimes means being a **genius**—a person with a very high I.Q. or a person with great mental capacity for being creative or inventive.

Having intelligence sometimes means being **shrewd**—having a keen mind, sharp insight, and cleverness in practical matters.

Having intelligence sometimes means being **astute**—being shrewd (see above) combined with being wise or being skillful in misleading other people.

EXERCISE 5a: Match each classified ad below with a vocabulary word from this lesson.

CLASSIFIED ADS

HELP WANTED

DO YOU HAVE a sharp mind and excellent insight when it comes to practical matters? We could use your skills. Send resume to KEEN ASSOCIATES.

1. ____________________

A PERSON OF TALENT and natural ability to take tests requiring either good mental or physical skills. Send your school records and recent test scores to BUREAU OF COLLEGE EXAMINATIONS.

2. ____________________

ARE YOU AT EASE with words? We will use you for many projects in communications. Stop by TALK, Inc. to make an appointment.

3. ____________________

SITUATIONS WANTED

EXPERT AT GIVING WISE counsel often inspired by the gods. I am descended from a tradition that goes back to Greek and Roman times. See me in action at Delphi.

4. ____________________

I AM BOTH shrewd and wise, with some talent for misleading others. One of my specialties is advertising. Write me at 007 MADISON AVENUE, New York City.

5. ____________________

I AM INTERESTED IN SCHOLARSHIP and all activities related to schooling. I would make an excellent teacher. Contact me at LEARNED ACADEMY.

6. ______________________

HAVE STRONG INTERESTS in advanced fields of knowledge. I like to spend my time reading and thinking. Write to me at PLEASURES OF THE MIND.

7. ______________________

NOT VERY SMART but willing to try to do whatever job you give me. Send your requirements to LO IQ VILLAGE.

8. ______________________

BOOKS FOR SALE

SHORT BIOGRAPHIES of highly intelligent inventors or creative thinkers, including Albert Einstein and Thomas Edison. Read BRILLIANT MINDS by U. R. Smart.

9. ______________________

A COLLECTION OF formal statements made by authorities on many subjects—based on facts and judgments of dependable experts. See TAKE IT FROM ME, by I. N. Formed.

10. ______________________

Lesson Two: The Vocabulary of Social Standards

The essay "What Is Intelligence, Anyway?" by Isaac Asimov includes words that are useful when you are discussing social standards.

complacent	(paragraph 2)
devised	(4)
intricate	(4)
absolute	(4)
function (of)	(4)
foist	(4)
arbiter	(4)
indulgently	(6)
smugly	(6)

 Name: ______________________ Date: ______________________

A person who always goes along with current social standards is often **complacent**—either self-satisfied and overly contented with oneself or pleasantly agreeable.

A person who always goes along with current social standards usually has **devised**—thought through or worked out—ways of adapting to what is expected.

A person who always goes along with current social standards is able to understand unspoken rules that are **intricate**—hard to follow or understand because they are full of puzzling details or relationships.

A person who always goes along with current social standards sometimes forgets that the standards are not **absolute**—perfect, complete, and definite.

A person who always goes along with current social standards sometimes forgets that the standards are a **function of**—they depend upon and vary with—the values and beliefs of one group.

A person who always goes along with current social standards sometimes wants to **foist**—impose in a hidden, sly way—those standards on everyone else.

A person who always goes along with current social standards often considers himself or herself the **arbiter** of—a person qualified or given the power to judge—what is right or wrong.

A person who always goes along with current social standards rarely reacts **indulgently**—in a kindly way that gives in to another's wishes or needs—when other people ignore those standards.

A person who always goes along with current social standards often behaves **smugly**—self-satisfied or overly contented with oneself to the point that other people become annoyed.

EXERCISE 5b: Using the vocabulary words in this lesson, fill in the blanks.

1. Frequently a union will ask for an ____________ to settle a dispute with management.

2. The police ____________ a complicated plan to capture the escaped prisoners.

3. Many health experts think that alcohol and drug abuse are a ____________ ____________ the pressures and stresses of everyday modern life.

4. Although Mayor Kilroy was confident of reelection, he refused to become ____________, and he began to work harder than ever on his campaign.

5. Because special situations sometimes call for the making of exceptions, all company rules do not have to be considered ______________.

6. The technician traced the computer's ____________________ circuitry to locate the cause of the malfunction.

7. The overly strict, hated factory foreman smiled ______________ as his superiors praised him for his enforcement of assembly-line discipline.

8. Most newspaper editorials expressed disapproval of the government's attempt to ______________ a new tax on homeowners.

9. Parents must be careful not to ______________ excuse a child's use of temper tantrums to get attention.

SPELLING

Lesson One: Spelling Demons

Here are some more words that are frequently misspelled. Using the helpful techniques given in Chapter One, you should make it a point to learn these new Demons, which are taken from "What Is Intelligence, Anyway?"

absolute	**expect**	**scissors**
actually	**function**	**similar**
against	**highly**	**simply**
answer	**intelligence**	**soldier**
anxiously	**intelligent**	**suppose**
consider	**listen**	**together**
customer	**question**	**where**
estimate	**receive**	**wrong**

Lesson Two: Capitalization

The misuse of capital letters is as serious an error as a misspelled word. Unfortunately, some careless writers do not realize this and ignore the rules of capitalization. As you read the material that follows, you will begin to realize that a key word to remembering capitalization is *particular.* If you keep this word in mind, you should have less trouble applying these simple and easy to understand rules when you write.

1. CAPITALIZE:

the name of a particular person	*Martin Luther King, Jr.* *Elizabeth Taylor*
a title that precedes the name	*President Lincoln* *Admiral Dewey*
a title that replaces the name	the *Pope* the *Secretary of State*
the name of a race of people	*Negro* *Indian*
the name of an organization or a department of the government	the *Knights of Columbus* *Republicans* *Congress* The *Coca-Cola Company*
the pronoun I	Slowly *I* turned the key in the lock.

2. CAPITALIZE:

the name of a particular place	*New York* *Great Britain*
the name of a particular region	the *South* the *Northeast*
the name of a particular street	*Fifth Avenue* *Elm Street*
the name of a particular building	*the Empire State Building* *Independence Hall*
the names of the planets and stars with the exception of earth, sun, and moon	*Mars* *Venus* the *Milky Way*

3. CAPITALIZE:

the names of languages	*French* *Spanish*
the name of a particular school course	*Physics 14A* *Geometry 26D*
the names of publications	the *New York Times* *People* magazine
the name of a particular school or college	*Van Buren High School* *Yale University*
brand names	*Heinz Ketchup* *Ford Mustang*

4. CAPITALIZE:

the days of the week and the months of the year	*Monday* *September*
the names of particular holidays	*Christmas* *New Year's Day*
the names of historical events and periods	*World War Two* the *Renaissance*

5. CAPITALIZE:

all words denoting a particular deity	*God* *Allah* *Buddha*
all words referring to God	We cannot understand *God's* ways, but *He* surely understands our ways.
all names of religions and religious writings	*Christianity* the *Bible,* the *Koran*

Now the firsts—which you know quite well.

6. CAPITALIZE:

the first word of a sentence and the first word of a direct quotation	The actor exclaimed, "Do not touch me!"
the first word and all important words in the title of a book, play, short story, essay, poem	*The Fall of the House of Usher* *Catcher in the Rye*
the first word and all nouns in the salutation of a letter	Dear Mr. Lyons: My dear Sir:
the first word of the close of a letter	Sincerely yours,

EXERCISE 5c: Capitalize whichever words need to be capitalized.

218 seminole street
west palm beach, florida 33409
october 29, 1985

mr. robert j. ringer
funk & wagnalls publishing company
the tishman building
666 fifth avenue
new york, new york 10017

 Name: ______________________ Date: ______________________

dear mr. ringer:

i have just finished reading your book *looking out for number one,* which i understand is so popular that it is on most of the best-seller lists here in the southeast and has already been translated into french, spanish, and german. this popularity is certainly disturbing, for most of what you have written reflects a cold, selfish attitude toward life. i was particularly upset by your comments about friendship: "can you buy friendship? you not only can, you must. it's the *only* way to obtain friends." making a friend, mr. ringer, is not like buying a box of wheaties or a can of maxwell house coffee.

on the contrary, a true friendship is built on trust, understanding, and shared interests, as my own experience has taught me. i first met my close friend tommy fong when we were both students in professor starr's astrology 38d class at the university of hawaii. while suffering through this course together, we came to enjoy each other's company and discovered that we were both interested in collecting items from the civil war period and in following the workings of congress. although tommy is oriental and i am puerto rican and we come from very different cultural backgrounds, our friendship has grown throughout the years since college. in fact, even though tommy now lives in san francisco, where he is president of the fongitron computer corporation, and i am here in florida writing articles for *tropical travel* magazine, we still speak with each other on the telephone frequently and manage to visit each other during the christmas holidays. thinking back to professor starr's astronomy class, i may not remember anything about venus or mars, but i gained something much more valuable than knowledge—a lifelong friendship.

indeed, when god created human beings, he gave us the ability to find great joy and comfort from sharing both the wondrous and sorrowful experiences of living. as it is written in the bible, "a faithful friend is the medicine of life."

sincerely yours,
manuel torres

EXERCISE 5d: Using the Spelling Demons in this chapter, fill in the blanks with any missing letters.

According to a university study, your intel____en___e can act____ly be affected by the position of your body. For example, when you are standing, your mind may fun___ion so quickly that when somebody asks you a q___st___n, you fail to con___ider your an___er carefully and may often blurt out the ___rong response. In addition, you may have trouble remembering w____re you left your s___is___rs or umbrella, for when you are standing, you can e___pe___t your memory to be at its worst. On the other hand, su___ose that you were a sold___r waiting an____sly for news of the enemy's location, or a c___st___mer being tempted to buy an unnecessary item. In these instances, standing would help to give you a feeling of a ___ sol___te control over the situation.

When you are lying down, your thoughts will probably come toge___er slowly, but they are likely to be creative. In a resting position, you also li___en very carefully and rec___ve suggestions with an open mind. Faced with a problem, you are apt to weigh one argument ag____st another and make any necessary est____tes before reaching an intel____nt decision. Of course, it is sim___y not possible to lie down every time you have some hi___ly important thinking to do. So you might try sitting, which will give you somewhat sim____r results.

 Name: ______________________ *Date:* ______________

The -S Verb Ending

As you already know from the discussion of sentence fragments, every complete sentence must have a subject and a verb, which can be either singular or plural in form. Logically, a singular verb should be used with a singular subject and a plural verb with a plural subject.

A Politician needs campaign funds.

Students need time to study.

George and Helen need a new car.

As you can see from the examples above, verb agreement centers on one letter: the *s*. Below is a quick way to check that you have used the *s* correctly. In the drawing, the *s* can take only one of the two roads available to it; therefore, if you use the *s* on the top road, you cannot use it on the bottom road.

s → subject / verb

s → chemicals / pollute

s → chemical / pollutes

Try It Out

Using the correct present tense forms of the verbs given in parentheses, fill in the blank spaces provided.

1. Today's preschoolers (to watch) ______________ an average of 54 hours of television a week.
2. Sunja, a 3,000-pound elephant at Cleveland's Sea World, (to ski) ______________ on giant twenty-one-foot-long water skis.
3. A person never (to sneeze) ______________ without being forced to close his or her eyes at the same time.

Name: ______________ Date: ______________

II Of course, the drawing on the preceding page will not help you when you use someone's name for a subject, when you use a pronoun (*I, you, he, she, it, we, they*) for a subject, and when you use plural words that do not end in *s* (*children, people*). Similarly, this drawing will not help you when the verb follows one of these words: *shall, will, would, could, should, might, must, can.* Verbs following these words do not end with *s* whether the subject ends with *s* or not.

☞ *Try It Out*

Using the correct present tense forms of the verbs given in parentheses, fill in the blank spaces provided.

1. Once it (to reach) ______________ maturity, the leaves of an oak tree (to discharge) ______________ seven tons of water a day into the atmosphere.
2. In the United States, women (to live) ______________ an average of eight years longer than men (to do) ______________.
3. She (to think) ______________ that she might (to drop) ______________ chemistry next semester if she could (to study) ______________ computer science instead.

III Some writers have trouble with the present tense forms of the verbs *to be, to have,* and *to do* because these verbs change their spellings to agree with different subjects. These verbs are used much more frequently than any others in the English language, so it is important to study them carefully.

to be	*to have*	*to do*
I am	I have	I do
you are	you have	you do
he is	he has	he does
she is	she has	she does
it is	it has	it does
we are	we have	we do
they are	they have	they do

 *Try It Out*

Using the correct present tense forms of the verbs given in parentheses, fill in the blank spaces provided.

1. Vatican City, which (to be) ______________ the smallest independent country on earth, (to be) ______________ the size of an average golf course.
2. (to do) ______________ you know that Kentucky (to have) ______________ a law requiring all citizens to take a bath once a year?
3. Arizona and Hawaii (to be) ______________ the only states that (to have) ______________ never adopted Daylight Savings Time.

EXERCISE 5e: Using the subject and verb given for each item below, write two complete sentences, one with a singular subject and one with a plural subject. Be sure to keep the verb in the present tense and to use the *s* wherever necessary. Use your own paper for this assignment.

Example: s→ airplane / use

An airplane uses a great deal of fuel.

Airplanes use a great deal of fuel.

1. s→ billboard / advertise
2. s→ person / argue
3. s→ store / display
4. s→ computer / calculate
5. s→ automobile / cost
6. s→ athlete / train

Name: ______________ Date: ______________

7. s→ marriage
could succeed

8. 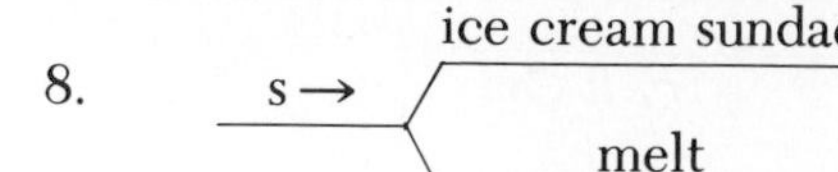

9. s→ student
worry

10. s→ musician
might play

11. s→ hospital
provide

12. s→ supervisor
order

13. s→ newspaper
print

14. s→ dancer
move

15. s→ radio
blast

EXERCISE 5f: Using the verb given in front of each sentence, fill in the correct form of the verb in the blank space provided. Keep all the verbs in the present tense.

1. *to have:* Shoelaces that ______________ starch in them will stay tied as long as desired.

2. *to consume:* Italy ______________ the most wine per person of any nation in the world.

3. *to strip:* According to the Agriculture Department, if a person ______________ the fat from pork and beef, they will taste the same.

4. *to have:* The world's smallest Bible ______________ pages approximately one-half the size of a postage stamp.

5. *to do:* Pigeons are the only birds that ______________ not raise their heads to swallow.

6. *to be:* According to many foot doctors, shoes that ______________ purchased in the late afternoon fit most accurately.

 Name: ______________________________ *Date:* ____________________

7. *to spread:* People ______________ cold germs as much by shaking hands as by kissing.

8. *to know:* When traveling by ship, every passenger should ______________ where the nearest lifeboats are located.

9. *to do:* The word "purple" ______________ not rhyme with any other word in the English language.

10. *to be:* A "hair's breadth" ______________ exactly one forty-eighth of an inch.

11. *to grow:* Fingernails ______________ faster than toenails.

12. *to be:* Poultry ______________ low in cholesterol and an excellent source of protein.

13. *to cause:* Emotions ______________ more perspiration than heat does.

14. *to contain:* A typical eyebrow ______________ 550 hairs.

15. *to survive:* Ninety million people ______________ on less than $75 per year.

16. *to have:* Africa ______________ more countries than any other continent.

17. *to be:* Because of its climate, Alaska ______________ the only state in the United States without houseflies.

18. *to raise:* A farm in Moorpark, California, ______________ over four million chickens at one time.

19. *to spend:* Americans ______________ a billion dollars a year for cold-relief medicines.

20. *to detect:* A rattlesnake can ______________ a change in temperature as small as one one-thousandth of a degree.

Agreement of Subject and Verb

If you have mastered the use of the *-s* ending for the present tense forms of verbs, you are now ready for these additional pointers about subject–verb agreement:

I (a) Words that come between a subject and its verb do not count as part of the subject. The verb, therefore, agrees with the subject, not with the words between.

The train with the beach crowds leaves at noon.

The men in the office work long hours.

I (b) Expressions introduced by such words as *together with, in addition to, including, except, as well as* do not count as part of the subject. The verb agrees only with the subject.

Professor Tobin, as well as his students, was surprised.

The President, together with his cabinet members, has left for vacation.

 *Try It Out*

In the following sentences cross out the incorrect verb form.

1. One of the jurors in the murder trial (is, are) under suspicion for having taken a bribe.
2. The captain of the fishing boat, along with his passengers, (was, were) eager to find the best place to catch bluefish.
3. The employees of the engineering department (has, have) decided to organize a bowling team.

 Name: ____________________ *Date:* ____________________

II (a) When subjects are joined by *either . . . or, neither . . . nor, not only . . . but also,* the verb agrees with the subject closer to it.

Neither Joe nor his sisters like to study.

Either the captains or the umpire calls time out.

II (b) Subjects joined by *and* are usually plural and take a plural verb. However, when *each* or *every* precedes singular subjects joined by *and,* a singular verb should be used.

Mike and Sally exercise every day.

Every man and woman has the need to accomplish something.

 *Try It Out*

In the following sentences cross out the incorrect verb form.

1. Neither the coach nor her players (was, were) pleased to look at the films of the previous game.
2. Either cookies or cake (is, are) offered for dessert.
3. Each doctor and nurse on the hospital staff (feel, feels) that more personnel should be assigned to each shift.

III (a) In sentences beginning with *here is, here are, there is, there are, where is, where are,* be especially careful to look ahead and find the subject. *Here, there,* and *where* are never subjects.

There are forty members in the commune.

Here is the latest innovation.

III (b) The introductory *it* is always followed by a singular verb.

It is the most appropriate gift possible.

It is the citizens who make the nation strong.

III (c) The title of a written work, or the name of a business company, even when plural in form or ending in *'s*, takes a singular verb.

The Grapes of Wrath is one of Steinbeck's best works.

Lever Brothers produces many household products.

 *Try It Out*

In the following sentences cross out the incorrect verb form.

1. *The Los Angeles Times* (is, are) highly respected for its coverage of the entertainment industry.
2. It (is, are) America's natural resources that help make the country strong.
3. There (is, are) the vultures hovering over the wounded deer.

IV (a) When used as subjects, *each, every, everyone, everybody, anybody, anyone, nobody, someone, somebody, something, everything, either, neither, nothing* regularly take singular verbs.

Everyone is fascinated with space exploration.

Each of us lives a rather complex existence.

IV (b) *None, some, any,* and *all* may be either singular or plural. Decide which is correct from the context of the sentence.

None are so appreciative as those who have little.

None is so appreciative as he who has little.

IV (c) *Class, number, family, group,* and all other collective subjects take a singular verb when the subject is regarded as a unit. A plural verb is used when the subject refers to the individuals of a group.

The whole family is going on the trip.

The family have gone their separate ways.

Try It Out

In the following sentences cross out the incorrect verb form.

1. The Russo family (own, owns) the old haunted house down the street.
2. Anyone over eighteen (is, are) eligible to register for adult education courses.
3. None (is, are) so wise as the person who knows when to be silent.

V (a) Words stating an amount (time, money, weight, etc.) are usually singular and take a singular verb.

Two weeks is the usual vacation.

Six ounces of cough syrup is what I ordered.

V (b) Subjects that are plural in form but singular in meaning usually take singular verbs. These include *economics, civics, mathematics, physics, news, measles, mumps, ethics.*

Economics is my favorite subject.

Measles is a common childhood disease.

V (c) The words *trousers, jeans, scissors, eyeglasses, thanks, riches,* and *means* usually take a plural verb.

The scissors are on the table.

The millionaire's riches are to be given to charity.

Try It Out

In the following sentences cross out the incorrect verb form.

1. Politics (is, are) a complicated—and often confusing—science.
2. One hundred and fifty thousand dollars (is, are) the minimum price for a house in that town.
3. The designer jeans (was, were) poorly made and uncomfortable to wear.

Name: ______________________ Date: ______________________

EXERCISE 5g: Using the verb given in front of each sentence, fill in the correct form of the verb in the blank space provided. Keep all the verbs in the present tense.

1. *to expect:* Every camper and counselor in the old cabin ______________ the roof to collapse in the storm.
2. *to persuade:* Neither your flowers nor your candy ______________ me to reconsider your proposal.
3. *to have:* The editor, along with her reporters, ______________ decided that the new crime wave is front-page news.
4. *to echo:* From every corner of the woods ______________ the sounds of startled birds whenever a supersonic airplane flies overhead.
5. *to be:* There ______________ 6,500 windows in the Empire State Building.
6. *to make:* General Foods ______________ breakfast cereals and cake mixes, among many other products.
7. *to lead:* Both tension and a high salt diet ______________ to high blood pressure.
8. *to be:* Alfred Hitchcock's movie *The Birds* ______________ one of his most admired films.
9. *to enable:* Mathematics ______________ scientists to calculate the distances between faraway stars and planets.
10. *to be:* Two hundred pounds ______________ too much to lift for a beginning weight lifter.
11. *to need:* Either the meteorologist or her assistants ______________ to figure out how to repair the computer before the storm strikes.
12. *to have:* The school's football team ______________ managed to lose every game this year.
13. *to give:* The male, not the female, seahorse ______________ birth to its young.
14. *to run:* Each of them ______________ two miles every day to keep in shape.

 Name: ______________________________ Date: ____________________

15. *to be:* Some people believe that there ______________ several continents, such as Atlantis, under the oceans.

16. *to use:* Many young married people who work and attend school at the same time ______________ almost every minute trying to catch up with some chore or assignment.

17. *to contain:* A four-ounce hamburger, the usual size in fast-food restaurants, ______________ almost as many calories as a large piece of apple pie does.

18. *to show:* Whales ______________ affection by slapping each other with their fins.

19. *to expose:* Pollution of our air, as well as hazardous chemical additives in our foods, ______________ everyone to cancer-causing agents.

20. *to be:* It ______________ Buffalo, New York, that has the largest average annual snowfall (88.6 inches) of any major city in the United States.

EXERCISE 5h: Rewrite each of the sentences given, making sure that the verb agrees with the new subject given.

Examples: The store *opens* for business at 6 A.M.
The stores *open* for business at 6 A.M.

1. Disease strikes both the youngest and oldest among us.

   Diseases ______________________________

   ____

2. At least two of the orchards were damaged by the frost.

   At least one ______________________________

   ____

3. Thunder and lightning frighten many people.

   Thunder ______________________________

   ____

4. Either a baked potato or French fries are served with the steak dinner.

Either French fries or a baked potato

5. The Air Force fighter pilots are performing at the air show this afternoon.

The Air Force

6. Both of her sisters are going to medical school.

One of her sisters

7. His sense of humor is in bad taste.

His jokes

8. Is that apartment a cooperative or a rental?

those apartments cooperatives or rentals?

9. His parents, as well as his college counselor, are encouraging him to apply to a medical school in the Caribbean.

His college counselor, as well as his parents,

10. Robots which were built especially for dangerous police work have won merit awards for heroism.

A robot

11. Almost all textbooks are expensive these days.

Almost every textbook

12. Included in his briefcase were two computer printouts.

a computer printout.

13. Neither laughter nor tears from the audience distract the actors during their performance.

Neither tears nor laughter

14. Those are the pyramids that attract millions of tourists to Egypt each year.

It

15. *Decision Making in the White House* is a famous book about John F. Kennedy.

A Thousand Days

16. Those two dancers rehearse every afternoon and evening.

The entire dancing class

17. Imagination, together with patience and care, makes a good chef.

Patience and care, together with imagination,

18. There are two raccoons living under my front porch.

a raccoon living under my front porch.

19. Both of my history professors were friendly with the students.

Neither of my history professors

20. The walls in old houses usually have to be restored.

The flooring in old houses

Name: ______ Date: ______

Irregular Verbs

I Most verbs are considered "regular verbs." These verbs use the *-ed* ending to form the past tense. However, some verbs are irregular. They usually change their spellings to form the past tense.

Regular Verbs: The driving instructor *smiled* nervously as his student *turned* the steering wheel sharply and the car *swerved* in front of an oncoming truck.

Irregular Verbs: Colonel Sanders, who *became* a millionaire when he *sold* his Kentucky Fried Chicken business, *gave* most of his money to charity.

☞ *Try It Out*

Using the verbs given in parentheses, fill in the correct past tense forms in the blank spaces provided. Consult the list of irregular verbs on pages 165–167. Be careful to spell the verb correctly.

1. In the early days of baseball, umpires (to sit) ______________ on rocking chairs which were covered with protective padding in case a pitcher (to throw) ______________ a wild ball.
2. During the American War of Independence, more men who (to make) ______________ their home in the American colonies (to fight) ______________ for the British than for the Americans.
3. The United States government (to pay) ______________ Russia $7,200,000 for Alaska; thus, the forty-ninth state (to cost) ______________ less than two cents an acre.

 Name: ____________________ Date: ______________

II The past participle is a frequently used verb form. This is the verb form that can be combined with forms of *to be* or *to have* to create many different verb tenses. The forms of *to be* are *am, is, are, was, were, be, being, been.* The forms of *to have* are *have, has, had, having.* To form the past participle, regular verbs use the *-ed,* and irregular verbs usually change their spellings. (For a list of the past participles of irregular verbs, see pages 165–167.)

Regular Verbs: The government's student loan program *is being investigated* because many college students *have failed* to repay the tuition money that they *had borrowed.*

Irregular Verbs: Pistachio nuts *are grown* in Turkey, Lebanon, and Afghanistan.

The United States *has begun* a trade program with China.

Shakespeare *had written* 38 plays before he died in 1616.

☞ *Try It Out*

Using the verbs given in parentheses, select either the past tense form or the past participle form, whichever is correct. Then fill in that form in the blank space provided. Consult the list of irregular verbs on pages 165–167. Be careful to spell the verb correctly.

1. When the United States exploration of space was first (to begin) ______________ in 1958, only three of eleven attempted liftoffs were successful.
2. The Russians had (to send) ______________ up Sputnik I before the United States (to build) ______________ and launched its first satellite.
3. Since then, the United States and Russia have (to fight) ______________ for control of outer space, and each country has (to spend) ______________ billions of dollars on the effort.

Name: ______________________________ Date: ______________________

III Like the other irregular verbs, the verb *to be* does not use the *-ed* ending to form the past tense and the past participle. Instead, the spellings change.

The Verb "to Be"

past tense		*past participle*
I	was	been
you	were	
he	was	
she	was	
it	was	
we	were	
they	were	

Examples: John Hanson *was* really the first President of the United States, but his powers of office *were* very limited.

Tennis *has been* popular for hundreds of years.

☞ *Try It Out*

Fill in the blank spaces below with the correct forms of the verb *to be*.

1. The first pizzeria in America ______________ opened in 1895 on Spring Street in New York City.

2. Thomas Jefferson ______________ the first person to serve French fries in America; they had ______________ popular in France, where he had served as U.S. ambassador.

3. When Commodore Perry opened Japan to Western trade in the 1850's, many goldfish ______________ brought back to America by his men, who ______________ fascinated with the hardy and colorful creatures.

COMMONLY USED IRREGULAR VERBS

Verb	*Past*	*Past Pa*
arise	arose	arisen
awake	awoke or awaked	awakec
be (is, am, are)	was, were	been
bear	bore	borne or born
beat	beat	beaten
become	became	become
begin	began	begun
bend	bent	bent
bet	bet	bet
bid (offer)	bid	bid
bid (command)	bade	bidden
bind	bound	bound
bite	bit	bitten or bit
blow	blew	blown
break	broke	broken
bring	brought	brought
build	built	built
burst	burst	burst
buy	bought	bought
cast	cast	cast
catch	caught	caught
choose	chose	chosen
cling	clung	clung
come	came	come
cost	cost	cost
creep	crept	crept
cut	cut	cut
deal	dealt	dealt
dig	dug	dug
dive	dived or dove	dived
do	did	done
draw	drew	drawn
drink	drank	drunk
drive	drove	driven
eat	ate	eaten
fall	fell	fallen
feed	fed	fed
feel	felt	felt
fight	fought	fought
find	found	found
flee	fled	fled
fling	flung	flung

Verb	*Past*	*Past Participle*
fly	flew	flown
forbid	forbade or forbad	forbidden
forget	forgot	forgotten or forgot
forgive	forgave	forgiven
forsake	forsook	forsaken
freeze	froze	frozen
get	got	got or gotten
give	gave	given
go	went	gone
grow	grew	grown
hang (suspend)	hung	hung
*hang (execute)	hanged	hanged
have	had	had
hear	heard	heard
hide	hid	hidden
hit	hit	hit
hold	held	held
hurt	hurt	hurt
keep	kept	kept
know	knew	known
lay	laid	laid
lead	led	led
leave	left	left
lend	lent	lent
let	let	let
lie	lay	lain
light	lighted or lit	lighted or lit
lose	lost	lost
make	made	made
mean	meant	meant
meet	met	met
pay	paid	paid
prove	proved	proved or proven
quit	quit	quit
**raise	raised	raised
read	read	read
rid	rid	rid
ride	rode	ridden
ring	rang	rung
rise	rose	risen
run	ran	run
say	said	said
see	saw	seen

Verb	*Past*	*Past Participle*
seek	sought	sought
sell	sold	sold
send	sent	sent
set	set	set
shake	shook	shaken
shine (glow)	shone	shone
*shine (polish)	shined	shined
shoot	shot	shot
show	showed	shown or showed
shrink	shrank	shrunk
sing	sang	sung
sink	sank	sunk
sit	sat	sat
slay	slew	slain
sleep	slept	slept
sling	slung	slung
speak	spoke	spoken
spend	spent	spent
spin	spun	spun
spring	sprang or sprung	sprung
stand	stood	stood
steal	stole	stolen
sting	stung	stung
stink	stank or stunk	stunk
stride	strode	stridden
strike	struck	struck
strive	strove	striven
swear	swore	sworn
sweep	swept	swept
swim	swam	swum
swing	swung	swung
take	took	taken
teach	taught	taught
tear	tore	torn
tell	told	told
think	thought	thought
throw	threw	thrown
understand	understood	understood
wake	woke or waked	waked or woken
wear	wore	worn
win	won	won
wring	wrung	wrung
write	wrote	written

* Not an irregular form. Shown here to emphasize contrast with other use of the same word.
** Not an irregular form. Shown here to emphasize contrast with the word *rise*.

EXERCISE 5i: Using the verbs given in parentheses, fill in the correct past tense or past participle forms in the blank spaces provided. Consult the list of irregular verbs on pages 165–167.

1. Until 1850, shoes were (to make) ____________ by hand and were "straight" so that they could be (to wear) ____________ on either foot.
2. Because a shrew has poisonous saliva, you would be in big trouble if you were (to bite) ____________ by this tiny, mouselike mammal.
3. As of 1981, one out of every six doctors in the United States (to be) ____________ a woman.
4. Both Kaiser Wilhelm, the German leader, and Joseph Stalin, the Russian premier, (to have) ____________ deformed left arms.
5. The first Cadillacs were (to sell) ____________ in 1903 for $750.00.
6. Before Edgar Allan Poe (to write) ____________ *The Murders in the Rue Morgue,* detective stories (to be) ____________ unknown in English and American literature.
7. In seventeenth-century Japan, no citizen (to be) ____________ permitted to leave the country, and anyone who was (to catch) ____________ disobeying this law (to be) ____________ executed immediately.
8. A large area of Honolulu was deliberately destroyed in 1900 when authorities (to set) ____________ fire to an area that had (to be) ____________ contaminated with bubonic plague.
9. The Empire State Building was (to strike) ____________ accidentally by a B-25 bomber on July 28, 1945, but the building (to be) ____________ not seriously damaged.
10. When Kleenex tissues (to be) ____________ invented, they were (to mean) ____________ to be used only as gas mask filters.

 Name: ____________ Date: ____________

11. Winston Churchill (to write) ____________ a fairly successful novel in 1900, but he (to find) ____________ such work boring, so he (to choose) ____________ to be a soldier, and eventually he (to become) ____________ prime minister of England.

12. The ancient Egyptians (to do) ____________ not sleep on soft pillows; they (to sleep) ____________ on pillows that (to be) ____________ made of stone.

13. When President Truman had a balcony (to build) ____________ on the second floor of the White House, U.S. Mint officials suddenly (to have) ____________ to take all twenty-dollar bills out of circulation and reprint them. Most people (to do) ____________ not know why. Do you?

14. Records show that Roderigo de Triana, a crewman on Christopher Columbus' ship the Nina, should have (to get) ____________ the reward which Queen Isabella had (to swear) ____________ to give to the first person who sighted land, but Columbus (to say) ____________ that he was the winner and was (to give) ____________ the prize.

15. In Western Brazil, over 6,000 lives were (to lose) ____________ to disease and attacks by hostile Indians and animals during the 42 years it (to take) ____________ to build the Madeira-Mamoré railway.

16. The Brazil record was (to break) ____________ by the Panama Canal, which claimed over 25,000 lives before it was completely (to dig) ____________ in 1914.

17. The construction of the Golden Gate Bridge (to leave) ____________ ten dead, and fourteen workers (to lose) ____________ their lives in erecting the Empire State Building. After these tragedies, U.S. safety regulations (to be) ____________ improved.

18. The first airplanes (to be) ____________ considered too fragile to transport cargo, but they were eagerly (to seek) ____________ after for carrying passengers and mail.

19. Ketchup, which was (to know) ____________ as "Dr. Miles's Compound Extract of Tomato," was (to sell) ____________ as a medicine in the 1830's.

20. Little (to do) ____________ Robert Louis Stevenson realize that while he (to be) ____________ entertaining his stepson one rainy day, the maps and stories he (to be) ____________ creating to amuse the boy would soon become the basis of his great novel *Treasure Island.*

EXERCISE 5j: Rewrite each of the following sentences so that all of the actions take place in the past.

Example: The water *freezes* when the temperature *falls.* (present)
The water *froze* when the temperature *fell.* (past)

1. The mail carrier arises every morning at 2 A.M., hours before the sun shines.

____

____

2. The escaped convict flees from the bloodhounds and hides in the woods.

____

____

3. The cranky baby flings his cereal across the room and hits his brother in the face.

4. When I lend money to friends, I tell them they have to repay me within a week, and they do.

5. The passing supersonic plane shakes my kitchen windows, but it also rids my house of rats.

6. My grandmother always wrings her hands and begins to shake whenever she hears a tornado warning.

7. José writes love poems to Gilda, but Gilda throws them away.

8. I say that one dollar an hour is not enough money to baby-sit for triplets, even if they are well-behaved.

Name: ______________________ Date: ______________

9. First, I take out life insurance; then I fly in a plane.

___

___

___

10. He runs the mile in four minutes and swims it in under an hour.

___

___

___

EXERCISE 5k: Write at least ten sentences using the subjects in column A, the verbs in column B, and the past participle forms of the verbs listed in column C. Try to use each verb in column B several times, but use each verb in column C only once. Use your own paper for this assignment.

	A	B	C	
Example:	The telephone	has	rung	for ten minutes.

A	B	C
werewolves	has	to take
Richard Nixon	have	to fly
fixing a flat tire	had	to wear
a chocolate kiss		to write
Mick Jagger		to speak
a pet snake		to fall
teachers		to sing
blind dates		to eat
migraine headaches		to feel
Johnny Carson		to cost
a female astronaut		to make
cable TV		to give

Name: ___ Date: ___

The *-ed* Verb Ending

The *-ed* verb ending has many uses in the English language. Most people tend not to pronounce the *-ed* ending clearly in everyday speech because it frequently comes at the end of an unstressed syllable or is immediately followed by a word that starts with a *t* or *d* sound. For example, read the following sentence aloud:

When Joe finished doing his homework, he was supposed to walk the dog, but he listened to his Rolling Stones albums instead.

Did you pronounce all three *-ed* endings clearly? If you didn't, you might forget to add the *-ed* when you need it in your writing. To help avoid this problem, listen carefully for the endings of words when you speak, and review these major uses of the *-ed:*

I The *-ed* ending is used to indicate the past tense of regular verbs. (The past tense forms of irregular verbs are discussed on pages 162–167.) Notice in the following sentences that all of the actions started and ended in the past:

As the crowds *cheered,* the marathon runner *stumbled* across the finish line and *collapsed* into her husband's arms.

The residents *decided* to leave the area before the volcano *exploded* again.

Try It Out

Add *-ed* endings wherever necessary in the following sentences. Use your own paper, if needed.

1. Walt Disney base the character of Mickey Mouse on a real mouse that he capture when he live and work in Kansas City.
2. Disney himself supply the voice of Mickey for twenty years.
3. Although Minnie Mouse appear as Mickey's leading lady in hundreds of cartoons, the two mice never marry.

Name: ______________________ Date: ______________________

II The *-ed* ending is added to regular verbs that follow a form of the verb *to have*. Because the verbs follow *to have*, they are in their past participle *-ed* forms. (The past participle forms of irregular verbs are discussed on pages 162–167.)

subject + [*has* / *have* / *had*] + verb + *-ed*

The rain + *has* + stopp*ed*.

Notice in the following sentences how this verb pattern changes the time when the action takes place:

Frank *worked* at McDonald's.	(*He doesn't anymore.*)
Frank *has worked* at McDonald's for two years.	(*He worked there in the past and he still does.*)
Frank *had worked* at McDonald's until he joined the Army.	(*He left his job before he joined the Army.*)

☞ *Try It Out*

Add -*ed* endings wherever necessary in the following sentences. Use your own paper, if needed.

1. It has snow on my birthday for the last ten years.
2. I had dine on lobster and steak before you invite me to go out for pizza.
3. Every year since Elvis Presley die, large crowds have gather at his grave on the anniversary of his passing.

III (a) The *-ed* ending is added to regular verbs that follow a form of the verb *to be*. Because the verbs follow *to be*, they are in their past participle *-ed* forms. (The past participle forms of irregular verbs are discussed on pages 162–167.)

subject + [*is* / *am* / *are* / *was* / *were*] + *verb* + *-ed*

The class + *was* + cancell*ed*.

In most English sentences, the subject is doing the action of the verb. But in this verb pattern the action of the verb is being done to the subject.

Da Vinci painted the Mona Lisa.	(*The subject,* Da Vinci, *is doing the action.*)
The Mona Lisa was painted by Da Vinci.	(*The subject,* the Mona Lisa, *is receiving the action.*)
We elect senators for six-year terms.	(*The subject,* we, *is doing the action.*)
Senators are elected by us for six-year terms.	(*The subject,* senators, *is receiving the action.*)

III (b) In the "to be" pattern above, helping verbs such as *has, have, had, will, would, could,* and *should* may be combined with *be, being,* or *been* to create many different verb tenses.

By the year 2000, home computers *will be used* by most Americans.

Natural gas *is being produced* from garbage.

Lotteries *have been established* in several states.

Try It Out

Add *-ed* endings wherever necessary in the following sentences. Use your own paper, if needed.

1. The hamburger patties were unwrap so they could be defrost in time.
2. Perfect hamburgers are flip only once and are serve medium rare.
3. Usually, meat that is refrigerate improperly turns bad.

IV (a) Many past participle forms of verbs can be used as adjectives. Adjectives are words that describe nouns or pronouns. (See page 284 for a more complete definition of an adjective.) Regular verbs use the *-ed* ending. (The past participle forms of irregular verbs are discussed on pages 162–167.) Notice in the following sentence that past participle adjectives often come in front of the words they describe.

An *educated* person should know not to play with a *loaded* gun in a *crowded* room.

IV (b) The past participle used as an adjective may also follow the word it describes:

subject + verb + descriptive verb + *-ed*
Edith + *was* + surpris*ed.*

The verb that links the subject with its adjective is often a form of the verb *to be: is, am, are, was, were.* Or, as the following sentences illustrate, the linking verb might also be a form of one of these verbs: *act, appear, become, feel, get, look,* or *seem.*

People who *are bored* easily usually *feel tired* most of the time.

Jack *got scared* when his wife *became interested* in raising rattlesnakes.

☞ *Try It Out*

Add -*ed* endings wherever necessary in the following sentences. Use your own paper, if needed.

1. The puppy seems frighten of the skinny, battle-scar alley cat.
2. The teenager was ashame to admit that he had eaten all the crumble cookies and had wiped up the spill milk with his newly iron shirt.
3. The very inexperience chef's assistant was nervous about his order: to prepare the grease cake pans, the scramble eggs, and the whip cream.

Just as some writers forget to use the *-ed* ending when it is needed, others use the ending when it is not needed.

V (a) The *-ed* ending is *not* added to most irregular verbs. Irregular verbs usually change their spellings to form the past tense and the past participle. (See pages 162–167 for more information on irregular verbs.)

Past Tense: On an average day in America last year, 2,740 children *ran* away from home, 3 million people *went* to the movies, and 10,000 people *took* their first airplane ride.

Past Participle: The forest fire has *driven* off all the wild animals.

The kite was *caught* in the TV antenna.

The *blown* tire was beyond repair.

V (b) The *-ed* ending is *not* added to a verb that follows *do, does,* or *did.*

The country *does need* a strong leader.

Levi Hutchins *did* not *earn* any money from his invention of the alarm clock.

V (c) The *-ed* ending is *not* added to the infinitive form of a verb. The infinitive is a verb preceded by the word *to.*

Many college students *have to work* part-time.

Because Thomas Jefferson *wanted to avoid* colds, he *used to soak* his feet in cold water every morning.

V (d) The *-ed* ending is *not* added to a verb that follows *can, could, should, would, may, might, must, shall,* or *will.*

Charles Atlas *could pull* a 145,000-pound railroad car down a track.

We *must save* the whale population of the earth.

Notice in the following sentences that the *-ed* ending is added when a form of the verb *to be* or *to have* is also included.

You *should have laughed* at the boss's joke.

Over 2 million American couples *will be married* this year.

 *Try It Out*

Make any necessary corrections in the verbs in the following sentences. You may have to remove *-ed* endings or change the spellings of the verbs. Use your own paper, if needed.

1. No one can breathed and swallowed at the same time.
2. Our neighbor has not forgetted our argument when I catched his dog as it creeped into my vegetable garden.
3. The old Pony Express did succeeded in getting the mail through; it failed only once in its first nineteen months of operation.
4. If you hoped to attended the rock concert, you should have purchased your tickets in advance.

Name: ______________________ Date: ______________________

A SPECIAL NOTE: The spelling of a regular verb sometimes changes slightly when *-ed* is added. (1) This happens sometimes when a verb ends with a *y*. See page 74 for more information. (2) This happens when the final consonant of some verbs has to be doubled. See page 419 for more information.

EXERCISE 5I: Rewrite each of the following sentences so that all of the actions take place in the past.

Example: After we *move* away, we *start* to miss everyone. (present)
After we *moved* away, we *started* to miss everyone. (past)

1. During basic training in the Army, the soldiers exercise, march, hike, and attend classes where they learn about military life.

____

____

____

2. The anaconda snake, which weighs about 300 pounds, moves as well in the water as it does on the land.

____

____

____

3. The young man composes a love letter to his sweetheart, types it, pastes a stamp on the envelope, and then decides to throw it away.

____

____

____

4. The magician who performs the trick of sawing people in two has four half-sisters.

____

____

____

 Name: ______________________ Date: ______________

5. The students claim that the math teacher's plant grows square roots.

6. The actor who plays a snake charmer faints whenever the stage manager hands him a real snake.

7. The acrobat climbs onto her partner's shoulders, grabs the rope, pushes off to swing across the stage, and lands perfectly on the elephant's back.

8. When the class starts to get noisy, the teacher yells, "Order, please!" and a student calls out, "I'll take a hamburger with onions."

9. The dog jumps in the lake and paddles around for a while whenever it wants to cool off on a hot day.

10. While the woman jogs five miles a day, she uses earphones to listen to her portable radio, which she hooks onto her belt.

____

____

____

EXERCISE 5m: Write at least ten complete sentences using the subjects listed in column A, the verbs listed in column B, and the past participle forms of the verbs listed in column C. Try to use each of the verbs in column B several times, but use each verb in column C only once. Use your own paper for this assignment.

	A	B	C	
Example:	The technicians	had	started	the experiment

before the lights suddenly went out.

A	B	C
the Army	has	to please
the mail-order catalog	have	to annoy
museums	had	to look
unidentified flying objects		to move
break dancing		to appear
Dan Rather		to disappear
after-shave lotion		to pass
all-night supermarkets		to purchase
the alarm clock		to succeed
sunglasses		to walk
Diana Ross		to land
jukeboxes		to act
pharmacists		to help
the final examination		to increase
cooking dinner		to improve

 Name: ______________________ Date: ______________

EXERCISE 5n: Rewrite each of the following sentences, using the new subjects provided on the blank lines.

Example: Every day, U.S. hospitals *treat* 7 million people.
Every day, 7 million people *are treated* at U.S. hospitals.

1. Each second, the sun burns 9 million tons of gas.

   Each second, 9 million tons of gas ____________________

   ____.

2. The color white reflects heat.

   Heat ____________________________________.

3. Surgeons are now using staple guns to close some wounds.

   Staple guns ________________________________.

4. Most people should avoid fatty foods.

   Fatty foods ________________________________.

5. The Black Plague destroyed half the population of Europe in the fourteenth century.

   Half the population of Europe ______________________

   ____.

6. The Puritans outlawed the singing of Christmas carols.

   The singing of Christmas carols _____________________

   ____.

7. By the end of this century, the United States probably will establish a permanent colony on the moon.

   By the end of this century, a permanent colony ______________

   ____.

8. The nuclear-powered aircraft carrier *Nimitz* requires a crew of over 6,000 sailors.

   A crew of over 6,000 sailors ______________________

   ____.

Name: ____________________ Date: ________________

9. Insect stings have killed almost 2,000 people this year.

Almost 2,000 people ______________________________

______________________________.

10. In 1939 Hollywood produced about two movies a day.

In 1939 about two movies a day ______________________________

______________________________.

EXERCISE 5o: For each item, first use the past participle form of a verb listed below to complete the sentence marked "a." Then place the same past participle verb in front of the subject provided in "b" and complete the new sentence by adding whatever words you think are reasonable.

Example: The table is *polished.*
The *polished* table reflects the sunlight.

to toast	to confuse
to scare	to tire
to relieve	to slice
to stain	to trap
to satisfy	to interest
to ruin	to use
to rescue	to bore
to repair	to decorate
to butter	to damage

1. a. The marshmallows seem ______________________.

   b. The ______________ marshmallows ______________.

2. a. The audience looks ______________________.

   b. The ______________ audience ______________.

3. a. The patient felt ______________________.

   b. The ______________ patient ______________.

4. a. The miners were ______________________.

   b. The __________________ miners __________________.

5. a. The winner acts ______________________.

   b. The __________________ winner __________________.

6. a. The rug looks ______________________.

   b. The __________________ rug __________________.

7. a. The actors became ______________________.

   b. The __________________ actors __________________.

8. a. The English muffin was ______________________.

   b. The __________________ English muffin __________________.

9. a. The wedding cake gets ______________________.

   b. The __________________ wedding cake __________________.

10. a. The sailors act ______________________.

    b. The __________________ sailors __________________.

EXERCISE 5p: Add the *-ed* ending wherever it is needed in the following sentences. Use your own paper for this assignment.

1. During World War II the Navajo language was use as a code by the United States. America's enemies never figure out how to break it.

2. Johnny Weissmuller's Tarzan yell combine three different sounds. It include his own unaid scream, a high C sung by a soprano, and a hyena's howl—all of which were record together and then play backwards.

3. Ernest Hemingway revise the last page of his novel *A Farewell to Arms* 39 times.

4. The first self-service elevators were locate in the Atlantic Refining Building in Dallas, Texas.

5. "Yankee Doodle," the unauthorize national anthem until "The Star-Spangle Banner" was adopt officially by Congress in 1931, was the first tune ever record on a record.

6. The average marry woman in seventeenth-century America conceive many children and deliver thirteen of them, but not all of them live to adulthood.

7. Only six out of thirty-three cars that start the 1966 Indianapolis 500 Race finish. A bad crash during the first lap stop nearly half the participants.

8. Baseball cards were first include in packs of cigarettes. Some ballplayers refuse to let their pictures be use because they did not want children to be encourage to smoke.

9. In Iceland, all employ citizens are require to have graduate from school and to have learn to speak three languages.

10. Bat Masterson, reform gambler and fame lawman of the Old West, is bury in the Bronx, New York City. He move to New York when he was 48 years old and serve as sports editor for the *Morning Telegraph*.

Name: ______________________ Date: ______________________

11. Coca-Cola was invent by retire Confederate officer John S. Pemberton. He mix the extract of the import cola nut with another extract which was derive from cola leaves, also the basis of cocaine. Long ago, of course, the formula was change.

12. Tennessee is call the "Volunteer State" because in 1847 its governor issue a call for 2,800 volunteers to fight in the Mexican War and 30,000 men answer.

13. The fictional lawyer Perry Mason first appear in *The Case of the Velvet Claws,* which was publish in 1932. Since then, the character has been feature in a television series and has been portray in numerous books and movies.

14. In the United States more than half the court cases are devote to matters concerning the automobile.

15. Davy Crockett desert his family. Later, he was elect to Congress, but within a short time he had develop a reputation for frequent absences.

16. After the Roman Empire and Persia had sign "The Endless Peace" treaty in 533 A.D., they start to fight again seven years later.

17. Benjamin Franklin never was marry, but he live with Deborah Reed for 44 years. Her husband had disappear and his death could not be verify.

18. The first state lottery was organize by New Hampshire in 1963 to provide funds for its underfinance school system, but even after the lottery start New Hampshire still rank last nationally in aid to education.

19. Most people are convince that Albert Einstein was award the Nobel Prize for physics for his famous Theory of Relativity, but he receive the honor for his work on the photoelectric effect which he had publish earlier.

20. A recent study has reveal that nearly half of all deaths in modern times have occur within three months following each person's birthday. One explanation is that older people consider a birthday a goal, and once it is reach they become depress.

EXERCISE 5q: REFRESHER

1. Add the *-d* or *-ed* ending wherever it is needed in the following paragraph.
2. Rework the sentences so that there are at least three examples of subordination.

Leslie Lemke is living proof that miracles do happen. Shortly after Leslie's birth, his parents abandon him. He had been born without eyes and had cerebral palsy. A middle-age couple name May and Joe Lemke agree to care for the brain-damage baby. He was like a vegetable; he did not move or make any sounds. Determine to help the boy overcome his handicaps, May Lemke work with Leslie regularly until he finally walk for the first time when he was sixteen. Next, May tried to stimulate the boy's mind by using an old piano, a record player, and a radio to fill the house with music for several hours each day. For three years Leslie gave no indication that he was listening. Then one night he suddenly sat down at the piano and start to play a difficult piece of classical music, which he follow with country-western, gospel, ragtime, and rock music as well. The Lemkes were shock to discover not only that Leslie could play the piano but also that he could sing everything from opera to show tunes and could imitate the voices of many popular singers. But the Lemkes' most amazing discovery was that Leslie could play even the most complicated piece of music after hearing it just once. Most musicians with normal minds do not possess this remarkable ability. Scientists are unable to explain Leslie's extraordinary talent. Many people believe that it is a miracle brought about by the loving care and concern of May and Joe Lemke.

 Name: ______________________ Date: ______________

SPRINGBOARDS TO WRITING

Using your knowledge of the writing process, explained on pages 12–14, write a paragraph or essay related to this chapter's central theme, *intelligence,* which is introduced on pages 136–139.

PREWRITING

To think of topics to write about, look at the lithograph and photograph, read the essay, and answer the questions that follow each. If you prefer, select one of the writing springboards below. (All paragraph numbers refer to the essay that starts on page 138.) To develop your ideas, use the prewriting techniques described on pages 15–20.

WRITING A PARAGRAPH (For help, see the Pointers on page 31.)

1. A person should (should not) know his or her I.Q.
2. Physical labor does (does not) require intelligence.
3. Does a person have to be educated to be smart? (see ¶ 6.)
4. How do you generally judge a person's intelligence?
5. Agree or disagree with this statement by Will Rogers: "There is nothing so stupid as an educated man, if you get off the thing he was educated in."

WRITING AN ESSAY (For help, see the Pointers on page 35.)

6. Give your answer to the question: What Is Intelligence, Anyway?
7. My Definition of an Educated Person
8. My Definition of a Smart Person
9. I Consider Myself a Genius at ______________________.
10. Tests of Mental Ability Do Not Tell the Whole Story about a Person
11. A Person Needs (Does not Need) a High I.Q. to Be Successful
12. Agree or disagree: Experience Is the Best Teacher
13. Agree or disagree: The More You Learn, the Less You Know
14. All High School Students Should (Should Not) Have to Pass Competency Tests to Graduate
15. What School Does Not Teach about Life
16. ______________________ Does the Type of Excellent Work that I Admire
17. People Are Not Always What They Seem

We have it on high authority that sharing the ride is a very good idea.

It made sense to Noah. After all, it was a whole lot more economical and efficient to get together and share the ride than it would have been for everybody to go their own way.

And that still holds true today.

Sharing the ride with just one other person can cut your commuting costs in half.

Think about it.

Share the ride with a friend. It sure beats driving alone.

Ad Council

A public service of this magazine, The U.S. Department of Transportation and The Advertising Council.

Courtesy of the Advertising Council, Inc.

UPI/Bettmann Archive.

SPRINGBOARDS TO THINKING

For informal, not written, response . . . to stimulate your thinking

1. How would you feel if you were driving in the heavy traffic shown in the photograph? Explain.
2. Every day many people have to drive back and forth to work or school in traffic like that shown in the photograph. What effects do you think this might have on a person? Explain.
3. What effects does heavy traffic have on the environment? What can be done to lessen the effects?
4. Do you agree with the message in the advertisement for car-pooling? Why or why not? If you have a car, do you car-pool to work or school? (Or if you had a car, would you car-pool?) Why or why not?
5. Why do so many people refuse to car-pool even when it is economical? Can anything be done to make car-pooling more attractive to car drivers? Explain.
6. Why do people sometimes want, and even need, the privacy of their own cars?

The Great American Love Affair

WILLIAM SAFIRE

(1) I drive to work. I say that defensively, fully expecting to incur the wrath of the car-haters, who are revving up their propaganda engines to bring to an end the great American love affair with the private car. They tell me that:

(2) I am polluting the atmosphere. We drivers of the nation's 108 million private automobiles churn out some 70 million tons of noxious fumes annually, poisoning our fellow citizens, be-smogging whole cities, and costing taxpayers billions of dollars in air-pollution-control equipment.

(3) I am slaughtering my fellow man. Safety-council experts inform me grimly that we drivers cause 46,000 deaths every year.

(4) I am aggravating an energy crisis. Autos gulp down 200 million gallons of gasoline every day, increasing U.S. dependence on foreign oil and placing our foreign policy in sheiky hands.

(5) I am selfishly standing in the way of providing clean, fast mass transportation. If the $26 billion a year we have been spending on highways went instead to public mass transit, we could beat our fenders into turnstiles, and soon all be living in an egalitarian world of zippy monorails, moving sidewalks and pulsating undergrounds.

(6) To the organized car-haters of the mass-transit lobby, I say: sorry about all that. You have made me feel guilty. But, like most other commuters, I intend to continue driving to work—no car pool, no hitchhikers, no excuses. Here's why.

(7) The private automobile is the last bastion of personal independence. Just as most people prefer single-family homes of their own—even though apartment houses are much more efficient—most people also prefer vehicles of their own. Certainly a strong reason must exist for commuters to go into hock to buy a car, to sweat out traffic jams, to groan over repair bills. That reason is, simply: the blessed orneriness called love of privacy.

(8) In the morning, when I go out to my car, it is there, waiting; it never leaves without me even if I am late. I have missed buses, trains, ships, but never my car. It is my slave. All its shafts, plugs, and mysterious pistons do my bidding, usually.

(9) Inside the private car, the driver is gloriously alone. In a world of people pressing at him in the office and kids needing him at home, of lines at the museum and crowds at the ballpark, he is at last sealed in his own climate-controlled cocoon. The man who dreams of riding with a chauffeur is a fool. The man who installs a telephone in his car is a communicaholic.

(10) Most of the time, if you want to be alone, you have to explain why. But not if you're driving to work. For a blissful half-hour, twice a day, I can talk to myself, and nobody thinks I'm crazy. I can sing, and nobody can complain. I can play whatever I want on the radio, loud or soft.

(11) Don't get me wrong, I'm no car nut. No tinkering with the engine, no long hours buffing the finish, no four-wheel fetishism for me. To keep the real sense of privacy, a car must be nondescript, a comfortable companion, so close that you never have to pay it any attention.

(12) Subway riders and other mass-transit freaks may scoff, but every commuter knows that after a couple of hundred trips back and forth, a car learns the way. When my car was in the garage recently for repairs, I took a rental car to work. Sure enough, while I was alternately singing and thinking through an essay, the car got lost. Rental cars don't know the way home: it takes a heap o' drivin' to make a car a heap.

(13) Of course, when asked, "*Why* do you commute, and congest, and pollute?" the driving commuter cannot simply say, "I want to be alone." So, to confound the mass-transitites, he must marshal facts like these:

1. The auto industry is the backbone of the American economy. Automobile owners spend well over $100 billion a year—close to ten percent of the gross national product—to satisfy their transportation lust. One of every six workers is directly or indirectly employed in the auto industry, and when car production drops ten percent—as it did last year—over 200,000 are thrown out of work.

2. Auto taxes feed hungry bellies. Private-car owners cough up billions of dollars to federal and state governments each year.

3. We're solving the pollution problem. Noxious emissions in today's cars have been cut 85 percent from those that come out of my 1968 wheezer.

4. Cars are drinking less. The 1976 models get 17 miles per gallon. By 1985, we'll be getting 27 m.p.g. *

5. Autos are safer than ever. Lower speed limits, bothersome belts and costly safety devices have cut traffic fatalities to the lowest point in more than a decade.

(14) Still, the real justification for the personal car is convenience. And social psychology. In an era that has nibbled away at the perimeter of our privacy, we need to hang onto every bit of personal freedom we've got.

(15) That's why Secretary of Transportation William T. Coleman, Jr.—speaking to busloads of car-hating, mass-transportation bureaucrats at their annual convention last year—told them to keep their eye on the line in the middle of the road. "Like it or not," he said, "the automobile is going to remain our preferred form of transportation. The great American love affair with the automobile is *not* over."

* Car manufacturers have met this goal; indeed, some cars now get 40 miles per gallon.

READING SURVEY

1. *Main Idea*

What is the central theme of this essay?

2. *Major Details*

a. Why do people prefer to drive to work alone rather than to car-pool or use public transportation?
b. What are the reasons a driver can offer in defense of congesting and polluting?
c. What did William T. Coleman, Jr., say at the annual convention of mass transportation bureaucrats?

3. *Inferences*

a. Read paragraph 4 again. What does William Safire mean by the expression "placing our foreign policy in sheiky hands"?
b. Read paragraph 12 again. How does making a car into a "heap" enable the car to learn the way back and forth?

4. *Opinions*

a. If given a choice, would you rather drive alone to work, car-pool, or use mass transportation? Explain.
b. Why do so many people have to escape to their cars to gain a small measure of independence and privacy?

VOCABULARY BUILDING

Lesson One: The Vocabulary of Traffic

The essay "The Great American Love Affair" by William Safire includes words that are useful when you are discussing traffic.

defensively	(paragraph 1)	**scoff**	(12)
wrath	(1)	**congest**	(13)
revving	(1)	**confound**	(13)
noxious	(2)	**emissions**	(13)
orneriness	(7)	**fatalities**	(13)

In heavy traffic, drivers should drive **defensively** by being on guard against harm or danger.

In heavy traffic, drivers often express their **wrath** or extreme anger and rage by honking their horns or by trying to cut in front of other cars.

In heavy traffic, drivers can often be heard **revving** up their engines even though they are standing still. Such people seem to feel powerful when they can speed up the action of their engines even when they cannot move.

In heavy traffic, drivers have to breathe **noxious** or harmful fumes.

In heavy traffic, drivers' **orneriness** often comes out in that the mean and ugly parts of their personalities emerge.

In heavy traffic, those drivers who pass by in an opposite direction with only light traffic might **scoff**—laugh with a sense of looking down on others—at the trapped drivers.

In heavy traffic, cars **congest** the roads in that the cars overcrowd the roads and almost stop the flow of traffic.

In heavy traffic, finding a way out of the jam can often **confound** or confuse and bewilder even the best drivers.

In heavy traffic, drivers have to breathe the **emissions** or the discharges of fumes of all the cars.

In heavy traffic, as in all kinds of traffic, careless driving can lead to **fatalities** or deaths by accident.

EXERCISE 6a: Each of the vocabulary words from this lesson is shown below in italics as the word appeared in context in the essay. Write an explanation of each word within the context of the material given. Use your own paper for this assignment.

1. From paragraph 1: "I drive to work. I say that *defensively,* fully expecting to incur the *wrath* of the car-haters, who are *revving* up their propaganda engines to bring to an end the great American love affair with the private car."
2. From paragraph 2: "We drivers . . . churn out some 70 million tons of *noxious* fumes annually. . . ."
3. From paragraph 7: "That reason is, simply: the blessed *orneriness* called love of privacy."
4. From paragraph 12: "Subway riders and other mass-transit freaks may *scoff*. . . ."
5. From paragraph 13: ". . . 'Why do you commute, and *congest,* and pollute?' "
6. From paragraph 13: "So, to *confound* the mass-transitites, he must marshal facts. . . ."
7. From paragraph 13: "Noxious *emissions* in today's cars have been cut 85 percent. . . ."
8. From paragraph 13: ". . . bothersome belts and costly safety devices have cut traffic *fatalities* to the lowest point. . . ."

Lesson Two: The Vocabulary of Government

The essay "The Great American Love Affair" by William Safire includes words that are useful when you are discussing government.

propaganda	(paragraph 1)	**marshal**	(13)
foreign policy	(4)	**gross national product**	(13)
egalitarian	(5)	**bureaucrats**	(15)
lobby	(6)	**convention**	(15)
bastion	(7)		

When the government uses **propaganda,** it wants to promote its own ideas at the expense of opposing ideas, usually by exaggerating the truth or by twisting it until it becomes misleading.

When the government sets **foreign policy,** it is concerned with the course of action it will take in its relations with foreign countries.

When the government supports **egalitarian** principles, it favors the belief that all people should have equal political, social, and economic rights.

When the government is influenced by a **lobby,** it is influenced by a group of people who have special interests that are not always the best for the entire country and who want the government to go along with their needs.

When the government is considered a **bastion,** it is seen as having strong defenses or as being a fortress.

When the government has to **marshal** evidence to support its point of view, it has to call forth its evidence and arrange it in good order.

When the government turns its attention to the **gross national product (GNP),** it is concerned with the total value of the nation's annual output of goods and services.

When the government is run by **bureaucrats,** it is run by people who follow a routine in a mechanical, unimaginative way by having people fill out forms and by insisting on unimportant rules.

When any group holds a **convention,** it calls a meeting of its members. These meetings are usually held on a regular basis, once every year or two.

EXERCISE 6b: Match the columns. Do not draw lines: writing the words will help you learn them better. Notice that there are two extra definitions, neither of which matches a word from this lesson.

propaganda
foreign policy
egalitarian
lobby
bastion
marshal
gross national product
bureaucrats
convention

__________ 1. unimaginative officials

__________ 2. to call forth and arrange

__________ 3. a group representing special interests organized to influence legislators

__________ 4. an assembly of members

__________ 5. the total value of a nation's yearly output

__________ 6. a country's way of dealing with other countries

__________ 7. a visiting foreign diplomat

__________ 8. a fortress

__________ 9. favoring equal rights for all

__________ 10. exaggerated promotion of particular ideas at the expense of other ideas

__________ 11. corrupt officials

Name: __________ *Date:* __________

SPELLING

Lesson One: Spelling Demons

Here are more words that are frequently misspelled. Using the helpful techniques given in Chapter One, you should make it a point to learn these new Demons, which are taken from "The Great American Love Affair."

aggravate	**device**	**pollution**
annually	**efficient**	**preferred**
atmosphere	**enough**	**propaganda**
certainly	**equipment**	**safety**
comfortable	**government**	**satisfy**
controlled	**independence**	**sense**
convenience	**mysterious**	**vehicle**
council	**personal**	**whole**

Lesson Two: Commonly Confused Words

You may sometimes misspell a word because you confuse it with another word that is similar in appearance. Unlike the Sound-Alikes given in Chapter Two, the sets of words listed below are not pronounced alike, but there is a close resemblance in their spelling; often the difference is just a letter or two. Because they are very commonly used words, you should try to learn them well.

I A/AN/AND. *A* and *an* are two forms of the same word; both *a* and *an* mean "one."

a. *An* is used before a word beginning with a vowel sound (*a, e, i, o, u*).

an *a*thlete an *o*nion an *u*mbrella

A is used before a word beginning with a consonant sound (all letters other than the vowels).

a *h*orse a *n*urse a *w*indow

☞ *Try It Out*

Fill in each blank with *a* or *an*.

________ class	________ teacher	________ snake
________ orange	________ insect	________ answer

---

b. *An* is used before a word beginning with a silent *h.*

an *h*our   an *h*onorable discharge

A is used before a word beginning with a vowel when that vowel sounds like a consonant. Note in the examples below that both the vowel *u* and the *Eu* vowel combination sound like the consonant *y.*

a *u*niform   a *Eu*ropean   a *u*nit

☞ *Try It Out*

Fill in each blank with *a* or *an*.

________ union	________ hour	________ university
________ honor	________ U-turn	________ honest answer

---

c. *And* joins two words or ideas together. *And* means "plus" or "in addition to."

Smith *and* Johnson are the most common last names in America.

The largest planet in our solar system is Jupiter, *and* the smallest is Pluto.

☞ *Try It Out*

Fill in each blank with *a, an,* or *and.*

1. _______ cat's tail contains three times as many muscles as _______ human hand _______ wrist do.

2. _______ elephant eats as much as 500 pounds of food _______ day _______ sleeps only two or three hours _______ night.

II OTHER COMMONLY CONFUSED WORDS

a. *accept* (to receive)
   I would be happy to accept the dinner invitation.
   except (excluding)
   Everyone except Joe passed the English test.

b. *advice* (a recommendation)
   My mother gave me good advice concerning my future plans.
   advise (to give a recommendation)
   I advised Jack to see a doctor.

c. *affect* (to change or influence)
   The bad weather will affect my plans for the day.
   effect (to cause; the result)
   The doctor is working to effect a cure.
   Alcohol has a strange effect on many people.

d. *breath* (an exhalation)
   I could smell liquor on his breath.
   breathe (to inhale and exhale)
   It is unhealthy to breathe polluted air.

e. *choose* (to select—present tense)
   Because I am lazy, I always choose the easiest courses.
   chose (to select—past tense)
   Ann chose a Buick as her next car.

f. *clothes* (garments)
Lou changed his clothes before going out for dinner.
cloths (pieces of fabric)
We have a drawer full of dusting cloths.

g. *costume* (a suit or dress)
Helen wore a gypsy costume to the masquerade ball.
custom (the usual course of action)
It is a custom to tip a waiter.

h. *desert* (to leave or abandon; a dry, wasted region)
Do not desert those in need.
The Sahara Desert is in North-Central Africa.
dessert (the last course of a meal)
Strawberry shortcake is my favorite dessert.

i. *later* (coming after)
Mike promised to do his homework later.
latter (the second of two things)
The millionaire has both a Rolls-Royce and a Jaguar XKE; the latter is a very expensive sports car.

j. *loose* (not tight)
The car has a loose wire.
lose (to misplace)
I had better tighten this button before I lose it.
loss (the fact of being misplaced)
Phyllis was upset about the loss of her watch.

k. *moral* (an ethical issue)
There is a moral to be learned from many children's fables.
morale (mental state)
The soldiers' morale was improved by the visiting entertainers.

l. *quiet* (silent)
You must be quiet in a library.
quite (completely)
She was quite tired after the long trip.

A SPECIAL NOTE: Memory tricks may help you to distinguish between these often confused words:
Remember that *ex*cept means *ex*clude.
The expression "cause and effect" will help you link *effect* with "to cause."
*S*trawberry *s*hortcake is a de*ss*ert.
Three vowels in a row are very q*uie*t.

EXERCISE 6c: Fill in each blank with *a*, *an*, or *and*.

1. ______ English medical journal claims that ______ overweight child who does not slim down by age seven will probably stay fat for ______ lifetime.

2. While it is growing, ______ banana inhales oxygen, exhales carbon dioxide, ______ creates its own heat.

3. ______ old Biblical saying insists that it is more difficult to find ______ honest person than it is for ______ camel to pass through the eye of ______ needle.

4. ______ ant is equipped with five different noses, each designed to accomplish ______ specific task.

5. ______ average seven-inch pencil is capable of drawing ______ line 35 miles long.

6. Felix Mendelssohn, the famous German composer ______ musician, had already written ______ opera, ______ overture, ______ several symphonies by the time he was seventeen.

7. ______ United Nations study says that Hungary has the highest recorded suicide rate ______ Mexico has the lowest.

8. ______ angry Los Angeles librarian took away ______ man's library card because the fellow had ______ unusual habit of using ______ strip of raw bacon as ______ bookmark.

9. ______ Japanese inventor has created ______ vending machine that freshly cooks ______ serves ______ plate of spaghetti with meat sauce in 27 seconds.

 Name: ____________________ *Date:* ____________

10. According to ______ recent study of color preferences, ______ intellectual person usually prefers blue ______ ______ athletic person usually prefers red.

11. ______ Georgia law makes it illegal to slap ______ friend on the back, ______ ______ Florida law makes it illegal to break more than three dishes ______ day.

12. The little metal or plastic tip on the end of ______ shoelace is called ______ aglet.

13. ______ ostrich can run twice as fast as ______ human being can.

14. ______thirsty camel can drink 25 gallons of water in half ______ hour.

15. In New Hampshire it is legal for ______ 14-year-old boy ______ ______ 13-year-old girl to get married.

EXERCISE 6d: Underline the correct word from each set of words in parentheses.

In certain parts of the world, it is the (costume, custom) to (accept, except) treatment from "doctors" who have had no medical training whatsoever but are apparently (quiet, quite) successful at giving medical (advice, advise) and performing a mysterious form of surgery. Perhaps the most famous of these healers was an uneducated Brazilian named Arigo, who in the (later, latter) years of his life (adviced, advised) more than two million people, some of whom came from as far away as Tokyo and the Sahara (Desert, Dessert). When a team of fourteen American scientists (choose, chose) to investigate his work, they traveled to his clinic in a (deserted, desserted) region of Brazil, where they watched what occurred between each of one thousand patients and Arigo. In about one minute's time, the (later, latter) would complete his examination and give an accurate diagnosis and the appropriate prescription to (affect, effect) a cure. To perform an operation, he wore his (loose, lose, loss) native (costume, custom) instead of the surgical (clothes, cloths) usually seen in hospitals. In one instance, he decided to (choose, chose) a pocket knife as his surgical tool and, as his patient took a deep (breath, breathe), Arigo inserted the dirty blade into the patient's arm and cut out an egg-shaped tumor. (Accept, Except) for a slight (loose, lose, loss) of blood, the surgery had no bad (affect, effect) on the patient's health.

Arigo's methods may have spread to the Philippine Islands and (affected, effected) a group of men who use their bare hands to perform operations and yet rarely (loose, lose, loss) a patient. In a typical operation, a woman complaining of a constant pain in her stomach lay down on a table while the surgeon dipped some cotton (clothes, cloths) in a bowl of water and then rubbed her abdomen with them. Soon a watery liquid that looked like blood began to gurgle up between the surgeon's fingers as they started to poke around inside the woman's belly. The patient continued to (breath, breathe) normally and remained (quiet, quite) throughout her ordeal; indeed, her (moral, morale) was very good. After removing a large round lump from her belly, the surgeon wiped her abdomen clean with a towel, leaving no wound whatsoever. The woman then got off the table, walked home, and managed to eat an entire dinner from soup to (desert, dessert). Although many American scientists are impressed by these apparently miraculous medical procedures, the (moral, morale) issue cannot be overlooked: Should individuals who have no medical training be permitted to practice medicine?

EXERCISE 6e: Unscramble the letters in parentheses to form the missing words in each sentence. If necessary, check your spelling with the list of Demons in this chapter.

1. The American (ETAFSY) ____________ (CILOUNC) ____________ warns that air (LLIONUTPO) ____________ must be (LLTROCONED) ____________ because it can

 Name: ____________ Date: ____________

(AINCERLYT) ______________ (GGATERAVA) ______________ many health conditions.

2. Although we have heard (OVEGENTMNR) ____________________ (PAGPRODAAN) ____________________ denying the existence of flying saucers, some of us have (RRFEEDREP) ________________ to believe the stories about (IUOMYSSRET) ____________________ (LESHICVE) ____________________________ soaring through the (PHATERMOSE) ________________.

3. New (VIDESEC) ____________________ are being invented to help handicapped people (FYISSAT) __________________ their need for (ALSONREP) ____________________________ (DEPENCINEEND) ________________.

4. McDonald's sells about three billion hamburgers (LLYNNAUA) ______________________, largely because the fast-food chain offers (IENVENCECON) __________________________, (CIEFFIENT) ______________________________ service, and (FORBLECOMTA) ________________ surroundings.

5. Because Gus did not have (GHOUEN) ________________ common (SESEN) ____________________ to buy any fishing (ENTUIPMEQ) ________________, when he went camping he ended up spending a (EOLWH) __________________ day trying to catch a trout with his hands.

EXERCISE 6f: PROOFREADING FOR SPELLING Use the proofreading techniques given in Chapter Four to find and correct any misspelled words in the following paragraph. If necessary, check your spelling with the list of Spelling Demons in this chapter.

The automobile of the future is going to contain all of the equiment needed to satify a driver's desire for safe, comforble transportation. For example, a radar devise in the bumpers of the vehical will sence an approaching obstacle and warn the driver of possible danger. For added convienance, tasks such as raising the antenna and turning on the heat will be controled by the driver's voice. Similarly, a misterous-sounding voice in the car will tell the driver when repairs are needed. But one repair will be a thing of the past: a driver will never be agarvated by a flat tire, for the tires will maintain enugh air pressure for the hole life of the car. Finally, this car will make such efficent use of fuel that only tiny amounts of polution will be released into the atmoshere. With these features to improve personel safty and comfort, the automobile will certanly continue to be most people's perfered means of transportation.

 Name: ______________________ Date: ______________

Pronoun Choice

A pronoun takes the place of a noun, a word that indicates a person, place, or thing. For example:

> In 1972 Michael Gallen established a new world's record for eating bananas; *he* consumed 63 of *them* in just 10 minutes.

In the sentence above, *he* takes the place of Michael Gallen, and *them* takes the place of the bananas. If the nouns were used instead of the pronouns, the sentence would become very wordy.

Pronouns have different forms—or cases—depending on how they function in a sentence. For example:

> Arnold Bly was able to write the entire Lord's Prayer on a single grain of rice. *He* demonstrated *his* remarkable lettering ability at the 1939 World's Fair in New York.

Notice that *He* and *his* both refer back to Arnold Bly. Yet the two pronouns differ in form. Some major forms of pronouns are:

- **I** Subject Pronouns
- **II** Object Pronouns
- **III** Possessive Pronouns
- **IV** Pronouns Ending in *-self* or *-selves*

I (a) SUBJECT PRONOUNS

Singular	*Plural*
I	we
you (one person)	you (more than one person)
he	they
she	
it	

These pronouns are the subjects of verbs. A subject explains who or what is doing the action of the verb.

She can whistle "The Star Spangled Banner."

In less than one hour *they* spent $3,000 on clothing.

Who or what can whistle? *She* can. Who or what spent? *They* spent.

Therefore, *she* and *they* are subject pronouns.

I (b) Subject pronouns are also used after a form of the verb *to be: am, is, are, was, were, be, been.*

My father thought it was *I* who dented the car.

It is *she* who runs the entire company.

I (c) A subject pronoun is used even when it is joined with other subjects in a sentence.

Joan and *I* fell into the quicksand.

If you are tempted to write "Joan and *me*" in the sentence above, check yourself by reading only the pronoun with the rest of the sentence. The correct pronoun will sound right.

Wrong: *Me* fell into the quicksand.

Right: *I* fell into the quicksand.

Also, notice that the pronoun *I* always follows the other subjects in a sentence. Thus, you would write "Joan and *I*," not "*I* and Joan."

☞ *Try It Out*

Underline the correct pronoun from each set of words given in parentheses.

1. It was (them, they) who covered the sidewalk with graffiti.
2. (He, Him) and (I, me) work part-time at the local Burger King.
3. When are you and (her, she) finally going to get married?

II (a) OBJECT PRONOUNS

Singular	*Plural*
me	us
you (one person)	you (more than one person)
him	them
her	
it	

These pronouns may be the objects of verbs. An object explains who or what is receiving the action of the verb. To find an object, simply ask *whom* or *what* after the verb.

Denise slapped *him* in the face.

The banker hid *them* under the mattress.

Denise slapped whom? She slapped *him. Him* is the object pronoun. The banker hid what? He hid *them. Them* is the object pronoun.

II (b) Object pronouns are also used after prepositions, such as *at, between, by, for, from, in, inside, into, near, next to, of, on, onto, over, through, under, with, without.*

The ground began to move *under him.*

The flying saucer landed right next *to me.*

II (c) An object pronoun is used even when it is joined with other objects in a sentence.

The roller coaster ride made my wife and *me* sick.

If you are tempted to write "my wife and *I*" in the sentence above, check yourself by reading only the pronoun with the rest of the sentence. The correct pronoun will sound right.

Wrong: The roller coaster ride made *I* sick.

Right: The roller coaster ride made *me* sick.

 *Try It Out*

Underline the correct pronoun from each set of words given in parentheses.

1. The police arrested Bob and (her, she) for using stolen credit cards.
2. I could not keep up with (he, him) and the other marathon runners.
3. After picking up the tip, the waiter gave Susan and (I, me) a dirty look.

III (a) POSSESSIVE PRONOUNS

Singular	*Plural*
my, mine	our, ours
your, yours	your, yours
his	their, theirs
her, hers	
its	

These pronouns show ownership or possession.

A hummingbird flaps *its* wings over 4,000 times a minute.

Your car is beautiful; *theirs* is a nightmare on wheels.

Notice that the possessive pronouns do not use apostrophes. Be careful not to confuse these pronouns with contractions such as: *it's* (it is), *you're* (you are), or *they're* (they are). (For more information on contractions, see pages 276–277.)

III (b) Possessive pronouns are used before an *-ing* verb that is used as a noun.

The audience was put to sleep by *his singing.*

My passing this course could mean the difference between summer school and a summer job.

What put the audience to sleep? *His singing.* Because *singing* functions as a noun, a possessive pronoun precedes it. What could mean the difference between summer school and a summer job? *My passing* this course. Because *passing* functions as a noun, a possessive pronoun precedes it.

Try It Out

Underline the correct pronoun from each set of words given in parentheses.

1. If (its, it's) very hungry, a camel will eat (its, it's) owner's tent.
2. My husband complains about (me, my) watching football games on television every Sunday afternoon.
3. (Your, You're) going to be late for (your, you're) own graduation.

IV (a) PRONOUNS ENDING IN -SELF OR -SELVES

Singular	*Plural*
myself	ourselves
yourself	yourselves
himself	themselves
herself	
itself	

These pronouns are used to indicate an action that affects the one who performs it.

I cut *myself* while shaving this morning.

The children got *themselves* into trouble with the police.

IV (b) These pronouns are also used for emphasis.

The chef *himself* could not eat the meal.

We do not understand punk rock music *ourselves.*

When you write these pronouns, be careful to form them correctly. There are no words such as *hisself, ourself, theirself, themself,* and *theirselves.*

IV (c) None of these pronouns can be used as the subject of a sentence.

Barbara and ~~myself~~ I refused to eat the chocolate-covered ants.

☞ *Try It Out*

Underline the correct pronoun from each set of words given in parentheses.

1. Jack always laughs whenever he looks at (himself, hisself) in a mirror.
2. The doctor and (I, me, myself) argued about his ridiculously high fees.
3. Nurses have to pay for their uniforms (theirselves, themself, themselves).

You probably use most pronouns correctly without having to think about rules of grammar. But here are a few types of sentence structure that may cause you trouble.

V (a) **COMPARISONS.** When making a comparison, be careful to select the correct pronoun to follow *than* or *as*. Some comparisons need subject pronouns to follow *than* or *as*.

You are lazier *than I.*

That old woman can run as fast *as he.*

Comparisons like these are shortened forms of longer ones. To check that the pronoun is correct, add the missing word or words to the comparison.

You are lazier than *I am.*

That old woman can run as fast as *he can run.*

With these comparisons completed, the pronoun *I* is clearly the subject of the verb *am*, and the pronoun *he* is clearly the subject of the verbs *can run.*

V (b) Some comparisons need object pronouns to follow *than* or *as.*

Our English teacher praises you more often *than her.*

Calculus confuses me as much *as them.*

When these shortened comparisons are completed, the pronouns *her* and *them* are clearly objects of verbs.

Our English teacher praises you more often than *he praises her.*

Calculus confuses me as much as *it confuses them.*

 Name: ______________________ *Date:* ______________________

Be careful to use the correct type of pronoun in a comparison; the type of pronoun that is placed after *than* or *as* can change the meaning of a sentence.

Dad loves my sister more than *I.* (more than I love her)

Dad loves my sister more than *me.* (more than he loves me)

To make sure that the reader does not misunderstand the meaning, it is always a good idea to write the complete comparison; avoid shortened comparisons.

 *Try It Out*

Underline the correct pronoun from each set of words given in parentheses.

1. Lisa is smarter than (I, me), but I have more money than (her, she).
2. The boss gave you a bigger raise than (her, she).
3. The other bowlers on the team are not as good as (us, we).

VI (a) WHO/WHOM, WHOEVER/WHOMEVER

Who and *whoever* are subject pronouns.

The jury convicted the thief *who* had robbed the supermarket.

Whoever made dinner needs cooking lessons.

In the first example above, *who* is the subject of the verbs *had robbed.* In the second example, *whoever* is the subject of the verb *made.*

Note that *who* or *whoever* may follow a preposition if the pronoun is the subject of a verb.

The college should give a scholarship to *whoever* needs one.

Although *whoever* follows the preposition *to,* the pronoun is not the object of the preposition; *whoever* is the subject of the verb *needs.*

VI (b) *Whom* and *whomever* are object pronouns.

To *whom* are you addressing that insult?

Tom always bores *whomever* he dates.

In the first example above, *whom* is the object of the preposition *to.* In the second example, *whomever* is the object of the verb *dates.*

Try It Out

Underline the correct pronoun from each set of words given in parentheses.

1. (Who, Whom) dropped that chocolate cream pie on the rug?
2. Some mothers are prepared to dislike (whoever, whomever) their sons marry.
3. With (who, whom) are you having dinner tonight?
4. The cereal company will give a free baseball to (whoever, whomever) sends in 500 box tops.

VII **WE/US.** The pronouns *we* and *us* are sometimes followed by a noun that identifies who *we* or *us* is.

We drivers need lower automobile insurance rates.

The television networks have been treating *us viewers* like idiots.

To determine the correct pronoun, simply read the sentence without the noun.

We need lower automobile insurance rates.

The television networks have been treating *us* like idiots.

Try It Out

Underline the correct pronoun from each set of words given in parentheses.

1. Mr. Higgins gave (us, we) students just five days to do a ten-page essay.
2. (Us, We) consumers are protected by many federal laws.

EXERCISE 6g: Underline the correct pronoun from each set of words given in parentheses.

1. Although (her, she) and her business partner are having financial problems, she is one of the few factory owners (who, whom) (us, we) workers can really trust when the time comes to negotiate a new contract.

2. Just between you and (I, me), (I, me) don't think that our gym teacher is as intelligent as (us, we).

3. (Its, It's) amazing that a giant clam may weigh up to 500 pounds, and (its, it's) shell may measure up to four feet across.

4. The other witness and (I, me, myself) thought it was (her, she) (who, whom) committed the crime.

5. (Me, My) father is not happy about (me, my) joining the Army because he (himself, hisself) was a Navy man.

6. Oscar invites you and (I, me) for dinner more often than (them, they); (them, they) are lucky, for Oscar is a terrible cook.

7. (Their, They're) offering a reward to (whoever, whomever) finds (their, they're) pet tarantula.

8. (Us, We) men had better get (ourself, ourselves) into shape if we hope to look better than (he, him).

9. Stella and (I, me, myself) are tired of being treated so poorly; indeed, (your, you're) treating (your, you're) cat better than (us, we).

10. Firefighters frequently put (theirselves, themself, themselves) in danger to help (whoever, whomever) they find in a burning building. I certainly do not have as much courage as (them, they).

11. (He, Him, His) playing the stereo at 3 A.M. got (us, we) neighbors so angry that we woke his wife and (he, him) at 6 A.M. to complain.

12. (He, Him) and Shirley are the people to (who, whom) you should turn for advice.

13. Our driving instructor must dislike you as much as (I, me); after all, (he, him) threw (us, we) both out of the car.

14. Al, (who, whom) has a newer car than (I, me), has more trouble with his car than (I, me) do with mine.

15. (Their, Them, They) constant complaining got (us, we) waiters so annoyed that no one will wait on (them, they) anymore.

EXERCISE 6h: Correct any pronoun errors in the paragraphs below. Use your own paper, if needed.

Us softhearted people can easily get ourself into a great deal of trouble. For example, last Saturday me and my friend Jack went into a local supermarket to get refreshments for a party. As we were walking down an aisle, we noticed an old man and woman whom seemed to be following us. Indeed, each time Jack and myself turned down another aisle we would hear people close behind us, and when we turned around it would be them again, staring at my friend and I. Finally, I could not take any more of them spying on us, so I turned and asked harshly, "Who are you staring at?" Immediately, the old couple started to tremble and they're eyes filled with tears. Upset by them crying, I quickly apologized.

"We're sorry," the old woman responded. "Its just that you remind we old people of our son. Your a little taller than him, but otherwise you look exactly like him."

"Big deal!" I shot back.

With more tears in her eyes, the woman explained, "Our son got hisself killed recently in a car accident."

My eyes lowered in shame as the old man spoke for the first time. "We would be very grateful if when we leave the store, you would wave good-bye to my wife and I and say, 'Bye, Mom and Dad!' "

His request sounded ridiculous, but I agreed anyway. Then Jack and myself went off looking for the rest of the party food. When we later got on the checkout line, we noticed that the couple were already at the counter chatting with the cashier. As the cashier finished packing they're groceries, the couple turned around and yelled, "Bye, son!" Feeling stupid, I waved and yelled back, "Good-bye, Mom and Dad!" With that, they smiled to theirselves and left the store. A few minutes later me and Jack finally reached the cashier. As she finished putting our groceries into a bag, she said, "That will be $83.40." Shocked, us fellows blurted out, "What?" After all, how could a six-pack of beer and some peanuts and pretzels cost that much?

Looking directly at me, the cashier explained, "You're parents said that your paying for everything."

"My parents!" I burst out. "I don't even know whom those people are."

EXERCISE 6i: For each of the words and phrases given below, write a complete sentence that uses the word or phrase correctly. Use your own paper for this assignment.

Example: her and her sister
The truck almost hit *her and her sister.*

1. we students
2. us Americans
3. himself
4. themselves
5. me and him
6. she and her boyfriend
7. my winning the state lottery
8. their laughing at my appearance
9. who
10. whom
11. its
12. it's
13. the coach and us
14. they and their families
15. better than me
16. longer than she
17. as rich as they
18. as much as us
19. your
20. you're

Name: ______________________ *Date:* ______________________

Pronoun Agreement

A pronoun must agree in number with the word or words for which it stands. If a pronoun stands for a singular word, the pronoun should be singular; if the pronoun stands for a plural word, the pronoun should be plural.

Mike said that he would fulfill his plans.

The astronauts left their space capsule to walk in space.

These examples are easy enough to understand. But there are some common problems in agreement of pronouns and the words for which they stand. These problems are like those discussed in the earlier section on the agreement of subject and verb. On the following few pages you will find the most important pronoun agreement rules. All other pronoun agreement rules are similar to those given for the agreement of subject and verb, pages 154–157.

1 (a) Use a singular pronoun to refer to such words as *somebody, someone, something, everybody, everyone, everything, nobody, no one, nothing, anybody, anyone, one, person, man, woman, either, neither, each.*

According to widely accepted traditional usage, the pronouns *he, him, his,* and *himself* are used to refer to these words. However, according to newer usage, the combinations *he or she, him or her, his or her, himself or herself* are used. Because of the word *or,* these combinations are singular, not plural.

Everyone can learn to benefit from his mistakes. (traditional usage)

Everyone can learn to benefit from his or her mistakes. (newer usage)

A person should practice what he preaches. (traditional usage)

A person should practice what he or she preaches. (newer usage)

For good style, try to avoid more than one combination in a sentence. Try to restructure your sentence. One way is to change to a plural subject, if possible.

Cluttered: When a person practices what he or she preaches, he or she tends to be somewhat cautious in giving advice.

Clear: When people practice what they preach, they tend to be somewhat cautious in giving advice.

I (b) Collective nouns such as *group, team, class,* and *family* take a singular pronoun when the noun refers to the group as a whole and a plural pronoun when the noun refers to the individual members of the group.

The team is practicing for its biggest game.

The team are going their separate ways after this game.

☞ *Try It Out*

Insert the correct pronouns in the spaces provided.

1. The oil company paid for television commercials that would improve ____________ public image.
2. Someone parked ____________ car on the sidewalk.
3. The rock band surprised ____________ audience by playing "The Beer Barrel Polka."

II (a) Use a plural pronoun when you are referring to two or more words joined by *and.* However, when *each* or *every* precedes singular words joined by *and,* a singular pronoun should be used to stand for these words.

Lynn and David are transforming their basement into a playroom.

Every girl and young woman needs to choose a career for herself.

II (b) When two words are joined by *either . . . or* or *neither . . . nor,* the pronoun should agree with the word that is closer.

Either Dan or Ted will read his article.

Neither the general nor his officers have revealed their secret.

Try It Out

Insert the correct pronouns in the spaces provided.

1. Neither the Virgin Islands nor Cuba has many colleges for ______________ citizens to attend.
2. Every waiter and busboy needs comfortable shoes, or ______________ feet will hurt at the end of ______________ work shift.
3. Dieters usually avoid eating butter and mayonnaise because ______________ contain a great deal of fat.
4. Either Paul or his friends will have to clean up the mess after ______________ party.

EXERCISE 6j: Underline the correct pronoun from each set of words given in parentheses.

Paul, along with his friend Frank, registered for an economics course to meet one of (his, her, their) degree requirements. When the two of them showed up for (his, her, their) first class, neither of them recognized (his, her, their) economics professor. Beginning to lecture, the professor stared at (his, her, their) notes and mumbled continuously while the class were trying to keep (itself, themselves) awake. After the lecture was over, the entire class quickly left the room and then regrouped (itself, themselves) in the hallway to discuss (its, their) problem. Neither Paul nor his classmates liked (his, her, their) economics teacher, and it soon became clear that either the students or their teacher would have to change (his, her, their) attitude. Since no one was willing to risk (his, her, their) grade by complaining directly to (his, her, their) teacher, everyone agreed that (he, she,

Name: ______________________ *Date:* ______________________

they) would just have to suffer through a semester of this boring class—everyone, that is, except Paul, who never came to any of the lectures again. Thus, when he appeared to take the final examination, each of the students in the room turned (his, her, their) shocked face in Paul's direction. The students were equally shocked when (he, she, they) saw the examination questions, which required a thorough knowledge of economics and (its, their) related areas. When the professor later marked Paul's examination paper, (he, she, they) was anxious to find many errors so (he, she, they), along with several of (his, her, their) colleagues, examined the paper carefully, but (he, she, they) could find only one small mistake. Because the professor was amazed, (he, she, they) called Paul to (his, her, their) office, where (he, she, they) told the student, "A person must usually attend my class regularly if (he, she, they) expects to pass the course." Meanwhile, Paul stared nervously at the huge stack of examination papers with a rubber band around (it, them). "Paul," the professor continued, "several colleagues and I went over your paper, and (I, we, they) found only one small mistake." Paul replied apologetically, "Gee, Professor, I'm sorry about the mistake. I wouldn't have made (it, them) if I hadn't been confused by your first lecture."

 Name: ______________________ Date: ______________________

EXERCISE 6k: Rewrite the following sentences, making sure to correct any errors in verb and pronoun agreement. Use your own paper for this assignment.

1. After a collection of ancient Egyptian art objects were found in the tomb of King Tut, they were displayed in many American museums.
2. Physics can be difficult to understand because they make use of complicated mathematical formulas.
3. The United States, as well as many other nations, are encouraging their citizens to use less energy.
4. Each of the television networks have their share of bad programs.
5. Through the thick African jungle glides deadly cobras, each looking for their next meal.
6. Neither the gorillas nor the zoo keeper want to have their picture taken with the visiting politician.
7. *Roots,* known for their extremely detailed history of a black family, were written by Alex Haley.
8. Because ten gallons of gasoline are so expensive nowadays, they would be a thoughtful gift for a driver.
9. Everyone were frozen with fear when they saw the flying saucers landing in the parking lot.
10. The scissors you lent me was so dull that I could not cut butter with it.
11. There stand the United Nations with their Secretariat building rising into the sky like a huge slab of glass.
12. The audience was relieved that the chorus was finally finishing their last song.
13. A reptile, unlike most creatures, have two lower jawbones that hinge to allow them to swallow food larger than their body.
14. The noise created by the supersonic jet engines were so loud that they broke windows in houses near the airport.
15. Because every person are vulnerable to disease or infection at various times during their life, doctors will always be prosperous.
16. Either prune juice or sauerkraut are sometimes used for their special powers.
17. None are so fortunate as he who loves the human race.

Name: ______________________ Date: ______________________

Pronoun Reference and Consistency

A pronoun should always refer clearly to a noun that has already been used, so that a reader will understand immediately which noun the pronoun is replacing. For example:

> In Petersburg, West Virginia, a farmer was planting horseradish when *he* found a shiny, greasy stone. Fifteen years later *he* discovered that *it* was a 32-carat diamond.

In the sentences above, the pronoun *he* clearly refers to the farmer and the pronoun *it* clearly refers to the stone.

If the relationship between a pronoun and its noun is not completely clear, your writing will not be easily understood.

1 (a) A pronoun usually refers to the closest noun that has just been mentioned. If a pronoun can possibly refer to more than one noun that has been mentioned, the reader will be confused.

Confusing: Whenever John plays tennis with Jimmy, *he* always wins.

Who always wins? John or Jimmy? The reader cannot be sure because the pronoun *he* could refer to either person. To avoid such a problem, either repeat the correct noun or restructure the entire sentence.

Clear: Whenever John plays tennis with Jimmy, John always wins.

OR

John always wins whenever he plays tennis with Jimmy.

I (b) A pronoun cannot refer to a noun in its possessive form.

Confusing: During the President's press conference, *he* announced a tax increase.

The pronoun *he* cannot refer to *President's,* which is a possessive form. The best way to correct this problem is to restructure the sentence.

Clear: The President announced a tax increase during his press conference.

 *Try It Out*

Revise these sentences to clarify the pronoun references. Use your own paper if needed.

1. A log fell right on my foot just as I was about to chop it in half.
2. Because many of Joan Crawford's movies are still shown on television, she will not be forgotten.
3. Snails are eaten by many people even though they are slimy creatures that live in the garden.

II The pronouns *this, that,* and *which* can be used in place of either a noun or a specific idea that has already been stated. If the pronoun seems to refer to more than one noun or idea, the reader will be confused.

Confusing: My new Pontiac Trans Am was stolen last week, but my insurance company may pay me almost its full value. I was really very upset about *that.*

What was I really upset about? That my Pontiac Trans Am was stolen last week? Or that my insurance company may pay me almost its full value? The reader cannot be sure because the pronoun *that* could refer to either idea. To avoid such a problem, either add a noun or restructure the sentences.

Clear: My new Pontiac Trans Am was stolen last week, but my insurance company may pay me almost its full value. I was really very upset about *the theft.*

OR

I was really very upset that my new Pontiac Trans Am was stolen last week, but my insurance company may pay me almost its full value.

The unclear use of the pronoun *which* can make a sentence seem unintentionally funny.

Confusing: Kathy gave herself a permanent the night before her wedding *which* made all of her hair fall out.

Did the wedding make all of her hair fall out? Or was the hair loss caused by the permanent?

Clear: The night before her wedding, Kathy gave herself a permanent which made all of her hair fall out.

 *Try It Out*

Revise these sentences to clarify the pronoun references. Use your own paper if needed.

1. After Senator Simmons was arrested for drunk driving, he entered an alcohol rehabilitation program. This may hurt his chances for reelection.
2. The city was completely paralyzed by just a few inches of snow. That really got many of the citizens angry.
3. Hal stopped using narcotics after he overdosed on heroin which made all of his friends happy.

III (a) A pronoun cannot refer to a noun that has been suggested but never actually stated.

Confusing: My mother is a lawyer, but I am not interested in *it.*

The reader will probably guess that *it* refers to the law, but this noun has not been stated. To correct this problem, replace the unclear pronoun.

Clear: My mother is a lawyer, but I am not interested in the law.

OR

My mother is a lawyer, but I am not interested in becoming one.

III (b) The pronouns *it* and *they* can be used only when the noun has already been clearly stated.

Confusing: On television last night, *they* said the heat wave will continue for another week.

Who is *they*? To clarify the sentence, supply the missing noun.

Clear: On television last night, the weather forecaster said the heat wave will continue for another week.

☞ *Try It Out*

Revise these sentences to clarify the pronoun references. Use your own paper if needed.

1. Mark got married a few months ago, but it lasted only six days.
2. In Washington, D.C., they just voted to increase defense spending.
3. In most classrooms it says "No Smoking."

IV (a) Pronouns have to be consistent with the nouns they refer to. For example, a sentence about criminals as its subject would consistently use the pronouns *they, them,* or *their* to refer to criminals. If the sentence suddenly shifted to a different pronoun, the reader would be confused.

Confusing: When criminals were convicted for stealing in ancient China, *you* would be punished by having *your* nose sliced off.

Notice in the example above that the subject shifts from criminals to the pronouns *you* and *your,* which do not refer to criminals.

Clear: When criminals were convicted for stealing in ancient China, *they* would be punished by having *their* noses sliced off.

The tendency to shift to the pronouns *you* and *your* is a common one. To avoid this problem, use *you* and *your* only when referring specifically to the reader.

IV (b) A sentence with *person* as its subject should consistently use *he* (or *he or she*) to refer to *person*. (See pages 215–216 for more information on the use of *he or she* instead of *he*.) A sentence with *people* as its subject should consistently use *they* to refer to *people*. If a sentence with *person* or *people* as its subject suddenly shifts to the wrong pronoun, the reader becomes confused.

Confusing: When a *person* is learning to cook, *they* make many mistakes at first.

Can *they* refer to *a person*? No. Use *he* (or *he or she*).

Clear: When a *person* is learning to cook, *he or she* makes many mistakes at first.

Similarly, the pronoun used with *people* should not shift incorrectly.

Confusing: Whenever I hear about *people* who work long hours, I wonder how *he or she* can manage to have time for relaxation.

Can *he or she* refer to *people*? No. Use *they*.

Clear: Whenever I hear about *people* who work long hours, I wonder how *they* can manage to have time for relaxation.

IV (c) Some careless pronoun shifts occur as a writer goes from one sentence to the next in a paragraph.

Confusing: *Muggers* do not care who *they* hurt. *He* can use a knife or a gun without even thinking about the victim. *They* are determined to get what *they* want.

In the example above, the writer lost sight of the pronoun *they* in the first sentence and shifted to *he* in the second sentence. In the third sentence the writer wandered back to the correct pronoun.

Clear: *Muggers* do not care who *they* hurt. *They* can use a knife or a gun without even thinking about the victim. *They* are determined to get what *they* want.

Try It Out

Correct any errors in pronoun consistency in the sentences below. Use your own paper if needed.

1. From where I was standing, you could see Mount Rushmore very clearly.
2. As a person gets older, their nose continues to grow larger.
3. Some people like to eat raw hamburger meat, but he or she runs the risk of getting sick from bacteria in the meat.
4. I will never forget my first airplane trip. The flight was so bumpy that you could not eat your meal without spilling it all over yourself.

If you use unnecessary pronouns, your sentences will be cluttered and confusing.

V (a) A noun and its pronoun should not be used immediately following one another.

Wordy: Susan B. Anthony *she* worked for women's rights.

Clear: Susan B. Anthony worked for women's rights.

Wordy: In the newspaper, *it* gives the winning lottery numbers.

Clear: The newspaper gives the winning lottery numbers.

V (b) The pronoun *this* can be used with a noun only if the noun has been mentioned before. Therefore, when the noun is mentioned for the first time, *a* or *an* should be used, not *this.*

Confusing: We were driving over the Golden Gate Bridge when suddenly *this* big truck crashed into our car.

Clear: We were driving over the Golden Gate Bridge when suddenly *a* big truck crashed into our car.

☞ *Try It Out*

Eliminate any unnecessary pronouns in the sentences below. Use your own paper if needed.

1. In the Pentagon they have 25,000 telephones.
2. Marie Curie, who discovered radium, she won two Nobel Prizes.
3. I stopped going out with Sharon because she had this annoying habit of picking her teeth.

EXERCISE 6I: In the following sentences correct any unclear pronoun references and errors in pronoun consistency. Also, eliminate any unnecessary pronouns. Use your own paper for this assignment.

1. When a person has "aviophobia," you suffer from a fear of flying.
2. To make one pound of butter, they use 21 quarts of milk.
3. Grasshoppers are used as food by some people; in fact, they are three times as nutritious as beefsteak.
4. Prison riots have been occurring more frequently because they are complaining that their poor living conditions are a violation of basic human rights.
5. People who jog should do muscle-stretching exercises before they start running so that you can prevent injuries as much as possible.
6. The Rivoli Theater may be torn down after Bruce Springsteen's concert. That should not be allowed to happen.
7. If a person started counting 24 hours a day at birth, they would not get to a trillion for 31,688 years.
8. In the newspaper it said that about 57 million Americans become victims of crime every year.
9. Many women need to eat a diet that is rich in iron; otherwise, you can easily become anemic.
10. An octopus can gather up as many as 25 crabs at one time in its eight arms. Then it eats them one by one.
11. An insect's skeleton grows outside its body.
12. Ralph Cambridge, the oldest bridegroom in history, he was 105 years old when he married this 70-year-old woman in South Africa in 1971.

 Name: ______________________ *Date:* ______________

13. Mark Spitz won seven gold medals for swimming in the Olympics at Munich, Germany, which really amazed everyone.

14. Child abuse has become such a widespread problem that several states are passing stricter laws to protect them.

15. When people use toothpicks or talk with toothpicks in their mouths, he or she is in danger because more people choke to death on toothpicks than on anything else.

16. They used to make gum from chicle, the milky juice of a tropical evergreen tree. Now they frequently make gum from plastics.

17. Back in the 1960's Americans took the nation's energy supply for granted. After all, you could buy a gallon of gasoline for just 29 cents.

18. According to this book of unusual facts, the oil used by jewelers to lubricate clocks and watches it costs about $3,000 a gallon.

19. Many people are donating money to help feed the millions of people who are starving throughout the world. This sounds like a good idea.

20. In ancient China and parts of India, they ate mice on special occasions.

21. The women's liberation movement has helped many of them to gain equal employment opportunities.

22. The members of a Philadelphia family have been written about in several well-known medical journals because they have no fingerprints.

23. Our coach told everyone that I had failed my gym class. That really got me upset.

24. They show advertisements in many movie theaters these days.

25. People are the only animals that can cry. He has tear ducts that respond to emotions or pain. Also, he is the only animal that will kill for pleasure.

EXERCISE 6m: Correct any unclear pronoun references and eliminate any unnecessary pronouns in the following paragraphs. Use your own paper for this assignment.

Martha she enjoyed working as a waitress at Joe's Diner because he treated her well. But she hated to wait on this regular customer named Mrs. Swope. Mrs. Swope she was this bad-tempered old woman who had this well-earned reputation as a complainer. Thus, she was not surprised on one particular day that the old woman started complaining as soon as she sat down at her table. "This water glass is dirty," she insisted as she pointed a finger across the table. Although it was sparkling clean, she got her another one. Then while ordering her meal, she demanded to have strips of bacon instead of fried onions with her broiled liver. When she pointed out that it clearly stated, "No substitutions allowed," the old woman she started to complain loudly enough to disturb the other diners. To quiet her, she quickly agreed to get them for her. Next, she brought her a bowl of steaming soup, which Mrs. Swope insisted was cold. Throughout all of this, she kept reminding herself that they had told her to be courteous at all times. So she hid her anger and did everything she could to please her.

But later in the meal, she shrieked, "Waitress!" and banged her hand forcefully on the table. At that moment, Martha realized that she could not take any more of this. "Waitress," Mrs. Swope repeated, glancing down at her plate with a look of disgust, "this baked potato is bad." Determined to stay calm, she smiled politely as she carefully lifted the potato from the customer's plate. Shaking a finger at it, Martha said angrily in a voice everyone could hear, "Bad potato! Bad, bad potato!" Then she replaced it on her plate and added, "Madam, if it gives you any more trouble, tell me right away and I shall punish it at once!" She remained silent for the rest of her meal and never again uttered a complaint in Joe's diner.

 Name: ______________________ *Date:* ______________

EXERCISE 6n: Find and correct any errors in pronoun consistency in the following paragraphs. Some pronoun changes may also require verb ending changes in order to maintain correct subject-verb agreement. Use your own paper for this assignment.

The Amish people, who live in their own farming communities in Pennsylvania and twenty other states, cling to the lifestyle of America's pioneer days. The Amish grow their own food, make their own clothes, and refuse most of the conveniences brought by technology. They live this way because of their religion. Guided by a strict interpretation of the Bible, the Amish are against anything not mentioned or accepted by the Bible. Thus, you cannot use electricity, telephones, automobiles, or most store-bought items. You travel by horse and buggy, heat your homes with wood-burning or coal-burning stoves, and create light with kerosene lamps. Moreover, your children go to a one-room Amish school for just eight years and then go to work in the fields or the home.

Amish children learn early in life that their highly structured world demands strict discipline and set roles for men and women. When an Amish boy reaches sixteen, he is given an open "courting buggy" and horse. With this buggy, you can attend hymn-singing sessions which are held for the young Amish on Sunday afternoons. These social events give you the opportunity to become acquainted with the single girls in your area. After meeting the right one, you must court her politely until you announce your desire to marry, usually when you are in your early twenties. The wedding, always held after the harvest in the fall, draws friends and relatives from several states. After they are married, the couple spend a month or two visiting relatives all over the country. During this honeymoon trip, you receive many wedding gifts, all of which are practical items needed by a farm family.

When you return home, you live with the husband's parents and become hard-working members of the household. Indeed, the young couple's workday, with the exception of Sunday, starts before sunrise and lasts until sundown. The husband tends the crops, fields, and livestock without the help of tractors and the other modern farm equipment that is banned by the Amish. Meanwhile, his wife takes care of the house and does cooking and canning. In your spare time, you also make new clothing or wash and mend the old clothing. Eventually, you will have several children to care for as well, since the Amish generally have large families. Although such work forms the backbone of Amish life, the couple do have some leisure-time activities. In the evenings and on Sundays, you can socialize at barn-raisings, quilting bees, auctions, and song fests. But you cannot go to a movie or relax in front of a television set, for such activities are not permitted.

To an outsider, this life may seem difficult because there are few conveniences and no luxuries in the Amish world. But to the Amish their way of life is quite peaceful and happy.

EXERCISE 6o: REFRESHER

1. Find and correct any irregular verb errors.
2. Find and correct any errors in pronoun agreement and vague pronoun reference.

A personal tragedy influenced Candy Lightner, a Los Angeles real-estate agent, to begin a national campaign against drunk drivers. When Mrs. Lightner returned home from a shopping trip on a spring day in 1980, they told her that her 13-year-old daughter, Cari, had been killed by a hit-and-run driver. Shortly after the accident, Clarence Busch was arrested for the crime. At his trial, his wife testified that he had drank so much liquor on the day of the accident that he actually creeped into bed on his hands and knees that night. In addition, they said that he had already been convicted of drunk driving three times, yet he had went to jail for a total of only 48 hours. Even after he had took Cari Lightner's life, he spended just 10 months in a work camp and halfway house. Then he was back out on the streets with a new driver's license. When Candy Lightner seen that someone could easily get away with little or no punishment after they had been convicted of drunk driving, she sweared to fight for tougher laws. So she quitted her job and established an organization called MADD, Mothers Against Drunk Drivers. Working quickly, they have already had some success in getting judges and lawmakers to support increased punishment for drunk drivers. They have also began an assistance program for victims of drunk driving accidents. Thus, young Cari Lightner's senseless death has led to positive action that may help to save many lives in the future.

 Name: ______________________ Date: ______________

SPRINGBOARDS TO WRITING

Using your knowledge of the writing process, explained on pages 12–14, write a paragraph or essay related to this chapter's central theme, *the automobile*, which is introduced on pages 188–191.

PREWRITING

To think of topics to write about, look at the advertisement and photograph, read the essay, and answer the questions that follow each. If you prefer, select one of the writing springboards below. (All paragraph numbers refer to the essay that starts on page 190.) To develop your ideas, use the prewriting techniques described on pages 15–20.

WRITING A PARAGRAPH (For help, see the Pointers on page 31.)

1. The American "love affair" with the car will (will never) end.
2. The 55-mile-per-hour national speed limit is (is not) a good idea.
3. We should (should not) have a national law requiring drivers and passengers to wear seat belts.
4. People convicted of drunk driving should (should not) have their driver's licenses permanently revoked.
5. The ________________ is the best-looking car on the road today.

WRITING AN ESSAY (For help, see the Pointers on page 35.)

6. The Advantages and Disadvantages of Car-Pooling
7. The Problems of Owning a Car (See ¶ 7.)
8. My Ideal Plan for Mass Transportation (see ¶ 5.)
9. The Problems of Using Today's Mass Transportation
10. What Makes a Safe Driver?
11. My Design for an Ideal Car
12. How Having a Car Has Changed (Would Change) My Life
13. Is a Car a Luxury or a Necessity?
14. The Joys of Tinkering with a Car
15. Paragraph 7 states: "The private automobile is the last bastion of personal independence." Agree or disagree.
16. Why People Sometimes Need to Be Alone (See ¶'s 9 & 10.)
17. Paragraph 14 states: ". . . we need to hang onto every bit of personal freedom we've got." Agree or disagree.

What he needs, money can't buy.

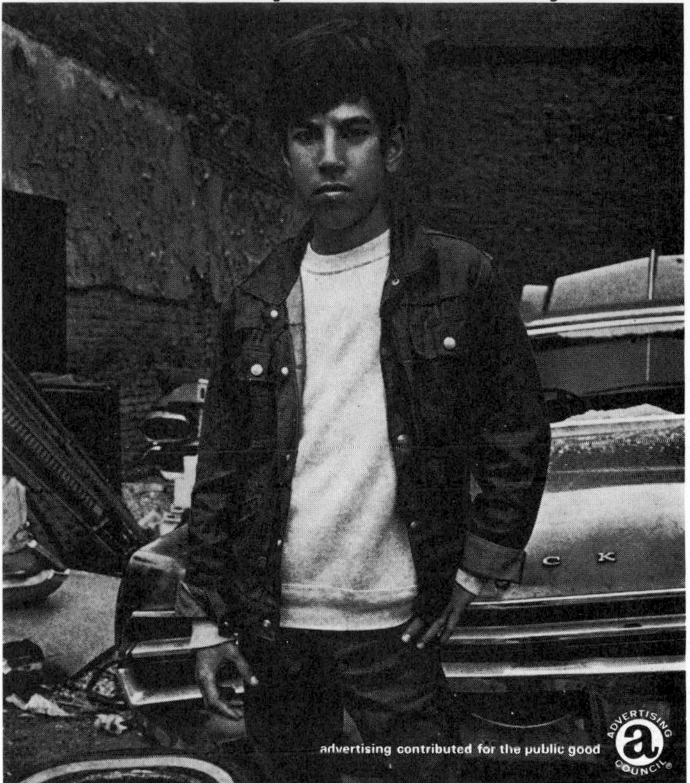

Frankie Covello's mother works in a hospital. She puts in a lot of overtime. So Frankie takes care of his five brothers and sisters.

Frankie never met his father.

Last summer, he and three buddies got arrested for stripping cars. He got off with a probation and a warning. Next time it'll be the state reform school.

Frankie's mother loves him, but he needs someone to talk to. Man to man. Someone who thinks there's more to life than gang fights, pushing drugs or rolling bums.

Someone like you.

We know lots of fatherless kids like Frankie who need you. And we know a lot of other people who need you, too. Guys in veterans' hospitals. Unwed mothers. Old people. Blind people. Patients in mental institutions.

If you can help, even for a few hours, call your local Voluntary Action Center, or write to: "Volunteer," Washington, D.C. 20013.

What we need money can't buy.

We need you.

The National Center for Voluntary Action.

Courtesy of the Advertising Council.

seven

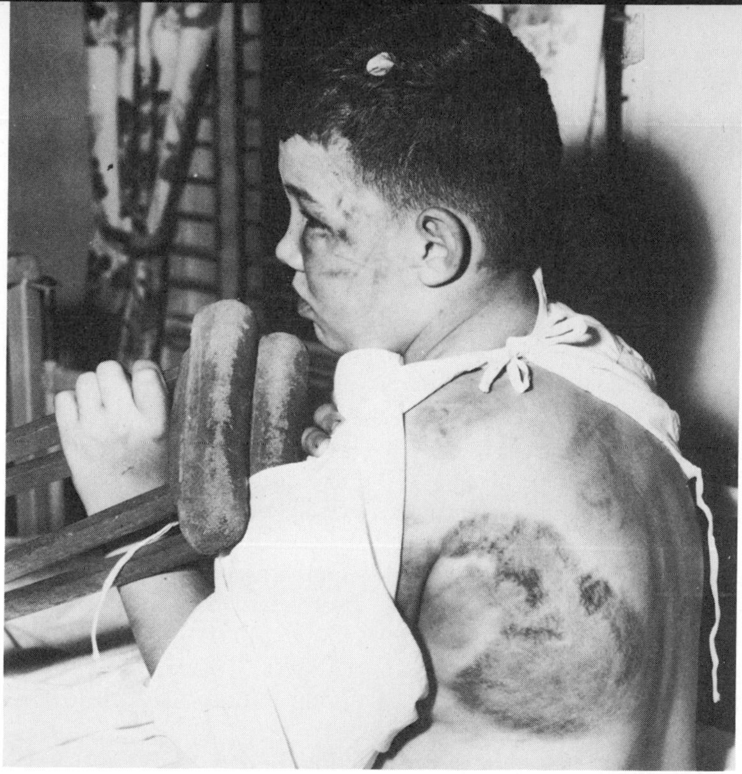

Wide World Photos.

SPRINGBOARDS TO THINKING

For informal, not written, response . . . to stimulate your thinking

1. The injuries suffered by the 9-year-old child in the photograph above came from a beating by an 18-year-old cousin. Why do some relatives beat and abuse young children? Why do some strangers beat and abuse young children?
2. What psychological effects does such abuse usually have on the children at the time and in later life? Explain.
3. Look at the advertisement on the opposite page. Why can't money buy what Frankie needs? Do you think that the suggestion given in the advertisement will help? Why or why not?
4. Why do many teenagers, from both wealthy and poor homes, get into trouble with the law today? Why are many teenagers insecure and troubled today?
5. What is the role of the family in helping children to grow into secure, honest teenagers and adults? What is the role of society in helping children to grow into happy, productive citizens?

Troubled Teenagers

STANLEY N. WELLBORN

(1) In a Milwaukee suburb, a teenage gang awarded points to members for vandalizing streetlights and lawns. A 16-year-old in Santa Clara County, California, took 12 classmates to look at the body of his ex-girlfriend. None of them told police. Later, the boy was charged with her murder. In Chicago's affluent North Shore suburbs, more than 40 teenagers have taken their own lives in the past two years. These episodes point up what many social scientists regard as one of the most significant—and disturbing—trends of recent years: A new generation of American teenagers is deeply troubled, unable to cope with the pressures of growing up in what they perceive as a world that is hostile or indifferent to them.

(2) Among thousands of teenagers, these experts report, alienation and a lack of clear moral standards now prevail to the point where individual lives, families, and in some cases, whole communities are threatened. To be sure, the vast majority of young Americans emerge from their teen years—always a troubled period—as well-balanced individuals. Observes Robert Bourdene, administrator of discipline and student services for Dallas public schools and a guidance counselor: "Generally, the youth of today are good, law-abiding, responsible youngsters." Yet authorities involved with youths from inner cities to suburbia suggest the process rarely if ever has produced such serious disorders—especially among middle-class children seemingly reared with every material advantage.

(3) Even those who emerge from adolescence today with few emotional scars undergo stresses far greater than those of earlier generations. Statistics that measure social behavior bear witness to those pressures. One third of major crimes are committed by people under 20 years of age. Alcoholism among youth has grown to epidemic proportions, with 15 percent of high schoolers considered problem drinkers. As many as a third of the nation's 27 million teenagers "seem unable to roll with life's punches," says one sociologist. "They grow up lacking the internal controls needed to stay on course."

(4) What has gone wrong? Why do today's teenagers seem to be in more trouble than those of previous generations? And what can be done about it? For answers, *U.S. News & World Report* correspondents talked to sociologists, psychologists, and counselors as well as teenagers themselves.

Why They Get Into Trouble

(5) Psychologists say many youngsters, bedeviled by pressures to enter the world of adults too early, become jaded by their midteens and are unable to cope with the breadth of problems facing them. "For these kids," says a Stanford University social scientist, "life in the fast lane isn't just a cliché. It's a fact." Some real-life examples:

- Mike is an 18-year-old from Long Island serving three years for murder and armed robbery. He is among those teenagers who account for 31 percent of all violent-crime arrests and 54 percent of property crimes. "It's a matter of trying to impress people," Mike explains. "If everybody on your block is stealing, you grow up thinking that's cool, and you start doing it, too."
- Sally, a pregnant 16-year-old near San Francisco, provides insight into why nearly one fifth of U.S. babies are born out of wedlock. "I guess I wasn't the daughter my parents were hoping for," she says. "I could never do anything to please them." When she told them she was pregnant, they threatened to disown her; when she told her boyfriend, "He cut out." Now she says, "Maybe things will work out. At least the baby will love me."
- Kate is 17, a high-school senior near Detroit. She swallowed 75 narcotic pills when she did poorly on a college-entrance exam, another in the thousands of teenage suicide attempts each year. "It's a dictatorship of peers," she says. "You have to measure yourself against everyone. It's either conform or burn out. For some people, suicide seems to be the only escape from the pressure."
- David is a 16-year-old hustler who sells sex to men and women near Times Square in New York—one of a million runaway and unwanted youths who roam big-city streets. His advice: "Stay home and be a child for as long as you can. Don't grow up too quick and don't try."

(6) Most adolescents seem to share the idea that these are hard times in which to mature to adulthood—harder, they believe, than their parents faced because of a pervasive drug culture and more broken families. Many teens suffer from stress and depression at being bounced from parent to parent after divorce. Youth from middle- and upper-income families often wilt under constant urgings to excel in sports or academics, to be popular, to win acceptance to good colleges or to aim for high-paying professional careers. Those in the inner city remain largely jobless and feel trapped in despair. "Burnouts" languish on street corners, in videogame arcades, in school parking lots and foster-care centers.

(7) One side effect: a rise in what experts call "sociopathic" subcultures, ranging from membership in far-out cults and extremist groups such as the Ku Klux Klan to the demented punk-rock underground. "As a society, we have come to imagine that it is good for young people to mature rapidly," says psychologist David Elkind, chairman of the Tufts University School of Child Development and author of the forthcoming book, *Hurried Child: Growing Up Too Fast Too Soon.* "We dress our children in miniature adult

costumes with designer labels; we expose them to gratuitous sex and violence and we expect them to cope with an increasingly bewildering social environment—divorce, single parenthood, homosexuality," adds Elkind. "Many adolescents feel betrayed by a society that tells them to grow up fast but also to remain childlike."

(8) Juvenile-court officials and school guidance counselors say they have seen a sharp erosion in the ability of parents to control their adolescent children in the past 10 years. Many place much of the blame on parents themselves. "Today's parents matured in the social upheaval of the '60s and early '70s," says Dr. Judianne Densen-Gerber, a psychiatrist and director of Odyssey House, a drug-and-runaway-counseling program in New York and several other states. "Many young persons lost their moorings in the turmoil over Vietnam, Watergate, racial unrest, rising drug use and violence. The 'me first, do your own thing' philosophy is the way these people are raising their children." The upshot, contend these experts, is that loneliness, boredom and rebelliousness are rampant among teenagers and that disaffection with life runs deep in youth from every level of society.

The Turn to Violence

(9) Rebellion among the young increasingly takes violent form. In Amarillo, Texas, a 17-year-old was charged in November with the strangulation and rape of a 76-year-old Franciscan nun. In Maryland, an 18-year-old woman hired a gunman and participated with four young men in the murder of her husband of two months. Teenagers account for nearly one third of all violent-crime arrests, including those for arson. Killings by teenagers, particularly urban gangsters who murder at random and without remorse, are a plague in many cities. In Philadelphia and a growing number of suburban communities elsewhere, 9 P.M. curfews have been set for anyone under 18. New York City deployed guards in its middle schools this year for the first time.

(10) Increasingly, the victims are the young themselves. In Los Angeles last year, 453 teenagers were murdered, often by other teenagers. "Shakedowns" of students by older students are commonplace in many schools. Statistics show that the rate of juvenile crime, while remaining high, has not risen since the mid-1970's. But, as Hunter Hurst, director of the National Center for Juvenile Justice in Pittsburgh, points out, "There is often more violence in a given crime: Instead of just robbing a supermarket, a youth may also shoot the manager and pistol-whip the clerk. It's not an increase in the quantity of violence, but in the quality of it."

(11) Behind such wanton actions runs a view of life that seems bizarre by most standards. In the words of a Massachusetts judge, too many youngsters adopt a philosopohy that "if you don't have something, you have a right to take it." Another authority, Thomas R. Evans, former director of Cleveland's Institute for Studies of Violence and Aggression, points to a "fatalism" that characterizes many youths, a feeling of "Why not? What

the hell?" "Inner-city kids see themselves as losers," Evans explains. "They don't see themselves as capable of attaining success." Thus, he says, "their tendency is to take what you can get when you can get it. That leads to violence."

(12) One of the most alarming trends involves teenagers who turn violence on their own parents. Last July, for example, the 14-year-old son of a wealthy oil executive in Dallas was arrested and charged with the shotgun deaths at their home of his mother and father. "Parent abuse" is also becoming evident in the courts, where parents seek restraining orders against their belligerent children. Deputy Inspector Thomas Gallagher of the New York Police Department's youth-services section—a father of seven—says flatly: "Some parents are afraid of their own children."

Throwaway Children

(13) Linda was 14 when she ran away from home. She had been sexually abused by her father since the age of 5, and says, "I waited for years for the chance to get out." One month after leaving home, Linda became a prostitute in Denver. She recalls: "It was easy to say 'Yes' to nice clothes and a nice place to live. I felt miserable at home. Being a prostitute was a lot better than going home to my father." Although her case may be extreme, Linda is only one of a million children who run away from home each year, according to estimates by the Senate Subcommittee on Juvenile Justice. Such children—often abused and neglected at home—become easy prey for adults who exploit them through pornography and prostitution, says John Rabun, manager of the Exploited Child Unit in Louisville, Kentucky. Many runaways are murdered, he notes.

(14) The Runaway Hotline, established in 1973, after the discovery of the mass murder of 27 youths in Houston, fields between 200 and 300 calls every day from teenagers, up nearly 100 calls a day over a year ago. Children may pass messages to their families, but few return home, authorities say. Lois Lee, director of Children of the Night, a program that employs 20 counselors to help youths break out of prostitution in Los Angeles, says many children are pushed out of their homes by uncaring parents and end up sleeping in parks or abandoned buildings. "These kids develop families on the street," she says. "They'll form groups and look out for each other." Increasingly, it is the parents who toss the children out, adds Nick Clark, director of Alternative House, a runaway center in McLean, Virginia. He observes more "throwaway children" whose parents drop them off at Alternative House, saying: "I can't handle you. You're too much." Clark says the average age of children coming to his center has dropped from 14 to 12. Some young people have run from problems at home so many times that they are resigned to self-loathing. One 16-year-old girl from Fairfax County, Virginia, a frequent runaway and drug user, shrugs: "I really don't want to care. If I care about things, it'll just be another thing I have to worry about. It's less painful if you don't care."

Trying to Cope with Pressures

(15) One of the most tragic aspects of the pressures many teenagers live under is the increasing number who self-destruct through suicide, alcohol and other drugs or who disrupt their lives with early pregnancy. The proportion of young people taking their own lives is rising. Among 15-to-24-year-olds, suicide is the third leading cause of death, after homicide and accidents. The number of teenage suicides has doubled in 10 years to around 2,000 annually, mostly males. Certain upper-income neighborhoods near Chicago have been plagued by an epidemic of teen suicides in recent years. In Kentucky, the teenage suicide rate has gone up 300 percent in the last 10 years. Such figures, say experts, are a measure of the panic youths feel when they fail to meet the expectations placed on them by parents and peers. Researchers at the National Institute of Mental Health report that suicide attempts outnumber actual suicides by 50 to 1. Dr. Cynthia Pfeffer, a psychiatrist at Cornell University, has found that 33 percent of adolescents have suicidal impulses, up from about 10 percent in the 1960's. Some physicians are alarmed about a rise in incidence of anorexia nervosa, a medical syndrome in which young people starve themselves into virtual skeletons in what may be a disguised form of suicide. The motive of a young suicide victim may be revenge on a parent, the trauma of a divorce or simply a cry for attention. A high-school senior from Wilmette, Illinois, slashed her wrists on the second anniversary of her friend's suicide. She recalls: "There was a part of me that wanted to say, 'Hey, I do feel bad,' but I was never able to let anybody know."

(16) Another index of teenage rebellion is drug abuse, particularly alcohol, which the National Institute on Alcohol Abuse and Alcoholism says is the Number 1 youth drug problem. About 15 percent of 10th to 12th graders and 11 percent of 7th to 9th graders are classified as problem drinkers, despite the fact that nearly 20 states have raised the legal drinking age to above 18 in the last five years. Many teenagers also drink while using other drugs or sniffing fumes from glue or other inhalants. The combination "can be lethal," says Bobbie Schanzenbach, director of the Northern Virginia Hotline. "And they don't even know it." Many teens are part of what counselors call "the six-pack syndrome." They do not drink every day, but become intoxicated once or twice a month. Police say drunkenness is the chief cause of auto accidents among young people. "That's the big danger, because teenagers are inexperienced drinkers and inexperienced drivers," says Howard T. Blane, professor of education and psychology at the University of Pittsburgh, who has done extensive research on teenage drinking. "Combine those things with the natural risk-taking that occurs in adolescence, and you have a volatile situation."

(17) For many teens, the initiation into alcohol is more a need for acceptance than an escape from problems. Notes one eighth grader from Silver Spring, Maryland, "If you're not willing to take a risk, you're not in. Being part of the group, being with a big bunch of friends is survival." For others, alcohol and drugs provide both an escape and a veneer to cover up other

problems, such as boredom and loneliness. "Most keep themselves medicated to avoid pain," believes Jeanne Androit, director of the Center for Counseling Families in Fairfax, Virginia. "Drugs are a complete and total escape," says Stan, a 19-year-old cocaine addict in California. "They're expensive, illegal and bad for you, but they can also make you feel incredibly good. The high you get from cocaine is beyond description, and once you experience it, you want it again and again."

(18) Pregnancy for teenagers usually brings an interruption of schooling and results in a failure of teenage parents to realize their career potential. Even worse, the problems of unwed teen parents usually fall upon their illegitimate offspring. Yet more than a million teenagers—1 out of every 10 girls ages 15 through 19—become pregnant every year, mostly out of wedlock. More than half of them decide to have their babies. Teenage sexual activity is increasing, too, even though young people's knowledge about sex is often limited. Before they are out of their teens, 80 percent of boys and 70 percent of girls have had sexual intercourse, latest surveys show. "There are some very sexually sophisticated kids, at least outwardly," says Kay Bard, executive director of Planned Parenthood of Atlanta. "But in most cases, a child just wants someone to love her, to hold her, to pay some special attention to her."

(19) Teenagers say that peer pressure plays a prominent role in determining whether or not to be sexually active. A 17-year-old Montgomery County, Maryland, high-school girl observes: "If your sexual life isn't like Luke and Laura's on 'General Hospital,' you ain't got it. Nobody lets things happen naturally." A growing number of experts—and teens themselves—say young persons are not sophisticated enough to cope with questions of birth control, abortion and suggestive advertising that appears to endorse sex at an early age. Beth, a 16-year-old junior at North Hollywood High School, agrees: "There's a lot of pressure in the media to be like Brooke Shields. You can't get away from that face on the billboards. I'm attractive, but I'm not going to be on any billboard. It's an unattainable goal."

Main Solution: Closer Families

(20) Today's maturing youth are at the tail end of the baby-boom years, and because of that the pressures facing them are not going to disappear. Many of their hopes may not be realized simply because of demographics. Landon Y. Jones writes in *Great Expectations: America & the Baby Boom Generation:* "The last baby boomers will grow up into a world already too crowded for them. Ahead of them, every base will be taken by their older brothers and sisters. Throughout their lives they will face the prospect of salaries that were not quite as large as they hoped, devalued education and difficult promotions."

(21) For clearly incorrigible youth, the solution suggested by many authorities is a tougher stance by society. Some states have attempted to drop the legal age at which minors become adults to as low as 12 years of age, and some experts say juveniles who commit "adult" crimes should be

treated as adults. "There is a percentage of violent juveniles that have to be dealt with stringently," declares Robert C. Trojanowicz, director of Michigan State University's School of Criminal Justice. "We can't change the mentality of a 16-year-old who blows somebody's brains out in a gas station."

(22) Many authorities have doubts about the effectiveness of government aid in dealing with troubled youth. The Reverend Bruce Ritter, director of New York City's Covenant House, has watched 20,000 runaways move through his Times Square shelter since 1977. He told a Senate subcommittee examining juvenile problems: "You could throw enormous amounts of money into it, and nothing would change. Our kids are not the problem. Our adults are the problem."

(23) Despite the concerns, some sociologists detect hopeful trends. More parents are reaching out for help in child rearing. Support groups for parents—from family counseling centers to home-nurse practitioners—now are available in many areas to advise adults on ways to cope with wayward children.

(24) Many experts are convinced that better communication between generations is the best way to bring troubled teenagers back toward fruitful lives, and parents must bear the brunt of the task. "The unhappiest kids in the world are those with the least parental supervision," asserts Bill Gregory, director of the Excelsior Youth Center in Denver. Says Tom Cottle, a Harvard University psychologist: "The parents are saying, 'I really think it is important for you to achieve, and when you do I'll think about loving you.' It is contingency love. Love on the bonus plan. It should be love no matter what. When kids are 14, 15 and 16, the essential bond is still with the parents."

READING SURVEY

1. *Main Idea*

What is the central theme of this essay?

2. *Major Details*

a. What makes most adolescents feel that these are hard times in which to grow up—harder, they believe, than their parents faced?
b. Explain the view of life that motivates many youngsters to commit the crimes mentioned in paragraphs 9 and 10.
c. According to paragraph 17, what are some major reasons why teenagers abuse alcohol and drugs?

3. *Inferences*

a. Read paragraph 15 again. Why is the proportion of actual suicides to attempted suicides so small (only 1 in 50)?
b. Read paragraph 16 again. If the legal drinking age has been increased in many states to above the age of 18, where are the young teenage problem drinkers getting their alcohol?

4. *Opinions*

a. What specifically can parents do to help their children overcome the difficulties described in this essay? Explain.
b. If you had a friend who was a "troubled teenager," how would you try to help him or her? Explain.

VOCABULARY BUILDING

Lesson One: The Vocabulary of Crime

The essay "Troubled Teenagers" by Stanley N. Wellborn includes words that are useful when you are discussing crime.

vandalizing	(paragraph 1)	**belligerent**	(12)
law-abiding	(2)	**prey**	(13)
betrayed	(7)	**lethal**	(16)
rampant	(8)	**incorrigible**	(21)
wanton	(11)	**wayward**	(23)

When crime is **rampant,** it spreads unchecked as a result of widespread violent and uncontrollable actions. Most criminals have a **belligerent** attitude in that they behave in a warlike manner and are always ready to start a fight or quarrel. Usually, these criminals are **wayward** in that they insist on having their own way in spite of good advice from others. The sad truth is that the majority of criminals are **incorrigible** because their bad habits are so established that they cannot be corrected or reformed. Also, many criminals are very dangerous because they use **lethal** or deadly weapons when they commit a crime.

Law-abiding citizens, people who obey the law, are seen by criminals as **prey** to be robbed or killed or otherwise made into victims. Good citizens know that criminals often commit **wanton** crimes that are uncontrolled, senseless, purposely cruel, and show not even the slightest sense of what is right. When law-abiding people have to stand by helplessly while criminals are robbing, stealing, and **vandalizing**—destroying personal or public property for no reason—they feel that the society has **betrayed** them because they think that society has failed or deserted them in their time of need.

EXERCISE 7a: For each word in italics below, circle the definition closest in meaning.

1. A person who is *vandalizing* is
   a. accidentally causing a car collision.
   b. ignoring directions from firefighters.
   c. apologizing for one's mistake.
   d. willfully damaging property.

2. A *law-abiding* person is someone who
   a. is studying law.
   b. has broken the law.
   c. obeys the law.
   d. enforces the law.

3. To have been *betrayed* is to have been
   a. deserted or let down in a time of need.
   b. rescued or warned about extreme danger.
   c. advised or coached by an expert.
   d. criticized or embarrassed by a coach.

4. A *rampant* disease
   a. has no known cure.
   b. cannot be identified.
   c. has been brought under control.
   d. is spreading unchecked.

5. A *wanton* act would be considered
   a. lacking in purpose.
   b. senseless and cruel.
   c. having a selfish motive.
   d. strong and courageous.

6. A *belligerent* person is generally
   a. quarrelsome and aggressive.
   b. lacking in common sense.
   c. hardworking and responsible.
   d. devoted to his or her family.

7. Animals that serve as *prey* for other animals are
   a. members of an endangered species.
   b. friendly and protective.
   c. tracked and hunted for food.
   d. unable to become domesticated.

8. Anything considered *lethal* would be able to
   a. cause death.
   b. relieve pain.
   c. produce pleasure.
   d. be eaten.

9. A convict who is *incorrigible* is
   a. a model prisoner.
   b. able to be rehabilitated.
   c. soon to be paroled.
   d. unable to be reformed.

10. A *wayward* person generally
    a. is able to earn his or her own living.
    b. ignores good advice from other people.
    c. likes to share his or her knowledge with others.
    d. has a good sense of direction.

Name: ______________________ Date: ______________

Lesson Two: The Vocabulary of Extremists

The essay "Troubled Teenagers" by Stanley N. Wellborn includes words that are useful when you are discussing extremists.

bedeviled	(paragraph 5)	**extremist**	(7)
conform	(5)	**demented**	(7)
sociopathic	(7)	**rebelliousness**	(8) . . . **rebellion** (9)
subcultures	(7)	**bizarre**	(11)
cults	(7)	**aggression**	(11)

Most people in a society like to **conform** in that they like to behave the way that the majority of people do, and they like to go along with accepted customs, traditions, and opinions. Every culture, however, usually has a number of **subcultures,** groups of people of the same ages, or social, economic, or ethnic backgrounds. A few of these groups consist of **extremists** who will often take severe and possibly dangerous action in support of their political (or sometimes religious) views that are extremely far from the views of the majority. Many extremists feel that **aggression,** the use of force or attacking behavior, is acceptable in the service of their "cause." Also, many extremists favor **rebellion** and are known for their **rebelliousness** because they want to organize either peaceful or armed opposition to authority.

The behavior of extremists is often **bizarre** because it is totally out of the ordinary and is usually very strange and startling. Some extremists have **sociopathic** personalities, which means that they are strongly antisocial. Others are **demented** in that they are mentally insane. Some extremists belong to **cults,** which are groups devoted to the extreme admiration of a person whom they worship, or of ideas and beliefs that they consider the only "true way." Some people who belong to cults are considered to be **bedeviled** in that they behave as if they are under a bad spell or their minds are totally confused.

EXERCISE 7b: For each word in italics below, circle the definition closest in meaning.

1. To be *bedeviled* is to
   a. be a member of a church or synagogue.
   b. behave as if under a bad spell.
   c. be admitted to a fraternity or sorority.
   d. feel as if sick with the flu.

2. People who *conform* prefer to
   a. go along with accepted customs.
   b. make hasty judgments of others.
   c. be in the company of others.
   d. avoid close human relationships.

 Name: ______________________ Date: ______________

3. A *sociopathic* personality belongs to a person who
   a. has unusual talents.
   b. is pitifully unfortunate.
   c. likes to socialize frequently.
   d. is strongly antisocial.

4. *Subcultures* are groups of people who
   a. are members of a political party.
   b. have some similarity of age or background.
   c. avoid being identified with any religion.
   d. prefer to work in hospitals or schools.

5. *Cults* are groups of people who
   a. frequently get together to play music or sing.
   b. are residents of a particular community.
   c. are extremely devoted to a person or a belief.
   d. are fans of the home baseball or football team.

6. An *extremist* is a person who
   a. is generally considered courteous.
   b. suffers from a severe physical handicap.
   c. is generally critical of others.
   d. favors or takes severe action.

7. *Demented* people are generally
   a. insane.
   b. depressed.
   c. intellectual.
   d. ambitious.

8. *Rebelliousness* is a condition characterized by
   a. extreme poverty.
   b. opposition to authority.
   c. approval of a leader's decision.
   d. attempts to abolish freedom.

9. A *rebellion* can be
   a. a public opinion poll.
   b. the impeachment of a president.
   c. an uprising against authority.
   d. the readiness of a nation's armed forces.

10. A *bizarre* act would be considered to be
    a. extremely kind and loving.
    b. somewhat ordinary and expected.
    c. very brave and skillful.
    d. unusually strange and startling.

Name: ______________________ Date: ______________________

11. *Aggression* can be described as
   a. attacking behavior.
   b. being aggravated.
   c. creating a scene.
   d. being in mourning.

SPELLING

Lesson One: Spelling Demons

Here are more words that are frequently misspelled. Using the helpful techniques given in Chapter One, you should make it a point to learn these new Demons, which are taken from "Troubled Teenagers."

acceptance	**description**	**miniature**
accident	**difficult**	**naturally**
adolescent	**discipline**	**philosophy**
afraid	**generally**	**previous**
amount	**guidance**	**quantity**
authority	**involve**	**sophisticated**
career	**knowledge**	**tendency**
crowded	**medical**	**write**

Lesson Two: Spelling Rule—*ie* and *ei*

Many of the words in Stanley N. Wellborn's essay can be learned easily with the help of this one simple spelling rule.

Use *i* before *e*
Except after *c*,
Or when sounded like *a*
As in *neighbor* or *weigh*

☞ *Try It Out*

Fill in *ie* or *ei* in each of the following words.

th_____f	rel_____ve	conc_____ted
_____ghth	rec_____pt	rev_____wer

Here are some examples:

f*ie*ld	dec*ei*ve	fr*ei*ght	conc*ei*ve	v*ei*l	y*ie*ld
b*ei*ge	ach*ie*ve	c*ei*ling	w*ei*ght	th*ie*f	rec*ei*pt

☞ *Try It Out*

Fill in *ie* or *ei* in each of the following words.

sl____gh　　pat____nce　　pr____st

br____fly　　rec____ver　　w____ght

A SPECIAL NOTE: Here are some words you see frequently which are exceptions to the above rule.

*ei*ther　　for*ei*gn　　w*ei*rd　　s*ei*ze　　l*ei*sure　　n*ei*ther

EXERCISE 7c: Insert *ie* or *ei* in each of the following words.

1. bel____vable
2. ch____fly
3. perc____ve
4. p____rce
5. ____ghteen
6. s____ze
7. gr____ve
8. front____r
9. c____ling
10. retr____ve
11. n____ghborhood
12. n____ther
13. ach____vement
14. v____l
15. conc____ve
16. handkerch____f
17. len____nt
18. r____gn
19. for____gn
20. sh____ld

Name: ______________________　　Date: ______________________

EXERCISE 7d: Using the definitions given as clues, fill in this puzzle. If necessary, check your spelling with the list of Demons in this chapter.

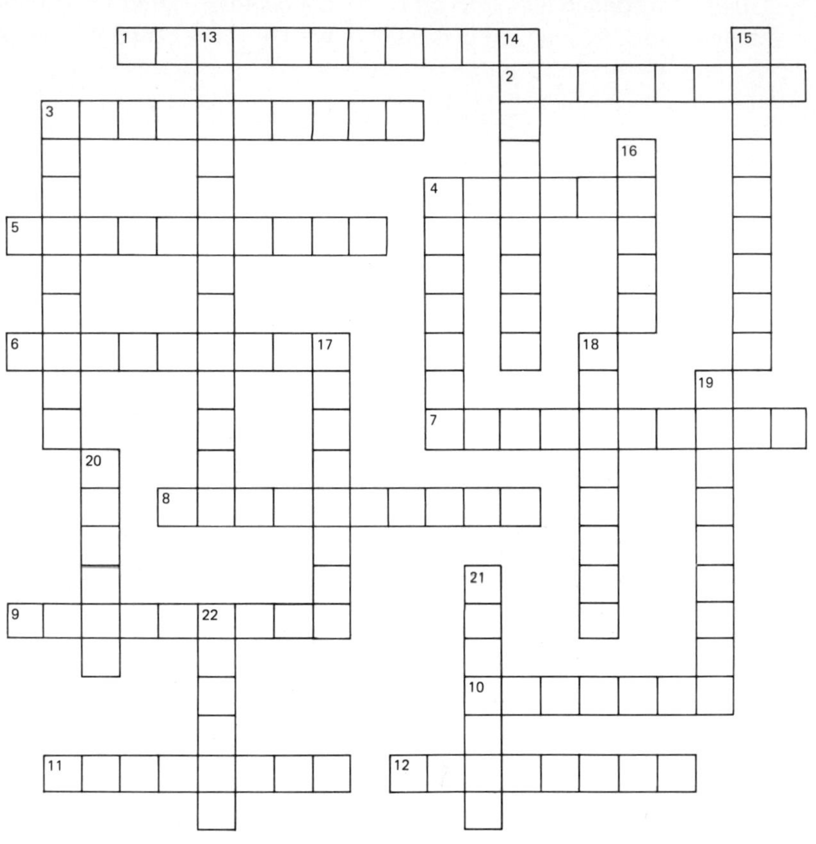

Across

1. The police wanted a __________ of the suspect.
2. Two people were injured in the automobile __________.
3. approval
4. profession
5. a way of life or of thinking
6. hard to do
7. punishment or self-control
8. teenager
9. for the most part, usually
10. I don't want to get __________d.
11. the one before this one
12. a number or amount of something

Down

3. an expert or a person in charge
4. packed with people
13. experienced in the ways of the world
14. of course
15. learning
16. to jot down or scribble
17. He has a __________ to exaggerate.
18. __________ counselor
19. a small copy of something
20. quantity
21. Doctors are members of the __________ profession.
22. fearful

 Name: ____________________ Date: ____________

From Paragraph Principles to Essay Writing

Frequently you will be required to write essays for some of your college courses. Such assignments usually require the presentation of information about a selected subject. An essay that is written to convey information is called *exposition.*

In many ways an expository essay has the same structure as a paragraph, except that the essay has more extended discussion and uses additional specific examples. If you have used any of the Springboards to Writing at the end of each chapter, you have written an expository essay. Perhaps a few pointers will guide you in planning your essays:

The Paragraph	*Purpose*	**The Essay**
the topic sentence	to state, limit, and control the main idea	the introductory paragraph
development with use of: facts; examples; incident; definition; comparison and contrast; or statistics, names, and the senses	to develop the main idea with specific points	the main body paragraphs (there should be at least three of them)
(in certain cases: the concluding sentence)	to conclude by coming back to the general main idea	the concluding paragraph

Notice from the comparison chart above that an expository essay should have at least five paragraphs. Keep this in mind when selecting a topic. Some topics might be suitable for a book but too broad for a five-paragraph essay; other topics might be suitable for a paragraph but too limiting for a five-paragraph essay. For example, suppose that you wish to write a five-paragraph essay on the general topic of *alcoholism:*

GOOD TOPIC: Some Causes of Alcoholism
TOO BROAD: Alcoholism Is a Serious Problem
TOO LIMITING: Alcohol Is a Clear Liquid

Before you can be sure that a topic is good for an essay, it is best to think ahead to *each of the three main points* that you will discuss in *each of the three paragraphs of the main body of the essay.* Try to think of three sensible, interesting main ideas, each of which can be stated in a good topic sentence and which can be developed with one of the six methods presented in Chapters One and Two. If you cannot, the chances are that the topic you have chosen is not suitable.

As you think ahead to the three main points that you plan to make, write them down. Looking at the three main points you have listed will make more visibly clear whether or not a topic is suitable for a five-paragraph essay. Compare the plan for each of the following topics, and notice the judgment made for each plan:

	A *Some Causes of Alcoholism*	**B** *Alcoholism Is a Serious Problem*	**C** *Alcohol Is a Clear Liquid*
Introduction	introduce the three main ideas that follow	←	←
Main Body (three main ideas)	I. curiosity II. peer group influence III. feelings of loneliness	I. crime II. deaths III. rehabilitation programs	I. what it looks like II. why it is clear III. how to identify it
Conclusion	summarize the three main ideas	←	←

Judgments:

A is fine; not too broad or too limiting.
B is too broad; each development would be shallow and general.
C is too limiting; the main points are similar and repetitious.

☞ *Try It Out*

Which topic is most suitable for a five-paragraph essay?

1. a. Dieting
   b. A Sensible Way to Lose Weight
   c. Pies Are Very Fattening

2. a. Cars
   b. Car Brakes Must Be Reliable
   c. The Pleasures of Driving a Car

3. a. How to Take Proper Care of House Plants
   b. How to Water House Plants
   c. The Different Types of House Plants

Many times even when students can sense that a topic is good, they cannot think of three main points for the three main body paragraphs. Often it is not difficult to think of two main points; it is the third point that can become troublesome. In planning, first allow yourself to come up with your own ideas. Use the prewriting techniques discussed in Chapter One to help stimulate new thoughts.

Essay Pattern

1. Introduction
2. Main Body I ______ main point one ______
3. Main Body II ______ main point two ______
4. Main Body III ______ main point three ______
5. Conclusion

If you run out of ideas, here are a few main idea patterns—which you should feel free to adapt, rearrange, modify, and change—to help you find three main points of value:

Main Body Idea Patterns

I. past II. present III. future	I. science II. business III. the arts
I. personal II. family III. social group	I. political II. economic III. social (or substitute for any: religious)
I. the individual II. the community (or nation) III. the nation (or world)	I. home II. business (or school) III. leisure time
I. childhood II. adulthood III. old age	I. physical II. psychological III. spiritual
I. personality II. character III. ability	I. students II. workers III. government officials (or bosses)

Here are some examples of how to use these idea patterns.

Women Are Superior to Men
- Introduction
  - I. personality
  - II. character
  - III. ability
- Conclusion

New Uses of the Computer
- Introduction
  - I. science
  - II. business
  - III. the arts
- Conclusion

Some Effects of War
- Introduction
  - I. political
  - II. economic
  - III. social
- Conclusion

What Makes People Feel Secure?
- Introduction
  - I. childhood
  - II. adulthood
  - III. old age
- Conclusion

EXERCISE 7e: For each essay topic given, think of three main ideas which you might use to develop the topic. You can refer to the suggested Main Body Idea Patterns for help in getting ideas.

1. A Person's Definition of Success Often Changes
   I. ______________________
   II. ______________________
   III. ______________________

2. What Makes a Good Friend?
   I. ______________________
   II. ______________________
   III. ______________________

3. Why Get Married?
   I. ______________________
   II. ______________________
   III. ______________________

4. Age Is a State of Mind
   I. ______________________
   II. ______________________
   III. ______________________

5. The Effects of Technology
   I. ______________________
   II. ______________________
   III. ______________________

6. How Drug Addicts Affect Our Society
   I. ______________________
   II. ______________________
   III. ______________________

7. Can an Individual Express Himself/Herself Fully in America?
   I. ______________________
   II. ______________________
   III. ______________________

Name: ______________________ Date: ______________________

8. Are Big Families a Good Idea?
   I. ______________________
   II. ______________________
   III. ______________________

9. How Has Women's Liberation Affected Our Lives?
   I. ______________________
   II. ______________________
   III. ______________________

10. Why We Have to Control Pollution
   I. ______________________
   II. ______________________
   III. ______________________

EXERCISE 7f: For each of the general topic areas given, create a suitable topic for a five-paragraph essay. In each case, think of three main ideas which you will discuss; your plan should clearly show that the essay topic you have created is suitable.

1. General topic area: love
   Suitable topic for a five-paragraph essay:

   ____

   Plan: Think ahead: Main Body I: ______________________

   Main Body II: ______________________

   Main Body III: ______________________

2. General topic area: outdoor life
   Suitable topic for a five-paragraph essay:

   ____

   Plan: Think ahead: Main Body I: ______________________

   Main Body II: ______________________

   Main Body III: ______________________

3. General topic area: politicians
Suitable topic for a five-paragraph essay:

____

Plan: Think ahead: Main Body I: ____________

Main Body II: ____________

Main Body III: ____________

4. General topic area: soap operas
Suitable topic for a five-paragraph essay:

____

Plan: Think ahead: Main Body I: ____________

Main Body II: ____________

Main Body III: ____________

5. General topic area: materialism
Suitable topic for a five-paragraph essay:

____

Plan: Think ahead: Main Body I: ____________

Main Body II: ____________

Main Body III: ____________

6. General topic area: social pressure
Suitable topic for a five-paragraph essay:

____

Plan: Think ahead: Main Body I: ____________

Main Body II: ____________

Main Body III: ____________

EXERCISE 7g: ESSAY ANALYSIS Although the essays in this book are each more than five paragraphs long, the authors have followed the pattern of introduction, main body, and conclusion. Answer these questions about the main body paragraphs of the following three essays:

1. In "Old Before Her Time," which appears at the beginning of Chapter Two, the main body is organized to present four major points. For each set of paragraphs listed below, give the major point presented. Select four from the list of six choices.

   paragraph 2 ____

   paragraph 3 ____

   paragraphs 4–22 ____

   paragraphs 23–26 ____

   (a) why Patty disguised herself
   (b) Patty's speeches about her experiences
   (c) how Patty changed because of her experiences
   (d) how Patty disguised herself
   (e) the Social Security problems of older people
   (f) the seven lessons that Patty learned

2. In "The Great American Love Affair," which appears at the beginning of Chapter Six, the main body is organized to present three major points. For each set of paragraphs listed below, give the major point presented. Select three from the list of five given.

   paragraphs 2–5 ____

   paragraphs 6–12 ____

   paragraph 13 ____

   (a) The car is the last bastion of personal independence.
   (b) The car is good for emergencies.
   (c) A car is an expensive investment.
   (d) Several facts support the use of automobiles.
   (e) Car-haters give four main reasons against auto use.

3. In "Troubled Teenagers," which appears at the beginning of Chapter Seven, the main body is organized to present six major points. For each set of paragraphs listed below, give the major point presented. Select six from the list of eight given.

   paragraphs 2–3 ____

   paragraphs 5–8 ____

   paragraphs 9–12 ____

   paragraphs 13–14 ____

   paragraphs 15–19 ____

   paragraphs 20–23 ____

   (a) the self-destructive behavior of teens
   (b) why teens get in trouble
   (c) the spread of venereal disease among teens
   (d) the seriousness of the problem
   (e) closer family ties as a solution
   (f) the violent form of teen rebellion
   (g) the vandalism of schools by teens
   (h) teens who run away from home

 Name: ____________________ Date: ________________

The Introductory Paragraph

It is important to write an introductory paragraph that will convince the reader that the essay is worth reading. To be completely effective, this opening paragraph must accomplish two things: it must *state the topic of the essay* and it must *capture the reader's interest.* Any one of several devices may be used to fulfill the latter purpose.

- **I** Emphasize the importance of the topic.
- **II** Ask a provocative question.
- **III** Use an appropriate quotation.
- **IV** State the divisions of the topic.
- **V** Use a stimulating incident or anecdote.

Naturally, the method that you choose will depend on the nature of the topic and on your own preferences. Any one of these devices can help make the reader receptive to an essay. After each device is explained below, there is an example of an appropriate introduction that could be used for an essay entitled: "The Case Against Experimenting with Drugs."

I EMPHASIZE THE IMPORTANCE OF THE TOPIC. The writer may impress the reader by explaining the current interest in the topic or by indicating that the subject may influence our lives. For example:

Every day the newspapers and television and radio news programs are flooded with stories about the tragic results of drug addiction. Indeed, in the past year over two thousand people died from drug abuse in this country alone. About two hundred of these victims were teenagers who were probably just satisfying their natural curiosity or were searching for a few thrills—and got more than they bargained for. Their deaths are the most potent evidence in the case against experimenting with drugs.

II ASK A PROVOCATIVE QUESTION. The reader's interest can be stimulated by the writer's asking a question that does not have an easy answer. The essay that follows should then be concerned with finding a possible answer. For example:

Should people be encouraged to try new things? "Of course!" one may likely answer. But what if heroin or LSD is new to someone? Why is it all right to taste new foods and to visit new places, but not to try out drugs? It is precisely this problem that is confusing young people who have been encouraged by their parents to experience all that life has to offer. To end this confusion, society must build a convincing case against experimenting with drugs.

III USE AN APPROPRIATE QUOTATION. A quotation is an easy and effective device to use—if it is used sparingly. The daily newspapers are a good source of quotations suitable for current topics. If the subject is of a more general nature, the book *Bartlett's Familiar Quotations,* which you can find in the reference section of the library, may provide appropriate material. For example:

"Heroin is a death trip. I really enjoyed it. But once you get the habit, you're in trouble. One good friend is in the hospital with an $80 a day habit. Another is almost dead from hepatitis. Two others I know, one a girl, died from overdoses. Every time you stick that needle in your arm you're playing with your life." This statement was made by a 19-year-old boy who, like many of his friends, had tried drugs out of curiosity and soon discovered that he was experimenting with danger.

IV STATE THE DIVISIONS OF THE TOPIC. A brief idea of the plan of the essay, if stated in an effective manner, can hint at the interesting points which you intend to cover. For example:

Many young people who have been using drugs for a short time are still filled with the excitement of trying something that is new and somewhat mysterious to them. But few of these drug users realize that their physical well-being may be permanently ruined, that their mental capacity may be destroyed to the point of insanity, and that their ability to maintain a normal social life may be lost. Surely, the initial thrill of experimenting with drugs is not worth the agony that can follow.

V USE A STIMULATING INCIDENT OR ANECDOTE. The use of an interesting incident or anecdote can act as a teaser to lure the reader into the remainder of the essay. Be sure that the device is appropriate for the subject and focus of what is to follow. For example:

Happy to be released after serving a six-month sentence for prostitution, Florence hurried toward the drug pusher who was waiting for her in the lobby of the jail building. According to a prearranged plan, she gave him twenty dollars in exchange for a needle filled with heroin. Because she was desperate for a fix, Florence then rushed into a nearby telephone booth, where she quickly injected the needle through her clothes and into her hip. When she later tried to leave the building, she was arrested by a plainclothesman who had viewed the entire incident. This woman is just one of thousands who have wasted their lives with shoplifting and prostitution in order to finance their own physical and mental destruction. They, better than most people, know the horrifying results of experimenting with drugs.

The Concluding Paragraph

Because no reader likes to be jarred by an abrupt ending, a concluding paragraph should be used to give the essay a feeling of completeness. An effective conclusion should *reemphasize the topic of the essay,* leaving the reader with a strong impression of what has been said. Any one of the following methods may be used:

I Make a plea for change.
II Draw the necessary conclusions from what has been said.
III Summarize the major points of the essay.

When choosing a method for ending an essay, remember that the conclusion should flow naturally out of the body of the paper; it should not appear to be tacked on. After each method is explained below, there is an example of a conclusion that could be used for an essay entitled: "The Case Against Experimenting with Drugs."

I MAKE A PLEA FOR CHANGE. A conclusion may make a plea for a change of attitude or for specific action. The following paragraph does both:

The parents, the schools, and the government must make a combined effort to educate young people about the dangers of drug abuse. Moreover, the whole society must change its attitude concerning such over-the-counter preparations as sleeping pills, diet pills, and tranquilizers. The careless use of these drugs creates an atmosphere that invites the use of illegal narcotics. When we realize our full responsibility in dealing with this problem, drug addiction may begin to disappear as a national menace.

II DRAW THE NECESSARY CONCLUSIONS FROM WHAT HAS BEEN SAID. Drawing on the facts given in the essay, you may use the concluding paragraph to form judgments about the topic. For example:

Thus it can be seen that the strong warnings about drug abuse heard on radio and television and seen in newspapers and magazines are not an exaggeration. The evidence is overwhelming and only one overriding conclusion can be drawn: drugs are deadly, and experimenting with them can lead people and, in fact, our entire society to the point of extinction.

III SUMMARIZE THE MAJOR POINTS OF THE ESSAY. A restatement of the major points—using new words—will help the readers to remember what they have read. A summary is usually most effective in a long theme; it would seem repetitious at the end of a short theme. For example:

Narcotics, then, can affect the user in a variety of ways, most of which are frightening and dangerous. When someone tries an illicit drug, he may experience immediate effects such as severe hallucinations, serious mental changes, and a loss of appetite. Taken over a long period of time, drugs may cause hepatitis, a complete mental breakdown—or even death from an overdose. If people can be made to truly understand these effects, the seductive appeal of drugs will disappear and thousands of useful lives will be saved from the terrifying results of narcotics addiction.

A SPECIAL NOTE: Aside from the methods given here, certain devices presented in the section on the introductory paragraph can be useful in concluding paragraphs: for example, the quotation, the question, and the incident or anecdote.

Common Errors to Avoid in Introductions and Conclusions

1. Never use expressions such as: "Now I will tell you about . . . ," "I would like to discuss . . . ," or "In my paper I will explain. . . ." Such expressions make the structure of your essay too obvious.

2. Avoid absolute statements such as "This proves that . . ." or "If we take this action, the problem will be solved." To be as accurate as possible, you need to qualify these statements: "This seems to prove that . . ." or "If we take this action, we will be helping to solve the problem."

3. Avoid using clichés and overworked quotations. An essay on marriage would not benefit from a reminder that love and marriage go together like a horse and carriage. "To err is human, to forgive divine" has long since lost its freshness and would add nothing to an essay.

4. Never apologize for what you are going to write or for what you have written. If you begin your theme with "I don't know very much about this subject," you will immediately lose the reader's interest. In addition, if you end a theme with, "Of course there are many other opinions about this subject, and I certainly do not know everything," you will destroy the impact of your essay. If you really do feel unsure about your opinions, change your topic to something that you can be more positive about.

5. The introduction and conclusion should not seem tacked on; make sure that they are an integral part of the whole essay. The introduction should state the topic of the *entire* theme, and the conclusion should relate to the general topic rather than one specific point.

6. The size of the introduction and conclusion should not be out of proportion to the size of the whole essay. An introduction or conclusion of 200 words would certainly be too long for a theme of about 500 words. However, a long paper may require a 200-word introduction or conclusion.

EXERCISE 7h: Referring to the list of errors to avoid, evaluate the effectiveness of the following sets of introductions and conclusions. Make any corrections that you think will improve these introductions and conclusions. Some of them may have to be completely rewritten.

1. The following introduction and conclusion are from a 500-word expository theme on the topic:

The Pressures of a College Student

Introduction

There are many pressures that a college student must face.

Conclusion

Perhaps the greatest pressure college students feel is the need to fulfill course requirements. A full-time student may have to spend at least three or four hours a night doing homework assignments and going over class notes. During any one semester, a student may also have to prepare three or four research papers, each of which requires several visits to the library and many days of organizing the information and writing and typing the final copy. In the midst of all this work, the student may spend an evening studying for a quiz and certainly several evenings studying for a major examination. Thus, it is not surprising that many students complain about not having enough free time.

2. The following introduction and conclusion are from a 500-word expository theme on the topic:

The Case Against Food Additives

Introduction

Would you drink a glass filled with glycerol ester of wood rosin, potassium sorbate, and sodium silico aluminate? Although the idea of drinking these substances seems horrifying, these man-made chemicals and a large number of others have been added to many of the foods you eat every day. As I will show in my essay, food additives can cause cancer and other deadly illnesses.

Conclusion

I must admit that my knowledge of this subject is somewhat limited and that the effects of food additives on the human body must be investigated further. But based on the evidence given, I believe that people should stop buying foods which contain unnatural chemicals.

3. The following introduction and conclusion are from a 500-word expository theme on the topic:

Today's Consumers Are Being Cheated

Introduction

I had never realized how underhanded and sneaky some businessmen could be until I recently purchased a clock radio. I arrived at a local appliance store at 9:15 A.M. on the first day of the sale to buy a clock radio that had been advertised for ten dollars less than its usual price. This clock radio had lighted digital numbers, a snooze alarm, and an imitation walnut case. After the fast-talking salesman informed me that the item I wanted was already sold out, he showed me another clock radio that was fifteen dollars more than the one I had come to buy. Although this was more than I wanted to spend, I bought this clock radio anyway because it was similar to the one I had originally wanted and I had gone to great trouble to get to the store in the first place. I had had to hire a baby-sitter and borrow my neighbor's car because mine was being repaired. As I was driving home, it suddenly occurred to me that if the less expensive clock radios had all been sold in just fifteen minutes, then the store had probably had very few of them and had advertised the sale to attract customers who would then be shown the more expensive clock radio. This incident made me start thinking about all of the ways that consumers are being cheated today.

Conclusion

Therefore, in an effort to reduce the number of instances of overpricing, false advertising, and the misrepresentation of merchandise by salespeople, the federal, state, and local governments must pass and strictly enforce stronger consumer protection laws and must also begin a large-scale consumer education program. In addition, consumers themselves must be on guard against being cheated when they shop. Although these actions will certainly not bring about a complete end to the problem, they will help to protect the public still further against the dishonest practices of greedy businessmen.

4. The following introduction and conclusion are from a 500-word expository theme on the topic:

The Need for Physical Exercise

Introduction

Physical exercise has become a popular pastime for many millions of Americans. More people than ever are going to health spas, public gymnasiums, and exercise classes offered by local schools and colleges. In addition, sales of bicycles, chinning bars, weights, and other exercise equipment have risen sharply in recent years. Indeed, even the federal government encourages physical exercise through the President's Council on Physical Fitness.

Conclusion

Therefore, you should participate in a daily program of active, lively exercise. In this way, you will prevent a deadly disease from striking and you will undoubtedly lengthen your life.

5. The following introduction and conclusion are from a 500-word expository theme on the topic:

The Need for Patriotism

Introduction

Because the United States faces so many serious problems such as poverty, unemployment, and the energy crisis, now more than ever the people must renew their patriotism in order to preserve American democracy. As Abraham Lincoln reminded us, "Democracy is the government of the people, by the people, for the people." Thus, we must give three cheers for the red, white, and blue to uphold the land of the free and the home of the brave.

Conclusion

As I have proven in my essay, if the people would become more patriotic, our way of life would improve and American democracy would be strengthened.

EXERCISE 7i: Look back at the essay topics and plans which you created for Exercise 7f. On separate paper, write an appropriate introduction and conclusion for each essay.

EXERCISE 7j: ESSAY ANALYSIS Answer each set of questions given below.

1. Look back at the essay "Old Before Her Time," which appears at the beginning of Chapter Two.

   a. What device does the author use as the basis for her introduction?

   ____

   b. With what words in the introduction does the author state the topic of the essay?

   ____

   ____

2. Look back at the essay "Why People Are Rude," which appears at the beginning of Chapter Three.

   a. What two devices does the author use as the basis for his introduction?

   ____

   ____

   b. With what words in the introduction does the author state the topic of the essay?

   ____

   ____

3. Look back at the essay "School for Marriage," which appears at the beginning of Chapter Four.

   a. What device does the author use as the basis for her three-paragraph introduction?

   ____

 Name: ______________________ Date: ______________

b. With what words in the introduction does the author state the topic of the essay?

____

____

4. Look back at the essay "Troubled Teenagers," which appears at the beginning of Chapter Seven.

   a. What two devices does the author use as the basis for his introduction?

   ____

   ____

   b. With what words in the introduction does the author state the topic of the essay?

   ____

   ____

5. What method is used to develop the conclusion of each of the following essays?

   a. "Why People Are Rude" (Chapter Three): ____________________

   ____

   ____

   b. "The Great American Love Affair" (Chapter Six): ____________

   ____

   ____

   c. "Troubled Teenagers" (Chapter Seven): ____________________

   ____

   ____

EXERCISE 7k: REFRESHER

1. Find and correct any errors in pronoun consistency.
2. Find and correct any errors in verb agreement.
3. Find and correct any sentence fragments.

Toughlove, a self-help program for the parents of problem teenagers, offer a strict approach to dealing with adolescents. Started in 1979 by two counselors, the Toughlove movement have grown to include 700 local groups throughout the country. At weekly meetings, you are encouraged to set a "bottom line" on your children's behavior. For example, you might set a midnight curfew for your 14-year-old son, who has gotten into the habit of staying out until 6 A.M. If the boy ignore the curfew, you would make him stay home for an entire weekend. In a more serious case, Lorraine Bauer were threatened with a butcher knife by her drug-dazed daughter, Diane. After escaping from the family home, Mrs. Bauer called some other members of her Toughlove group. Who immediately came over to take charge of the situation. First, they called several hospitals until they found one that would take Diane that night. Then they offered Diane the "bottom line": If she did not go into the hospital to recover from her addiction. She would have to leave home permanently. Faced with this choice, the girl decided to enter the hospital. However, if she had not decided to go for treatment, she would have had to move out. Taking only her personal belongings and a note listing the names of Toughlove families that was willing to take her in if necessary. Although Toughlove's no-nonsense approach may seem harsh, many parents claims that it has enabled them to take control of their own families again.

 Name: ______________________ Date: ______________

SPRINGBOARDS TO WRITING

Using your knowledge of the writing process, explained on pages 12–14, write a paragraph or essay related to this chapter's central theme, *troubled teenagers*, which is introduced on pages 232–240.

PREWRITING

To think of topics to write about, look at the advertisement and the photograph, read the essay, and answer the questions that follow each. If you prefer, select one of the writing springboards below. (All paragraph numbers refer to the essay that starts on page 234.) To develop your ideas, use the prewriting techniques described on pages 15–20.

WRITING A PARAGRAPH (For help, see the Pointers on page 31.)

1. Paragraph 24 states: "The unhappiest kids in the world are those with the least parental supervision." Agree or disagree.
2. Read the Refresher on page 266. What do you think of the Toughlove program?
3. React to the philosophy that "if you don't have something, you have the right to take it!" (See ¶ 11.)
4. Teenagers should (should not) be allowed to drink alcoholic beverages.
5. What do you think of the philosophy of "me first, do your own thing"? (See ¶ 8.)

WRITING AN ESSAY (For help, see the Pointers on page 35.)

6. Society Does (Does Not) Pressure Young People to Grow Up Too Quickly (See ¶ 7.)
7. The Major Pressures Faced by Teenagers Today
8. Agree or disagree: "These are hard times in which to mature to adulthood." (See ¶ 6.)
9. What Can Be Done to Help America's Troubled Teenagers?
10. Paragraph 22 states: "Our kids are not the problem. Our adults are the problem." Agree or disagree.
11. I Have (Have Not) Lived Up to My Parents' Expectations of Me
12. The Menace of Child Abuse
13. What Makes a Good (Bad) Parent?
14. How I Want to Raise (Am Raising) My Children
15. Paragraph 24 states: ". . . better communication between generations is the best way to bring troubled teenagers back toward fruitful lives, and parents must bear the brunt of the task." Agree or disagree.
16. My Life Is (Is Not) Boring
17. The Government Should (Should Not) Ban Pornography

"We're afraid to have a baby"

"There's hardly enough room to turn around. Food is scarce, so the cost is sometimes more than we can afford. And then there are the poachers. What chance does a kid have in a world like this?"

Save their world. A contribution to the African Wildlife Leadership Foundation will help buy this lion and his lioness room, food, and safety. And help make the place they live the kind of place where you can raise a family.

Please send your contribution (tax deductible) to: African Wildlife Leadership Foundation Box 661, Washington, D.C. 20044.

Save their world. It's your world, too.

African Wildlife Leadership Foundation

eight

This 4,000-year-old good luck charm could be yours.

The authentic oriental gong. Traditionally invested with powers to ward off bad luck by millions of Chinese. Now gong fever is sweeping America.

Feeling down? Frustrated? Anxious? Feel like hitting something? Hit a gong! Experience its unique, soothing, mystical tones. Feeling up? Let it ring! Having a party? What could be more fun than having your own gong show? Looking for a special gift? What's more unusual, decorative or functional?

The Paiste family has been making the definitive oriental gong for generations, never compromising a grand family tradition of hand workmanship. Each is a unique collector's item adding elegance and mystery to any room. Supplied with stand and mallet.

Please ship:

____ 7" gong(s) at $41.50 ppd.
____ 10" gong(s) at $56.50 ppd.
____ 13" gong(s) at $78.50 ppd.
____ 16" gong(s) at $121.50 ppd.
____ 20" gong(s) at $206.50 ppd.
(sizes represent gong's diameter)

☐Check Enclosed ☐BankAmericard
☐Master Charge ☐Central Charge

Card No. ____ Exp. Date ____
Name ____
Street ____
City ____ State ____ Zip ____

Drums unlimited® inc.
Percussion Merchants to the World
4928 St. Elmo Ave. Bethesda, Md. 20014

Courtesy of Drums Unlimited, Inc., Bethesda, Maryland.

SPRINGBOARDS TO THINKING

For informal, not written, response . . . to stimulate your thinking

1. Why are the lions afraid to have a baby? Do you think it is important that we preserve wildlife on this planet? Why or why not?
2. Look at the advertisement above for the good luck charm, an oriental gong. Why do some people like to own things from cultures other than their own? Why do some people like to own things that are handed down from past generations?
3. What is your most prized possession? Might someone else think it is unimportant or junk? Why or why not? What makes something valuable?
4. If you were given $45 and told that you had to choose between spending it *only* on helping the African Wildlife Leadership Foundation or on buying an oriental gong, which would you choose? Why?
5. Do you think people should be free to spend their money as they wish? Why or why not? Do you think there should be controls on what is offered for sale or on what is advertised? Why or why not?

Take It Away!

RUSSEL J. THOMSEN

(1) America can well afford, indeed deserves, a recession! *Please* let me explain that.

(2) A few weeks ago, I left my home among the wheat and pea fields of the Walla Walla Valley way out in the breadbasket of Washington State, got on a small plane, flew to Spokane to where the big jets are and then set off on a 2,000-mile trip to the nation's Capital. There I delivered a *ten*-minute speech to a somewhat bored and boring group of scientists, turned tail and flew back the same 2,000 miles to my home in the wheat and pea fields.

(3) I figure that the cost of my ten-minute speech ran to about $100 a minute. And even though I am egocentric enough to feel that during those few minutes I might have said something that will help protect the health of thousands of women, I still am faced with the nagging question: "What sane society can consider such extravagance as an expected privilege for its common citizenry?"

(4) And even if my thousand-dollar ten minutes prove life-saving for other citizens, on that plane were persons with less compelling missions and motives. There were college students on last-minute flings before returning to their diversions, businessmen who could have conducted their business by phone, servicemen caught up in the perpetual and often senseless moving associated with the military and others who just were trying to fly away from themselves.

Materialism as Right

(5) The almost immoral American "way of life" manifested by flying has often been brought home to me at the small but sleek airport serving the prosperous Monterey peninsula south of San Francisco. Home of some of California's truly rich and pseudo-rich, Monterey boasts of its Fisherman's Wharf, Seventeen-Mile Drive and Pebble Beach Golf Course. From its airport dapper businesspeople leave each morning for commuter flights to San Francisco. As casually as your child might walk to school, these people have built into their life standard a daily commuter flight of about 200 miles round-trip. To them, such is not a luxury but part of their American birthright—and damn the rest of the world.

(6) Another picture: A nurse's aide working with my hospitalized patients confided to me during a moment of introspection that her 16-year-old daughter wanted a certain *new* car, which the nurse's aide was trying

to supply by working double shifts. "Why should you work so hard just so your daughter can have a car?" I asked in friendly perplexity. "Because her friends have cars and because she deserves a car," was the reply.

(7) Since when do teenagers deserve cars? Why does mere employment as a soda jerk entitle the nation's young to the guaranteed privilege of hot cars, hot women, hot clothes? Is there no end in this nation to the supposed rights to enjoy nauseating materialism?

Illusion as Standard

(8) A different scene: San Francisco's Golden Gate Park is favored real estate that should give children and adults living at its fringes a strip of green in which to run, turn somersaults, exult in the preliminaries of love-making or simply meditate. Instead, it is one of the largest piles of dog manure in the nation. Morning and evening, the apartment dwellers in the area unleash their caged canines (usually the size of German police dogs or Saint Bernards) to do their thing in the park. Simply put, here are Americans who have been nurtured on the right of being American, including the right to use public or private property to dispose of Coke cans, dog droppings or any other unwanted material.

(9) I propose that America's standard of living is an illusion bordering on insanity. I further assert that many *things* could disappear from our lives and leave us not in a state of economic recession, but in a far healthier reality—good for body and soul. Here are a number of *things* that could and should just disappear. You can easily add to the list:

- The comic page in newspapers.
- The box in which a well-known hamburger chain puts its Big Mac.
- Recreational vehicles. Ford's production genius gave to America the promise of a Tin Lizzie in front of every house. Then it was two cars—one for the him and one for the her. Then the American Dream blossomed to the three-car-plus family. Now, the same workaday families expect motorcycles, campers, snowmobiles, gliders, planes, boats.
- Parsley served on food in restaurants.
- Junk mail. I realize that what is junk mail to one person might be truth, beauty or advertising to another—especially the purveyor. But my daily mail is cluttered with throwaways that I have neither the time nor desire to open. Multiplied across the nation, this is a mountain of material that first requires the rape of our forests, then clogs our postal system and finally overflows our garbage dumps.
- Horse farms of less than 10 acres. Stray or unwanted animals.
- At least a significant portion of the nudie magazines, massage parlors, body paint shops, and the like that dredge the muck of a neurotic society.
- Cigarettes. And the fires, disease and death caused by the weed.
- Cars heavier than 3,000 pounds.

- Aerosol spray cans. America is engulfed in spray cans and their contents. Underarm deodorants and drying agents. Frying pan unstickers and hair stickers. Spray paints that have become an ecological disaster in the senseless defacing of America and its monuments.
- Ditto for pop and beer cans.
- The bagging of one-or-two-item purchases in the market.
- Hats—except for hazardous duty in the military.
- Trinkets. Whether in the glut of vending machines or hanging by the row in every store, plastic and tin toys, puzzles, charms and other worthless junk-in-the-making could disappear overnight and have only positive effect on our lives.

(10) Along the roads of my Walla Walla Valley lie the discarded things of a profligate and sick society. The trails to the tops of our tallest mountains are lined with similar trash. And such junk clutters the life-being of each American. Take it away! But don't call it a recession. Let it be known as a breath of fresh air!

READING SURVEY

1. *Main idea*

What is the central theme of this essay?

2. *Major Details*

a. What effect would the removal of many "things" in our lives have upon us?
b. What does Russel J. Thomsen think should happen to trinkets?
c. In mentioning the litter along the roads of the Walla Walla Valley, how does Russel J. Thomsen label our society?

3. *Inferences*

a. Read paragraph 5 again. What does the expression "damn the rest of the world" say about the attitudes of the Monterey flying commuters toward other human beings?
b. Read paragraph 6 again. Why does a nurse's aide use the term "deserve" in expressing her wish to give her daughter a new car?

4. *Opinions*

a. Do you agree with Russel J. Thomsen's point of view about our materialistic society? Explain.
b. If our materialistic society is so wasteful, what steps do you think should be taken to correct the problem?

VOCABULARY BUILDING

Lesson One: The Vocabulary of Materialism

The essay "Take It Away!" by Russel J. Thomsen includes words that are useful when you are discussing materialism.

extravagance	(paragraph 3)
immoral	(5)
materialism	(7)
dredge	(9)
muck	(9)
ecological disaster	(9)
defacing	(9)
glut	(9)
profligate	(10)
clutters	(10)

In our society, **extravagance** means that people spend money beyond reasonable limits to the point of being wasteful.

In our society, when people are **immoral** they act in ways that are against accepted standards of right and wrong.

In our society, when people are overly concerned with **materialism,** they put a higher value on the possession of things than on the pursuit of intellectual goals.

In our society, when people **dredge** up **muck** about others, they dig up and search for all available uncomplimentary, disgusting information they can find.

In our society, people create **ecological disaster** when they destroy the complex relations of organisms in our environment.

In our society, when people are **defacing** the environment, they are spoiling the appearance of our lands, buildings, and the like.

In our society, when there is a **glut** of a product, that product floods our markets far beyond the need or demand for it.

In our society, when people are **profligate,** they are shamelessly wasteful.

In our society, people often realize that a great deal of junk **clutters** our world, but they feel helpless to do anything about such messy crowding.

EXERCISE 8a: Each of the vocabulary words from this lesson is shown below in italics as the word appeared in context in the essay. Write an explanation of each word within the context of the material given. Use your own paper for this assignment.

1. From paragraph 3: "What sane society can consider such *extravagance* as an expected privilege for its common citizenry?"
2. From paragraph 5: "The almost *immoral* American 'way of life' manifested by flying has often been brought home to me at the small but sleek airport serving the prosperous Monterey peninsula. . . ."
3. From paragraph 7: "Is there no end in this nation to the supposed rights to enjoy nauseating *materialism*?"
4. From paragraph 9: ". . . massage parlors, body-paint shops, and the like that *dredge* the *muck* of a neurotic society."
5. From paragraph 9: "Spray paints that have become an *ecological disaster* in the senseless *defacing* of America and its monuments."
6. From paragraph 9: "Whether in the *glut* of vending machines or hanging by the row in every store . . . worthless junk-in the making could disappear overnight. . . ."
7. From paragraph 10: "Along the roads of my Walla Walla Valley lie the discarded things of a *profligate* and sick society."
8. From paragraph 10: "And such junk *clutters* the life-being of each American.

Lesson Two: The Vocabulary of Business

The essay "Take It Away!" by Russel J. Thomsen includes words that are useful when you are discussing business.

recession	(paragraph 1)	**nurtured**	(8)
missions	(4)	**standard of living**	(9)
motives	(4)	**assert**	(9)
prosperous	(5)	**purveyor**	(9)
entitle	(7)		

In business, a **recession** means a temporary falling off of business activity throughout a large part of the country.

In business, people usually set **missions** or goals for themselves based on the profits they hope to make.

In business, people have desires and inner drives—known as **motives**—which usually lead them to action designed to increase profits.
In business, **prosperous** people are those who have continued success.
In business, some people feel that they are **entitled** to cheat because they think that is their right.
In business, successful people are usually those who have been **nurtured**—raised, fed, and trained—on the business point of view.
In business, a **standard of living** is the level of income that permits people to pay for needs and comforts.
In business, many successful people are able to **assert** themselves in that they can state their point of view with great confidence.
In business, a **purveyor** is someone who supplies products, usually food.

EXERCISE 8b: Each of the vocabulary words from this lesson is shown below in italics as the word appeared in context in the essay. Write an explanation of each word within the context of the material given. Use your own paper for this assignment.

1. From paragraph 1: "America can well afford, indeed deserves, a *recession!*"
2. From paragraph 4: ". . . on that plane were persons with less compelling *missions* and *motives.*"
3. From paragraph 5: ". . . at the small but sleek airport serving the *prosperous* Monterey peninsula south of San Francisco."
4. From paragraph 7: "Why does mere employment as a soda jerk *entitle* the nation's young to the guaranteed privilege of hot cars? . . ."
5. From paragraph 8: "Simply put, here are Americans who have been *nurtured* on the right of being American. . . ."
6. From paragraph 9: "I propose that America's *standard of living* is an illusion bordering on insanity."
7. From paragraph 9: "I further *assert* that many things could disappear from our lives. . . ."
8. From paragraph 9: "I realize that what is junk mail to one person might be truth, beauty or advertising to another—especially the *purveyor.*"

SPELLING

Lesson One: Spelling Demons

Here are some more words that are frequently misspelled. Using the helpful techniques given in Chapter One, be sure to learn these new Demons, which are taken from "Take It Away!"

across	**enjoy**	**privilege**
area	**especially**	**realize**
beauty	**genius**	**require**
cigarette	**group**	**scene**
citizen	**guarantee**	**scientist**
desire	**luxury**	**since**
disappear	**magazine**	**speech**
disease	**material**	**those**

Lesson Two: The Apostrophe

Disregarding or misusing the apostrophe is as serious an error as misspelling the word. Careless writers do not realize that the apostrophe is as much a part of the word as each letter. Because it has only three major uses, the apostrophe is easy to learn and use properly.

I CONTRACTIONS. The apostrophe is used in contractions to indicate that a letter or letters have been left out.

It is = it's	do not = don't
let us = let's	we have = we've
have not = haven't	they had = they'd

☞ *Try It Out*

Form contractions out of the following sets of words. Be sure to use the apostrophe where needed.

are + not = __________	we + have = __________
I + will = __________	they + are = __________
let + us = __________	does + not = __________

 Name: __________ *Date:* __________

II PLURALS. To form the plural of a letter of the alphabet, a number, or a symbol, use *'s.*

6's three c's &'s

If the number is written out, use only the *s.*

fours sevens nines

Try It Out

Insert any necessary apostrophes in the following sentences.

1. Although Wendy got three 50s and two 60s on her final examinations, she passed her courses with three Bs and two Cs.
2. The bookkeeper lost his job because his 5s looked like Ss and his 6s looked like bs.

III POSSESSION. To form possessives, first write the name of the possessor—whether it be singular or plural.Then add *'s* to the end of the name. If it already ends in *s*, add just the '.

Helen's hat	Dickens' *Tale of Two Cities*
man's fate	the ladies' club
the class' suggestion	two boys' uniforms

To form the possessives of noun combinations, use the apostrophe only after the last noun in the combination.

my sister-in-law's car the chief of police's remarks

A SPECIAL NOTE: Do not use an apostrophe with the possessive pronouns: *his, hers, yours, ours, theirs, its, whose.*

Try It Out

Rewrite each of the following phrases to form a possessive that uses an apostrophe.

the advice of the father-in-law ____________________

the rights of the women ____________________

the food of the restaurant ____________________

EXERCISE 8c: Follow the directions for each section.

1. Form contractions out of the following sets of words.

a. I + would = ______________
b. who + is = ______________
c. Jeff + is = ______________
d. were + not = ______________
e. we + are = ______________
f. where + is = ______________
g. I + am = ______________
h. could + not = ______________
i. she + will = ______________
j. that + is = ______________
k. can + not = ______________
l. there + is = ______________
m. he + had = ______________
n. you + are = ______________
o. did + not = ______________
p. could + have = ______________
q. will + not = ______________
r. it + is = ______________
s. who + would = ______________
t. have + not = ______________

2. Rewrite each of the following phrases to form a possessive that uses an apostrophe.

a. the rifle of the soldier ______________
b. the rifles of the soldiers ______________
c. the strength of Edith ______________
d. the earthquake of last year ______________
e. the teacher of the children ______________
f. the decision of the attorney general ______________
g. the new cars of General Motors ______________
h. the duty of everyone ______________
i. the problems of the community ______________
j. the problems of the communities ______________

 Name: ______________ Date: ______________

k. the population of the world ______________________

l. the roar of the lion ______________________

m. the latest hit of the rock group ______________________

n. the girlfriend of Carlos ______________________

o. the weather of yesterday ______________________

p. the popularity of the magazine ______________________

q. the uniforms of the police officers ______________________

r. the speed of the airplane ______________________

s. the fees of the doctor ______________________

t. the fees of the doctors ______________________

3. Insert apostrophes where necessary in the following sentences.

   a. If youre going to become a secretary, youd better remember that "sincerely" contains two es and "concerning" contains two cs and three ns.

   b. Linda Ronstadts album of songs from the 30s and 40s, which was one of the biggest hits in recent years, renewed the publics interest in music from the "big band era."

   c. Its the parents responsibility to make sure that they dont buy childrens toys with sharp edges that can cut a youngsters tender skin.

   d. When the temperature is in the 90s, a person shouldnt sit in the sun for too long, for the suns hot rays can cause the bodys heat-regulating mechanism to stop working.

   e. Ive just read that a cats face always has four rows of whiskers, that an elephants diet doesnt include meat, and that the worlds fastest animal is the cheetah.

   f. Isnt it a shame that football players salaries have gotten so high that the teams owners arent able to keep ticket prices at last years level?

EXERCISE 8d: Follow the directions for each item. Each Spelling Demon given in this chapter should be used only once.

1. Six of the Demons have double letters in them. Write them here and either circle or enlarge any letter(s) that seem difficult.

_______________ _______________

_______________ _______________

_______________ _______________

2. Several of the Demons contain more vowels (a, e, i, o, u) than consonants. Write four of them here and either circle or enlarge any letter(s) that seem difficult.

_______________ _______________

_______________ _______________

3. Several of the Demons contain an equal number of vowels (a, e, i, o, u) and consonants. Write five of them here and either circle or enlarge any letter(s) that seem difficult.

_______________ _______________

_______________ _______________

____

 Name: _______________ Date: _______________

4. Each of the following Demons contains one or more smaller words in its spelling. Using one of these smaller words and the original Demon, compose a sentence that will help you to associate the two.

   Example: courtesy   We must show *court*esy in court.

   a. enjoy ______________________________

   b. since ______________________________

   c. those ______________________________

5. Using each set of Demons given below, create a complete sentence that makes sense.

   Example: caution, disease, population, particular
   We must *caution* the *population* against the spread of a *particular disease.*

   a. group, citizen, scientist ______________________________

   ____

   ____

   b. luxury, privilege, scene ______________________________

   ____

   ____

The Comma

Although the comma seems to be a troublesome mark of punctuation, you can master it by learning just six principles that cover the great majority of uses. It is also helpful to remember that the comma represents a short pause in speech. However, since not all people pause in exactly the same places, rules must be relied upon for correct usage. Be sure that you have a reason for every comma that you use. If you are not sure that a comma is needed, it is usually wise to leave it out. Use the comma:

I to separate items in a series
II to separate two complete sentences joined by *and, but, for, nor, or, so, yet*
III to separate coordinate adjectives
IV to set off introductory material
V to set off interrupters
VI to set off certain conventional material

I THE COMMA IS USED TO SEPARATE ITEMS IN A SERIES. Each item may be just one word or a whole string of words, but the series must have at least three items.

Patterns: Item 1, Item 2, Item 3

OR

Item 1, Item 2, and Item 3

Examples: The restaurant is small, elegant, expensive.
Three popular professions are data processing, electrical engineering, and drafting.
The convict ran across the yard, climbed over the wall, and escaped to freedom.
The students complained that the course was too hard, that the grades were too low, and that the teacher was too boring.

Try It Out

Insert any necessary commas in the following sentences.

1. Overeating fried food cream-filled pastries and smoked meats can shorten a person's life.

2. Paramedics need to know how to diagnose injuries quickly how to set bones how to administer certain medications and how to transport patients safely.

II THE COMMA IS USED TO SEPARATE TWO COMPLETE SENTENCES JOINED BY *AND, BUT, FOR, NOR, OR, SO, YET.* The two sentences to be joined should be related in thought and of equal importance. (See Chapter Four, page 113, for a more complete discussion of coordination.) It is important to remember that the comma is used only when one of these seven words is being employed to join *two complete sentences.*

Pattern: Complete Sentence, [*and* / *but* / *for* / *nor* / *or* / *so* / *yet*] Complete Sentence.

Examples: She had prayed he would live, *but* she knew he would die.
She would never forget his face, *nor* would she forget his warm eyes.

A SPECIAL NOTE: If the two sentences are very short, the comma may be omitted. For example: The elephant bellowed wildly and its mate answered.

Try It Out

Insert any necessary commas in the following sentences.

1. Scientists all over the world are working hard to develop a cure for the common cold yet they are making little progress due to the large number of different cold viruses.

2. The flying fish can leap out of the water and then use its winglike fins to glide through the air for as much as 500 feet.

III THE COMMA IS USED TO SEPARATE COORDINATE ADJECTIVES.

An *adjective* describes a noun or pronoun; it makes the meaning of a noun or pronoun more specific. The adjective is usually placed as close as possible to the word it describes. The slot method can be used to identify adjectives. Start with this basic sentence:

That is (a) ________________ thing.

Now let's use some words from "Take It Away!" to test the method.

That is a *new* thing.

That is a *small* thing.

That is a *worthless* thing.

When two or more adjectives are used to modify the same word, the adjectives are coordinate and must be separated by commas.

Pattern: Adjective, Adjective Noun
Example: bright, colorful shirts

Two tests may be used to determine if the adjectives are coordinate: (a) try to put *and* between them or (b) try to reverse their order in the sentence.

Coordinate Adjectives: bright, colorful shirts
Test One: bright and colorful shirts
Test Two: colorful, bright shirts

Not Coordinate Adjectives: several colorful shirts
Test One: several and colorful shirts (illogical)
Test Two: colorful several shirts (illogical)

Try It Out

Insert any necessary commas in the following sentences.

1. Chinese typewriters are such large complicated machines that even an intelligent skilled operator cannot type at a rate of more than three or four words per minute.
2. Several famous movie stars are willing to appear in televised public-service announcements without charging a fee.

IV THE COMMA IS USED TO SET OFF INTRODUCTORY MATERIAL. The introductory material may be just a single word such as *however, therefore, moreover, nevertheless,* or *furthermore* . . . or a short expression such as *on the contrary, in fact, for example, on the other hand, in the first place, in general, to tell the truth, of course, in addition.*

Pattern: Introductory Word or Expression, Complete Sentence.

Examples: Nevertheless, the world's population will continue to grow.
In fact, the world's population will double by the year 2000.

The introductory material may also be a lengthy phrase or a subordinate section. (See Chapter Four, page 118, for a more complete discussion of subordination.)

Pattern: Introductory Material, Complete Sentence.

Examples: During the coldest months of the year, a flu epidemic may spread throughout the nation.
Although an elephant can weigh up to 14,000 pounds, its brain weighs only about 11 pounds.
Revving up his car's powerful engine, the driver waited for the traffic light to turn green.
To feel calm and relaxed, some people take tranquilizers.

 *Try It Out*

Insert any necessary commas in the following sentences.

1. Whenever there is a severe snowstorm my parents talk about moving to the Sunbelt.
2. According to experts at the U.S. National Weather Service the largest snowflake on record measured 8 inches in width.
3. After being frozen in a block of ice for six months some fish remain alive and can swim around as usual as soon as they are defrosted.

Name: ____________________ Date: ____________________

V COMMAS ARE USED TO SET OFF INTERRUPTERS. An interrupter may be any one of the single words or short expressions that can be used to introduce a sentence. (See rule IV.) Be sure that a comma is placed both *before* and *after* the interrupter.

Pattern: Complete, Interrupter, Sentence.

Examples: The nation is, of course, under the rule of the majority.
I believe, however, that the majority is capable of making a mistake.

An interrupter may also be a subordinate section that usually begins with *who* or *which.*

Pattern: Complete, *who* OR *which* ~~~~~~~~, sentence.

Examples: Juan, who is worried about pollution, plans to be an ecologist.
The S.S. Norway, which is docked at Pier 67, is crippled by a dock workers' strike.

In the pattern above, commas are used to surround the subordinate section because the subordination merely adds information about a specific *subject.* In the examples above, Juan is a specific man and the S.S. Norway is a specific ship. Therefore, the information given in the subordinate section is ADDED INFORMATION not basic for identification of the subject and you need to ADD COMMAS. NO COMMAS are used to surround the subordinate section when the INFORMATION IS NEEDED for basic identification.

Examples: The man who is worried about pollution plans to be an ecologist.
The ship which is docked at Pier 67 is crippled by a dock workers' strike.

If the *who* and *which* sections were removed from the examples above, we would have no idea of which man and which ship are being discussed. Because the subordinate information is needed to clearly identify the subject, commas are *not* used. (See Chapter Four, page 126, for additional discussion of this case of subordination.)

A SPECIAL NOTE: The *who* or *which* and its verb may sometimes be omitted from the subordinate section, but the same rule still applies: If the subordinate section is merely *added information,* then *add commas.* If the subordinate section is needed to identify the subject, then commas are *not* used.

Examples: Mark, a professional soldier, is a patriotic man.
(Mark, who is a professional soldier, is a patriotic man.)
The lamp sitting on the desk belongs to me.
(The lamp which is sitting on the desk belongs to me.)

 *Try It Out*

Insert any necessary commas in the following sentences.

1. Winners of state lotteries must of course pay taxes on what they receive.
2. It took two tries to hang Captain Kidd the famous English pirate because both he and the hangman were too drunk to stand up unaided.
3. Ian Fleming who is best known as the creator of James Bond served in the British Intelligence Service during World War II.

VI THE COMMA IS USED TO SET OFF CERTAIN CONVENTIONAL MATERIAL.

Conventional material may consist of dates, addresses, or titles.

On June 6, 1944, the allies invaded Normandy.
My aunt has lived at 24 Oak Street, Austin, Texas 78712, for the last thirty years.
J. T. Racken, M.D., is the President's new physician.

Conventional material may also consist of statistics.

957,357,268 page twelve, line ten
five feet, six inches Act II, scene iv

Conventional material may also consist of the complimentary close and the opening in an informal letter.

Sincerely yours, Dear Joe,
Very truly yours, Dear Uncle George,

A SPECIAL NOTE: In a formal letter the opening is followed by a colon.
Dear Sir: Dear Mr. Riggs: Dear Ms. Hartley:

Try It Out

Insert any necessary commas in the follow material.

1. As of September 1 1986 the address of N.O. Payne D.D.S. will be 22 Root Canal Avenue Chicago Illinois 60600.
2. Page 50 paragraph two of my history textbook states that the ancient city of Sparta had 25000 citizens and 500000 slaves.
3. Dear Mr. Walsh Sincerely Dear Aunt Joyce

EXERCISE 8e: Insert commas wherever they are necessary in the following sentences. Be prepared to justify the use of each comma or set of commas.

1. A multimillionaire from Lyon France died of shock upon learning that his fortune had shrunk to a mere $20000. As strange as it seems his nephew poverty-stricken all his life died of joy when informed that he was about to inherit the $20000.

2. The biggest money in the world which is used on the Pacific island of Yap consists of enormous heavy boulders that stand twelve feet high weigh over a ton and are shaped like doughnuts. When a piece of money is to be spent the new owner must carve his or her name into it for the boulder is too large to be moved from the original owner's front yard.

3. The federal government encourages all American voters to cast their ballots at each election but citizens have the right not to vote if they so choose. In Australia on the other hand it is against the law not to vote. In fact an Australian who does not vote risks getting a four-dollar fine.

4. A 32-year-old Columbian man announced to everyone's surprise that he was in love with a 100-year-old woman that he had already married her and that they planned to have children. Although all his friends and relatives thought that his family plans were unrealistic his 100-year-old wife nevertheless gave birth one year later to a beautiful healthy baby boy. This woman was without a doubt the oldest new mother in the world.

5. In recent years a huge hairy apelike giant has been seen walking around on its two back legs throughout the wilderness area of Humboldt County California. Whenever the creature has appeared it has

Name: ______________________ Date: ______________

carried off road-building equipment weighing hundreds of pounds or it has made terrifying high-pitched shrieks and then run off into the woods. Named "Bigfoot" by investigators this beast may be the missing link between humans and the apes or it may be just one of the biggest practical jokes in history.

6. When ball-point pens were first introduced to the American public at a New York department store on October 29 1945 10000 of them were sold the very first day for $12.50 each. Today of course a sturdy reliable ball-point pen can be bought for as little as 19 cents.

7. Nimrod Robertson who was an Alaskan hunter lost all of his teeth. Thus when he shot a bear one day he could not eat it nor could he stand to leave it for the wild animals to eat. To solve his problem he made the bear's teeth into a set of false teeth and then he proceeded to eat the bear with it.

8. A lake which is situated on the island of Java blows bubbles six feet in diameter. Formed from steam and gases these bubbles like giant balloons sail high into the air and explode with a loud noise.

9. John Wesley Hardin a famous outlaw of the Old West killed 43 men and was sentenced to 25 years in prison. After studying law in his cell he was pardoned became a licensed lawyer and worked to defend the law.

10. To determine the best qualified human pincushion the country people of Bohemia which is a section of Czechoslovakia hold annual pin-sticking contests. Bagro king of the local gypsy tribe stuck 3200 needles in his arm for 31 hours and thus he holds the contest record.

11. While a person is often said to be "as busy as a bee" this comparison is not accurate nor is it necessarily complimentary. Working only a very small fraction of the time a bee is actually rather lazy.

12. Pirate treasure and lost gold mines together with many other forms of wealth are buried throughout the country. Indeed it is estimated that more than $4000000000 in lost treasure is just waiting to be found. To become rich therefore get a shovel and start digging!

13. On September 13 1847 a railroad worker was preparing an explosion for a construction project when to his great surprise the dynamite blew up sooner than he had expected. The explosion drove a crowbar three feet seven inches long completely through the man's head. In spite of his terrible injury the worker did not even lose consciousness made a full recovery and lived many more years.

14. The Karaya Indians who live in the Amazon Valley of South America speak through their noses instead of through their mouths. As if this were not extraordinary enough the males of the tribe do not speak the same language as the females making communication between the sexes very difficult. As a result the tribe is also known for its many happy peaceful marriages.

15. John W. Horton an entertainer from Wellington Kansas made his living by eating whatever was placed before him. On any one occasion he could consume large quantities of egg shells glass newspapers or books. Although he also managed to eat a sack of dry dusty cement he later admitted apologetically that it had made him a little sick.

16. According to leading psychiatrists over 14000000 adult Americans suffer from phobias fears that are senseless and unusual. For example people have been known to suffer from a fear of beds work or hair. Perhaps the most dreaded fear however is arachibutyrophobia the fear of peanut butter sticking to the roof of the mouth.

17. Benjamin Franklin who was best known as a government leader and philosopher organized the first street-cleaning department and the first fire department. Furthermore he invented the harmonica the rocking chair and the street lamp.

18. By adding olive oil and cheese to large flat crackers Roman soldiers actually created the first pizza more than 2000 years ago. Introduced into the United States about fifty years ago pizza has obviously become one of our favorite foods for there are now more than 30000 pizzerias in this country.

19. Carlton Fredericks Ph.D. as well as many other nutritionists has claimed that sugar robs the body of B vitamins interferes with the digestion of calcium and contributes to hardening of the arteries. If these claims are true it is alarming to find on page 20 line 19 of a recent Department of Agriculture report that the average American consumes over 100 pounds of sugar each year.

20. Harvey Kennedy who created the first shoelace made $2500000 from his invention. Realizing that other new devices can also earn large sums of money individuals have patented such items as a parakeet diaper and an alarm clock that squirts the sleeper in the face but these inventions were never successful.

Name: ______________________ Date: ______________________

EXERCISE 8f: Follow the directions for each item. Be sure to use commas wherever necesary.

1. Write a statement about Martin Luther King, Jr., using two complete sentences joined by *and.*

____

____

____

2. Using coordinate adjectives, describe the dirtiest place you have ever seen.

____

____

3. Using *because* to begin the sentence, write a statement about a vacation spot you would like to visit.

____

____

4. Write a statement about a billboard, using a short expression to interrupt the sentence.

____

____

5. State your home address as part of a sentence.

____

____

6. Write a sentence about a politician, starting with the person's name and using an interrupter which states his or her position in government. Do not use the word *who.*

____

____

____

Name: ______________________ Date: ______________________

7. Use an introductory word or expression to begin a sentence about the need for trust in a relationship.

____

____

8. Complete the following sentence, giving three actions that you believe should be taken.

   There would be fewer divorces if ______________________

____

____

9. Write a statement about crash diets, using two complete sentences joined by *for*.

____

____

____

10. Using *when* to begin the sentence, write a statement about reruns on television.

____

____

11. Write a sentence about Mexico or Puerto Rico. Use an interrupter that is a subordinate section requiring commas.

____

____

____

12. Use an introductory word or expression to begin a sentence about taxicabs in your city or town.

____

____

____

 Name: ______________________ *Date:* ______________

13. Describe your favorite animal using coordinate adjectives.

____

____

14. Write a sentence about the worst thing that has happened to you this year. Give the date at the beginning of the sentence.

____

____

____

15. Using at least three items in a series, describe the prettiest wedding gown you have ever seen.

____

____

____

16. Write a sentence about a disco or restaurant you like to go to. Use an interrupter that is a subordinate section requiring commas.

____

____

____

17. Write an opening and complimentary close for a letter complaining about service in a gas station. (Make up the name of the gas station.)

____

____

____

18. Using *although* to begin the sentence, write a statement about going to college.

____

____

Other Marks of Punctuation

Punctuation not only is necessary but also is extremely useful in adding color and style to your writing.

The Period

Use after a complete statement.	The campaign was successful.
Use after most abbreviations.	U.S. Mr. etc. B.A.

The Question Mark

Use only after a *direct* question.	Did the dog bite you? (direct) [not: I asked if the dog bit you. (indirect)]

The Exclamation Point

Use after a word, expression, or complete sentence that conveys strong emotion.	Oh! What a surprise! It's an engagement ring!

The Semicolon

Use between two full sentences that are closely related in thought and are of equal importance. (Notice that the sentence following the semicolon does *not* begin with a capital letter.)

Joe is a very poor reader; it takes him three days to read a comic book.

Use between items in a series when the items themselves contain commas.

At the party I met Frank Parks, a bank president; Elaine Warren, a history teacher; and Mimi Carson, a professional singer.

The Colon

Use after an opening statement to direct attention to the material that follows, which is usually an explanation of the opening statement.

I need the following groceries: ketchup, napkins, and cereal.
You made one big mistake: You used a generalization to prove your argument.

Use after the opening of a formal letter, between a title and a subtitle, between numbers indicating chapter and verse of the Bible, and between numbers indicating hours and minutes.

Dear Sir:
Dear Ms. Hernandez:
Taking Action: Writing, Reading, Speaking, and Listening Through Simulation Games
We read Matthew 6:11.
Theresa left at 12:30.

The Dash

Use to signal a dramatic pause: Use a single dash to emphasize what follows, and use a set of dashes as you would a set of commas. (The dash should be used sparingly in formal writing.)

It was one thing she really needed—a mink toothbrush.
The man walked for hours—as he often did—until it was dark.

Parentheses

Use sparingly to set off an interruption that is not as important as the main material.

Thomas Wolfe (1900–1938) wrote *Look Homeward Angel.*

Sailing (not to be confused with cruising) is difficult.

Quotation Marks

In all of the examples below, notice where the quotation marks are placed in relation to the other marks of punctuation. For example, *the commas and the period are always placed to the left of the quotation marks.*

Use to set off the exact words that someone has said when he or she is quoted directly. (Notice that when the wording of a person's statement is changed to form an indirect quotation, you do *not* use quotation marks.)

Susan said, "I will leave tomorrow." (direct)

Susan said that she would leave tomorrow. (indirect)

"I believe," said Peter, "that we are sinking."

"What makes you say that?" gurgled his wife.

Use to set off the titles of stories, magazine articles, short poems, and chapters in books. (The titles of longer works, including books and plays, should be underlined or italicized.)

"Old Before Her Time" is one of the essays in this book.

The first poem in *Leaves of Grass* is entitled "Song of Myself."

Use to set off words that are being used in a special sense.

Health food is "in" today.

"Charisma" is a difficult word to define.

EXERCISE 8g: Follow the directions for each item. Be sure to use whatever punctuation is required.

1. Write a direct quotation about holding hands. Then change it to an indirect quotation.

Direct: ______________________________

____

Indirect: ______________________________

____

 Name: ____________________ *Date:* ____________________

2. Write an exclamation about getting a surprisingly low grade on an examination.

____

____

____

3. Using hot dogs as your subject, write two complete sentences that can be joined by a semicolon.

____

____

____

4. Write a direct question about the closing of a local factory. Then change it to an indirect question.

Direct: ______________________________________

____

Indirect: ____________________________________

____

5. Using a dash for emphasis, write a sentence about a law that you think is unfair.

____

____

____

6. Using T-shirts as your subject, write two complete sentences that can be joined by a colon.

____

____

7. Using an interrupter, write a sentence in which you define an intelligent person. Use parentheses to set off the interrupter.

____

____

Name: ______________________ Date: ______________________

8. Use a complete sentence to state the title of your favorite poem or song.

9. Write a sentence about your three closest friends, giving each one's name and special qualities. Be sure to use semicolons for clarity.

10. In a complete sentence, list at least three of the changes that happen to a person who owns a car for the first time. Use a colon to direct attention to your points.

11. Using direct quotations, present a three-line dialogue between a teacher and a student who wants permission to hand in a report late. For each line, identify the speaker in a different place in the sentence.

12. Write a brief note to your sweetheart explaining why you have had to cancel your date suddenly. Use three common abbreviations and three marks of punctuation that are appropriate in a letter.

 Name: ______________________ Date: ______________

13. Write a direct question about private citizens applying to be passengers on American space shuttles. Then change it to an indirect question.

Direct: ______________________________

____

Indirect: ______________________________

____

14. Using traffic jams as your subject, write two complete sentences that can be joined by a semicolon.

____

____

15. Using the cost of groceries as your subject, write two complete sentences that can be joined by a colon.

____

____

16. Using dashes to set off an interrupter, write a sentence about ghosts.

____

____

17. Write a direct quotation about teenagers in trouble. Then change it to an indirect quotation.

Direct: ______________________________

____

Indirect: ______________________________

____

18. Write a sentence about your favorite candy, using parentheses to set off an interrupter.

____

____

EXERCISE 8h: First use the chart below to find out what number you are. Then to find out what your number means, add all necessary punctuation and capital letters to the paragraphs that follow so that sensible sentences are created. Be sure to include all marks of punctuation presented in this chapter.

FIND OUT THE TRUTH ABOUT YOURSELF!

Using the most familiar form of your name, turn each letter into a number as listed:

1	2	3	4	5	6	7	8
A	B	C	D	E	U	O	F
I	K	G	M	H	V	Z	P
Q	R	L	T	N	W		
J		S			X		
Y							

Now add the numbers!

(If your total has more than one digit, add the digits until you get one number.)

Sample: P A T T Y M O O R E
8+1+4+4+1 4+7+7+2+5= 43

Since 4+3 = 7, SEVEN will tell the truth about Patty Moore.

although it is based on a complicated historical system numerology can provide an easy form of enjoyment for us today numerologists believe that a persons character is contained in the letters of his or her name how well do the following numerological descriptions fit you your family and your friends

if your number is one you are a human dynamo you are independent forceful ambitious and inventive when people do what you want you can be kind and generous on the other hand you have a violent temper and can be quite nasty if you are opposed

the number two an evil and female number has all the opposite characteristics people whose names add up to two make good servants for they enjoy being subservient quiet and helpful however they also have some negative qualities cruelty and dishonesty

 Name: ____________ Date: ____________

three which is the luckiest number belongs to charming sophisticated people who easily make money and conquests in love because they are anxious to gain the approval of their peer group they tend to lavish their efforts wastefully an American numerologist states they prefer opera to jazz when living true to their higher nature

four the number of the earth is very gloomy and belongs to people who are lethargic and conventional they may seem calm and composed on the surface but there may be violent eruptions of feeling underneath unfortunately four is the number of disappointment and defeat it does not hold out much prospect of success dont you know an unlucky Four

jumping from one project to another those whose number is five are clever energetic and impulsive they are in addition known for their mental and physical agility because five is the number of sex the word sex adds to five they have great love-lives whenever you are near a Five you can be sure of one thing he or she will be bragging a great deal

people with the number six are reliable and kindly and at the same time are also gossipy and narrow-minded their interests always lie in the same direction the home like the number four six belongs to those who are peaceful and conventional lets have peace they will insist strife can only lead to our downfall

seven belongs to scholarly philosophical people they value things of the mind are uninterested in money and often seem to be serious and dignified they also dislike other peoples opposition to their ideas although the Sevens ideas are good other people are as a rule left in a state of confusion

by contrast eight stands for involvement in the workings of everyday life to forge ahead to success people with this number must work feverishly and with great concentration when worldly success is achieved it is usually in one of three areas money-making business or politics some famous people with the number eight are John F Kennedy the late President Frank Sinatra the singer and actor and Michael Jackson the teen idol wouldnt you agree that they all fit the description of an Eight

nine which is the number of high spiritual achievement belongs to those who are energetic emotional and passionate moreover they have a great sense of duty to others this feeling in turn creates an intense hatred of poverty old age and ugliness those with the number nine are often condemned for the same reason wildness according to a well-known numerologist they may also undergo many operations by a surgeons knife

in his article Youre Ruled by Your Name JD Krank MD presents a rather convincing argument in favor of numerology its true he admits many scientists think that its just a numbers game if they took the time to determine their own numbers however they might discover some essential truths about themselves

EXERCISE 8i: REFRESHER

1. Make any corrections that will improve the effectiveness of the following introduction and conclusion.
2. Plan ahead by listing three main ideas.
3. Correct any errors in verb agreement.

What We Can Do to Cut Down on Waste

Introduction

Although the population of the United States account for only 5 percent of the earth's inhabitants, each year Americans consumes nearly half of the world's production of raw materials, and we creates 300,000,000 tons of solid wastes. If we continues to use up our natural resources at this rate, we will eventually run out of them and, at the same time, we will have filled all of our garbage dumps to overflowing. But we can prevent these problems by taking the necessary steps to cut down on waste in our society. In my essay, I will discuss some of these steps.

Main Body I. ______________________________

Main Body II. ______________________________

Main Body III. ______________________________

Conclusion

Of course, I has to admit that I doesn't know very much about this topic. But I thinks that if we all followed my suggestions, America would no longer be a wasteful society.

 Name: ______________________ Date: ______________________

SPRINGBOARDS TO WRITING

Using your knowledge of the writing process, explained on pages 12–14, write a paragraph or essay related to this chapter's central theme, *our materialistic society*, which is introduced on pages 268–272.

PREWRITING

To think of topics to write about, look at the two advertisements, read the essay, and answer the questions that follow each. If you prefer, select one of the writing springboards below. (All paragraph numbers refer to the essay that starts on page 270.) To develop your ideas, use the prewriting techniques described on pages 15–20.

WRITING A PARAGRAPH (For help, see the Pointers on page 31.)

1. ________________ is one product that is a waste of money.
2. Junk mail should (should not) be banned.
3. A law requiring consumers to pay a deposit on soda and beer bottles is (is not) a good idea.
4. Does every teenager deserve a car? (See ¶'s 6 & 7.)
5. I will never forget a time when I wasted my money foolishly.

WRITING AN ESSAY (For help, see the Pointers on page 35.)

6. Disposable Products: Convenience or Waste?
7. Today's Consumer Is Being Cheated!
8. I Am (Am Not) Wasteful
9. Agree or disagree: ". . . many *things* could disappear from our lives and leave us not in a state of economic recession, but in a far healthier reality—good for body and soul." (See ¶ 9.)
10. The "Things" I Would Like to See Disappear from American Society
11. New "Things" I Would Like to See Invented
12. I Am (Am Not) a Materialist
13. Material Things I Treasure: What They Mean to Me
14. People Can Become Controlled by Their Possessions
15. How Can Consumers Protect Themselves Against Inferior Products?
16. Should Pornography Be Banned?
17. Agree or disagree: We live in "a profligate and sick society." (See ¶ 10.)

YAHOO! I got a "96" on my Biology Final Exam!!
You DID...?!? I thought that Biology was your worst subject!
IT WAS!! But I discovered a NEW METHOD for getting high marks on final exams!
What method is that??
I make use of VISUAL AIDS!
Gee! That's sort of old fashioned!! How do you employ that method to pass a Biology Final??
I COPY from the guys next to me!!

The world is getting really rotten these days! There's no honesty left! There are no more scruples! You can't TRUST anybody any more!!
This morning, somebody passed me some funny money... a bogus bill... a counterfeit twenty!!
Really...?? Show it to me!!
I can't!
I got rid of it at the Supermarket!!

nine

"The truly amazing thing about our new and improved product is that it's seventy-three per cent more effective than our previous product, which, in turn, was eighty-five per cent more effective than our original product, which, it must be admitted, wasn't really effective at all."

SPRINGBOARDS TO THINKING

For informal, not written, response . . . to stimulate your thinking

1. What is the underlying message in the top cartoon panel on the opposite page? Why do some students cheat on tests? What is your frank opinion of people who cheat on tests? Would you cheat on a test? Why or why not?
2. What is the underlying message of the bottom cartoon panel on the opposite page? Is behavior like that shown common today? Why or why not?
3. What is the underlying message in the cartoon above?
4. In general, do you think most people you know personally are honest or dishonest in their dealings with you? In their dealings with stores? In their dealings with government (paying taxes, applying for unemployment insurance or welfare, etc.)? Explain your answers to each question.
5. In general, do you think that most politicians and government officials are honest? Why or why not?

Honesty: Is It Going Out of Style?

STACIA ROBBINS

(1) • In the spring of 1980, students from five schools faced a New York State grand jury for allegedly selling advance copies of state Regents exams.

• A college student quickly became an ex-student when he turned in a term paper with the purchase receipt for it still inside the pages.

• A clerk ran his own Christmas cards through the office postage meter. He was found out when he sent one to the company treasurer.

• Travelers ripped off so many towels last year that it cost a major motel chain $3 million to replace them.

• FBI undercover agents, posing as representatives of Arab businessmen, offered bribes for favors to several members of Congress. As a result, six Congressmen, so far, have been indicted on bribery charges.

Reports like these may prompt a person to ask, "Is anybody truly honest?" And, occasionally, the answer appears to be "No!" As disclosures of cheating, lying, bribery, embezzlement, and fraud crowd our newspaper pages and TV news, it seems that honesty is a rapidly vanishing value. But, is that really so? Is dishonesty more widespread now than it was 20 . . . 50 . . . 100 years ago? If so, what's behind it?

(2) When the Gallup organization recently polled high school students on whether they had ever cheated on exams, 61 percent said they had cheated at least once. It can be argued that such a response may not mean much. After all, most students have, at one time or other, been faced with the temptation to peek at a neighbor's test paper. And students can be very hard on themselves in judging such behavior. However, there are other indications that high school cheating may be on the rise.

(3) More and more states are requiring students to pass competency tests in order to receive their high school diplomas. And many educators fear that an increase in the use of state exams will lead to a corresponding rise in cheating. They cite the case of students in New York State who faced criminal misdemeanor charges for possessing and selling advance copies of state Regents examinations. Approximately 600,000 students take the Regents exams. And it proved impossible to determine how many of them had seen the stolen tests. As a result, 1,200 principals received instructions from the State Education Commissioner to look for *unusual scoring patterns* that would show that students had the answers beforehand. This put a cloud over the test program. Students making special efforts in preparing

for particular exams ran the risk of getting "unusual scores" and thus being suspected of cheating. This showed that a single cheating incident can have a ripple effect—touching the lives of people who had nothing to do with it. Educators in New York are not the only ones worried. If students can figure out a way to steal closely guarded exam papers in New York State, they can steal them in other states as well. If students are worried enough about their test scores to cheat in New York, they're equally nervous in Idaho or Connecticut.

(4) Cheating is now considered to be a major problem in colleges and universities. How to cope with it has become a favorite topic of conversation at faculty meetings and conferences. Several professors say they've dropped the traditional term paper requirement. Why? Many students buy prewritten term papers. And faculty members say they can't track down all the cheaters anymore. "I may be wrong," said one professor wistfully, "but I think the situation has gotten worse in the past few years. I used to catch students making up footnotes. Today they simply buy the whole paper."

(5) Some college faculty members across the nation have decided to do more than talk about the rise in student cheating. For instance, professors of the Department of Psychology at the University of Maryland launched a campaign to clamp down on one form of cheating. As 409 students filed out of their exam in *Introduction in Psychology,* they found all but one exit blocked. Proctors (monitors) asked each student to produce an ID card with an attached photo. Students who said they'd left theirs in the dorm or at home had a mug shot taken. The purpose of the campaign was to flush out "ringers," students who take tests for other students. The majority of students at the University of Maryland applauded the faculty strategy. The campus newspaper editorialized, "Like police arresting speeders, the intent is not to catch everyone but rather to catch enough to spread the word."

(6) With today's growing awareness of dishonest practices, it is sometimes implied that in the "good old days" Americans were better, happier and more honest. Were they more honest? Maybe yes, a long time ago when life was very different from what it is today. Long ago, all schoolchildren knew the story of how Abraham Lincoln walked five miles to return a penny he'd overcharged a customer. It's the kind of story we think of as myth. But in the case of Lincoln, the story is true . . . unlike the story of George Washington and the cherry tree. Washington's first biographer, Parson Weems, invented the tale of little George saying to his father, "I cannot tell a lie. I did it with my ax." What is important in both stories, however, is that honesty was seen as an important part of the American character. And these are just two stories out of many. Students in the last century usually didn't read "fun" stories. They read stories that taught moral values. Such stories pointed out quite clearly that children who lied, cheated, or stole came to bad ends. Parents may have further reinforced those values. It's difficult to know. We do know that children didn't hear

their parents talk of cheating the government on income taxes—there weren't any.

(7) A clue as to why Americans may have been more honest in the past lies in the Abe Lincoln story. Lincoln knew his customer. They both lived in a hamlet. Would a check-out person at a large supermarket return money to a customer? It's less likely. On the other hand, would overnight guests at an inn run by a husband and wife steal towels? It's less likely. Recently, a woman who works as a consumer advocate "admitted" that she peels off the higher price stickers to expose the earlier, lower price stickers on many food items. She does that at her local supermarket. But she never does the same thing at her corner delicatessen. "I couldn't do that to Louie," she says. She knows Louie. She doesn't know the owners of the big supermarkets. Perhaps this tells us that people need to know one another to be at their honest best.

(8) Some critics of American society say that dishonesty is also rampant in the Federal government. One example they cite took place during March and April, 1980. For a whole month, they say, the United States lied to its allies. Cyrus Vance, who was then Secretary of State, was given the task of telling Great Britain, Japan, France, West Germany and others that the United States would not take military action against Iran as long as we had the cooperation of our allies. Secretary of State Vance knew that the raid to get out the American captives was already planned while he was talking to our allies. But he also knew that the reason for this deliberate lying was to save lives. The primary purpose of the deception was not to trick our allies but to mislead the Iranian kidnappers so that a rescue attempt could take place. Many students of ethics believe that lying for the sake of one's country is justified—in certain cases. In this case, having lied for the sake of his country, Secretary Vance secretly wrote a letter of resignation before the raid took place. By submitting his resignation before the raid, he showed that the result had nothing to do with his resignation. It can be said that former Secretary of State Vance deceived other governments only for humanitarian reasons. Then, once he had lied, he resigned. In that case, it is argued, lying may be justified. Without the deception, the rescue mission could not have taken place.

(9) Of course, dishonesty in government—at local, state and national levels—does not always have such noble reasons. A prime example is the so-called Watergate affair. During President Nixon's first term (1969–73), a Committee to Reelect the President was formed. The committee is said to have authorized a group of men to break into the Democratic national headquarters in the Watergate hotel. The idea was to take a peek at the files of the Democratic party. When the burglars were caught, many politicians began scrambling to cover up the story. And President Nixon may have been involved. Most Americans were surprised and outraged by news of the break-in and cover-up. But many Europeans were surprised at our surprise. Some European observers explained that they tend to think of lying, cheating, deception and corruption as part of politics and government.

(10) The vast majority of Americans still believe that honesty is an important part of the American character. For that reason, there are numerous watchdog committees at all levels of society. Although signs of dishonesty in school, business and government seem much more numerous in recent years than in the past, could it be that we are getting better at revealing such dishonesty? There is some evidence that dishonesty may ebb and flow. When times are hard, incidents of theft and cheating usually soar. And when times get better such incidents tend to go down.

(11) Cheating in school also tends to ebb and flow. But it doesn't seem linked to the economy. Many educators feel that as students gain confidence in themselves and their abilities, they are less likely to cheat. Surprisingly, some efforts to curb cheating may actually encourage cheating—a person may feel "they don't trust me anyway," and be tempted to "beat the system." Distrust can be contagious. But, so can trust!

(12) Then there's always that small voice called conscience whispering in everyone's ears. The United States Treasury even gave that name to a special fund—back in 1811. It was started when an anonymous citizen sent in $5, perhaps to ease his conscience over some affair. Contributions have been steady ever since. A nickel was sent in by a boy who found it on the street. But most contributions are much more substantial than that. At the end of last year the fund stood at $3,824,486.42. Contributions to the fund often come with a conscience-easing letter like this: "Here's $6,000 I owe for back taxes. I haven't been able to sleep nights. If I still can't sleep, I'll send you the rest."

READING SURVEY

1. *Main Idea*

What is the central theme of the essay?

2. *Major Details*

a. What objection might be made for requiring high school students to take competency tests before receiving their diplomas?

b. What is learned from stories about the high moral values of George Washington, Abraham Lincoln, and others?

c. What are the two examples of dishonesty in the Federal government given by critics of American society?

3. *Inferences*

a. Read paragraph 3 again. Why do you suppose more and more states are requiring students to pass competency tests in order to receive their high school diplomas?

b. Read paragraph 12 again. What is implied about the honesty of the taxpayer who returned $6,000 in back taxes?

4. *Opinions*

a. Read paragraph 6 again. Do you think that people were more honest in the "good old days"? Explain.
b. From your personal experience and observations, do you think Americans today are honest? Explain.

VOCABULARY BUILDING

Lesson One: The Vocabulary of Dishonesty

The essay "Honesty: Is It Going Out of Style?" by Stacia Robbins includes words that are useful when you are discussing dishonesty.

allegedly	(paragraph 1)	**proctors**	(5)
bribes	(1) . . . **bribery** (1)	**moral values**	(6)
embezzlement	(1)	**ethics**	(8)
fraud	(1)	**deceived**	(8) . . . **deception** (8)
temptation	(2)	**corruption**	(9)

Dishonest people are said to have **allegedly**—supposedly—done something wrong if clear proof is not available.

Dishonest people might take **bribes**—gifts of money or other things of value in return for doing something wrong or illegal. People who engage in **bribery** give or take bribes.

Dishonest people might engage in **embezzlement**—using fraud (see below) to steal money that has been entrusted to them.

Dishonest people might commit **fraud**—trickery and lying to cheat honest people out of their property.

Dishonest people usually cannot resist **temptation**—the powerful attraction or tendency to do something against their better judgment.

Dishonest people find it difficult to cheat on tests if **proctors**—monitors or supervisors of examinations—are watching.

Dishonest people rarely have a sense of **moral values**—social standards built on principles of right and wrong as defined by the society.

Dishonest people rarely think about **ethics**—standards of conduct and judgment based on society's view of what is right and what is wrong.

Dishonest people often engage in **deception**—the act of making people believe what is not true. When people are **deceived,** they are misled by dishonest people who want personal gain from the deception.

Dishonest people often are involved in **corruption**—bribery (see above) or similar dishonest dealings or behavior that is wicked and evil.

EXERCISE 9a: Using the vocabulary words in the lesson, fill in the blanks.

1. When the shortage of funds was uncovered, the cashier was suspected of ______________ although she had been a loyal, long-time employee.
2. Religious leaders usually have excellent ______________ which inspire other people.
3. In some countries, police officials expect ______________ before releasing people who have committed minor offenses.
4. A magician has to be a master of the art of ______________ when pulling rabbits out of a hat.
5. Although most large stores have elaborate security measures, some people cannot resist the ______________ to shoplift.
6. The student, ______________ having cheated on his final exams, was questioned by the dean.
7. Videotapes showing the exchange of money have been used to support charges of ______________ against some business and government leaders.
8. The ______________ of a doctor can be challenged by a review board if he or she has a history of making money by doing unnecessary tests on patients.
9. People who buy jewelry at extremely low prices from a street vendor often discover later that they have been ______________ into buying junk.
10. The students taking the college entrance examination were supervised by very alert ______________.
11. People who use stolen credit cards are committing ______________.
12. The construction company went bankrupt because its top executives were engaged in widespread ______________ that included giving bribes to building inspectors, filing false income tax returns, and charging personal expenses to the company.

Name: ______________________ Date: ______________

Lesson Two: The Vocabulary of Police Work

The essay "Honesty: Is It Going Out of Style?" by Stacia Robbins includes words that are useful when you are discussing police work. Some additional commonly used words about police work are also given below.

indicted	(paragraph 1)	**mug shot**	(5)
disclosures	(1)	**felony**	
misdemeanor	(3)	**larceny**	
suspected	(3)	**arraigned**	
clamp down	(5)		

In police work, for a person to be charged officially with having committed a crime, the person must be **indicted**—formally accused of the crime on the basis of positive legal evidence and usually by the action of a grand jury that requires the person to be brought to trial.

In police work, the case against someone often depends on **disclosures**—information or evidence revealed or uncovered.

In police work, a **misdemeanor** is a relatively minor offense compared with a felony (see below). The penalty is usually a fine and/or less than one year in prison.

In police work, someone is **suspected** of a crime when that person is believed to be guilty although there is little or no evidence to prove the police's guess.

In police work, from time to time the authorities **clamp down** on—become more strict about—certain types of crimes.

In police work, anyone arrested has to permit the taking of a **mug shot**—a photograph of the face of a suspect.

In police work, a **felony** is a major crime such as murder, arson, or rape. The penalty is usually imprisonment in a penitentiary from one year to life; in some states the penalty may be death.

In police work, **larceny** is theft or the unlawful taking and keeping of another's property.

In police work, when a suspect is **arraigned,** the suspect is brought before a court of law to be informed officially of the charges against him or her; after hearing the charges, the suspect states for the record a plea of guilty or not guilty.

EXERCISE 9b: Using the vocabulary words in the lesson, fill in the blanks.

1. Because of an alarming increase in drug-related crime, the mayor ordered the police commissioner to ______________ ______________ on drug dealers.

2. Littering a city's sidewalks is a ______________ for which a person can be fined or, in rare cases, imprisoned.

3. The suspect pleaded not guilty when she was brought to court and formally ______________ for her role in the bank robbery.

4. Since the evidence was clear, the grand jury quickly recommended that the suspect be ______________ for murder.

5. After examining hundreds of photographs, the mugging victim suddenly saw the ______________ ______________ of her attacker.

6. From the ______________ given by many reliable informers, no doubt about the identity of the arsonist existed.

7. ______________ is often committed by drug addicts to support their habits.

8. Tax evasion is a serious ______________ that can lead to a long prison sentence.

9. After his attorney arrives, the ______________ auto thief will be thoroughly questioned by police detectives.

SPELLING

Lesson One: Spelling Demons

Here are some more words that are frequently misspelled. Using the helpful techniques given in Chapter One, be sure to learn these new Demons, which are taken from "Honesty: Is It Going Out of Style?"

approximately	**favorite**	**politician**
attempt	**further**	**possess**
campaign	**increase**	**professor**
committee	**likely**	**psychology**
conscience	**nervous**	**several**
cooperation	**numerous**	**substantial**
doesn't	**organization**	**surprise**
encourage	**particular**	**themselves**

Lesson Two: Plurals

I FORMING PLURALS

a. REGULAR PLURALS. A plural is usually formed by adding *s* to the singular word.

matters
sources
groups

If the plural creates an extra syllable, add *es* to the singular.

churches
lunches
kisses

b. Y PLURALS. If a word ends with a *y* that is preceded by a consonant, change the *y* to *i* before added endings.

centuries
countries
fallacies

If the *y* is not preceded by a consonant, the *y* is not changed.

monkeys
alleys

c. NOUN COMBINATIONS. If the noun combination is more than one word, add *s* or *es* to the most important word.

mothers-in-law
commanders-in-chief
brigadier generals

If the noun combination is written as one word, add *s* or *es* to the end of the word.

spoonfuls
handfuls
stepsons

d. O PLURALS. If a word ends with an *o* that is preceded by a vowel, add *s* to form the plural.

radios
patios
rodeos

If a word ends with an *o* that is preceded by a consonant, add *es* to form the plural.

potatoes
heroes
Negroes

A SPECIAL NOTE: Here are some words you frequently see that are exceptions to the above rule. Notice that many of the exceptions are musical terms borrowed from Italian.

sopranos	altos	autos	Eskimos
pianos	solos	tobaccos	dynamos

e. F PLURALS. Some words ending in *f* or *fe* merely add *s*, whereas some change the *f* or *fe* to *ves*. Because there is no rule for this change, you must learn each word individually and use a dictionary when necessary.

calf—calves
knife—knives
life—lives
roof—roofs
belief—beliefs
safe—safes
self—selves

f. SINGULARS THAT ARE PLURAL. Some words have the same form for both the singular and the plural. Notice that most of these words refer to animals, fish, or grains.

deer	wheat
sheep	rye
bass	series
trout	

g. IRREGULAR ENDINGS. A few common words have irregular plural endings.

man—men
woman—women
tooth—teeth
goose—geese
mouse—mice
ox—oxen

h. FOREIGN WORDS. Many foreign words form their plurals according to the rules of the foreign sources. Some of the plurals you may already know; others you will have to look up in the dictionary.

alumnus—alumni
fungus—fungi
bacterium—bacteria
analysis—analyses
axis—axes
basis—bases
crisis—crises
parenthesis—parentheses
chateau—chateaux

II PROOFREADING FOR THE PLURAL *-S* ENDING

While working on the first draft of a paragraph or essay, you might be so involved in getting your ideas on paper that you may leave out some word endings, especially the *-s* ending for plurals. If you do tend to forget the *-s* ending when it is needed, then you should use the techniques given in this section when you proofread your writing.

a. AS YOU PROOFREAD, WATCH FOR MARKER *WORDS* THAT INTRODUCE EITHER PLURAL NOUNS OR SINGULAR NOUNS.

MARKER WORDS FOR SINGULAR NOUNS	MARKER WORDS FOR PLURAL NOUNS
a	all
an	both
another	few
each	many
every	most
much	several
one	some
that	these
this	those
	two (or any number except one)

In the examples below, notice how the marker words indicate when the plural *-s* ending is and is not needed.

I look forward to *each holiday.*

I look forward to *most holidays.*

☞ *Try It Out*

Fill in each blank with an appropriate noun. Be sure to add the *-s* ending wherever it is needed.

this ____________ every ____________

many ____________ these ____________

nine ____________ another ____________

---

b. AS YOU PROOFREAD, WATCH FOR MARKER *PHRASES* THAT INTRODUCE PLURAL NOUNS.

MARKER PHRASES FOR PLURAL NOUNS

one of	none of
each of	a number of
many of	a group of
all of	a pair of
some of	a bunch of
most of	both of

Notice that two of the marker phrases make use of *each* and *one.* When these words are not combined with *of,* they introduce singular nouns; however, when combined with *of, each* and *one* become marker phrases for plural nouns that refer to members of a group of more than one item.

One problem is crime.

One of the *problems* is crime.

A marker phrase can also be expanded so that several words may come between the marker and the plural noun. When you proofread, be sure to look for the noun at the end of the marker phrase.

One of the *problems* is crime.

One of the city's worst *problems* is crime.

☞ *Try It Out*

Fill in each blank with an appropriate noun. Be sure to add the -*s* ending wherever it is needed.

each of my ______________________ some of your ______________________

a group of ______________________ one of the ______________________

one ______________________ each ______________________

both of ______________________ all of ______________________

Name: ______________________ Date: ______________________

C. NOT ALL PLURAL NOUNS ARE INTRODUCED BY MARKER WORDS OR PHRASES. Therefore, you need to get into the habit of proofreading slowly, taking special note of each noun in a sentence. Whenever you spot a noun, you should immediately ask yourself if it is supposed to refer to more than one person, place, or thing. If it is, have you used the *-s* ending when necessary? For more proofreading suggestions, see page 108.

☞ *Try It Out*

Insert *-s* endings wherever they are needed in the following sentences.

1. A housefly beats each of its wing about 20,000 time a minute.
2. Most dinosaur lived to be more than 100 year old.
3. Ice cream is one of America's favorite dessert; the average person eats about 23 quart of it each year.

EXERCISE 9c: Form the plurals of the following words.

1. politician ____________
2. brush ____________
3. company ____________
4. brother-in-law ____________ ____________
5. echo ____________
6. mouse ____________
7. radius ____________
8. thief ____________
9. class ____________
10. tablespoonful ____________
11. donkey ____________
12. campaign ____________
13. radio ____________
14. loaf ____________
15. box ____________
16. attorney general ____________ ____________
17. parenthesis ____________
18. deer ____________
19. piano ____________
20. knife ____________

 Name: ____________ *Date:* ____________

EXERCISE 9d: Fill in each blank with an appropriate noun. Be sure to add the -*s* ending wherever it is needed.

1. All of the ________________ were gone when I got to class.
2. Most ________________ are not worth what they cost.
3. One of the President's ________________ is missing.
4. The criminal begged for another ________________.
5. Helen sat on a bunch of ________________ by mistake.
6. Some ________________ cheat the consumer.
7. A number of world-famous ________________ make television commercials.
8. These ________________ once belonged to Michael Jackson.
9. Put each of your ________________ on the table.
10. The politician spoke to a group of ________________ last night.
11. Both of your ________________ look weird.
12. The salesperson showed us some of the store's finest ________________.
13. None of my ________________ remembered my birthday.
14. The pair of ________________ split open right on the seam.
15. The comedian told several dirty ________________.
16. This ________________ is better than those ________________.
17. Every ________________ should have at least a few ________________.
18. The overweight plumber ate six ________________ in just ten ________________.
19. Each ________________ takes many ________________ to learn.

Name: ________________ Date: ________________

EXERCISE 9e: Add the plural -*s* ending wherever it is needed in the following paragraphs. In some instances, you may have to change the spelling of a word before adding the plural ending. If necessary, refer to the rules for forming plurals.

Chang and Eng Bunker certainly had fascinating life. Born in Siam (now Thailand) in 1811, the twin boy were connected at their chest by a thick band of flesh about five inch in length. As they grew up, the twin learned to deal with this physical difficulty so that it did not interfere with their ability to walk or their many daily activity. By the time they reached their teen, the boy had become successful merchant who sold duck egg and peacock feather for a living. Then when the twin were eighteen, a foreign businessman convinced them to make personal appearance in other part of the world. Eventually, their travel brought them to the United State, where they held performance in large town and city. Thousand of curious people paid 50 cent apiece to see "The United Brother" and to ask them question. For an additional 12½ cent, the member of the audience could also buy a pamphlet which included photograph of the twin and all of the important detail of their life.

After several year, Chang and Eng stopped making these appearance because they wanted to be regarded as human being, not as freak. So they became naturalized American citizen and bought a farm in North Carolina. There they tamed wild horse, raised farm animal, and grew wheat, corn, oat, and potato. Then when the brother were 31, they married two Southern sister. Eager to enjoy normal married life, Chang and Eng asked some doctor to separate them surgically. But most of the doctor warned that such an operation would probably kill both of the brother. For the first ten year of their marriage, the two couple lived together, but a growing number of argument finally led to the decision that each of the twin should have his own home. Therefore, the men bought a second farm two mile away and set up a regular schedule which required them to move back and forth between the two farm every three day. Over the year, the two couple produced a total of 21 children, all of them physically normal. The brother lived quiet, happy life until they were 63 year old. Then Chang caught pneumonia and died. Less than two hour later Eng died also, most likely of grief and fright about his own health.

Although there were over 100 reported case of physically joined twin before Chang and Eng were born, they achieved the greatest amount of fame. During their lifetime, story about them appeared in hundred of newspaper and magazine. Indeed, the twin were even used as character in play, poem, and novel. And since the death of these wonder of nature, all physically connected youngster are commonly called "Siamese Twin."

 Name: ______________________ *Date:* ______________________

EXERCISE 9f: Using the Spelling Demons in this chapter, fill in the blanks with any missing letters.

1. During political camp ______ns, polit______________________ns at__em__t to win the support of com__it____es that pos______s the power to influence a sub____an_______l number of voters to back a part_______l__r candidate.
2. A well-known p_________ology pro_______sor claims that a person with a guilty con_______en__e is lik____y to experience n__rv_____s tension and perhaps even an incr______e in blood pressure.
3. The English teacher was s____pri__ed to hear her fav______te student say that he d_______n't write well, which could not be f_____ther from the truth.
4. Using num__r____s television advertisements, sev__r__l org__n_______tions have __nc_____r__ged drivers to protect themse_______s by wearing seat belts; unfortunately, these messages have not won the c____p__r__tion of most Americans, for a__pro_____m__t____y 85 percent of all drivers still do not "buckle up for safety."

Name: ______________________________ Date: ____________________

The Unified Essay

A unified essay is one in which all ideas are related and all points link. Many of the skills previously discussed in this book will help you achieve a unified essay. A quick review will illustrate:

Skill Topic	*How It Helps You Achieve a Unified Essay*
Topic Sentence and Paragraph Development	The main idea of each paragraph is clearly stated at its beginning. The rest of the paragraph develops that topic sentence.
Arrangement of Details	Details do not jump around but instead are put in an order that makes sense and flows smoothly.
Paragraph Principles in Essay Writing and Introductions and Conclusions	The total design of the basic expository essay is five paragraphs. The introduction launches the topic, and the conclusion summarizes it. Each of the three main body paragraphs presents and develops one main idea.
Logical Thinking	All points are logical and related so that a sensible train of thought is presented.

These aids help you in the external plan and design of your essay. Equally important, however, are devices of *internal* unity. Internal unity is achieved with the use of certain words and types of wording that link sentences and even paragraphs more successfully. They are:

I Words of Transition

II Key Words: Deliberate Repetition

I Words of Transition

When moving from one idea or example to the next, you might feel that the change is too abrupt.

Too abrupt: People who lose their temper often become irrational. They might get very angry at the wrong person.

Smoother: People who lose their temper often become irrational. For example, they might get very angry at the wrong person.

To avoid abrupt changes, you can use words of transition. A full list of such words is given here in a chart.

When selecting a word of transition, do it with care. Be certain of the type of signal you need—addition, contrast, and so on. Then look through all the words listed in the appropriate signal group until you locate the one most suitable and appropriate for the sentences you wish to connect.

Words of transition should be used sparingly. If you overuse them, your writing will become bulky. Remember that the mind automatically links statements that follow each other. Therefore, you should use words of transition only when they are needed for clarity. As a general, informal rule, a maximum of three or four words of transition should be used in a paragraph of 150 words.

☞ *Try It Out*

Write a complete sentence both before and after the words of transition provided. Be sure that there is a period after the first sentence so that you do not write a run-on.

1. *about motorcycles:* ______________________.

   However, ______________________.

2. *about dictionaries:* ______________________.

   Moreover, ______________________.

3. *about shoplifting:* ______________________.

   In spite of this, ______________________.

WORDS OF TRANSITION

Directions: Two steps should be used when you consult this list. First, determine the type of signal you need. Next, select from that signal group the word that is most appropriate to the meaning of your sentences.

Type of Signal	*Words to Use; Signal Group*
To signal an addition:	in addition, furthermore, moreover, also, equally important,
To signal an example:	for example, for instance, thus, in other words, as an illustration, in particular,
To signal a suggestion:	for this purpose, to this end, with this object,
To signal emphasis:	indeed, truly, again, to repeat, in fact,
To signal granting a point:	while it may be true, in spite of this,
To signal a summary:	in summary, in conclusion, therefore, finally, consequently, thus, accordingly, in short, in brief, as a result, on the whole,
To signal the development of a sequence:	*Value Sequence:* first, second, secondly, third, thirdly, next, last, finally, *Time Sequence:* then, afterward, next, subsequently, previously, first, second, at last, meanwhile, in the meantime, immediately, soon, at length, yesterday, today, tomorrow, eventually, *Space Sequence:* above, across, under, beyond, below, nearby, nearer, opposite to, adjacent to, to the left/right, in the foreground, in the background,
To signal a relationship:	*Similarity:* similarly, likewise, in like manner, *Contrast:* in contrast to, however, but, still, nevertheless, yet, conversely, notwithstanding, on the other hand, on the contrary, at the same time, while this may be true, *Cause and Effect:* consequently, because, since, therefore, accordingly, thus, hence, due to this, as a result,

EXERCISE 9g: Many of the paragraphs written for this book have good examples of the correct use of words of transition. Refer to the following three paragraphs and underline or list all words of transition:

1. Chapter One, page 22, "New cars can be purchased. . . ."
2. Chapter Two, pages 60–61, "Is it really possible. . . ?"
3. Chapter Two, pages 61–62, "A street carnival easily draws. . . ."

EXERCISE 9h: Insert an appropriate word of transition in each blank. In some cases you may decide that no word is needed. Although signal groups are repeated, try to vary the words you select.

1. Some states have strange laws. ________________, in Idaho it is against the law for a person to give someone else a box of candy that weighs more than fifty pounds. ________________, in Alaska it is illegal to look at a moose from the window of an airplane.
2. Birds have very sensitive hearing. ________________, some birds can hear the sound of an earthworm crawling under the grass.
3. Most people think that flowers usually have a beautiful odor. ________________, more than 90 percent of all flowers have either an unpleasant odor or no odor at all.
4. It is easy to determine how far away a thunderstorm is located. ________________, wait for a lightning flash. ________________, count the seconds that pass until you hear the sound of thunder. ________________________, divide the number of seconds by five. ________________, if ten seconds pass between the lightning flash and the thunderclap, the storm is about two miles away.
5. Arnold Rothstein, a famous American gambler in the 1920's, never went out without $100,000 in cash in his wallet. ________________, he was known among gamblers as "The Big Bankroll."

Name: ________________________________ Date: ________________________

6. Although Hetty Green was a millionaire, she was so tight with money that she would resell the morning newspaper after she had finished reading it. ________________, John Elwes was worth a fortune, but he was so eager to avoid spending money that he frequently ate spoiled food that others had thrown out and once even ate a dead bird that a rat had pulled from a river.

7. In 1976 a Los Angeles secretary named Jannene Swift actually married a fifty-pound rock. ________________, the ceremony was witnessed by more than twenty people.

8. More than half of all Americans suffer from occasional headaches. ________________, it is not surprising that about 27 million pounds of aspirin are manufactured in the United States each year.

9. Alcohol can irritate the stomach, damage the liver, and destroy brain cells. ________________, drinking large quantities of alcohol is bad for one's health.

10. A drawing of a pyramid appears on the back of the one-dollar bill. ________________ the pyramid is a triangle with a human eye in it. ________________ the pyramid is a banner that proclaims, "Novus Ordo Seclorum" or "A New Order of the Ages."

11. Law schools turn out about 5,000 more lawyers each year than are actually needed by the legal system. ________________, many parents would still like their children to become lawyers.

12. Blue whales gain weight very quickly. ________________, a young one puts on weight at a rate of two to three hundred pounds a day.

13. In his best-selling book *How to Make Friends and Influence People*, Dale Carnegie offers three major suggestions for making and keeping friends. ________________, become really interested in others and try to see things from their point of view. ________________, be a good listener, letting others do a good deal of the talking. ________________, praise people as much as possible.

Name: ________________________________ *Date:* ________________________

14. We must discourage people from mistreating pets and other animals.

_________________, the federal government should enact laws that provide harsh penalties for those who harm animals of any kind.

15. Americans eat about fifteen pounds of meat per person each month.

_________________, the Japanese eat only about eight ounces of meat per person each month.

EXERCISE 9i: Choose three of these five paragraphs to write. Use separate paper. In writing these paragraphs, do not overuse words of transition; use them only where needed for clarity.

1. Write a paragraph about the costs involved in spending a day at an amusement park. Use appropriate words of transition which signal examples.
2. Write a paragraph describing the view from your bedroom window. Use appropriate words of transition which signal space sequence.
3. Write a paragraph in which you describe the perfect way to celebrate New Year's Eve. Use appropriate words of transition which signal time sequence.
4. Write a paragraph in which you explain how you are different from either your mother or your father. Use appropriate words of transition that signal the relationship of contrast.
5. Write a paragraph which explains why some students cheat on tests. Use appropriate words of transition which signal the relationship of cause and effect.

II Key Words: Deliberate Repetition

Ideas can be connected by the deliberate repetition of certain key words. It is best that the word you choose for deliberate repetition be closely related to the main idea of the paragraph or essay. Of course, while such repetition should occur often enough to achieve unity, it should not be overdone.

a. KEY WORDS IN A PARAGRAPH. Here is a paragraph which was presented in Chapter One as an illustration of a topic sentence developed by example. Notice how key words are used to create internal unity.

Some couples who are determined to reveal their individuality are getting married in unusual ceremonies. For example, a couple employed as linemen for the Southwestern Bell Telephone Company exchanged their wedding vows clad in jeans and climbing equipment atop a brightly decorated telephone pole while the justice of the peace shouted instructions from the ground. Elsewhere, a couple dressed in swimsuits were married on the high diving board of a local swimming pool because they felt that swimming was an important part of their lives. Furthermore, one couple was wed at the firehouse where the groom was a fireman because the bride wanted to make their wedding just a little different. Another wedding was held in a 747 jet as it flew over Washington State at an altitude of 10,000 feet. Thus, the wedding ceremony has become another example of how more and more people are showing their individuality today.

☞ *Try It Out*

Referring to the paragraph above, answer these questions.

1. What word is deliberately repeated throughout the paragraph? ________

   ________ Why is it, more than any other, a key word? ________

   ____

2. What words are used in the paragraph to mean "got married"?

   ________ ________

   Why isn't "got married" merely repeated each time?

   ____

3. What words of transition are used in the paragraph?

   ________ ________

   ________ ________

4. What two words are used in both the first and last sentences—but nowhere else—in the paragraph?

   ________ ________

 Name: ________ Date: ________

b. KEY WORDS TO LINK PARAGRAPHS. Paragraphs, as well as sentences, can be linked with the use of key words. Of course, in an expository essay paragraphs are related to each other as long as they follow the essay pattern presented in Chapter Seven and reviewed in this chapter. However, if you wish to achieve internal unity as well, it is possible to link paragraphs by finding a key word in the final sentence of one paragraph and deliberately repeating it in the opening sentence of the next paragraph. Notice these sentences, which are taken from a five-paragraph expository essay:

Title:	How to Study for an Examination
The last sentence of one paragraph:	In short, studying for an examination is easier if the student has adequate light and a comfortable study area.
The opening sentence of the next paragraph:	While suitable physical surroundings are important, studying for an examination also calls for a disciplined review of class and reading notes.

Try It Out

Referring to the above, answer these questions.

1. How many times is the word *studying* used? ______
2. What other word is deliberately repeated? ______
3. How many times is it repeated? ______
4. Why are both *studying* and the other word you found key words? ______

______

If you wish to link paragraphs, it is useful to employ subordination for one or both of the linking sentences. Use the subordinate section to refer to the idea just finished and the independent section to refer to the new idea you are going to discuss. The following is an example of subordination in a linking sentence which opens a new paragraph:

> While suitable physical surroundings are important, studying for an examination also calls for a disciplined review of class and reading notes.

You can see that the main idea *just finished* concerns the physical surroundings needed for studying for an examination, and the main idea *being introduced* concerns proper review of class and reading notes.

The use of subordination in sentences that link paragraphs will serve as an extra check for unity: Remember that for correct subordination the two ideas must be *logically related, with one idea more important than the other or one idea closely following the other.* Here is another example:

> Although rock music employs intricate sound patterns, country music explores life more directly.

☞ *Try It Out*

Assume that the above is a final sentence of one paragraph which is to link with the next paragraph.

1. What would you guess is the topic of the paragraph being closed?

   ____

2. What would you guess is the topic of the coming paragraph? __________

   ____

3. Would this sentence be an appropriate link if used as the first sentence of a paragraph? ______________________________

   Why or why not? ______________________________

Sentence structures other than subordination can be used for linking sentences. In all linking sentences, the pattern is the same: The topic just finished is mentioned first and the topic being introduced is mentioned second. Here are some examples:

> A problem closely related to crime in the streets is the increase in drug addiction in today's big cities.

> Not only will uncontrolled gambling ruin a person's home life, it will also seriously threaten a person's job.

> For the elderly, health care is as important as an active social life.

 Name: ______________________ *Date:* ______________________

EXERCISE 9j: Many of the paragraphs in this book are good examples of the correct use of key words. Refer to the following three paragraphs and underline all key words.

1. Chapter One, page 30, "The cockroaches that inhabit. . . ."
2. Chapter Two, pages 61–62, "A street carnival easily. . . ."
3. Chapter Seven, page 258, "Many young people who have. . . ."

EXERCISE 9k: For three of the following topic sentences, write a unified paragraph using the deliberate repetition of key words. While such repetition should occur often enough to achieve unity, it should not be overdone. Use your own paper for this assignment.

1. The children of working mothers do (do not) receive enough attention.
2. My grandparents are (were) very much in love.
3. I prefer (do not prefer) to go to a female doctor.
4. When older students return to school, they sometimes have special adjustments to make.
5. Taking care of a very sick person can be a difficult challenge.

EXERCISE 9l: For each of the following you are given the title of an essay and the three main ideas which the essay will cover in its main body paragraphs. Write a linking sentence to start the second main body paragraph and write another linking sentence to start the third main body paragraph. Use your own paper for this assignment.

1. Let the Army Educate You
   Introductory paragraph
   I. technical training
   II. college-level courses
   III. tuition for college after discharge
   Concluding paragraph

2. Word Processors: Will They Replace the Typewriter?
   Introductory paragraph
   I. for business
   II. for professional writers
   III. for students
   Concluding paragraph

3. The Benefits of Owning a Dog
   Introductory paragraph
   I. provides companionship
   II. provides affection
   III. provides protection
   Concluding paragraph

4. Part-Time Work in Fast-Food Restaurants
   Introductory paragraph
   I. low pay
   II. bad hours
   III. lack of advancement opportunities
   Concluding paragraph

5. The Disappearing Small Farmer
   Introductory paragraph
   I. long hours and exhausting work
   II. high expense of modern farming machinery
   III. price competition from larger farms
   Concluding paragraph

EXERCISE 9m: For each of the following you are given the title of an essay and the three main ideas which the essay will cover in its main body paragraphs. Write a linking sentence to end the first main body paragraph and write another linking sentence to end the second main body paragraph. Use your own paper.

1. Are We Alone?
   Introductory paragraph
   I. evidence that there were visitors from outer space in ancient times
   II. recent sightings of Unidentified Flying Objects (UFO's)
   III. testimony of people claiming to have been on UFO's
   Concluding paragraph

2. Our Roads and Bridges Are Falling Apart
   Introductory paragraph
   I. past neglect
   II. current condition
   III. what must be done
   Concluding paragraph

3. Make Your Own Job
   Introductory paragraph
   I. assess your abilities
   II. decide on your possible customers
   III. advertise yourself
   Concluding paragraph

4. The Rewards of Becoming a House-Husband
   Introductory paragraph
   I. changing the pace of life
   II. learning new skills
   III. getting closer to one's children
   Concluding paragraph

5. The Population Explosion Is Serious
   Introductory paragraph
   I. causes hunger and starvation in some countries
   II. overburdens our natural resources
   III. reduces people's living space
   Concluding paragraph

EXERCISE 9n: ESSAY ANALYSIS Answer these questions about the essay "Honesty: Is It Going Out of Style?"

1. In paragraph 2, what words of transition are used to create unity? ______________________________
2. In paragraph 3, what key words are deliberately repeated to create unity? ______________________________
3. In paragraph 6, what key words are deliberately repeated to create unity? ______________________________
4. a. In paragraph 7, what words in the first sentence help to link that paragraph with the preceding one? ______________________________
   b. In the same paragraph, what words of transition are used to create unity? ______________________________
5. In paragraph 8, what words of transition are used to create unity? ______________________________
6. In paragraph 9, what words in the first sentence help to link that paragraph with the preceding one? ______________________________
7. In paragraph 11, what words in the first sentence help to link that paragraph with the preceding one? ______________________________

EXERCISE 9o: REFRESHER

1. Find and correct any comma splices and run-on sentences.
2. Make any necessary corrections in punctuation and capitalization.

a group of milwaukee teenagers known as the 414's has broken into more than 60 business and Government computer systems in the United States and Canada. Using home computers and devices that allow computers to send information over the telephone lines the 414's have managed to gain entry to the computerized records stored at such locations as Los Alamos National Laboratory, Security Pacific National Bank in Los Angeles, and New Yorks Memorial Sloan-Kettering Cancer Center. Officials at Sloan-Kettering revealed that some accounting information had been erased from their computer's memory but that the patients therapy records had not been touched. Executives at many of the companies that have had computer break-ins have refused to reveal the exact nature of the damage, in fact, some companies have not reported computer crimes at all for fear of the bad publicity.

why have the teenagers been committing these illegal acts. For the 414's, breaking into a computer is like climbing a mountain, both of these activities offer an exciting challenge that ends with the thrill of accomplishment. In addition the 414's do not share society's view of morality. As one of the computer hobbyists has stated, Philosophically, we dont believe in property rights." According to this philosophy, the information stored in a computer is not private property it belongs to anyone who has enough skill to uncover it. However, most computer experts insist that these break-ins are not merely harmless games they are actually dangerous destructive crimes.

SPRINGBOARDS TO WRITING

Using your knowledge of the writing process, explained on pages 12–14, write a paragraph or essay related to this chapter's central theme, *honesty*, which is introduced on pages 304–309.

PREWRITING

To think of topics to write about, look at the cartoons, read the essay, and answer the questions that follow each. If you prefer, select one of the writing springboards below. (All paragraph numbers refer to the essay that starts on page 306.) To develop your ideas, use the prewriting techniques described on pages 15–20.

WRITING A PARAGRAPH (For help, see the Pointers on page 31.)

1. Agree or disagree: "As students gain confidence in themselves and their abilities, they are less likely to cheat." (See ¶ 11.)
2. I would (would not) report someone I found cheating on a test.
3. What do you think of the University of Maryland's campaign to clamp down on cheating, as described in paragraph 5?
4. Even a small lie can lead to big problems.
5. Agree or disagree: Anyone caught cheating in high school or college should be permanently expelled.

WRITING AN ESSAY (For help, see the Pointers on page 35.)

6. Is Honesty a "Rapidly Vanishing Value" in America? (See ¶ 1.)
7. Is Honesty Always the Best Policy?
8. My Conscience Is (Is Not) Always My Guide (See ¶ 12.)
9. Why Do Some Students Cheat on Tests?
10. Why Do Some People Lie?
11. Agree or disagree: "Distrust can be contagious, but so can trust." (See ¶ 11.)
12. How Parents Influence Their Children's Values about Honesty
13. Why Do Some People Cheat on Their Income Tax?
14. Most Politicians Are (Are Not) Honest
15. The Government Does (Does Not) Tell Us the Truth
16. Why Do Some People Shoplift?
17. Today's Consumers Are (Are Not) Frequently Cheated

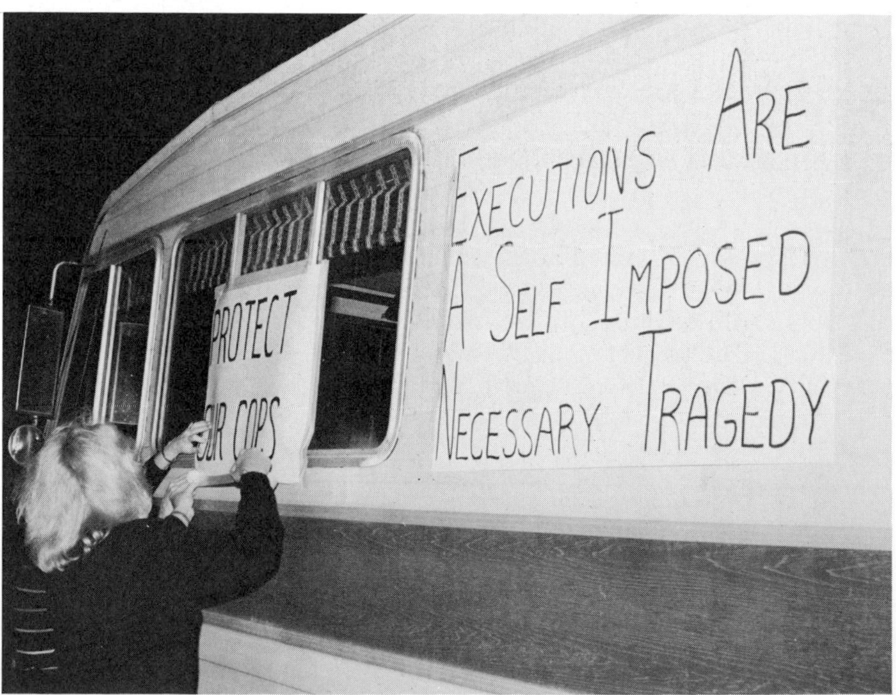

Wide World Photos.

ten

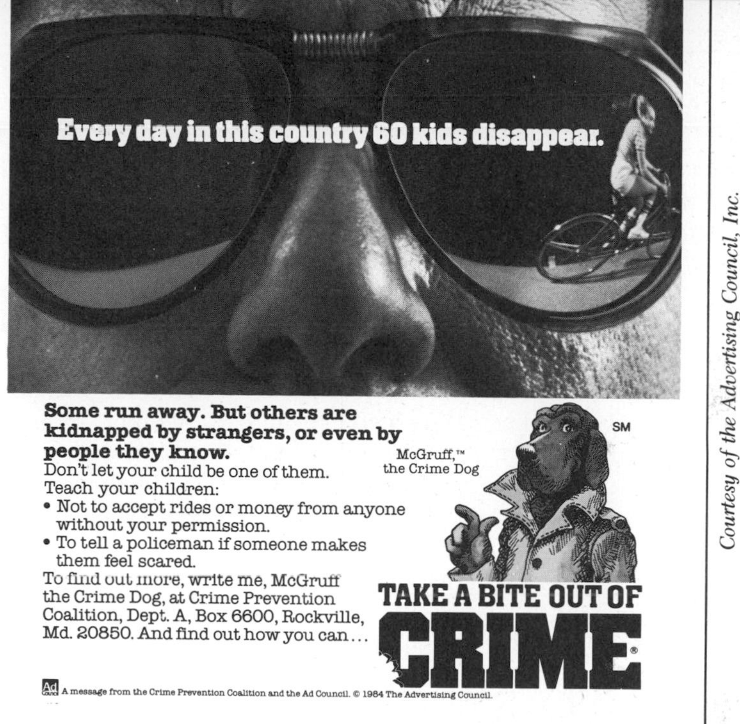

Courtesy of the Advertising Council, Inc.

SPRINGBOARDS TO THINKING

For informal, not written, response . . . to stimulate your thinking

1. What is the story implied by the photograph shown in the advertisement above?
2. Why is child kidnapping more common in the United States today than ever before in its history? Why are most crimes more common today than ever before?
3. Look at the two photographs on the opposite page. They show two sides of what issue related to crime and punishment? What is your position on this issue? Explain.
4. Many crimes are committed by children and teenagers. Do you think children and teenagers should be treated differently from adults by the criminal justice system? Why or why not.
5. If someone you loved were hurt or killed by a criminal, or if someone you loved committed a crime, would your point of view change about any of the questions you just answered? Why or why not?

Reflections on My Brother's Murder

DAVID FINN

(1) Several months ago, my brother, Herbert Finn, a prominent civil rights lawyer from Phoenix, Arizona, was shot and killed while visiting my family in New York. We had been to the opera—Herbert, his wife, my wife, my sister, my daughter, and I—and the six of us drove to the quiet residential neighborhood of Riverdale, where my daughter lives. I left the car for a few minutes to take her to her apartment. While I was gone, several young black men held up the rest of the family, taking pocketbooks from my wife and sister and grabbing my brother's wallet as he took out his money for them. Although no one is quite sure what happened, we think my brother reached out to retrieve the credit cards in his wallet because he was planning to leave the next day on a trip to Egypt and Israel. One impatient robber fired a single .22-caliber bullet, and all of them fled. A moment later I arrived on the scene to find the women screaming and my brother dead.

(2) All that night I repeated four words—*I can't believe it*—so often that they must be imprinted on my brain. The murder took place just after midnight, and we finished with the police interrogation at 5:30 the next morning. My wife and I had a couple of drinks to try to calm our nerves, but the alcohol didn't work. I couldn't stop myself from shivering (although I wasn't cold) and repeating the four words endlessly. In desperation, I took a pad from the drawer next to my bed and wrote "I can't believe it" 26 times, as if writing it out would serve as a cathartic for disbelief. But it was no help. I truly could *not* believe it. I went on repeating the words to myself all through the next day as I sat with my wife, sister, and sister-in-law in three different police stations, going through hundreds of mug shots and answering questions posed by various teams of detectives. While I could not absorb the reality of what had happened, neither could I get the sight of it—the sight of my brother slumped in the back seat—out of my mind.

(3) About two weeks later, four suspects were arrested. Their ages were 19, 17, 17, and 15. Newspaper accounts stated that three of them came from middle-class homes in Mt. Vernon, New York.

(4) Two of the youths confessed. The story they told deepened the crease of incredulity in my brain. It went something like this: One boy borrowed his mother's car to go to a high-school dance. He changed his mind and instead picked up three friends, drove to a pizzeria, then to a disco, and finally went for a ride in Riverdale. As they were cruising, the four boys thought of sticking up an ice-cream store, but by the time they got there it

was closed. Later, they passed our car, saw the people in it, and thought it looked like an interesting target. They pulled into a driveway, and three of them said they'd check our car and be right back. The fourth boy waited, listening to his car radio. A minute later he heard a noise and the three ran back screaming, "Get out of here, get out of here." As they sped away, one of the boys kept asking another, "Why did you do it? Why did you shoot him?" "I had to," he answered and then said reassuringly, "Don't worry about it." They argued for a while. Finally, one of them distributed $44 to each of the others. "You shot [this guy] for less than $200? That's stupid," one of the boys remarked. "Don't worry," the murderer insisted.

(5) As told by the two who confessed, the casualness of the whole incident—taking my brother's life to get some money for fun—makes the tragedy all the more unbearable. It was apparently just a matter of going after easy pickings and striking down a victim who might have been trying to hold out. It was like swatting a fly. That was all there was to it.

(6) In the months that followed, the shock waves of what we initially took to be a private nightmare radiated farther than any of us could have imagined. People from all over the world called and wrote to give some expression to the pain they felt. I could almost hear the whispers echoing in the atmosphere as anybody who had the slightest connection to us passed the story on. What dumbfounded acquaintances was the senselessness, the chilling irony, of Herbert's death. Dying from an illness is no better than dying from a robber's bullet, but we learn to accept death from disease as fate, while murder threatens to undermine the assumption that man can control societal forces.

(7) A friend who served for many years as Chief of Police in the Bronx, Anthony Bouza, has likened the unchecked spread of crime to a cancer that will destroy our society unless we attack its cause—poverty and unemployment. People who can't speak the language, can't get jobs, and can't find decent places to live are excluded from society. They come to feel that robbing and killing are the only ways they can survive. Desperation, Chief Bouza believes, overwhelms morality and the law. What is worse, he says, is the more recent development. As the poor increasingly resort to their desperate solutions, more fortunate youths adopt the same measures to accomplish their own ends. Robbing and killing fill the emptiness caused, not by hunger, but by boredom and a lack of purpose in their lives. The cancer that begins in the burned-out buildings of our cities metastasizes to the rest of society.

(8) A number of people, reacting to my brother's death, are seeking cures for the disease Bouza describes. Some say they will work for stricter gun-control laws. Others want tougher sentences for convicted criminals. Still others want to reinstate the death penalty. And some want to work for a stronger and better equipped police force. But it seems to me that these efforts, many of which are clearly necessary, are unlikely to rid us of the cancer; they treat the symptoms, not the disease. The cancer itself can be arrested, I believe, only if we minister to its root cause. We must stop the decay in our cities and the deterioration of our values. We must have faith

in our own power to cure the disease and the determination to exercise that power.

(9) The shock of my brother's death has in itself given rise to some innovative ideas that illustrate the kind of determination called for. While talking about Herbert's death, for example, a friend who heads an influential foundation raised the question of relating education to work opportunities. He proposed an unusual plan for a pilot project: If a small group of underprivileged students would promise to finish their college education, he would arrange jobs for them in advance, guaranteeing them positions on graduation. The companies for which they would work would pay only half their salaries, and his foundation would pay the rest. If the project succeeds, he would encourage other foundations to do the same thing for thousands of young people. His idea could be the small beginning of a major accomplishment.

(10) My brother's death was cruel, inhuman, personally devastating; but I do not want to believe it was futile. Taking initiatives to cope with the disease rather than despairing at its ravages is the only sane response to our tragedy. If we who have been subjected to such horrors can show the world that we have not lost our faith, if out of our pain we can help to awaken the forces within our society that are capable of curing the disease, his death and the deaths of other martyrs of the streets will not have been in vain.

READING SURVEY

1. *Main Idea*

What is the central theme of the essay?

2. *Major Details*

a. How does the Chief of Police in the Bronx, Anthony Bouza, explain the unchecked spread of crime?
b. Why does David Finn think that stricter gun control laws, tougher prison sentences, and the reinstatement of the death penalty cannot cure the "cancer" that pervades our society?
c. A friend of the Finns who heads an influential foundation proposed an unusual plan for a pilot project as one possible solution to the crime problem. What was his plan?

3. *Inferences*

a. Read paragraph 2 again. Why did David Finn find it impossible to accept the reality of what happened?
b. Read paragraph 7 again. Why should emptiness, boredom, and lack of purpose exist in the lives of "more fortunate youths"?

4. *Opinions*

a. Read paragraph 2 again. David Finn thought that it would be "cathartic" to write "I can't believe it" over and over. Does writing personal notes to yourself or keeping a personal diary sometimes help you cope? Why or why not?

b. Read paragraph 9 again. Besides the pilot program proposed, what else might be done to control random youthful violence?

VOCABULARY BUILDING

Lesson One: The Vocabulary of Despair

The essay "Reflections on My Brother's Murder" by David Finn includes words that are useful when you are discussing despair.

desperation	(paragraph 2)	**devastating**	(10)
incredulity	(4)	**futile**	(10)
tragedy	(5)	**despairing**	(10)
dumbfounded	(6)	**ravages**	(10)
undermine	(6)	**martyrs**	(10)

People who suffer from feelings of despair feel a total loss of hope. People who are **despairing** are deeply sad and discouraged by this loss of hope.

People who suffer from feelings of despair sometimes are overcome with **desperation** or feelings of extreme hopelessness and depression that can lead to violence.

People who suffer from feelings of despair sometimes view life with **incredulity** or a general unwillingness or inability to believe what is going on.

People who suffer from feelings of despair often have experienced a **tragedy** or a disaster or terribly sad event.

People who suffer from feelings of despair often react to life by being **dumbfounded** or speechless because of shock or great amazement.

People who suffer from feelings of despair often have experienced something that **undermined** them or weakened them in ways that are not easily noticed but are nevertheless very damaging.

People who suffer from feelings of despair often experience a hopelessness that is **devastating** or overwhelmingly destructive.

People who suffer from feelings of despair often feel that their efforts are **futile** or useless, worthless, and complete failures.

People who suffer from feelings of despair often feel that they are victims of life's **ravages** or a series of destructive troubles that create much damage over an extended period of time.

People who suffer from feelings of despair sometimes see themselves as **martyrs** or people who choose to or who are forced to sacrifice themselves or suffer in order to arouse feelings of guilt or pity in others.

EXERCISE 10a: For each word in italics below, circle the definition closest in meaning.

1. *Desperation* is a feeling of
   a. uncertainty.
   b. hopelessness and depression.
   c. delight.
   d. optimism and strength.

2. *Incredulity* is
   a. a lack of self-control.
   b. a willingness to understand another point of view.
   c. an unwillingness to believe what is going on.
   d. the ability to take charge.

3. A *tragedy* is a
   a. terribly sad event.
   b. violent act of nature.
   c. Broadway show.
   d. close race.

4. A person who is *dumbfounded* can be described as
   a. having a low I.Q.
   b. being speechless because of shock or amazement.
   c. having been abandoned as an infant.
   d. being deaf and mute.

5. To *undermine* something is to
   a. dispose of it by burying it at sea.
   b. improve its performance.
   c. temporarily change its appearance.
   d. weaken it in small, hardly noticeable stages.

6. A *devastating* event is
   a. barely able to be observed.
   b. delightful to watch.
   c. overwhelmingly destructive.
   d. easily predicted.

7. A *futile* effort is
   a. of great value.
   b. of questionable value.
   c. unknown to others.
   d. a complete failure.

8. A *despairing* person is likely to be
   a. deserving.
   b. cheerful and energetic.
   c. unattractive.
   d. sad and discouraged.

 Name: ______________________________ *Date:* ____________________

9. Life's *ravages* can best be described as
   a. damaging troubles over an extended period of time.
   b. a person's accomplishments over a lifetime.
   c. a person's inherited characteristics.
   d. the standards by which people are judged.

10. *Martyrs* are people who
   a. seek a place in history.
   b. sacrifice themselves to arouse others.
   c. hurt others to advance themselves.
   d. die in accidents.

Lesson Two: The Vocabulary of Hope

The essay "Reflections on My Brother's Murder" by David Finn includes words that are useful when you are discussing hope.

retrieve	(paragraph 1)	**minister to**	(8)
cathartic	(2)	**innovative**	(9)
societal forces	(6)	**initiatives**	(10)
morality	(7)	**cope**	(10)
reinstate	(8)		

To regain feelings of hope about society, people have to be able to **retrieve**—get back or recover—their positive feelings about society.

To regain feelings of hope about society, people might do something **cathartic**—action that leads to the reduction of emotional tensions, fears, or problems.

To regain feelings of hope about society, people need to feel confident in and comfortable with **societal forces**—the controls and influences that make our society function.

To regain feelings of hope about society, people need to see the positive aspects of society's **morality**—the principles concerning what behavior is right or wrong.

To regain feelings of hope about society, people need to **reinstate**—instate again or put back into its former position—their confidence in society.

To regain feelings of hope about society, people might **minister to**— give help to or attend to the wants of—people in need.

To regain feelings of hope about society, people can try to come up with ideas that are **innovative**—that introduce new devices or methods of doing things.

To regain feelings of hope about society, people can try to undertake **initiatives**—the first steps toward creating a new or original idea or method.

To regain feelings of hope about society, people need to know how to **cope**—to face up to and deal successfully with problems or troubles.

EXERCISE 10b: Match each classified ad with a vocabulary word from this lesson.

CLASSIFIED ADS

HELP WANTED

LOST PROPERTY our speciality. Do you have the mental ability to save or recover lost things? Apply in person to GOTCHA ASSOCIATES on Memory Lane.

1. ______________________

ARE YOU A SELF-STARTER? We need someone who can take the first steps needed to come up with a new idea. Begin by calling ACTION, INC. right away.

2. ______________________

VACATION SPOTS

CREATIVE PEOPLE are our business. If you like to come up with new ideas or methods, you will find our setting an inspiration. Send for our brochure about beautiful DaVINCI ISLAND.

3. ______________________

GIVE OF YOURSELF! Come and help serve the needs of others less fortunate than you. You will find your reward within yourself. CAMP HAND-IN-HAND.

4. ______________________

LIKE TO STUDY about the controls and influences that shape our society? Attend our seminars and live on our lovely organic farm, THE HUMAN CONDITION. Discounts for families.

5. ______________________

SELF-HELP COURSES

RELEASE your emotional tensions and reduce the fears that trouble you. We guarantee that you will feel better afterwards. Taught by Professor P. Urge.

6. ______________________

 Name: ______________________ Date: ______________________

DO YOU KNOW THE DIFFERENCE between right and wrong? Go on a retreat and learn the principles of good judgment that govern proper behavior. Send for information from THE ETHICAL ASSOCIATION.

7. ______________________

LEARN TO DEAL SUCCESSFULLY with problems or troubles you encounter. You will feel more in command of your life. Come to THE SUCCESS INSTITUTE.

8. ______________________

GET BACK THAT OLD FEELING and find your former "you" again. Spend a long weekend at THE RENEWAL FARM.

9. ______________________

SPELLING

Lesson One: Spelling Demons

Here are more words that are frequently misspelled. Using the helpful techniques given in Chapter One, you should make it a point to learn these new Demons, which are taken from "Reflections on My Brother's Murder."

absorb
accomplish
acquaintance
alcohol
apparently
attack
beginning
despair
exercise
fourth
influential
interest
matter
necessary
neighborhood
prominent
response
sentence
succeed
symptom
through
tragedy
various
writing

Lesson Two: To Split or Not to Split

Some word combinations cause a great deal of confusion because the writer is not sure if the words should be joined or separated. In some cases, the written form will depend on how the words are used in the sentence. In other cases, it is necessary to memorize the proper spelling.

I WORDS THAT MAY OR MAY NOT SPLIT. Because the spelling of each of these words will vary according to its meaning, pay special attention to the definitions given.

already (previously)
The movie had already started when I arrived.
all ready (completely prepared)
We are all ready for the work ahead.

altogether (completely)
My answer is altogether different from yours.
all together (in a group)
The children were all together in the park.

anyone (any person at all)
Anyone can count to a hundred.
any one (one person or thing in a specific group)
Any one of these detergents will do the job.

Note: This also applies to: everyone—every one; someone—some one

maybe (perhaps)
Maybe I will join the Peace Corps.
may be (the verb form meaning "might be")
This may be his last public appearance.

II WORDS THAT NEVER SPLIT

another	nearby
bathroom	nevertheless
bedroom	northeast
bookkeeper	percent
cannot	playroom
downstairs	roommate
everything	schoolteacher
granddaughter	yourself

III WORDS THAT ARE ALWAYS SPLIT. Because the English language is so changeable, you should rely on an up-to-date dictionary for the current spelling of a word combination. Below are some of the common word combinations that are still written as two words.

a lot	in fact
all right	in spite
dining room	living room
high school	no one

IV WORDS THAT ARE JOINED BY A HYPHEN. Because there are no rules to cover all the uses of the hyphen, you should rely on a dictionary whenever you are in doubt. There are, however, a few principles to guide you:

a. Use a hyphen to join compound numbers from twenty-one to ninety-nine.

forty-seven	seventy-eight

b. Use a hyphen (or hyphens) to join two or more words that are combined to refer to the same person or thing.

mother-in-law	fighter-bomber
cure-all	court-martial
drive-in	forget-me-not

c. Use a hyphen (or hyphens) to join two or more words that form a single adjective before a noun.

ten-year-old boy	bluish-green eyes
absent-minded professor	first-rate performance
well-known poet	

d. Use a hyphen to join certain prefixes and suffixes to the main word.

co-owner	anti-communist
self-sacrifice	bell-like
ex-president	pro-American

EXERCISE 10c: Underline the correct word from each set of words in parentheses. If necessary, consult a dictionary.

As amazing as it (maybe, may be), more American homes now have television sets than have (bathtubs, bath tubs). According to the most (up to date, up-to-date, uptodate) studies, the majority of these television sets are on for over six hours a day, with the typical viewer spending over (twenty six, twenty-six, twentysix) hours each week in front of the small screen. (In fact, Infact), by the time (some one, someone) reaches the age of eighteen, he or she will have (all ready, already) spent an average of (twenty five, twenty-five, twentyfive) thousand hours—two years, eleven months—watching television. Naturally, all of this viewing has affected (every one, everyone) in many ways.

For example, the (day to day, day-to-day, daytoday) activities of the family have been greatly influenced by the presence of the television set. A poll taken on this very subject found that (fifty five, fifty-five, fiftyfive) (per cent, per-cent, percent) of the families in the study (re-arranged, rearranged) their (meal times, mealtimes) around their favorite programs and that television acted as a (made to order, made-to-order, madetoorder) (baby sitter, baby-sitter, babysitter) in (seventy eight, seventy-eight, seventyeight) (per cent, per-cent, percent) of the families and (re-adjusted, readjusted) the sleeping patterns of sixty (per cent, per-cent, percent) of the families. In (households, house-holds) with two or more sets, family (get togethers, get-togethers, gettogethers) were becoming more and more unusual. (In stead, Instead) of gathering (all together, altogether) around one set in the (living room, livingroom), the members of the family (split up, split-up, splitup) (in to, into) viewing groups. Thus, the (teen-agers, teen agers, teenagers) might have been in the (down stairs, downstairs) (play room, playroom) watching a (night time, nighttime) game show, their parents might have been having a snack in the (dining room, dining-room) while watching a comedy special, and the (grand parents, grandparents) might have been in their (bed room, bedroom) relaxing in (arm chairs, armchairs) while watching a (soap opera, soapopera).

It has also been claimed that television is a safety valve because it helps relieve (anti-social, antisocial) pressures in families that might explode

 Name: ____________ Date: ____________

(with out, without) this (non stop, non-stop, nonstop) electronic entertainment. This point was made in a study in which 184 people living in the (South West, Southwest) were paid to give up television for a year. (With in, Within) a short while after this experiment began, family squabbles flared up, (wife beating, wife-beating) increased, and the individuals' (self control, self-control, selfcontrol) broke down. By the end of five months, the (long suffering, long-suffering, longsuffering) volunteers were (all ready, already) to return to their screens, tensions lessened, and (every thing, everything) seemed (all right, alright) once again. Life was apparently (all together, altogether) too difficult (with out, without) television programs to take the people's minds off (them selves, them-selves, themselves) and their personal problems.

While these programs are helping to relieve the pressures of (every day, everyday) life, the commercials are (brain washing, brain-washing, brainwashing) the viewing audience as no (sales man, salesman) ever could. (In deed, Indeed), most (eighteen year old, eighteen-year-old, eighteen-yearold) viewers have (all ready, already) seen about 350,000 commercials, many of which repeat the same messages over and over again. For instance, a television advertising campaign for McDonald's, the (fast food, fast-food, fastfood) chain, forced (a lot, alot) of us to learn the ingredients in a Big Mac (with out, without) even trying. Similarly, commercials sell politicians like hamburgers or (soap flakes, soapflakes) so that many citizens make almost (every one, everyone) of their voting choices based on which candidate projects the best (over all, overall) image of a (red blooded, red-blooded, redblooded) American rather than on which candidate has the best qualifications. (May be, Maybe) this marketing of a politician as just (an other, another) product seems ridiculous. (Never the less, Never-the-less, Nevertheless), these commercials work, for in a recent election campaign, over $200 million was spent on television advertising.

Thus, television's powerful effect on politics as well as on family life and the release of tension (can not, cannot) be denied. Does this (wide spread, wide-spread, widespread) influence do more harm than good? (No one, No-one, Noone) knows for sure. (How ever, However), time and further research may provide the answer.

EXERCISE 10d: Unscramble the letters in parentheses to form the missing words in each sentence. If necessary, check your spelling with the list of Demons in this chapter.

1. It is (SSCEARYNE) ______________ for us to know the (IOURSVA) ______________ (TOMYMPSS) ______________ of (HOCOALL) ______________ abuse so that we can identify any (AINCESACTANQU) ______________ who (RENTPPA-LYA) ______________ seem to be headed for (GEDTRAY) ______________.
2. A good way of (NNGIINGBE) ______________ an essay is by (INGITWR) ______________ a (NCESENTE) ______________ that will (EESUDCC) ______________ in catching the reader's (TERINEST) ______________.
3. As the (ENTMINPRO) ______________ and (UENFLIALINT) ______________ politician walked (GHTHOUR) ______________ the crumbling (BORGHEIOODHN) ______________, she refused to be overcome by a feeling of (AIRPESD) ______________.
4. The body's (PONSEESR) ______________ to (CISEREXE) ______________ includes an increase in circulation, which helps the blood to (SORABB) ______________ more oxygen.
5. On the (THOURF) ______________ of July, we should not (CKAATT) ______________ our country's weaknesses but instead give thanks that we have the freedom to (LISHACCPOM) ______________ our goals, no (TTMAER) ______________ how unusual they may be.

 Name: ______________ *Date:* ______________

Using the Right Word

Errors in some words, more than others, are often used as yardsticks to measure a person's maturity and level of education. While many such errors are made in everyday speech, they should not be made in formal written English. There are three major yardsticks:

- **I** Comparisons
- **II** Verbs
- **III** Expressions

I COMPARISONS. When you are comparing two things, never use the superlative form. It is reserved for a comparison of three or more things. For example:

Joe is the older of the two brothers.
Joe is the oldest of the three brothers.

For most short words, form the comparative by adding an *-er* ending and form the superlative by adding an *-est* ending. For most longer words (of three syllables or more), form the comparative by using *more* and the superlative by using *most.*

Positive	*Comparative*	*Superlative*
old	older	oldest
green	greener	greenest
fast	faster	fastest
slow	slower	slowest
beautiful	more beautiful	most beautiful
optimistic	more optimistic	most optimistic
easily	more easily	most easily

Some words have irregular comparative and superlative forms:

Positive	*Comparative*	*Superlative*
good, well	better	best
bad	worse	worst
little	less	least
many, much	more	most

☞ *Try It Out*

In the following paragraph correct any errors in forming comparisons. Cross out the error and write the correct form directly above it. If necessary, check your answers in a dictionary.

Mexico City has the unusualest combination of sights. In the heart of the city are some of the most newest and modern hotels and office buildings in the Western hemisphere. These skyscrapers overlook a ghetto that is probably worser than any in the United States. Begging outside of the expensiver restaurants are small children with the leastest amount of education and the most empty stomachs. Even more strange is the sight of one of the city's popularer churches next to a hamburger stand. On the outskirts of the city, the most efficienter factories are just down the road from the ancient pyramids, which draw the mostest number of tourists of any attraction in the country. All over Mexico City one finds these combinations of the old and the new, the rich and the poor. One can only guess about which of these two contrasts the visitor finds most fascinating.

II COMMONLY CONFUSED VERBS. Certain verb forms may cause confusion because, while they look or sound very much alike, they are really quite different in meaning.

lay, lie

The verb *lay* means to place. (The action is in progress.)
The verb *lie* means to rest. (There is no action.)

lay	*lie*
Please *lay* the book on the table.	The children *lie* on mats.
Yesterday the hen *laid* six eggs.	Yesterday I *lay* in bed all day.
Jack *has laid* out the map.	The dog *has lain* there for an hour.
He *is laying* my coat on the chair.	The deed *is lying* on the desk.

learn, teach

Learn means to gain knowledge.
Teach means to give knowledge.

Professor Higgins tried to teach me biology, but I must admit that I did not learn very much.

leave, let

Leave means to depart from.
Let means to permit or allow.

I will leave for Florida tomorrow if you will let me make the trip.

raise, rise

The verb *raise* means that the subject is making something move upward.
The verb *rise* means that the subject is moving.

raise	*rise*
Raise your hand if you want to speak.	The temperature *rises* during the summer months.
Helen *raised* carrots in her garden.	The sun *rose* through the morning mist.
The teacher *has raised* an interesting question.	The men *have risen* to greet the general.

sit, set

Sit means to be seated.
Set means to place or put.

If you will sit in this chair, I will set the cushion at your feet.

stay, stand

Stay means to remain.
Stand means to be in an upright position.

He had to stay in bed for three days before he was allowed to stand up for a few minutes.

☞ *Try It Out*

In the following paragraph correct any verb errors. Cross out the error and write the correction directly above it.

Recently, my friend Fran was trying to learn me how to take notes when the teacher leaves the class have a discussion. First, Fran advised, I should never lie my pencil down. Rather, I should keep my notebook open so that I can write down the key points the students are rising. In addition, as I set there listening to the discussion, if I have an idea or a reaction I want to contribute, I should sit it down in my notes. Then, once I think that I will not forget what I want to say, I should rise my hand. Now that I have started using these suggestions, not only has the teacher's opinion of my work raised, but also after a class discussion, I no longer find that I remember nothing and that I might just as well have stood at home that day.

III COMMONLY CONFUSED EXPRESSIONS

among, between

Use *among* for three or more things, people, etc.
The club treasury was divided among all ten members.
Use *between* for only two things, people, etc.
What is the difference between an alligator and a crocodile?

amount, number

Use *amount* to refer to the total mass of something.
A large amount of food is wasted every day.
Use *number* to refer to things that can be counted.
A large number of people suffer from a neurosis.

bad, badly

Use *bad* with nouns and generally after verbs that refer to the senses: look, feel, smell, taste, and hear.

I feel bad.

Use *badly* after most other verbs.

Many people drive badly.

can, may

Use *can* to indicate the ability to do something.

My brother can stand on his head.

Use *may* to indicate permission or possibility.

May I leave the room?

can hardly (not: can't hardly)
can scarcely (not: can't scarcely)
could hardly (not: couldn't hardly)
could scarcely (not: couldn't scarcely)

I can hardly (not: can't hardly) see straight.

could have (not: could of)
would have (not: would of)
might have (not: might of)
should have (not: should of)

Tony could have (not: could of) done it better.

different from (not: different than)

Neurosis is different from (not: different than) psychosis.

fewer, less

Use *fewer* to refer to things that can be counted.

Fewer jobs are available for unskilled workers.

Use *less* to refer to quantity, value, or degree.

Many people have less education than they really need.

former, latter

Use *former* to refer to the first of two items that have been named. Use *latter* to refer to the second of two items that have been named. (If three or more items are referred to, do not use *former* and *latter;* instead use *first* and *last.*)

Las Vegas and San Juan are two popular resorts; the former is in Nevada and the latter in Puerto Rico.

good, well

Use *good* to describe a noun or pronoun only.
Muriel is a good swimmer.
Use *well* to describe a verb only.
She also bowls well.

☞ *Try It Out*

In the following paragraph correct any errors in using the yardsticks. Cross out the error and write the correct form directly above it.

Because Jack always took care of his garden good, people often admired it. Indeed, his flowers could of won prizes in a flower show. To please his friends, each year he planted varieties that were different than those he had used the year before. Last year, for example, he filled his garden with a large amount of roses, zinnias, and carnations. The latter were his favorite type of flower. Placed between all these flowers there was a sign that read: ''You can look—but do not pick!'' Well, one couldn't hardly blame him for feeling badly when one day he discovered that a thief had visited his garden, leaving behind less flowers than there would be after a tornado. It is no wonder that this year Jack has planted poison ivy.

---

is when, is where, is that

Never use *when* or *where* to refer to a thing; use *that.*

Awkward: A sonnet is when a poem has fourteen lines.
Corrected: A sonnet is a poem that has fourteen lines.

kind, sort

Never mix singular and plural. Use *this* or *that* with *kind* and *sort;* use *these* or *those* with *kinds* and *sorts.*

This kind of flower is very rare, but those kinds are grown everywhere.

like, as (as if)

Use *like* when no verb appears in the section that follows.
Use *as* (or *as if*) when a verb does appear in the section that follows.

If you do as I tell you, you will look like a movie star.

ought (not: had ought)

People ought (not: had ought) to be honest.

the reason is that (not: the reason is because, the reason is due to, the reason is on account of)

The reason is that (not: because) no one cares.

so, so that

Never use *so* to join two complete sentences when you want to show purpose; instead use *so that.*

The rocket increased its speed so that (not: so) it could withstand the gravitational pull.

try to (not: try and)

Please try to (not: try and) drive carefully.

used to, supposed to

Never leave out the final *d;* use *supposed to* and *used to.*

Although Jeff was supposed to be a stingy man, he used to spend a good deal of money on clothes.

where, that

Never use *where* to refer to things; use *that.*

I read in the newspaper that (not: where) Mr. Blowhard is running for mayor.

☞ *Try It Out*

In the following paragraph correct any errors in using the yardsticks. Cross out the error and write the correct form directly above it.

It is unfortunate that we are always reading in the newspapers where some parents are upset because their children are taking a sex education class in school. The reason for this concern is because the parents fear that such a class will encourage loose morals. But this will not happen, for the class will be taught by a specially trained instructor who will plan the course so the students will have a complete understanding of the subject. The sex education class is also when the teacher is suppose to try and answer the students' personal questions, those kind of questions which most parents are too embarrassed to answer honestly. Moreover, the teacher will discuss human sexuality in great detail; he or she will no longer stop with a discussion of guppies and puppies like the science teachers use to do. Parents really had ought to give the sex education classes a chance to prove their worth.

 Name: ______________________ *Date:* ______________________

EXERCISE 10e: For each item below, write as many fully and interestingly developed sentences as are necessary to follow the directions.

1. Using comparison forms of *sweet* correctly, compare three of your favorite desserts.

____

____

2. Using forms of *teach* and *learn* correctly, tell about someone who showed you how to play a particular sport.

____

____

3. Using *good, better, best* correctly, compare three enjoyable ways to spend a Saturday night.

____

____

4. Using comparison forms of *difficult* correctly, compare three hard courses that you have taken in school.

____

____

5. Using *stay* and *stand* correctly, tell about waiting on line in the rain to get tickets for a movie while your friends remained in the car.

____

____

____

6. Using the comparative form of *strong* correctly, compare your strength with that of your best friend.

____

____

____

Name: ______________________ Date: ______________________

7. Using *little, less, least* correctly, compare three types of music that you do not care for too much.

____

____

____

8. Using *lay* and *lie* correctly, tell about someone serving you a meal while you are resting in bed.

____

____

9. Using comparison forms of *funny* correctly, compare three comedians that make you laugh.

____

____

10. Using *bad, worse, worst* correctly, compare three restaurants that you dislike.

____

____

11. Using *rise* and *raise* correctly, tell about putting up the American flag as the sun comes up in the morning.

____

____

____

12. Using comparison forms of *interesting* correctly, compare three movies that you have enjoyed.

____

____

____

 Name: ______________________ Date: ______________

13. Using *let* and *leave* correctly, tell about someone who allows you to use his car when he goes away on vacation.

____

____

____

14. Using *much, more, most* correctly, compare the salaries for three different jobs.

____

____

____

15. Using *set* and *sit* correctly, tell about putting down your books before taking a seat in class.

____

____

EXERCISE 10f: Referring to the section on "Commonly Confused Expressions," select a word from the choices listed below and fill in the blanks.

Choices:	amount, number	like, as	former, latter
	good, well	bad, badly	can, may
	among, between	fewer, less	

1. Most snakes ____________ live for an entire year without eating any food at all.
2. The country of Tonga once issued a stamp shaped ____________ a banana.
3. Can you tell the difference ____________ a donkey and a pony?
4. Studies show that nonsmokers get far ____________ colds than smokers do.

5. The play was written so ________________ that the audience felt ________________ for the poor actors.

6. The body needs a small ________________ of copper to help in the formation of red blood cells.

7. A ________________ job not only pays ________________ but also provides an opportunity for advancement.

8. Fish can catch colds just ________________ you and I can.

9. Both soccer and football use eleven players on a team. However, the ________________ is played with a round ball whereas the ________________ is played with an almond-shaped ball.

10. If you are not on a diet, you ________________ have another ice cream cone.

11. The United States is importing ________________ oil now than it did ten years ago.

12. When Eleanor Ritchey died in 1968, she left a $4,500,000 fortune to be divided ________________ her 150 dogs.

13. A large ________________ of people are injured each year by falling out of bed.

14. You might be surprised to know that an elephant ________________ swim ________________.

15. The durian is an unusual fruit that tastes ________________ but smells ________________ a garbage dump.

EXERCISE 10g: Referring to the section on "Commonly Confused Expressions," fill in the blanks.

1. I ________________ hardly believe that mosquitoes are found at the North Pole, but they really are.

2. Most people should try ________________ eat some liver because it is ________________ to contain a great deal of iron.

3. Although sweet potatoes and yams look similar, they are actually quite different ________________ each other.

4. Texas ________________ to be the largest state in the United States, but now the largest state is Alaska, which is almost three times the size of Texas.

5. I read in a magazine ________________ each minute another four handguns are sold over the counter in America.

6. The real-estate man with 114 empty lots for sale should ________________ advertised the land as "The Greatest Earth on Show."

7. The Biltmore House, a private home in Asheville, North Carolina, is a popular tourist attraction; the reason is ________________ the house contains 250 rooms.

8. You ________________ to learn the Heimlich maneuver ________________ you will be prepared to help if someone chokes on a piece of food.

9. Although most Americans eat only one ________________ of rice, there are actually 15,000 different ________________ of rice growing in the world.

10. Robert Matern ________________ scarcely stand up after he set a world's record by eating 83 hamburgers on May 3, 1973.

11. The most complicated musical instrument is ________________ to be the organ.

12. The pyramids in Mexico are very different ________________ those in Egypt.

13. Iran ________________ to be called Persia.

14. I heard on the radio ________________ a man named Richard K. Brown rode a skateboard at a speed of almost 72 miles an hour.

15. If you had bought a copy of *The New York Times* on Sunday, October 10, 1971, you would ________________ lugged home a 972-page newspaper weighing over seven pounds.

Name: ________________________________ *Date:* ________________________

Informal Language

Different language is appropriate for different situations. When you speak, you usually adjust your choice of words and way of talking to suit your audience and the occasion. You might tell a friend, "My old man is a head shrinker," but to a possible employer you would probably say, "My father is a psychiatrist." Your choice of words when you are writing should also suit your audience and the occasion. Thus, the language you use when you write a letter to a close friend will likely be very different from the words you choose when writing an essay.

▌ How do you think someone who expects you to be formal would react to the following paragraph?

> If you read the classified ads in the papers, you'll get an idea of what jobs are available now. But it may be a couple of years before you'll be done with school. How'll you know what jobs will be available then? According to a recent report, by 1990 70% of all new workers will be between the ages of 16 and 34. If the U.S. maintains the economic patterns of the last 30 or 40 yrs., these here young people will be competing for some of the following positions. There'll be a demand for college profs. with a Ph.D. in bio. or math. As mass communication systems increase, the television industry and the phone co. will offer many job opportunities, especially in N.Y. and Calif. Because the population will continue to grow, the need for Drs. and other medical personnel will also kind of increase. This here will give you sort of an idea of what jobs will be available for them people with the proper education.

Here are some basic principles to help you rewrite the above paragraph in the formal English usually required in an essay.

FORMAL WRITING CUSTOMS. Numbers under 100 should be written out in words. When your writing includes numbers both over and under 100, the numerals are generally used to maintain consistency. The % sign should be written out as *percent* after numbers.

Because the pronoun *you* tends to give an informal tone to writing, many writers avoid using *you* when they are writing a formal essay. *Person* or *people* can often be substituted. Other pronouns such as *he, she, we,* or *they* may also be used.

SHORTENED FORMS. Many writers avoid using contractions in formal English whenever possible. However, sometimes a contraction may be necessary to prevent a very awkward-sounding sentence. "Are not the trees beautiful?" would sound much better as: "Aren't the trees beautiful?"

Do not use most abbreviations. However, forms such as *Mr., Mrs., Ms., Ph.D., Dr.,* and *Jr.* are permissible when they are used with a person's name. The initials of various organizations may also be used if the organization is usually referred to by its initials. FBI, UNESCO, NASA, VISTA, and GOP are some that are commonly used.

Shortened words such as *phone, photo,* and *ad* are commonly used in everyday speech. However, many writers use the full words when writing formal English.

ADJECTIVES. Most writers avoid using certain informal adjectives in formal writing:

Instead of:	**Use:**
a couple of	a few
this here that there	this that
them ("them people")	those
kind of / sort of (meaning somewhat)	somewhat, rather

 *Try It Out*

Referring to the yardsticks given, on separate paper rewrite Paragraph I about future job opportunities, using more formal English.

II How do you think someone who expects you to be formal would react to the following paragraph?

> A part-time job doesn't always pan out. I had really banked on getting the job at the local bank because I needed lots of dough so that I could buy a swell set of wheels and take in a movie sometimes. It was a lousy job as a janitor, but it paid plenty of bread. Although the job had sounded like a snap, I goofed it up on the first day. While I was slaving away real hard, I was also getting a gander at all the loot in the vault. I reckoned that there must have been at least a million bucks. Because I wanted to do a mighty good job, I made sure to pick up each scrap of paper and put it through the paper shredding machine. Well, did I flip when I figured out that I had mistakenly shredded a bag containing a lot of checks that were worth over a hundred grand. The next day the bank hired some groovy chicks who tried to put the checks back together, but the broads couldn't do it no how. The guy who had hired me was awfully mad and he took it out on me. I was sacked, which didn't bother me. I needed the long green in the worst way, but that banking jazz sure was a drag.

Here are some more basic principles to help you rewrite the above paragraph in the formal English usually required in an essay.

WORDS OF EMPHASIS. Everyday conversation is filled with many informal words that are used to add strength to a statement. However, formal English also has a wide selection of emphasis words. Most writers choose them when writing an essay.

Instead of:	**Use:**
awfully, mighty, so, plenty, real (used for emphasis)	very, extremely, exceedingly, acutely
in the worst way	very much, acutely, exceedingly
a lot, lots of	a great deal, many
sure (meaning "certainly")	certainly, surely, absolutely, truly
no how	not at all
lousy	bad, terrible, inferior
swell, super, some (used for emphasis)	good, excellent, outstanding, notable, distinguished

SLANG. Although slang is often colorful, it should be avoided in writing formal English. Words such as *guy, kid,* and *out of sight* are fine for a conversation with friends, but they rarely fit comfortably into an essay written in formal English. Also, it is more accurate to write *agreement* or *transaction* instead of *deal,* for example. When you are in doubt about whether or not a word is slang, consult your dictionary.

VERBS. Most writers avoid using certain informal verb expressions when writing formal English.

Instead of:	Use:
to figure to reckon	to suppose, to guess, to think
to bank on	to rely on
to take in a movie	to go to a movie
to take up with	to become friendly with
to take it out on	to release anger at

Try It Out

Referring to the yardsticks given, on separate paper rewrite Paragraph **II** about the costly mistake.

EXERCISE 10h: Each statement given below might appear as a headline in an informally written newspaper. Rewrite each statement as it would appear in the formal writing of an expository essay. Use normal formal English; do not use very stiff or pompous language.

1. **6 HOODS BUMPED OFF OVER PHONY PORNO DEAL**

   Cops Figure They Were Ripping Off the Mob

   ____

   ____

2. **PREZ AND COMMIE BIG SHOTS RAP ABOUT NUKES**

   Reds Warned to Hang Loose or They're Gonna Get Creamed

3. **A COUPLE OF DUDES SPOT UFO'S IN L.A.**

   Claim Them Saucers Were Out of Sight

4. **PHONE CO. BLOWS A BUNDLE ON RITZY ANNIVERSARY BASH**

   Workers Hit the Ceiling Cause They Weren't Invited

5. **ACTOR HITS THE BOTTLE & THEN A TREE IN SNAZZY HOT ROD**

   Promises to Kick the Habit if He's Not Thrown in the Clink

6. **D.A. GRILLS STOOL PIGEON ABOUT 100-G BANK HEIST**

   Stoolie Kind of Uptight about Snitching on His Buddies

7. **SMALLTIME BOXER KO'S CHAMP IN FRISCO SLUGFEST**

Champ Dumped with an Awfully Hard Belt to the Kisser

8. **HERE'S THE LOWDOWN ABOUT A HOTSHOT DOC**

He's Hooked on Dope & Hanging Around with Some Strung-Out Punks

9. **TV EXEC GETS CANNED FOR SHOOTING OFF HER TRAP**

Says a Lot of New Shows Stink

10. **H.S. GRADS GRIPE ABOUT LOUSY JOB MARKET**

Lots of 'Em Can't Find Work No How

11. **CON TO GET THE HOT SEAT FOR RUBBING OUT WARDEN**

He'll Fry Tomorrow!

Name: ______________________ Date: ______________________

12. **PARK AVE. SHRINK SUED OVER HOT NEW BOOK**

She Dishes Out Inside Info. about Patients' Hang-ups

13. **GOV WANTS TO JACK UP TAXES 18%**

We Gotta Kick This Guy Out of Office

14. **DOPEY HORROR FLICK IS A REAL TURKEY**

You've Gotta Be a Jerk to Fork Over Dough to See This Off-the-Wall Movie

15. **2 VIP'S CROAK DURING MEAL AT REAL CLASSY RESTAURANT**

It Sure Takes Guts to Eat at This Here Clip Joint

 Name: ____________________ Date: ____________________

EXERCISE 10i: Using a more formal version of each of the clue words, fill in the crossword puzzle. (If there is more than one word in an answer, do not leave space between words.)

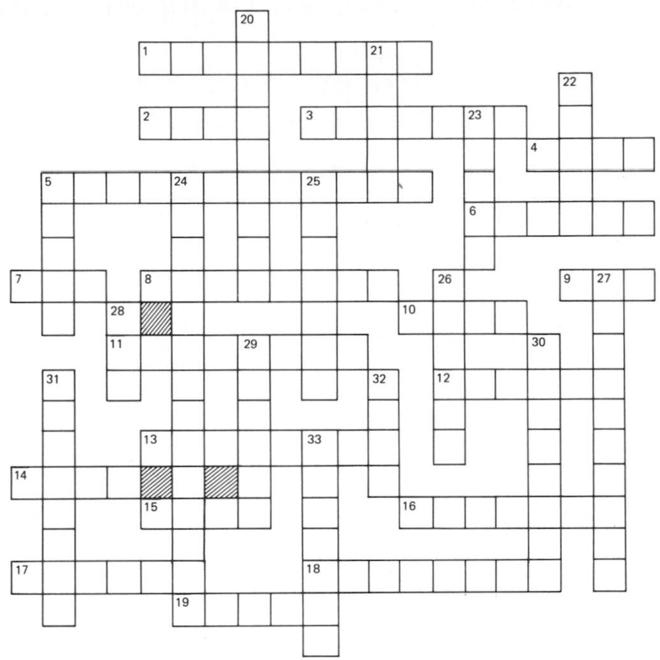

Across

1. I *gotta* get a car.
2. *that there* book
3. gonna
4. *a lot of* people
5. You *goofed!*
6. st.
7. guys
8. in the worst way
9. a *couple of* flowers
10. a *cool* movie
11. no how
12. He is *nuts!*
13. lousy
14. *real* lazy
15. *awfully* hungry
16. I *figure* that I can get a job.
17. can't
18. kids
19. The shoplifter is going to *rip off* some merchandise.

Down

5. a wallet filled with *dough*
20. It *sure* is hot today.
21. I *reckon* that the storm is over.
22. we're
23. *them* boots
24. ads
25. a hassle
26. the cops
27. *play around* with drugs
28. &
29. 30
30. chill out
31. *kind of* expensive
32. He *kicked the bucket.*
33. bike

EXERCISE 10j: REFRESHER

1. Correct any errors in punctuation in the following paragraphs.
2. Insert words of transition needed to help create unity.

Have you ever been punched, slapped, or shoved by someone you were dating. Recent studies indicate that such violent behavior is common among college couples. At Arizona State University, 60 percent of the unmarried upper-class students admitted that they had experienced violence while dating. This physical abuse can take many forms pushing, kicking, beating, or even biting. Some students have been threatened with guns and knives. According to the research, these acts of cruelty often creep into a campus romance because of jealousy over a third person. In other instances, the violent blowups grow out of arguments over sex or drinking. These studies may have overlooked the real reason for the problem stress. Experts point out that many young people are under a tremendous strain brought about by financial educational and sexual pressures.

Considering the suffering caused by these wild dangerous attacks you may wonder why over half of the students who have been assaulted choose to continue the relationship? One major reason is the fear of loneliness or of losing the status that comes from having a steady date. A study done at Oregon State University revealed, that 30 percent of the couples saw physical abuse as a sign of love, and more than one-third felt that hitting actually improved their relationship. These findings indicate that violence and romance will, unfortunately, remain closely linked until young people develop the maturity and self-control needed for a healthy satisfying relationship.

 Name: ______________________ Date: ______________________

SPRINGBOARDS TO WRITING

Using your knowledge of the writing process, explained on pages 12–14, write a paragraph or essay related to this chapter's central theme, *murder in the streets,* which is introduced on pages 336–340.

PREWRITING

To think of topics to write about, look at the advertisement and two photographs, read the essay, and answer the questions that follow each. If you prefer, select one of the writing springboards below. (All paragraph numbers refer to the essay that starts on page 338.) To develop your ideas, use the prewriting techniques described on pages 15–20.

WRITING A PARAGRAPH (For help, see the Pointers on page 31.)

1. If you were ever a victim of a crime, or if you ever witnessed a crime, describe exactly what happened.
2. I would (would not) come to the aid of a person being mugged or raped.
3. The job guarantee program described in paragraph 9 is (is not) a good idea.
4. Some states and cities now reward a person who comes to the aid of another citizen in trouble. Do you think such a program is a good idea?
5. Why does the author feel that "the casualness of the whole incident—taking my brother's life to get some money for fun—makes the tragedy all the more unbearable"? (See ¶ 5.)

WRITING AN ESSAY (For help, see the Pointers on page 35.)

6. What Makes People Turn to a Life of Crime? (See ¶ 7.)
7. Should Teenagers Who Commit Serious Crimes Be Given the Same Punishment as Adults Are?
8. A Plan to Reduce Crime in My Town (My City)
9. The Case for (against) Gun Control
10. The Case for (against) Capital Punishment
11. TV and the Movies Do (Do Not) Encourage Violence
12. The Police Are (Are Not) Doing the Best They Can in Dealing with Crime
13. The Courts Are Not (Are) Firm Enough in Dealing with Criminals
14. Agree or disagree: Our Prisons Do Not Rehabilitate Criminals
15. The Case for (against) Neighborhood Vigilante Groups
16. The Law Today: Protection for Criminals or for Victims?
17. How to Cope with the Loss of a Loved One

1
2
3
4
5
6

eleven

SPRINGBOARDS TO THINKING

For informal, not written, response . . . to stimulate your thinking

1. What do you think the chick sees when he looks around?
2. What is the chick telling us about what he sees?
3. Do you ever feel that you would like to crawl into a warm place and close off the world around you? What does or does not make you feel this way?
4. Do you find that some people act like the chick? Explain. What would happen if everyone acted this way?
5. What makes some people feel that the world's problems are too great to solve? What is your opinion? If you were free to start solving some of the world's problems, which would you start with? Why?

Once Upon a Time— A Fable of Student Power

NEIL POSTMAN

(1) Once upon a time in the City of New York civilized life very nearly came to an end. The streets were covered with dirt, and there was no one to tidy them. The air and rivers were polluted, and no one could cleanse them. The schools were rundown, and no one believed in them. Each day brought a new strike, and each strike brought new hardships. Crime and strife and disorder and rudeness were to be found everywhere. The young fought the old. The workers fought the students. The whites fought the blacks. The city was bankrupt.

(2) When things came to their most desperate moment, the City Fathers met to consider the problem. But they could suggest no cures, for their morale was very low and their imagination dulled by hatred and confusion. There was nothing for the Mayor to do but declare a state of emergency. He had done this before during snowstorms and power failures, but now he felt even more justified. "Our city," he said, "is under siege, like the ancient cities of Jericho and Troy. But *our* enemies are sloth and poverty and indifference and hatred." As you can see, he was a very wise Mayor, but not so wise as to say exactly how these enemies could be dispersed. Thus, though a state of emergency officially existed, neither the Mayor nor anyone else could think of anything to do that would make their situation better rather than worse. And then an extraordinary thing happened.

(3) One of the Mayor's aides, knowing full well what the future held for the city, had decided to flee with his family to the country. In order to prepare himself for his exodus to a strange environment, he began to read Henry David Thoreau's *Walden,* which he had been told was a useful handbook on how to survive in the country. While reading the book, he came upon the following passage:

> Students should not play life, or study it merely, while the community supports them at this expensive game, but earnestly live it from the beginning to end. How could youths better learn to live than by at once trying the experiment of living?

(4) The aide sensed immediately that he was in the presence of an exceedingly good idea. And he sought an audience with the Mayor. He showed the passage to the Mayor, who was extremely depressed and in no mood to read from books, since he had already scoured books of lore and

wisdom in search of help but had found nothing. "What does it mean?" said the Mayor angrily. The aide replied: "Nothing less than a way to our salvation."

(5) He then explained to the Mayor that the students in the public schools had heretofore been part of the general problem whereas, with some slight imagination and a change of perspective, they might easily become part of the general solution. He pointed out that from junior high school on up to senior high school, there were approximately 400,000 able-bodied, energetic young men and women who could be used as a resource to make the city livable again. "But how can we use them?" asked the Mayor. "And what would happen to their education if we did?"

(6) To this the aide replied, "They will find their education in the process of saving their city. And as for lessons in school, we have ample evidence that the young do not exactly appreciate them and are even now turning against their teachers and their schools." The aide, who had come armed with statistics (as aides are wont to do), pointed out that the city was spending $5-million a year merely replacing broken school windows and that almost one-third of all the students enrolled in the schools did not even show up on any given day. "Yes, I know," said the Mayor sadly. "Woe unto us." "Wrong," said the aide brashly. "The boredom and destructiveness and pent-up energy that are now an affliction to us can be turned to our advantage."

(7) The Mayor was not quite convinced, but having no better idea of his own he appointed his aide Chairman of the Emergency Education Committee, and the aide at once made plans to remove almost 400,000 students from their dreary classrooms and their even drearier lessons, so that their energy and talents might be used to repair the desecrated environment.

(8) When these plans became known, there was a great hue and cry against them, for people in distress will sometimes prefer a problem that is familiar to a solution that is not. For instance, the teachers complained that their contract contained no provision for such unusual procedures. To this the aide replied that the *spirit* of the contract compelled them to help educate our youth, and that education can take many forms and be conducted in many places. "It is not written in any holy book," he observed, "that an education must occur in a small room with chairs in it."

(9) Some parents complained that the plan was un-American and that its compulsory nature was hateful to them. To this the aide replied that the plan was based on the practices of earlier Americans who required their young to assist in controlling the environment in order to insure the survival of the group. "Our schools," he added, "have never hesitated to compel. The question is not, nor has it ever been, to compel or not to compel, but rather, which things ought to be compelled."

(10) And even some children complained, although not many. They said that their God-given right to spend 12 years of their lives, at public expense, sitting in a classroom was being trampled. To this complaint the aide replied that they were confusing a luxury with a right, and that, in any case, the community could no longer afford either. "Besides," he added,

"of all the God-given rights man has identified, none takes precedence over his right to survive."

(11) And so, the curriculum of the public schools of New York City became known as Operation Survival, and all the children from 7th grade through 12th grade became part of it. Here are some of the things that they were obliged to do:

(12) On Monday morning of every week, 400,000 children had to help clean up their own neighborhoods. They swept the streets, canned the garbage, removed the litter from empty lots, and hosed the dust and graffiti from the pavements and walls. Wednesday mornings were reserved for beautifying the city. Students planted trees and flowers, tended the grass and shrubs, painted subway stations and other eyesores, and even repaired broken-down public buildings, starting with their own schools.

(13) Each day, 5,000 students (mostly juniors and seniors in high school) were given responsibility to direct traffic on the city streets, so that all the policemen who previously had done this were freed to keep a sharp eye out for criminals. Each day, 5,000 students were asked to help deliver the mail, so that it soon became possible to have mail delivered twice a day—as it had been done in days of yore.

(14) Several thousand students were also used to establish and maintain day-care centers, so that young mothers, many on welfare, were free to find gainful employment. Each student was also assigned to meet with two elementary students on Tuesday and Thursday afternoons to teach them to read, to write, and to do arithmetic. Twenty thousand students were asked to substitute, on one afternoon a week, for certain adults whose jobs the students could perform without injury or loss of efficiency. These adults were then free to attend school or, if they preferred, to assist the students in their efforts to save their city.

(15) The students were also assigned to publish a newspaper in every neighborhood of the city, in which they were able to include much information that good citizens need to have. Students organized science fairs, block parties and rock festivals, and they formed, in every neighborhood, both an orchestra and a theater company. Some students assisted in hospitals, helped to register voters, and produced radio and television programs which were aired on city stations. There was still time to hold a year-round City Olympics in which every child competed in some sport or other.

(16) It came to pass, as you might expect, that the college students in the city yearned to participate in the general plan, and thus another 100,000 young people became available to serve the community. The college students ran a "jitney" service from the residential boroughs to Manhattan and back. Using their own cars and partly subsidized by the city, the students quickly established a kind of auxiliary, semipublic transportation system, which reduced the number of cars coming into Manhattan, took some of the load off the subways, and diminished air pollution—in one stroke.

(17) College students were empowered to give parking and litter tickets, thus freeing policemen more than ever for real detective work. They were

permitted to organize seminars, film festivals, and arrange lectures for junior and senior high school students; and on a U.H.F. television channel, set aside for the purpose, they gave advanced courses in a variety of subjects every day from 3 P.M. to 10 P.M. They also helped to organize and run drug-addiction rehabilitation centers, and they launched campaigns to inform people of their legal rights, their nutritional needs, and of available medical facilities.

(18) Because this is a fable and not a fairy tale, it cannot be said that all the problems of the city were solved. But several extraordinary things did happen. The city began to come alive and its citizens found new reason to hope that they could save themselves. Young people who had been alienated from their environment assumed a proprietary interest in it. Older people who had regarded the young as unruly and parasitic came to respect them. There followed from this a revival of courtesy and a diminution of crime, for there was less reason than before to be angry at one's neighbors and to wish to assault them.

(19) Amazingly, most of the students found that while they did not "receive" an education, they were able to create a quite adequate one. They lived, each day, their social studies and geography and communication and biology and many other things that decent and proper people know about, including the belief that everyone must share equally in creating a livable city, no matter what he or she becomes later on. It even came to pass that the older people, being guided by the example of the young, took a renewed interest in restoring their environment and, at the very least, refused to participate in its destruction.

(20) Now, it would be foolish to deny that there were not certain problems attending this whole adventure. For instance, there were thousands of children who would otherwise have known the principal rivers of Uruguay who had to live out their lives in ignorance of these facts. There were hundreds of teachers who felt their training had been wasted because they could not educate children unless it were done in a classroom. As you can imagine, it was also exceedingly difficult to grade students on their activities, and after a while, almost all tests ceased. This made many people unhappy, for many reasons, but most of all because no one could tell the dumb children from the smart children anymore.

(21) But the Mayor, who was, after all, a very shrewd politician, promised that as soon as the emergency was over everything would be restored to normal. Meanwhile, everybody lived happily ever after—in a state of emergency, but quite able to cope with it.

READING SURVEY

1. *Main idea*

What is the central theme of the essay?

2. *Major Details*

a. What problems created a state of emergency in New York City?
b. Briefly describe "Operation Survival."
c. What "extraordinary things" happened to the people and their environment as a result of "Operation Survival"?

3. *Inferences*

a. Is this fable only about New York City?
b. Read paragraph 20 again. What do you think is the author's opinion of the conventional form of education described?

4. *Opinions*

a. What do you think of the idea that students "will find their education in the process of saving their city"?
b. If "Operation Survival" were tried, what type of service would you want to give? Why?

VOCABULARY BUILDING

Lesson One: The Vocabulary of a Troubled Society

The essay "Once Upon a Time—A Fable of Student Power" by Neil Postman includes words that are useful when you are discussing our troubled society.

strife	(paragraph 1)	**affliction**	(6)
bankrupt	(1)	**desecrated**	(7)
siege	(2)	**hue and cry**	(8)
sloth	(2)	**alienated**	(18)
woe	(6)	**parasitic**	(18)

A society that is torn by **strife** is torn by bitter disagreement, struggle, and conflict.

A society that is considered to be **bankrupt** is considered to be an utter failure with nothing left to offer, not even money to pay back what it owes.

A society that is under **siege** is under persistent attack by destructive forces which threaten to destroy it completely.

A society that is the victim of **sloth** is the victim of laziness and lack of drive.

A society that is marked by **woe** is marked by sorrow, grief, and misfortune.

A society that is troubled by **affliction** is troubled by the curse of continued misfortune, suffering, and illness.

A society that is **desecrated** is abused and made to seem unholy when it should be protected and honored.

A society that puts up a **hue and cry** shouts and clamors in protest.

A society that is **alienated** has many people who are indifferent and withdrawn because they no longer find a common bond with the society.

A society that is **parasitic** survives by depending on others without making any useful contribution of its own.

EXERCISE 11a: Match the columns. Do not draw lines because writing the words will help you learn them better. Notice that there are two extra definitions, neither of which matches a word from the lesson.

strife
bankrupt
siege
sloth
woe
affliction
desecrated
hue and cry
alienated
parasitic

____________________ 1. great sorrow

____________________ 2. clean and orderly

____________________ 3. a troubled society

____________________ 4. the damaged condition of something holy or valued

____________________ 5. conflict

____________________ 6. failed and having no money

____________________ 7. indifferent and unattached

____________________ 8. surviving at the expense of others

____________________ 9. misfortune

____________________ 10. unwillingness to work or exert oneself

____________________ 11. a long-lasting attack

____________________ 12. screams and clamors

Lesson Two: The Vocabulary of a Renewed Society

The essay "Once Upon a Time—A Fable of Student Power" by Neil Postman includes words that are useful when you are discussing the renewal of society.

civilized	(paragraph 1)
morale	(2)
salvation	(4)
rehabilitation	(17)
revival	(18)
courtesy	(18)
restoring	(19)

A society that is **civilized** has developed beyond its primitive state and is now technically advanced, refined, and educated.

A society that has good **morale** has a sense of purpose and is confident of the future.

A society that has found its **salvation** has saved itself from danger and total decay.

A society that is dedicated to its **rehabilitation** wants to put itself back into good condition.

A society that is undergoing a **revival** has renewed interest in coming back to life.

A society that practices **courtesy** acts with helpful politeness and consideration.

A society that is interested in **restoring** itself wants to repair and reestablish itself to its original desirable form.

EXERCISE 11b: Match the columns. Do not draw lines because writing the words will help you learn them better. Notice that there are two extra definitions, neither of which matches a word from the lesson.

civilized morale salvation	______________	1. being saved from danger or evil
rehabilitation revival courtesy	______________	2. bringing back to a former condition
restoring	______________	3. culturally advanced and refined

 Name: ______________ Date: ______________

______________________ 4. mental condition of confidence and purpose

______________________ 5. great celebration

______________________ 6. gracious politeness

______________________ 7. coming back into use after disuse

______________________ 8. an improvement in condition

______________________ 9. a society in need of change

SPELLING

Lesson One: Spelling Demons

Here are some more words that are frequently misspelled. Using the helpful techniques given in Chapter One, you should make it a point to learn these new Demons, which are taken from "Once Upon a Time—A Fable of Student Power."

adequate	**experiment**
appreciate	**familiar**
audience	**ignorance**
bankrupt	**immediately**
children	**merely**
controlling	**permit**
courtesy	**practice**
criminal	**procedure**
curriculum	**resource**
desperate	**situation**
destruction	**substitute**
expense	**useful**

Lesson Two: Dropping the Final *e*

Many of the words in this essay can be learned easily with the help of this one simple spelling rule.

> Words ending in silent *e* usually drop the *e* before a suffix beginning with a vowel and keep the *e* before a suffix beginning with a consonant.

Try It Out

Add the suffixes indicated to the following words.

	-ing	-ment	-able
require	________	________	________
advise	________	________	________
achieve	________	________	________

Here are some examples:

guide + ance = guidance

care + less = careless

decide + ing = deciding

complete + ness = completeness

imagine + able = imaginable

grace + ful = graceful

 *Try It Out*

Apply the final *e* rule to the following words.

use + able = ________

grace + ful = ________

write + ing = ________

complete + ly = ________

survive + al = ________

create + ion = ________

A SPECIAL NOTE: Here are some words you see frequently that are exceptions to the above rule.

true + ly = truly

argue + ment = argument

notice + able = noticeable

agree + able = agreeable

courage + ous = courageous

canoe + ing = canoeing

 Name: ________ *Date:* ________

EXERCISE 11c: Apply the final *e* rule to these words.

1. appreciate + ion = ____________________
2. separate + ly = ____________________
3. imagine + ary = ____________________
4. believe + able = ____________________
5. state + ment = ____________________
6. pure + ity = ____________________
7. exercise + ing = ____________________
8. realize + ation = ____________________
9. force + ful = ____________________
10. grieve + ance = ____________________
11. agree + able = ____________________
12. substitute + ion = ____________________
13. refuse + al = ____________________
14. nine + ty = ____________________
15. response + ible = ____________________
16. home + less = ____________________
17. practice + ing = ____________________
18. argue + ment = ____________________
19. sincere + ly = ____________________
20. guide + ance = ____________________

Name: ____________________ Date: ____________________

EXERCISE 11d: Using the definitions given as clues, fill in this puzzle. If necessary, check your spelling with the list of Demons in this chapter.

Across

1. "__________ makes perfect."
2. to have knowledge of = to be __________ with
3. youngsters
4. to be thankful for or to admire
5. good manners
6. Oil is a natural __________.
7. the cost or price
8. driven to take any risk
9. without delay
10. a course of study
11. the lack of knowledge
12. A __________ person needs to have power and be in charge.

Down

1. a way of doing something
13. The __________ applauded.
14. acceptable
15. unable to pay the bills
16. allow
17. The scientist is performing an important __________.
18. a replacement
19. helpful
20. Nuclear war would cause total __________.
21. TV __________ comedy
22. one who commits a crime
23. only

 Name: __________ Date: __________

Sentence Logic

Logic in thinking, as discussed in Appendix I, refers to clear and effective reasoning. Logic in sentences, the topic of this chapter, refers to the correct form and placement of words in a sentence. Three aspects of sentence logic are:

Parallelism

Logical word placement for precise meaning

Logical relationship between a "set-off" section and the main sentence

Parallelism

In math . . . parallel lines run in the same direction and are the same distance apart from each other so that they never meet. Thus, *they correspond or match.*

In English . . . parallelism means that when words express equal or parallel ideas, *they must match or be parallel in form.*

We know that if a car tire goes flat and cannot be fixed, it must be replaced with a tire that is exactly the same size as the other three tires. If a different size is used, the car will sit awkwardly and drive poorly or not at all. Thus it is with sentences: Equal (parallel) ideas must be expressed in matching (parallel) form so that all parts of the sentence work properly.

If you use words that are parallel in form, your writing style can improve a great deal. At times it will be necessary for you to rewrite a sentence so that your word order will be parallel; however, the result will be a more balanced and smoother product.

A SPECIAL NOTE: The spelling of the word *parallel* can be remembered from its meaning: *All* lines are par*all*el (and the double *l* looks like parallel lines!).

I WORDS IN A PAIR OR A SERIES MUST MATCH IN FORM.

Nancy likes fishing
and
bowling.

Steve likes to swim,
to fish,
but not
to hike.

Sue wants to be a lawyer
or
a nurse.

Bob never smokes
nor
drinks.

Notice that the items in a pair or a series can be connected with *and, but, or,* or *nor.*

☞ *Try It Out*

Fill in the blanks with words that are logical and that match in form.

1. The truck driver was steering his rig, talking on his CB radio, and

   ________________________________.

2. The student protesters wanted the university to increase financial aid

   and to________________________________.

3. To win the three-event competition the athlete must swim 6 miles,

   ________________________________, and jog 20 miles.

II WORDS THAT FOLLOW "SET-UP" WORDS MUST MATCH IN FORM.

Some "set-up" words: *if, that, who, which, could, a* (*an*), *the, so that, of, at, when*

If we stop trying to participate in government,
if we prefer not to feel pity for others,
and
if we refuse to take risks,
then we are headed for disaster.

Try It Out

Fill in the blanks with words that are logical and that match in form.

1. A good sales manager is a person who can create interest in the product and who ______________________________.

2. If the battery is dead and if ______________________________ ______________, we are definitely going to be late for class.

Notice that the section that must match in form can start at a few different places. The number of words you decide to match should depend on the emphasis and style you want to achieve. Here are some good ways of writing a parallel sentence:

> The pilot told us that the plane would be delayed and that the plane would be crowded.
>
> The pilot told us that the plane would be delayed and the plane would be crowded.
>
> The pilot told us that the plane would be delayed and would be crowded.
>
> The pilot told us that the plane would be delayed and crowded.

Note that the second section of each sentence above started at a different place. As long as the two sections of the sentence are parallel, the second section can start wherever it sounds best in what you are writing. Which way is best? No one way.

Try It Out

Based on the model above, write all the ways the second section of this sentence could begin:

> Once the cleanup was finished, the students thought that the city looked clean and that the city looked prosperous.

III WORDS THAT GO WITH PAIRS OF "SET-UP" WORDS MUST MATCH IN FORM.

Some pairs of "set-up" words:

both	*and*	*not only*	*but also*
either	*or*	*which*	*and which*
whether	*or*	*that*	*and that*
neither	*nor*	*who*	*and who*

David is *both* strong
and handsome.

Bill is a man *who* likes responsibility
and who enjoys a challenge.

The politician liked *not only*
to meet people
but also
to sign autographs.

Neither
blankets
nor
hot drinks
were available to
the storm victims.

☞ *Try It Out*

Fill in the blanks with words that are logical and match in form.

1. My mother is not only an accomplished guitarist but also ____.

2. The young couple decided neither to get married nor ____.

3. Olympic stars are athletes who practice many hours a day and who ____.

 Name: ____________________ Date: ____________________

EXERCISE 11e: In each of the sentences given, one parallel section does not match in form. Underline that section and rewrite the section making any changes necessary for correct parallelism. The goal is to make all parallel parts match; in some cases, there is more than one possible form for the sections, and no one form is more correct than another.

1. After flying into the room through an open window, the bird panicked and was crashing into the walls in an attempt to get out.

2. The relay team had an early lead but then was lagging behind.

3. Whether to accept the case or refusing to take it was an important decision for the lawyer.

4. The animal trainer had to select which pair of lions to tame and what equipment he should be using.

5. Designing a computer program is easy; to write it accurately is not.

6. Once the warm liquid is added to yeast, it bubbles and then it is producing pockets of gas which make bread rise.

7. The mail clerk finds both operating the postage meter and to sort the mail simple to do.

____

____

____

8. The family wanted to relocate to a part of the country that was neither too hot in the summer nor had winters that were very cold.

____

____

____

9. Helping campers in trouble and to protect wildlife are two of the many responsibilities of a forest ranger.

____

____

____

10. Whenever drivers are not intoxicated and if they do not exceed the speed limit, car accidents are rare.

____

____

EXERCISE 11f: Fill in the blanks with words that are logical and that match in form. For effectiveness use more than one word in each of the matching parts.

1. For their wedding, the bride and groom planned to _______________ _______________ and to _______________.

2. Both _______________ and _______________ would improve America's schools.

3. Neither _______________ nor _______________ can cure a headache.

4. The team would win more games if ______________ and if ______________.

5. During our tour of the candy factory, we were told that ______________ and that ______________.

6. Anyone who runs for President of the United States must be the kind of person who ______________ and who ______________.

7. To have sufficient money when you retire, you should ______________ and you should ______________.

8. Shopping malls are both ______________ and ______________.

9. Drive-in movies usually are ______________ and ______________.

10. The physically handicapped not only can ______________ but also can ______________.

EXERCISE 11g: Using parallelism, write a sentence about each of the following topics. Use as many types of parallelism with as many "set-up" words and pairs of "set-up" words as possible. Do this assignment on your own paper.

1. a deserted street
2. your Social Security number
3. matches
4. drinking fountains
5. the rearview mirror in a car
6. boredom
7. secretarial schools
8. crying
9. a term paper
10. the kitchen sink
11. sunglasses
12. germs
13. family photographs
14. tacos
15. first love
16. closets
17. body building
18. keys
19. electricians
20. posters

Name: ______________ Date: ______________

Logical Word Placement for Precise Meaning

The position of a word or group of words can affect the meaning and logic of a sentence.

I EACH WORD MUST BE PLACED AS CLOSE TO WHAT IT DESCRIBES AS POSSIBLE. Incorrect placement of one word can completely change the meaning of a sentence.

For example, let's consider the sentence: *He said that she was pretty.* When the word *only* is inserted in various places in the sentence, the meaning of the sentence changes completely:

ONLY	ONLY	ONLY	ONLY	ONLY	ONLY
He	said	that	she	was	pretty.
No one else said it.	*He did not mean it.*	*He said nothing else.*	*No one else was pretty.*	*She was nothing else.*	*She was pretty, but not gorgeous.*

☞ *Try It Out*

Insert the word *only* in as many places as possible. Explain the meaning that each placement creates.

The police report said that the burglar had been wounded.

____

____

____

____

____

____

____

____

A SPECIAL NOTE: Avoid putting a word between the two words in the infinitive form of the verb, such as *to* run, *to* go, *to* be, *to* have, *to* think, etc.

 Name: ______________________ *Date:* ______________

II GROUPS OF WORDS MUST BE PLACED AS CLOSE TO WHAT THEY DESCRIBE AS POSSIBLE. Incorrect placement of groups of words can result in illogical—and unintentionally funny—sentences.

We took the broken chair to the carpenter with only three legs.
. . . a freak carpenter?

Ted kept a little black book with the telephone numbers of all the girls he had ever dated in his back pocket.
. . . that must have been a big pocket!

Try It Out

Explain the meaning of each sentence *as it stands.* Then underline the group of words that is incorrectly placed in the sentence. Finally, draw an arrow to where the group of words belongs.

1. The waiter served the chicken in a gorilla suit.
   meaning: ____

2. The old car was discovered by the police stuck in the mud.
   meaning: ____

EXERCISE 11h: For each list of words, write out all of the possible logical orders for a sentence. In some cases there is only one logical order, but in many cases there are more than one. If the latter applies, explain any differences in meaning among the sentences. Use your own paper for this assignment.

1. most
   enjoy
   teachers
   students
   senses of humor
   who have

2. for mail order catalogs
   every day
   Avery
   collects
   mailing lists

3. a physician
   to be
   Kristen hopes

4. carefully
   at his desk
   Jerry
   wrote the book

5. fishing rod
his own
Don
fixed
only

6. to fix
cars
twenty-two-year-old
Douglas
likes

7. killed
the police officer
with a bomb
the terrorist

8. ate
usually
an apple
the doctor
each day

9. knew
no one
the man
why
cried

10. in her studio
needed
watercolor paints
the artist

EXERCISE 11i: Find the word or group of words that is not as close to what it describes as it could be. Rewrite the sentence with all words correctly placed.

1. Albert Einstein never wore socks known as one of the world's greatest scientists.

____

____

2. After rolling in spilled paint, the puppy raced out of the garage with a pink bottom.

____

____

____

3. Parents should lock up medicines to prevent young children from always poisoning themselves accidentally.

____

____

____

 Name: ____________________ Date: ____________________

4. The girl operated the computer wearing a baseball cap.

____

____

5. Some actors have won awards for playing women such as Jack Lemmon and Dustin Hoffman.

____

____

____

6. The cookies were eaten by the doctor with chocolate chips.

____

____

7. Timidly, the stern professor was asked a question by the shy student.

____

____

8. The karate demonstrator showed them how to stop an attacker and then left skillfully.

____

____

____

9. The flag was handed to the woman with red and white stripes.

____

____

10. The Dingo is a wild dog found only in Australia with cold, mean eyes.

____

____

____

Name: ____________________ Date: ____________________

Logical Relationship Between "Set-off" Section and Main Sentence

A section that adds material to the main sentence is often "set off" either by a single comma (if the added section comes at the beginning or end of the sentence) or by a set of commas (if the added section comes in the middle of a sentence).

If there is no subject in the set-off section, its subject must be given in the main sentence. Thus, the set-off section must logically and clearly connect with the subject of the main sentence. If the relationship is not logically clear, the result can be illogical—and unintentionally funny.

Climbing a ladder, my head struck a branch.
. . . *a head that climbs a ladder?*

Crossing the street, the Empire State Building came into view.
. . . *the Empire State Building walks?*

A SPECIAL HINT: To find the subject of a set-off section, ask of its verb, "Who?" or "What?" The answer is the subject; it is this subject that *must* be clearly given either in the set-off section or in the main sentence.

☞ *Try It Out*

Explain why each of the following is illogical.

1. Eating at the kitchen table, the conversation turned to politics.

   ____

2. Protected against the cold, the jacket was buttoned up tight.

   ____

3. When walking to school, my textbooks weighed me down.

   ____

4. Strumming a guitar, the song was about social injustice.

   ____

 Name: ______________________ *Date:* ______________________

This error can be corrected either (1) by using the logical subject in the main sentence or (2) by inserting the logical subject into the set-off section.

1. Climbing the ladder, *I* struck my head against a branch.
2. As *I* was climbing a ladder, my head struck a branch.

☞ *Try It Out*

Correct each of the four sentences in the previous Try It Out exercise.

1. ______________________________

____

2. ______________________________

____

3. ______________________________

____

4. ______________________________

____

A SPECIAL NOTE: Errors in sentence logic can be slippery: When reading your own writing, you often tend subconsciously to add what is missing. Because it is more difficult to see what is illogical in your writing when you are too involved with it, plan your study time so that you can write, correct, *and then leave the product alone for a while.* Do not look at it for a day or two. When you come back to it, you will be more objective and, therefore, more able to recognize your errors.

Name: ______________________ *Date:* ______________________

EXERCISE 11j: Read each sentence given to see if the subject of the set-off section is clearly stated. If not, rewrite the sentence employing one of the two correction methods given above.

1. Chopping onions, tears ran down my face.

____

____

____

2. To feed the family, vegetables are growing in the former flower bed.

____

____

____

3. While eating an apple, a worm turned up.

____

____

____

4. Knowing about the fire drill, the teacher delayed the beginning of the test.

____

____

____

5. Dressed up for the party in a lovely gown, Horace proposed to Yolanda.

____

____

____

 Name: ______________________ *Date:* ______________________

6. To make new friends, the student lounge is a good place to visit.

____

____

____

7. Upset about the major crime wave, community meetings were held all over the city.

____

____

____

8. After shampooing the rugs, the windows were washed.

____

____

____

9. Frightened by the stampeding elephant, the circus tent was emptied by the audience.

____

____

____

10. Laughing at her clever jokes, the television talk show entertained millions of people.

____

____

____

Name: ______________________ Date: ______________________

EXERCISE 11K: REFRESHER

1. On separate paper, rewrite the following paragraph, correcting any errors in usage and informal language.
2. Correct any errors in parallelism, in logical word placement, and in logical relationship between "set off" sections and the sentences they are attached to.

Disney World, the huge amusement park in Orlando, Fla., is making use of lots of technical advances that make it perhaps the importantest city planning lab in the U.S. The park has, for example, a waste treatment plant that turns liquid sewage into a clear fluid that's then used to water a large amount of trees. Similarly, recycled waste heat is used good to power the cooling system to kind of cut costs and making maximum use of energy. Even wilder is the park's garbage transportation system, which speeds as much as 50 tons of trash daily through underground vacuum tubes to a disposal plant hidden from view outside the park which presses the garbage into real small bundles. The most spectacular achievement, however, is the enormous service basement that spreads beneath the entire park. Eliminating the need for tearing up streets to service utilities, a couple of guys can easily fix all the water, electric and sewage lines, which run through the basement hallways. In addition, a lot of tractors travel through these here hallways to make all deliveries so less trucks crowd the streets aboveground. Although today's cities can't hardly benefit from some of these super Disney World achievements no how, cities of the future may be built using these kind of amusement park advances.

 Name: ____________ Date: ____________

SPRINGBOARDS TO WRITING

Using your knowledge of the writing process, explained on pages 12–14, write a paragraph or essay related to this chapter's central theme, *our troubled society,* which is introduced on pages 374–379.

PREWRITING

To think of topics to write about, look at the cartoon, read the essay, and answer the questions that follow each. If you prefer, select one of the writing springboards below. (All paragraph numbers refer to the essay that starts on page 376.) To develop your ideas, use the prewriting techniques described on pages 15–20.

WRITING A PARAGRAPH (For help, see the Pointers on page 31.)

1. I would (would not) like to take part in "Operation Survival." (See ¶'s 11–17.)
2. Agree or disagree with these words by Henry David Thoreau: "How could youths better learn to live than by at once trying the experiment of living?" (See ¶ 3.)
3. Prayer should (should not) be allowed in public schools.
4. Physical punishment should (should not) be permitted in school.
5. Grades should (should not) be abolished in school.

WRITING AN ESSAY (For help, see the Pointers on page 35.)

6. My Plan for "Operation Survival" Where I Live (See ¶ 11–17.)
7. My Community Is (Is Not) Becoming Unlivable
8. Civilized Life Has (Has Not) Nearly Come to an End in America's Cities (See ¶ 1.)
9. Would it be good if ". . . no one could tell the dumb children from the smart children anymore?" (See ¶ 20.)
10. Agree or disagree: Children sit in "dreary classrooms" where they learn "dreary lessons." (See ¶ 7.)
11. What Is Good (Bad) About Today's High Schools?
12. Why Do Students Drop Out of School?
13. Higher Education Should (Should Not) Be Available to Everyone
14. The Advantages (Disadvantages) of Going to College
15. The Pressures for Going to College
16. What I Have Learned from Having a Job
17. Discuss this idea from paragraph 8: "People in distress will sometimes prefer a problem that is familiar to a solution that is not."

DO PEOPLE LIKE YOU?

JUNIUS ADAMS

Just about everybody in the whole world wants to be liked. Many of us, in fact, worry about the subject. Are we popular? Do we fit in with the gang? How well do we please our friends, neighbors, fellow workers, and relatives? How do people feel about *you*? Take this quiz and find out. Be sure to answer all the questions—there are no right or wrong answers—checking the response which seems closest to your own feeling or opinion. Then turn to page 413 to see how to compute your score.

1. How much room for improvement do you feel there is in your character, attitudes, skills, and habits?
   a. a great deal
   b. some
   c. just a little

2. Are your friends all pretty much similar to you in lifestyle, occupation, interests, income bracket, and so forth, or do some of them come from very different backgrounds?
   a. mostly similar
   b. similar with one or two exceptions
   c. have a number of "different" friends

3. Do people often take you aside to confide in you, tell you their troubles, or ask for personal advice?
   a. sometimes
   b. fairly often
   c. rarely

4. Generally, do you feel rather competent and efficient in handling your life, both professionally and in private?
   a. highly competent
   b. pretty competent
   c. just average

5. When a friend or acquaintance expresses an opinion you think is wrong, do you disagree or remain tactfully quiet?
   a. often disagree
   b. sometimes disagree
   c. usually keep quiet

6. Are you usually most enthusiastic and friendly when you first meet someone, or does your appreciation grow as you get to know the person better?
   a. like people right off
   b. get to like them gradually
   c. neither

7. In your particular circle, do people look to you for leadership when there's an emergency or something important needs to be done?
   a. frequently
   b. sometimes
   c. rarely

8. How would you rate yourself on build, looks, general personal appearance, and attractiveness?
   a. good appearance
   b. fairly good
   c. average or below

9. When you're someplace where you don't know anyone and have to approach a stranger for help or directions, how easy is it for you?
   a. quite easy
   b. sometimes easy, sometimes not
   c. a little awkward or embarrassing

10. If you got into bad trouble such as being arrested for a serious offense or losing your job and your savings, on whom could you count for help, excluding immediate relatives?
   a. hardly anyone
   b. a good friend or two
   c. a number of people

11. If you were taking a date to a large social gathering and at the last minute he or she decided not to go, would you:
   a. send regrets and not attend
   b. find someone else to go with
   c. go alone

12. How often do people seem to ask you for favors, assistance, small loans and the like?
   a. quite often
   b. fairly often
   c. occasionally

twelve

Courtesy Saturday Review *and the artist, Scott Val Taber.*

SPRINGBOARDS TO THINKING

For informal, not written, response . . . to stimulate your thinking

1. How do you think the bear in the cartoon feels? Explain. How do you think the man feels? Explain. If you were walking by, would you buy yourself a friendly bear hug? Why or why not?
2. Traditionally, a ''bear hug'' is a great big, friendly, warm, close hug. Do you like to give bear hugs? Why or why not? Do you like to get bear hugs? Why or why not?
3. In general, why do people need affection? Why do people need friends? Do you like to have a few close friends or a large group of friends? Explain.
4. Try out the quiz on the opposite page and then turn to page 413 to find out your score. Do you think that your score is a true reflection of you? Explain. Do you agree with Junius Adams' advice about being popular, which is given in his last paragraph on page 413? Why or why not?
5. Do you think that today's American society makes it difficult for people to make and keep friends? Why or why not? In general, do you think that loneliness is a problem in America today?

Lonely America: Looking for a Friend

RUTH WINTER

(1) Anyone who has listened to those phone-in radio programs or read the advice columns in newspapers can't help but realize there are thousands upon thousands of desperately lonely people in our society. They are so lonely, in fact, that they are willing to pour their hearts out in public to commercial pseudo-friends.

(2) Those media-made, pseudo-friends have been created specifically to capitalize upon people's need for human contact. The lure of "friendship" is used to sell products such as newspapers, deodorants, real estate—name it. But what about your own personal friends? Are they any more real or reliable than those commercial ones? How far can you—or should you—trust those you call close friends?

(3) Before you answer that you have to consider that your definition of "a friend" may be different from other people's. In reality, it may be very different from the concept held by your friend and that's where trouble may begin.

(4) Even the experts can't agree on the meaning of friendship. A Canadian psychiatrist, Thomas Verny, maintains a friend is a person with whom you can be yourself: "You don't have to play games; you don't have to pretend you are better than you really are. A friend is a person you can count on . . . and he can count on you for emotional support and even economic help, if necessary, in times of stress. A friend," Dr. Verny continues, "is someone who will listen to you at a time when you need somebody to talk to. . . . A friend is a person with whom you are comfortable . . . you can take off your mask and be yourself." And yet, another psychiatrist, Dr. Ari Kiev, chairman of the department of social psychiatry at Cornell Medical School in Manhattan, has a very different viewpoint. He agrees that a friend is very important but he believes a good friend is someone who does not allow you to lean upon him or her. In fact, when he chooses his staff at Cornell, he asks the applicant if he or she would lend money to a friend. If the answer is "yes," he does not hire the person.

(5) "A friend is many times someone who is going parallel with you on his own track," Dr. Kiev explains. "You can think of life as a tight-rope wire. If you are on it, it's kind of exhilarating to be on it alone but it is even more exhilarating if someone is on a tight-rope wire right next to you, exchanging notions. It's the sharing of some mutual experience. If, for in-

stance, someone has the same writing problem as you in the middle of the night—a mutual understanding like that can probably be one of the best moments in a friendship. It's a question of balance on the tight-rope wire. . . . You don't want to lean on the person beside you. You don't want to pull him down and you don't really want to run to catch up to him. You want to be beside him, sharing a mutual experience."

(6) Dr. Kiev maintains that friendship is "an act in a moment of time. . . . You build a relationship around shared activities. Life is a series of relationships," he muses. "You have a relationship with your spouse, child, parents . . . and then when they are all together, it's another kind of relationship. Everybody has something to contribute."

(7) Sociologist Dr. William Sadler Jr. of Bloomfield College in New Jersey, has a broad, rather than an individual, view of friendship. His main field of interest is the study of loneliness and he believes that we Americans don't have a real appreciation of friendship. "Our definition of it is superficial: 'a good companion' or 'somebody who likes you.' We say we have 'lots of friends,' but in Europe, people believe in having just one or two really good friends. In Germany, you have to know someone a long time before you call him a friend. In America, after three minutes, we are on a first name basis."

(8) Another expert who looks at the broad view of friendship, Dr. George Morren, professor of anthropology at Rutgers University in New Brunswick, New Jersey, agrees that Americans have a hard time making good friends and he thinks it is cultural and it starts at the moment of birth.

(9) "As soon as an infant is born in the United States, it is separated from its mother in the hospital. Then, when the baby is brought home, it is given its own room and has to cry to get any sort of attention. In the majority of societies, the child is in almost constant bodily contact with the mother and feeds whenever it's hungry. In this country, where we talk so much about independence, our customs foster just the opposite. The child is physically and emotionally separated from its mother and is on a very rigid, dependent schedule as far as feeding is concerned, which means the child is not self-sufficient in any way."

(10) According to the anthropologist, the most fundamental aspects of our culture are loneliness and separation of people, and our institutions maintain this state of affairs in many ways. We are compartmentalized and segregated from nursery school through senior citizens' housing. "In most cultures, little kids are taught by older kids in a natural way," Dr. Morren explains. "Our schools are not organized to take advantage of this near-peer learning. Children are sorted according to age and then taught by adults."

(11) Added to this unnatural separation which discourages friendship between age groups, the anthropologist said we have a highly competitive society which makes such relationships, even for peer groups, difficult to achieve. "Although men are supposed to have a lot of communicative behaviors which allow them to interact with complete strangers on a seemingly friendly basis, our competitive society does not allow true friendships

to be formed. For example, two business people who meet are soon on a first name basis and they exchange pleasantries. They may even talk about their families. They go out to lunch, have a few drinks; there is entertainment involved, and pretty soon they are old golf buddies. Yet, they are locked in rivalry. Neither one has a genuine feeling of friendship towards the other."

(12) For women, friendship is even more difficult to achieve, according to the anthropologist: "Our society traditionally has placed an actual barrier between women so that they are not allowed to interact in significant contacts with each other." Indeed, we have many women today in solitary confinement, as even the most naive social observer can see. They are locked up with toddlers in suburban homes or trapped in city apartments afraid to walk the streets because of the omnipresent danger of being attacked. But Dr. Morren feels that the isolation of many women is more than physical separateness. It is the inability of the whole to work well together as friends.

(13) He says that in New Guinea, where he did his field work, women have a "terrific amount" of public solidarity as a group. "They cluster together in public, arms around each other. They cooperate with each other and have real interdependence. Women are involved in the economy of the New Guinean society in a way that's just as significant as men's. There is a division of labor by sex. There is a separation of men and women but women as a group have a whole area where they operate in a very important way, just as men do."

(14) Despite the fact that we have many stellar civic and voluntary women's organizations here in America, Dr. Morren believes that real solidarity among women is rarely achieved in our society. "Women traditionally have not had such a role," he explains. "So when the feminists say that women can interact in a more significant way with each other—what they are really saying is that the barriers that exist can be broken down and the situation can be improved. Women may approach the solidarity of American men but American men are still isolated from one another, so it is a relative thing. It will be a long time before Americans of either sex reach the solidarity you find among women in New Guinea."

(15) Dr. Morren points out that people who work side by side and hand each other tools may very well have a much firmer basis for something approaching real friendship. People who work in separate offices and talk to each other by phone don't.

(16) A child care expert told me recently that one of the problems with American families today is the washing machine. When women gathered at the stream to wash clothes and talk over mutual problems, a lot of tensions were released and this view seems to fit in with what Dr. Morren contends.

(17) The Rutgers professor also maintains that the mobility of today's Americans makes it difficult for them to develop real friendships. Fifty percent of the population changes residences every year. There are rela-

tively few neighborhoods where a significant portion of the citizens have lived for ten years, let alone grown up knowing all generations of people. You don't have to be an anthropologist to see that if you don't stay in one place long enough, friendships are not going to take root and blossom. Nor do you have to be a psychiatrist to agree with Dr. Stefan A. Pasternack of Georgetown University, Washington, D.C., that friendships take time and most of us are in too much of a hurry.

(18) Dr. Pasternack says there must be ample opportunity for people to stay in contact with each other to preserve the integrity of friendship. "You have to go to lunch with a colleague or have someone meet you after dinner for a beer or make a home visit to a friend to straighten out a problem and that takes time. You can't have friendship if you are not going to put time into it. Everybody is in a hurry today as if human relationships didn't deserve attention. It's a paradox that we are supposed to have shorter work weeks now than ever before but nobody has any time. Everybody is so busy doing their own thing, they're not doing things with the people they ought to be doing them with. . . . So it's a challenge finding time to care for each other."

(19) Do we really need friends in our society? Anthropologist Morren points out that friendship is good for one's mental health: "It's not just being able to talk to someone but being able to talk to somebody and being constantly reinforced in your beliefs . . . it's knowing that what you are saying is meaningful and that it is not going to be used against you. The problem in our society is also one of trust because of its competitive nature." He says the vast majority of people are cogs in the wheel: "Contrast this to New Guinea where every person can do everything and every person sees himself or herself as his or her own master. Nobody has a corner on any particular specialty or any particular resource.

(20) "In New Guinea," he continues, "there is a sense of kinship. If you need something, you can get it from someone in the family. But here, in America, community and extended family bonds have loosened and even the nuclear family is breaking up, so we have a greater need for friendship than ever before." As the community and extended family bonds began to untie 75 years ago, says Morren, secondary associations such as the civic and common interest groups burgeoned, but now even those kinds of bonds are diminishing and people are becoming more and more isolated.

(21) How can you find and keep a friend? According to social scientists, the search for friendship and discussions about loneliness have replaced sex as the number one topic on college campuses. But not only the young are in search of this human relationship. Loneliness affects everyone—old and young, rich or poor, smart or dumb. And yet, it is becoming obvious that it is more difficult today than ever before to establish good, true friendships.

(22) Psychiatrists Verny and Kiev both believe that in order to have friends, you have to like and understand yourself first. "The only people who can really have a deep kind of friendship are those who have a fairly good understanding of themselves," Dr. Verny says. "You must be in touch

with your feelings and you must be able to share your feelings. You must be able to risk yourself a little bit and be vulnerable to rejection. Otherwise, you will have a superficial acquaintanceship."

(23) Dr. Kiev maintains that if you take care of yourself first, then you begin to recognize the autonomy of other people: "You recognize their special natures, their different rhythms, their uniqueness, their talents, their similarities and differences from you, and then you respect their territory and you don't intrude on it. You don't talk about things that might be distressing to them. You can take the lead from them. Just as you protect yourself, you realize that other people have the desire to protect themselves."

(24) This desire to protect oneself from being hurt or uncomfortable, however, is just what makes many people lonely, according to Santa Monica, California, psychologist Dr. Jerry Greenwald. He says lonely people are so afraid of being rejected that they withdraw. Dr. Greenwald, who is the author of *Be the Person You Were Meant to Be* (Simon and Schuster), divides behavior up into nourishing (good) and toxic (destructive). "The lonely person lacks development of his self-nourishing potentials. He feels an emptiness within himself and looks to the world to fill it in. His cry is: 'Here I am. Somebody please love me.' He proclaims to the world that he has a lot to give if only he could find the right person or someone to appreciate him."

(25) Dr. Greenwald describes a number of types which have trouble making and keeping friends. Perhaps you recognize someone you know among them:

(26) *The storm troopers.* Consider themselves very outgoing and extroverted. They may hang on to your every comment, ask a barrage of questions as they physically move towards you, or may argue as a form of "stimulating discussion." After listening intently in order to show interest, they proceed to monopolize the conversation, remaining oblivious to the boredom of others.

(27) *The psychic anesthetized.* They use alcohol and drugs to relax for social occasions and to be more outgoing. Superficially, the goal is accomplished; conversation flows more easily; tension is reduced. But fears are anesthetized along with tensions and the result is psychological dependency on alcohol or drugs, while loneliness increases.

(28) *The jokers.* They must be the life of the party when others are present. The message is: "I joke all the time. Don't take me seriously or think I need anything more. All I want is to have fun!" Chronic jokers are also subtle saboteurs. Serious or intimate conversations sometimes do occur but they are apt to be short-lived. Just at the point where the other people may feel some real closeness, they are undercut by the joker's ubiquitous humor which wipes out the previous intimacy.

(29) *The I-can't-stand-to-be-alones.* The avoidance of being alone may become compulsive. They have systematic routines of activities and contacts to fill any voids of being alone even for a single evening. They may

have a priority list of people they can contact should gaps in schedules occur. They use people for their immediate needs which are to avoid being alone.

(30) *The expert relaters.* This is a new brand of lonely people who are a manifestation of the age of psychology. These are the "enlightened" who have been psychoanalyzed, psychotherapized and encounter-groupized. They have learned to call the other person a dirty son of a bitch without flinching or feeling guilty. Their warmth and affection is readily demonstrable by their willingness to hug, kiss and "relate." Only gameplayers, their daily life remains as empty as ever.

(31) Dr. Greenwald concludes that "no matter how rich and gratifying a relationship may be, when a person seeks from others something which he must find from within himself, he dooms himself to a lonely, alienated existence. It is absurd to ask another person to remedy another's loneliness, no matter how caring and loving that person may be."

(32) Dr. Kiev puts it even more strongly. He believes that we should not rely on our friends to get us out of trouble by loaning us money or interceding in our behalf: "All those people who are disappointing you by not giving you what you think they should may be your best friends. Adversity is oftentimes one of the best ways to make you realize what you can do. A really good friend lets you become more of yourself and encourages you to handle matters yourself." Which means friends let us be ourselves.

READING SURVEY

1. *Main idea*

What is the central theme of this essay?

2. *Major Details*

a. According to Dr. George Morren, why do Americans have difficulty in making friends?
b. Even though business people form many business and social relationships, why don't genuine feelings of friendship develop?
c. According to psychiatrists Verny and Kiev, what kind of person is the only type who can form a deep friendship?

3. *Inferences*

a. Read paragraph 4 again. Why does Dr. Kiev feel that a good friend is someone who doesn't allow you to lean upon him or her?
b. Read paragraph 18 again. If the work week is shorter now than ever before, why is everybody so busy that people have no time to form close friendships?

4. *Opinions*

a. Read paragraphs 4 to 7 again. What is *your* definition of friendship?
b. Since our culture makes the formation of true, lasting friendship difficult, what recommendations do you have to help people overcome barriers to friendship?

TAKE THE QUIZ "DO PEOPLE LIKE YOU" BY JUNIUS ADAMS, PAGE 404. THEN FIND YOUR SCORE BY USING THE CHART BELOW, AND READ THE ANALYSIS TO LEARN MORE ABOUT YOURSELF.

Find the point value of each answer you checked and add up your total score.

1.	(a)	1	(b)	4	(c)	2	7.	(a)	2	(b)	4	(c)	1
2.	(a)	1	(b)	2	(c)	4	8.	(a)	4	(b)	2	(c)	1
3.	(a)	2	(b)	4	(c)	1	9.	(a)	4	(b)	2	(c)	1
4.	(a)	2	(b)	4	(c)	1	10.	(a)	1	(b)	2	(c)	4
5.	(a)	4	(b)	2	(c)	1	11.	(a)	1	(b)	2	(c)	4
6.	(a)	1	(b)	4	(c)	2	12.	(a)	2	(b)	4	(c)	1

34 points or more:

Most people find you likable and easy to get along with. Even if you sometimes argue or get angry with them, they feel good about knowing you and see you as basically well-intentioned and trustworthy.

23 to 33 points:

Respect rather than affection is what you tend to command. Though people might want to get to know you better, you often seem too superior or reserved to give them much encouragement. Your style is more to have a small circle of good friends than to be widely popular.

12 to 22 points:

If anything, you're a little too friendly and eager to please. Since they sense they needn't make much of an effort with you, people often take you for granted and fail to give you the consideration you deserve. You tend to lack self-confidence, and if someone wants to know you, they must work hard to gain your confidence.

Would you like to be more popular? Then you should cultivate the traits which, according to psychologists, contribute most to "social attractiveness." Here are the main ones: (1) physical beauty, handsomeness, or impressiveness of appearance; (2) self-confidence, superiority, or competence, softened by some evidence of human weakness such as making occasional mistakes; (3) a seeming tendency to like people despite differences rather than because of similarities in background and opinions; and (4) an attitude which may show reluctance but offers more and more approval as time goes by.

VOCABULARY BUILDING

Lesson One: The Vocabulary of Friendship

The essay "Lonely America: Looking for a Friend" by Ruth Winter includes words that are useful when you are discussing friendship.

reliable	(paragraph 2)	**interact**	(11)
mutual	(5)	**solidarity**	(13)
foster	(9)	**kinship**	(20)
peer	(10)	**intimate**	(28) . . . **intimacy** (28)
communicative	(11)	**gratifying**	(31)

Most people like to have friends. A friend is often a **peer,** someone who is the same age or who has similar abilities. A good friend is usually **reliable** in that he or she can be counted upon when needed. Also, good friends often share the same interests. Such **mutual** interests help develop and stimulate—and thereby **foster**—friendships.

Very close friends are usually **communicative** in that they talk openly and easily with one another. Thus, by reacting and acting together, they **interact** and become very personal, private, **intimate** friends. This **intimacy** or personal familiarity in a good friendship often leads to a sense of **solidarity,** a feeling of complete, solid unity. Such **kinship,** which is a close relationship sometimes but not always based on family ties, is usually very **gratifying** in that it is pleasing and satisfying.

EXERCISE 12a: Match each classified ad shown with a vocabulary word from the lesson.

CLASSIFIED ADS

HELP WANTED

TALK WITH others easily? We need you in our front office to help our employees talk and exchange information with one another. Drop in for an interview at the SILENT-T RANCH.

1. ______________________

WANT A SATISFYING, pleasing experience? Here you can be creative and feel good about yourself. Send résumé to ACHIEVEMENT WORKS, Inc.

2. ______________________

 Name: ______________________ Date: ______________________

WE BELIEVE IN solid relations between management and labor. Unity is all! Call for information about an opening for a loyal personnel manager at GIBRALTAR'S, Ltd.

3. ______________________

SITUATIONS WANTED

DEPEND ON ME to come through every time. Always there when needed. Call anytime: 735-4225, ext. 3.

4. ______________________

MY TALENT is in developing and stimulating your workers to greater achievements. Very creative methods. Contact Stephen at his Old Kentucky Home.

5. ______________________

I ACT AND REACT well with people. Very good at working in response to others. Use me for a job in customer relations. Call Joe at 468-3722, ext. 8.

6. ______________________

PERSONAL NOTICES

ARE YOU LIKE ME? Let's find out if we are the same age, for example. Maybe we can be friends or we can start a club of others like us. Write Mr. Lookingglass at Box 7337.

7. ______________________

PERHAPS WE HAVE similar interests. We can share as we relax and discover each other. Call at night, 631-6000

8. ______________________

I AM LOOKING FOR A good friendship, perhaps with a relative. Want that feeling of closeness in my life. If you are for me, write Ms. A. Bond at Friendly House.

9. ______________________

LET'S GET FAMILIAR! Private relationships my specialty. Reveal your most personal secrets and life to me. Find me at the PRIVATE-PERSON'S BAR.

10. ______________________

Name: ______________________ Date: ______________________

Lesson Two: The Vocabulary of Loneliness

The essay "Lonely America: Looking for a Friend" by Ruth Winter includes words that are useful when you are discussing loneliness.

superficial	(paragraph 7)
dependent	(9)
segregated	(10)
competitive	(11)
rivalry	(11)
isolated	(14)
vulnerable	(22)
rejection	(22)
intrude	(23)
saboteur	(28)

People sometimes feel lonely because they have **superficial** relationships which are shallow and limited in that they are concerned only with obvious surface features or behavior.

People sometimes feel lonely because they feel **dependent** in that they rely on someone else's influence and control.

People sometimes feel lonely because they are, or they feel they are, **segregated** or set apart from the main group and put into a group of their own.

People sometimes feel lonely because they are **competitive** in that they always compete with others, thinking that everything is a contest. This battle of striving for the same goal often leads to unfriendly competition known as **rivalry.**

People sometimes feel lonely because they feel **isolated** or alone and away from other people.

People sometimes feel lonely because they feel **vulnerable** in that they feel open to being easily hurt, either by physical attack or by criticism.

People sometimes feel lonely because they suffer from a feeling of **rejection** or being discarded or being passed over as worthless and useless.

People sometimes feel lonely because they are afraid to **intrude,** in that they do not want to force themselves into a situation without permission or an invitation.

People sometimes feel lonely because they feel someone else is a **saboteur** or someone who intentionally destroys or gets in the way of an activity or an effort.

EXERCISE 12b: Using the vocabulary words in this lesson, fill in the correct words in the parentheses.

CAMPUS NOTICE

A FRIEND IS NEAR

Do you feel all alone (1. ________________) and set apart from the main group and forced into your own group (2. ________________)?

If you have these bad feelings or if you are afraid of being ignored and considered worthless (3. ________________), dial FRIENDS (374-3637), our friendly Dial-A-Friend Service. Some people say we offer only shallow, surface (4. ________________) friendship, but we disagree.

Don't let someone get in your way (5. ________________). Reach out to your phone and call us. We do not want to force ourselves into your life without permission (6. ________________). We can, however, offer you advice if you, for example, rely on others too much (7. ________________). Or perhaps you feel too easily open to hurt (8. ________________). Or perhaps you want to stop seeing everything as a contest (9. ________________), a behavior pattern that locks you into unfriendly striving for the same goal as others have (10. ________________). These and many other problems can be talked out—call us today.

Name: ________________________ Date: ________________

SPELLING

Lesson One: Spelling Demons

Here are some more words that are frequently misspelled. Using the helpful techniques given in Chapter One, be sure to learn these new Demons, which are taken from "Lonely America: Looking for a Friend."

allowed	**easily**	**parallel**
appreciation	**entertainment**	**proceed**
basis	**individual**	**recognize**
busy	**loneliness**	**relative**
competitive	**lonely**	**schedule**
definition	**nuclear**	**separate**
difference	**operate**	**subtle**
discourage	**opposite**	**sufficient**

Lesson Two: Spelling Rule — Doubling

Many of the words in Ruth Winter's essay can be learned easily with the help of this one simple spelling rule.

When a suffix is added to a word, the final consonant of the word is doubled if the word meets all of these three tests:

1. The suffix begins with a vowel.
2. The word ends with a single vowel followed by a consonant.
3. The word is one syllable or has its accent on the last syllable.

☞ *Try It Out*

Add the suffixes indicated to the following words.

	-ing	-ed	-ment
equip	________	________	________
establish	________	________	________
ship	________	________	________

 Name: ________________ *Date:* ________________

Here are some examples:

begin + ing = begi*nn*ing	drop + ed = dro*pp*ed
hot + est = ho*tt*est	forget + ful = forge*t*ful
cost + ing = cos*t*ing	happen + ed = happe*n*ed

 *Try It Out*

Apply the doubling rule to the following words.

shift + ed = __________	appear + ance = __________
stop + ing = __________	forbid + en = __________
fat + er = __________	develop + ment = __________

EXERCISE 12c: Apply the doubling rule to these words.

1. wrap + ed = __________
2. permit + ing = __________
3. mean + est = __________
4. rot + en = __________
5. forget + able = __________
6. broil + ed = __________
7. beg + ar = __________
8. occur + ence = __________
9. drug + ist = __________
10. visit + ing = __________

Name: __________ *Date:* __________

11. refer + al = ______________________

12. shop + er = ______________________

13. happen + ed = ______________________

14. admit + ance = ______________________

15. slim + est = ______________________

16. fit + ness = ______________________

17. swim + ing = ______________________

18. war + ior = ______________________

19. clean + er = ______________________

20. plan + ed = ______________________

EXERCISE 12d: Using the Spelling Demons in this chapter, fill in the blanks with any missing letters.

1. Some people have tried to d__ sc____r__ge the United States from participating in the com___t_____ve nuc______r arms race that has led to the creation of a su__fi______nt number of atomic weapons to destroy the earth.

2. Dictionary def______tions fail to point out the su____le dif____r__n__e between being "lon____y" and being "alone." A person suffering from lon______ness lives a sad, painful existence while an ind__v__d____l who is alone may keep b____y with many rewarding activities that form the bas__s for a happy life.

 Name: ______________________ Date: ______________________

3. To obtain a driver's license, a person must prove that he or she has learned to reco____i__e traffic signs, to park a car pa__al____l to a curb, and to op______te a car safely and eas____y.

4. Stingy Stella al____wed her rel__t__ves to voice their ap__re______tion for her delicious dinner before she presented each of them with a sep__r__te check for the meal.

5. In spite of viewer protests, the television network pro____ded with its plan to s____ed__le its best enter________ment programs directly o__p______te those of the other networks.

The Essay: EXPLAINING A PROCESS CONSTRUCTING A DEFINITION ARGUING AN OPINION

There are many types of expository essays. In this chapter, three of the most frequently assigned types will be discussed. They are:

Explaining a Process
Constructing a Definition
Arguing an Opinion

If you refer to Chapter Seven of this book, you will be reminded that an expository essay is written for the purpose of conveying information. Thus, any of the specific types of expository essays listed above are merely alternative approaches to the main purpose—to convey information. In addition, you will be reminded that in many ways an expository essay has the same structure as a paragraph, except that the essay has more extended discussion and uses additional specific examples.

This chart summarizes the connections between the paragraph and the essay:

The Paragraph	*Purpose*	**The Essay**
the topic sentence	to state, limit, and control the main idea	the introductory paragraph
development with use of facts; examples; incident; definition; comparison and contrast; or statistics, names, and the senses	to develop the main idea with specific points	the main body paragraphs (There should be at least three of them.)
(in certain cases, the concluding sentence)	to conclude by coming back to the general main idea	the concluding paragraph

Explaining a Process

Curiosity to explore and understand the unknown is typical of the human mind. Expository essays that explain a process should encourage the reader's natural curiosity. There are three basic types of process essays:

I The most familiar is the *How to* . . . type of process essay. It gives directions which should be clearly stated step by step so that the reader can learn, for example, how to make pizza or how to clean a bolt-action rifle.

II A favorite of many people is the *How . . . Was Done* type of process essay. It describes how something unusual and complicated was achieved so that the reader can learn, for example, how the United States won the race to the moon or how I lost ninety pounds in six months.

III Of particular interest to many people is the *How . . . Works* type of process essay. It explains, in nontechnical language, how scientific and complex processes work so that the reader can learn, for example, how the atomic bomb is detonated or how radio waves are transmitted.

In all process essays, the introduction should state **what the process is and why it is important.** Then, the main body paragraphs should clearly and logically describe the steps in the process.

☞ *Try It Out*

For each process given, tell why it is important.

1. How to Make a Good Impression on Your Boss. Why important? ______________

____

____

2. How to Plan an Exciting Party. Why important? ______________

____

____

In explaining a process, you should also **make your essay lively** so that it encourages curiosity and entertains as it teaches. To do more than merely recite a recipe or give a dry list of facts and dates, you can try to include one or more of the following—if they clearly relate to the process: (1) an amusing or dramatic incident, (2) an unusually surprising fact, (3) a conclusion that challenges the reader to think and explore further.

☞ *Try It Out*

Specifically, how would you make the following process essays lively and interesting?

1. Think of how you learned to play a sport. If you had to write an essay that tells how this process was done, what might you include to make it more lively and interesting?

   A surprising fact: ____________________

   ____

   An amusing or dramatic incident: ____________________

   ____

   A challenge to think and explore further: ____________________

   ____

2. Assume that you must write a process essay that tells how an appliance in your home works. (Consult the appliance manual for information.) What might you include to make it more lively and interesting?

   A surprising fact: ____________________

   ____

   An amusing or dramatic incident: ____________________

   ____

   A challenge to think and explore further: ____________________

   ____

 Name: ____________________ *Date:* ____________________

POINTERS FOR EXPLAINING A PROCESS

1. The *introduction* should always tell what the process is and why it is important.

2. The *main body paragraphs* should give the parts of the process in an order that is appropriate for the clear and logical presentation of a topic. Time is the most common type of order; it presents what happened first, second, third, etc.
   Here are the most useful types of order:

The order (or its reverse)	*For example:*
BY IMPORTANCE:	How I Lost Ninety Pounds in Six Months Introductory paragraph I. will power II. dietetic foods III. doctors and drugs Concluding paragraph
BY LOCATION:	How to Clean a Bolt-Action Rifle Introductory paragraph I. the bore II. the breech III. the stock Concluding paragraph
FROM SIMPLE TO COMPLEX:	How the Atomic Bomb is Detonated Introductory paragraph I. bomb design II. Uranium-235 III. the implosion chamber Concluding paragraph
FROM KNOWN TO UNKNOWN:	How the U.S. Won the Race to the Moon Introductory paragraph I. billions of dollars II. dedicated specialists III. scientific breakthroughs Concluding paragraph

OF TIME: How to Make Pizza

Introductory paragraph

I. the proper ingredients

II. hands, utensils, and oven

III. the masterful combining of ingredients

Concluding paragraph

3. To avoid being dull, tease the reader's curiosity with a particularly interesting piece of information or arouse the reader's interest with an amusing or dramatic incident.

4. In order to achieve a unified essay, use words of transition and the deliberate repetition of key words which will tie the parts together.

5. The *conclusion* can challenge the reader to think and explore thoroughly.

EXERCISE 12e: For each process essay title given, select the type of order that would be most effective. Then list three major parts of the process by indicating the main idea of each paragraph.

1. How to Make Friends Order: ______________

Introductory paragraph

I. ____________________________________

II. ____________________________________

III. ____________________________________

Concluding paragraph

2. How to Improve Your Appearance Order: ______________

Introductory paragraph

I. ____________________________________

II. ____________________________________

III. ____________________________________

Concluding paragraph

 Name: ______________________ *Date:* ______________

3. How Television Influences Young People — Order: ______

Introductory paragraph

I. ______

II. ______

III. ______

Concluding paragraph

4. How to Write an Effective Essay — Order: ______

Introductory paragraph

I. ______

II. ______

III. ______

Concluding paragraph

5. How to Save Money on Expensive Purchases — Order: ______

Introductory paragraph

I. ______

II. ______

III. ______

Concluding paragraph

6. How to Make a Bedroom Truly Comfortable — Order: ______

Introductory paragraph

I. ______

II. ______

III. ______

Concluding paragraph

7. How to Make a Perfect Hamburger Order: ____________

Introductory paragraph

I. ______________________________

II. ______________________________

III. ______________________________

Concluding paragraph

8. How to Reduce Crime in My Neighborhood Order: ____________

Introductory paragraph

I. ______________________________

II. ______________________________

III. ______________________________

Concluding paragraph

9. How to Select a Good Stereo System Order: ____________

Introductory paragraph

I. ______________________________

II. ______________________________

III. ______________________________

Concluding paragraph

10. How to Keep a Car Clean and Shiny Order: ____________

Introductory paragraph

I. ______________________________

II. ______________________________

III. ______________________________

Concluding paragraph

 Name: ______________________ *Date:* ______________

11. How the Public School System Can Be Improved

Order: ______________

Introductory paragraph

I. ______________________________

II. ______________________________

III. ______________________________

Concluding paragraph

EXERCISE 12f: Are the following introductions to process essays appropriate? Why or why not? As you evaluate them, refer to the Pointers for Explaining a Process in this chapter, and to the list of Common Errors to Avoid in Introductions and Conclusions, in Chapter Seven.

1. *Title:* How to Survive in the Wilderness

   Introduction:

   Do you know how to search for water in the wilderness? Do you know what roots and berries are safe to eat? If so, you will have more of a chance of surviving if you are lost in the wilderness. Without a doubt, if people would learn basic survival techniques for the wilderness, many lives would be saved every year.

   Question: Appropriate? Why or why not?

   ____

   ____

   ____

   ____

   ____

   ____

2. *Title:* How to Take Notes in Class

Introduction:

In this essay, I will tell you how to take notes in class. After all, education means everything today. You must concentrate because daydreaming will lead to trouble. Also, you need good supplies such as paper and pens or sharpened pencils.

Question: Appropriate? Why or why not?

____

____

____

____

____

____

3. *Title:* How to Make People Hate You

Introduction:

Making people hate you is not very hard. With some determination, you can learn a few tricks and become an expert. Then you can have all the time you want to be alone and do all the things you want to do by yourself. Of course, if you would like to have the opposite effect on people, this advice can be a guide to what you should avoid in your relationships with other people.

Question: Appropriate? Why or why not?

____

____

____

____

____

____

 Name: ______________________ *Date:* ______________

4. *Title:* How to Recognize Sex Roles

Introduction:

My mother is a good woman who always stays home and cares for her children. She loves her family, and so she does not go running around the streets. I don't know much about sex roles because I have been brought up the true American way, but I will try to discuss what I know in this essay.

Question: Appropriate? Why or why not?

____

____

____

____

____

____

5. *Title:* How to Avoid Getting Mugged

Introduction:

Want your purse or wallet taken? Or perhaps you might like your watch and jewelry "borrowed" by force permanently? Crime statistics show that murder and arson in our large cities are increasing, and burglary and auto theft in our suburbs and rural areas are becoming huge problems.

Question: Appropriate? Why or why not?

____

____

____

____

____

____

Constructing a Definition

In writing an essay that constructs a definition, you have the opportunity to approach a subject with more thoroughness and spirit than the efficient, short dictionary definition does. A well-built definition essay **breaks a subject into parts** that can be clearly understood.

Usually a definition essay is constructed so that it will have **the effect of stimulating thought and providing a fresh approach** to a topic. This type of essay is always written for a specific purpose. Some of the more popular types of definition essays are:

ESSAYS WRITTEN TO SUGGEST A NEW OR ENLARGED WAY OF LOOKING AT SOMETHING. For example:

What Is Love?

Immediately, many people will think of the relationship, often sexual, between a man and a woman. But consider these other types of love:

parent for child
person for God
person for money
child for a pet
animal for its master
dictators for their power
person for learning
scientist for science
person for country
person for self

Try It Out

List eight possible ways of looking at the question: What is wealth? Try to include some types of wealth not often thought about.

_______________ _______________

_______________ _______________

_______________ _______________

_______________ _______________

II ESSAYS WRITTEN TO ILLUSTRATE AND COMMENT ON AN ASPECT OF HUMAN NATURE, SOCIETY, ETC. Often this is done by the construction of a definition of an event, a person, or a place.

 *Try It Out*

Answer these questions by referring to the essay "Lonely America: Looking for a Friend," which appears at the beginning of this chapter. Use your own paper.

1. What two aspects of society are being discussed?
2. What key term is defined in the first two paragraphs?
3. What key term is discussed in paragraphs 4 through 6?
4. In paragraph 7, sociologist Sadler compares friendship patterns in various places. How does he describe friendship in (a) Europe? (b) Germany? (c) America?
5. In paragraph 11, anthropologist Morren explains how our competitive society makes friendship difficult. What is his explanation?
6. In paragraphs 26 through 30, psychologist Greenwald describes five types of people who have trouble making friends. List his types and briefly describe each.

III ESSAYS WRITTEN TO CLARIFY AN EXISTING PRACTICE AND PERHAPS TO PRESENT A NEW PLAN OF ACTION. Often this type can persuade the reader.

Try It Out

Answer these questions by referring to the essay "Once Upon a Time—A Fable of Student Power" by Neil Postman, which appears in Chapter Eleven. Use your own paper.

1. In order to clarify the existing situation, Neil Postman defines city life in paragraph 1. What does he say?
2. In order to clarify the existing feeling about school, what does the author say in paragraph 10?
3. In paragraph 11, what plan for the schools is suggested?
4. What is the author's definition of "Operation Survival"?
5. What is the author's new definition of education as given in paragraph 19?
6. Why, if the author wished to clarify an existing situation and present a new plan of action, did he write it in the form of a fable?

Name: ______________________ Date: ______________________

POINTERS FOR CONSTRUCTING A DEFINITION

1. The *introduction* should state what is being defined. You should avoid using a dictionary definition because it provides too narrow a start (and because it is a technique vastly overused by students). The introduction might consider such questions as, "What or whom does it affect?" "Why is it significant?" "When did it take place?" when such questions are appropriate for the subject being defined.

2. The *main body paragraphs* should break what is being defined into its major parts. A separate paragraph should be devoted to each of these major parts. If what you are defining is:
   ... *an object,* such as an automobile, the parts are concrete;
   ... *an idea, person,* or *place,* such as love, President Lincoln, or Cape Canaveral, the parts can be things that are not concrete because they concern abstract ideas such as spirit and feelings.

3. The *parts that you select* will reflect your judgment, point of view, and major purpose, such as:
   a. to suggest a new or enlarged way of looking at something.
   b. to illustrate and comment on an aspect of human nature, society, etc.
   c. to clarify an existing practice and perhaps present a new plan of action.

4. The *order* in which the selected parts are presented should be clear and logical. Look back at the Pointers for Explaining a Process on pages 425–426 for a more complete explanation of these orders: by importance, by location, from simple to complex, from known to unknown, and of time.

5. If your definition seems too shallow, try to enrich your perception of the subject. Try thinking about your subject in terms of:
   a. its physical properties (through all five senses: sight, touch, hearing, smell, taste).
   b. its uses—and dangers.
   c. its effect on: people, history, attitudes, etc.
   d. what it is not.

6. Whenever possible, illustrate with specific examples, facts, or incidents. A definition that merely recites synonyms goes around in circles because it avoids being specific.

EXERCISE 12g: The parts listed for each of the definition essays given are too shallow for the scope and purpose of the title given. Referring to the Pointers for Constructing a Definition, tell why the definition is shallow and then list parts that would be more appropriate for the title.

1. TV Advertisements—An Insult to the American Public

	Revised Parts
Introduction	Introduction
I. Ads are frequent.	I. __________
II. Ads interrupt good programs.	II. __________
III. Ads try to sell products.	III. __________
Conclusion	Conclusion

Why shallow? ____________________

____

2. Is College Necessary?

	Revised Parts
Introduction	Introduction
I. College educates people.	I. __________
II. A college education is a good idea.	II. __________
III. College is not for everyone.	III. __________
Conclusion	Conclusion

Why shallow? ____________________

____

3. Vanishing Wildlife—A Tragic Loss

	Revised Parts
Introduction	Introduction
I. Wildlife is an asset.	I. ______
II. We need wildlife.	II. ______
III. Wildlife enriches our lives.	III. ______
Conclusion	Conclusion

Why shallow? ______

______

______

______

4. Success Cannot Be Measured by Money Alone

	Revised Parts
Introduction	Introduction
I. Money is not everything.	I. ______
II. Success means more than wealth.	II. ______
III. Successful people I know.	III. ______
Conclusion	Conclusion

Why shallow? ______

______

______

______

5. Indoor Plants Can Brighten your Life

	Revised Parts
Introduction	Introduction
I. Plants are living things.	I. __________
II. Plants need to be fed.	II. __________
III. Plants need care.	III. __________
Conclusion	Conclusion

Why shallow? ____________________

____

____

____

6. Exercise Builds Bodies

	Revised Parts
Introduction	Introduction
I. Exercise is healthy.	I. __________
II. Exercise is good for you.	II. __________
III. The body needs exercise.	III. __________
Conclusion	Conclusion

Why shallow? ____________________

____

____

____

____

Name: ____________________ Date: ____________________

7. A Good Friend Is a Treasure

	Revised Parts
Introduction	Introduction
I. A good friend is rare.	I. __________
II. A good friend is hard to find.	II. __________
III. Loneliness is a sad feeling.	III. __________
Conclusion	Conclusion

Why shallow? __________

8. Professional Sports—Just Another Business

	Revised Parts
Introduction	Introduction
I. Players are property.	I. __________
II. Players are owned.	II. __________
III. Players are often traded.	III. __________
Conclusion	Conclusion

Why shallow? __________

 Name: __________ Date: __________

9. Life Is Not Fair

	Revised Parts
Introduction	Introduction
I. Things don't always work out.	I. ____________
II. We all have some bad luck.	II. ____________
III. The "bad" comes with the "good."	III. ____________
Conclusion	Conclusion

Why shallow? ____________

____

____

____

EXERCISE 12h: Construct a definition for each topic given. First, decide on a purpose for your definition. Next, select the parts that should be discussed in order to achieve your purpose.

1. Topic: wastefulness

Your purpose: ____________

____

____

____

Parts selected: I. ____________

II. ____________

III. ____________

2. Topic: cars

Your purpose: ______________________________

____

____

____

Parts selected: I. ______________________________

II. ______________________________

III. ______________________________

3. Topic: a favorite relative

Your purpose: ______________________________

____

____

____

Parts selected: I. ______________________________

II. ______________________________

III. ______________________________

4. Topic: noise pollution

Your purpose: ______________________________

____

____

____

Parts selected: I. ______________________________

II. ______________________________

III. ______________________________

 Name: ______________________________ Date: ______________________________

5. Topic: diets

Your purpose: ______________________________

____

____

____

Parts selected: I. ______________________________

II. ______________________________

III. ______________________________

6. Topic: trees

Your purpose: ______________________________

____

____

____

Parts selected: I. ______________________________

II. ______________________________

III. ______________________________

7. Topic: an apple

Your purpose: ______________________________

____

____

____

Parts selected: I. ______________________________

II. ______________________________

III. ______________________________

Arguing an Opinion

Most people would like to have reasonable, well-thought-out opinions on many of the subjects that are of major concern in life. Intelligent opinions should be **based on evidence that is factual and logical.** Such opinions, however, should not be rigidly unchangeable; if an argument presents either new evidence or a new approach to already known evidence, people should be open-minded enough to alter their opinion.

In arguing an opinion, your purpose is to **tell the reader *why* you have your opinion and to persuade the reader to agree with you.** By the use of facts, reasons, examples, authorities, and other evidence, you should build a forceful and convincing argument.

To evaluate the effectiveness of an essay that argues an opinion, you should ask two questions:

I IS THE OPINION BASED ON FACTS AND SPECIFIC EVIDENCE RATHER THAN ON PERSONAL JUDGMENTS AND EMOTIONAL REACTIONS? A fact is something that can be clearly measured or observed; specific evidence is something that comes from a recognized authority, such as an encyclopedia, a book, or a person who is an expert.

☞ *Try It Out*

Select which of each set is a fact:

1. ________ a. In 1776 a person with an income of $4,000 a year was considered to be very wealthy.

   ________ b. If every American household earned at least $20,000 a year, the country's problems would be solved.

2. ________ a. Grizzly bears are mean, ugly animals.

   ________ b. A grizzly bear can run as fast as a horse.

3. ________ a. The essay "Lonely in America: Looking for a Friend" by Ruth Winter explains that many people are lonely today because they are unable to form good friendships.

   ________ b. The essay "Lonely in America: Looking for a Friend" by Ruth Winter presents a convincing case about the importance of having friendships in today's society.

II DOES THE METHOD OF PRESENTING THE OPINION HAVE ENOUGH IMPACT TO PERSUADE THE READER TO AGREE? Some of the devices you can use when planning an effective argument can be borrowed from the other types of expository essays discussed in this chapter:

a. To support an opinion, include a dramatic incident which illustrates the main point.

b. To explain an opinion, describe the process of how something is, was, or might be.

c. To clarify an opinion, construct a clear definition of a key term or concept.

Try It Out

Refer to the essay "The Tube Syndrome," which appears at the beginning of Chapter One.

1. In paragraph 1 thc author describes a process. What is it?

 ____

 ____

2. What incident does the author use in paragraph 6?

 ____

 ____

3. In paragraph 7 the author defines the impact of television on the intellectual abilities of viewers. Summarize the definition.

 ____

 ____

4. In paragraph 10 the author describes a process. What is it?

 ____

 ____

Name: ______________________ *Date:* ______________________

POINTERS FOR ARGUING AN OPINION

1. The *introduction* should lead into the reasons for your opinion. This can be done by:
   a. stating your opinion at the outset.
   b. giving an appropriate incident which will clearly illustrate and give impact to your opinion.
   c. asking a provocative question which will stimulate thought on the subject of your opinion.

2. The *full statement of your opinion* should appear where it has the most impact. This can be done in the introduction, main body, or conclusion.
   a. If your opinion is in the introduction, all reasons given must relate directly back to your basic position and the conclusion should include a restatement of your opinion.
   b. If your opinion is in the main body, it should smoothly follow the device used in the introduction.
   c. If your opinion is in the conclusion, it should not come as a surprise; all the reasons presented must build to the inevitable climax or conclusion.

3. The *support for your opinion* should be based on facts, examples, authorities, and other specific evidence. This support must be strong enough to stand on its own. The reader should be able to form an intelligent opinion from the evidence you have presented; you should not have to insist that you are correct.

4. Your argument should be logical. Refer to Appendix I for a more complete discussion of logic so that you will be reminded not to make errors such as oversimplification, generalization, attacking the person, and so on.

5. For impact try these argument techniques:
   a. To illustrate:
      . . . use a dramatic incident.
      . . . explain the process of how something was, is, or might be.
   b. To clarify:
      . . . give a clear definition of a key term.
      . . . ask an organizing question to give focus.
      . . . anticipate an objection by stating it and then answering it.
   c. To dramatize:
      . . . give the dangers of the present system.
      . . . make a comparison to something else.

EXERCISE 12i: Read each of the following statements carefully. Label each either *fact* or *opinion.*

_________ 1. The famous Washington, D.C., cherry trees were a gift from the mayor of Tokyo in 1912.

_________ 2. "Sanka" comes from the French phrase *sans caffeine,* meaning "without caffeine."

_________ 3. The giant panda is a cuddly, adorable animal that everyone loves to admire.

_________ 4. Colleges should provide day-care services for the children of adult students.

_________ 5. Elvis Presley owned 18 televisions sets.

_________ 6. Benjamin Franklin campaigned unsuccessfully to have the turkey declared our national symbol.

_________ 7. The White House has 132 rooms.

_________ 8. All politicians are corrupt.

_________ 9. While he was hanging by his heels 40 feet above ground, the magician Harry Houdini escaped from a straight-jacket.

_________ 10. John F. Kennedy was a handsome man.

_________ 11. Responsible for saving thousands of lives during World War II, a carrier pigeon was given a medal by the Lord Mayor of London.

_________ 12. Virginia has the perfect climate

_________ 13. Robins get drunk if they eat the red berries of the Florida holly bush.

_________ 14. When glass breaks, the cracks move at the speed of almost a mile a second.

_________ 15. Reading the daily newspaper is an important habit for good citizens to develop.

_________ 16. Everyone knows the correct way to change a tire.

Name: ______________________ Date: ______________________

_________ 17. The Rockies are the most beautiful mountains in the world.

_________ 18. Cranberries were one of the first crops exported from the American colonies.

_________ 19. It is hard to tell the difference between a fact and an opinion.

EXERCISE 12j: Many essays in this book are excellent examples of arguing an opinion. It can help your writing to notice the methods of other writers. Use your own paper for the answers to the following:

1. Refer to "The Tube Syndrome" by Pete Hamill, which appears at the beginning of Chapter One.
   a. In paragraph 1, what two techniques does the author use to introduce his argument?
   b. What argument technique does the author use in paragraph 7? In paragraph 8?
   c. What two argument techniques does the author use in paragraph 10?
   d. How does the author support his opinion in paragraphs 3 and 4? In paragraph 5?
   e. In paragraph 11 what technique does the author use to summarize his arguments?
   f. *Your reaction:*
      ... Do you think that the author gives enough support for his opinion? Why or why not?
      ... Do you think that this is an effective argument? Why or why not?

2. Refer to "What Is Intelligence, Anyway?" by Isaac Asimov, which appears at the beginning of Chapter Five.
   a. In Paragraph 1 what two techniques does the author use to introduce his argument?
   b. What argument technique does the author use in paragraph 2? In paragraphs 3 and 4?
   c. What is the author's opinion as stated in paragraph 4?
   d. In paragraphs 5 through 7, what argument technique does the author use to provide additional support for his opinion?
   e. *Your reaction:*
      ... Do you think that the author gives enough support for his opinion? Why or why not?
      ... Do you think that this is an effective argument? Why or why not?

3. Refer to "The Great American Love Affair" by William Safire, which appears at the beginning of Chapter Six.
   a. Read paragraphs 1 through 5. What technique does the author use to introduce his argument?
   b. What argument technique does the author use in paragraph 9? In paragraph 11?
   c. What two argument techniques does the author use in paragraph 13?
   d. How does the author support his opinion in paragraph 10? In paragraph 12? In paragraph 13?
   e. In what paragraphs does the author summarize his opinion?
   f. Why does the author end his argument by quoting William T. Coleman?
   g. *Your reaction:*
      ... Do you think that the author gives enough support for his opinion? Why or why not?
      ... Do you think that this is an effective argument? Why or why not?
4. Refer to "Take It Away!" by Russel J. Thomsen, which appears at the beginning of Chapter Eight.
   a. What is the author's opinion as stated in paragraph 1?
   b. At the beginning of paragraph 9 the author expands upon his opinion. What is the author's opinion as stated at the beginning of paragraph 9?
   c. In paragraphs 2 and 3 what incident does the author use to illustrate wastefulness in society?
   d. What argument technique does the author use in paragraph 6? In paragraph 9?
   e. In what paragraph does the author summarize his opinion?
   f. *Your reaction:*
      ... Do you think that the author gives enough support for his opinion? Why or why not?
      ... Do you think that this is an effective argument? Why or why not?

EXERCISE 12K: REFRESHER

1. Correct any errors in parallelism, in logical word placement, and in logical relationship between set-off sections and the sentences to which they are attached.
2. On separate paper rewrite the paragraph, rearranging the sentences in a more logical order for a process essay.

Pennsylvania State University offers a special course to help people overcome shyness. After this first success, the instructor stages a variety of other common situations such as a job interview and a cocktail party. By the end of the semester, this training will give most members of the class the skill and confidence needed to communicate effectively at school, at work, and socially. Next, the students go through a preparation period during which they think through the situation: the best, the worst, and the most likely things that could happen to them. They must develop an alternative strategy for each of these three possibilities. At this point, the instructor tries to convince the students that they have only 50 percent of the responsibility in any situation. When something goes wrong, it may be the other person's fault, not their own. To begin the training program, the instructor asks each student to select one goal. This goal might consist of asking a question in a history class or to ask someone for a date. Using the basic plans developed during the preparation period, the situations are then acted out in small groups. Now the students are ready to accomplish the goals that they selected at the beginning of the course. Because it is especially important that this first task be completed successfully, the instructor will frequently make telephone calls to smooth the way for the students. Thus, the history professor will be prepared in advance to offer encouragement when the shy student asks a question in class finally.

 Name: ____________________ Date: ____________________

SPRINGBOARDS TO WRITING

Using your knowledge of the writing process, explained on pages 12–14, write a paragraph or essay related to this chapter's central theme, *loneliness and friendship in America,* which is introduced on pages 404–411.

PREWRITING

To think of topics to write about, take the friendship test and look at the cartoon, read the essay, and answer the questions that follow each. If you prefer, select one of the writing springboards below. (All paragraph numbers refer to the essay that starts on page 406.) To develop your ideas, use the prewriting techniques described on pages 15–20.

WRITING A PARAGRAPH (For help, see the Pointers on page 31.)

1. My closest friend and I have similar (different) personalities.
2. Agree or disagree with this from paragraph 4: "... a good friend is someone who does not allow you to lean upon him or her."
3. Is it better to have a great many friends or just one or two really good friends? (See ¶ 7.)
4. It is (is not) a good idea to lend money to a friend.
5. Should a person always be truthful with a friend—even if the truth will hurt?

WRITING AN ESSAY (For help, see the Pointers on page 35.)

I In planning one of the following, try to use the technique of explaining a process. Remember to select the order that will be most effective for your purpose.

6. How to Make (Lose) Friends
7. How to Be a Good Friend
8. How to Overcome Loneliness
9. How Shyness Affects My Life
10. How to Overcome Shyness
11. How to Become a More Interesting Person

II In planning one of the following, try to use the technique of constructing a definition. Remember to decide first on a purpose for your definition, and then select the parts that will reflect your purpose.

12. What Is a Friend?
13. What Is Loneliness?
14. Being Lonely Is Not the Same As Being Alone
15. The Me Nobody Knows
16. My Friends Do (Do Not) Live Up to My Expectations of Them
17. How I Rate Myself as a Friend

III In planning one of the following, try to use the technique of arguing an opinion. Remember to support your opinion with specific facts and evidence and to include devices that have enough impact to persuade the reader to agree with you.

18. Is America a Country of Lonely People?
19. Why We Do (Do Not) Need Friends (See ¶ 19.)
20. Friendship Is (Is Not) a Complex Relationship
21. The Value of Having Friends of All Ages (See ¶ 10.)
22. Agree with this statement by the poet Kahlil Gibran: "Friendship is always a sweet responsibility, never an opportunity."
23. Should Close Friends Enter into Business Relationships?
24. A Man and a Woman Can (Cannot) Have As Close a Friendship As Two Men or Two Women Can Have
25. Agree or disagree: "The mobility of today's Americans makes it difficult for them to develop real friendships." (See ¶ 17.)
26. Agree or disagree: The fact that Americans have "a hard time making friends" is "cultural" and "starts at the moment of birth." (See ¶ 8.)

appendix

APPENDIX I: CLEAR THINKING—LOGIC

An essay—even one with proper grammar—will not be successful if it is built on faulty reasoning. You must think and write clearly, giving effective evidence to support well-thought-out ideas.

I As you read the following paragraph about the draft, pay close attention to the reasoning used to build the argument:

> I wholeheartedly disagree with Senator Claghorn's proposal to establish a universal national draft. The stupidity of the plan is apparent when one considers that the Senator has been divorced three times and is now being sued for back alimony payments by his last wife. In addition our enemies, the Russians, use this draft system, which makes me wonder if perhaps the Senator is a Communist. Instead of drafting fine young men, the government should send all of the convicted murderers to fight our wars. After all, these criminals like to kill people. This would be the democratic thing to do in the home of the free and the land of the brave.

ANALYSIS: The writer of this paragraph seems to have some very strong feelings about his subject but, unfortunately, he gives no proof to support his argument that a universal national draft is a bad idea. The Senator's marital troubles may indicate that he is not a good marriage risk, but these problems certainly have no bearing on the worth of the man's idea. Instead of discussing the plan, the writer prefers to **attack the man** who proposed it.

The writer then reasons that the plan cannot be any good because our enemies already use it. We may have ideological differences with the Russians, but that does not mean that everything they do is necessarily bad. **Guilt by association** is being used to destroy the proposal.

The counterproposal will not hold up under examination because, while it may be true that some murderers enjoy committing their crimes, it is ridiculous to assume that this is true of all killers. Thus, it is a **generalization** to say that all convicted murderers like to kill people.

Even if it were true that all murderers like to kill, too many questions have not been considered in formulating this new proposal: Can murderers be trusted? Is there a moral argument against such a plan? When dealing with a complex problem, you need to analyze and examine your subject from many points of view before coming to any conclusions. The writer, who has created a plan based only on his own personal feelings, is guilty of **oversimplifying** his solution.

The writer ends his argument by carefully linking his own proposal with democracy, freedom, and bravery—words that have good connotations for Americans. With the same purpose in mind, the writer identifies Senator Claghorn's plan as Communistic, a term that has negative connotations. Thus, the writer has tried to **feed our prejudices.**

 *Try It Out*

The following paragraph is built on some of the same confused thinking that has just been discussed. Find the errors and label each with its appropriate name. On separate paper, explain why it is wrong.

> The taking of vitamin C will protect the American people from catching the dreaded common cold. Doctors obviously agree with this because they always tell people who have colds to drink a great deal of orange or grapefruit juice, both of which are filled with health-giving vitamin C. Dr. Arthur Mometer, who conducted a research study on vitamin C, claims that the vitamin neither prevents nor cures colds. However, his claim cannot be true when one considers that he is a money-hungry quack who was recently found guilty of not paying all of his taxes. Even his own sister, Annie Mometer, was just arrested for practicing medicine without a license. Therefore, the federal government should ignore Dr. Mometer's findings and should force all food manufacturers to add large quantities of vitamin C to their products. If this is done, Americans will be forever free of the menace of the common cold.

II As you read the following paragraph about college life, pay close attention to the reasoning used to build the argument.

> College students should concentrate on having a good time and should never pay attention to intellectual growth. Studying too much can lead to serious consequences. Just last week R. T. Zank, the school bookworm, suffered a nervous breakdown right after his chemistry final. However, Sammy Swinger, the handsome football quarterback who never opens a book, is sure to succeed because he is so well liked.

ANALYSIS: The writer of this argument makes his first error in logic when he indicates that there are only two alternatives: a student spends all of his time either studying or having a good time. But there are other courses of action which have not been mentioned. For example, a student may spend part of his time studying and part of his time socializing. The situation is not as black and white as the writer's **either-or-argument** would have us believe.

The story of R. T. Zank proves only that the writer is not a very clear thinker. It is highly doubtful that studying was the sole cause of Zank's nervous breakdown. If the writer had explored the case, he probably would have discovered that Zank had some serious personal problems. Thus, a **false cause** is being used to prove the argument.

The case of Sammy Swinger falls apart under examination because the writer does not supply the proper evidence to prove that the football player will succeed. The fact that Sammy is well liked certainly does not mean that he will be successful. **Irrelevant evidence**—that is, evidence that has no logical relationship to the topic—should not be used to back up an argument.

Try It Out

The following paragraph is built on some of the same confused thinking that has just been discussed. Find the errors and label each with its appropriate name. On separate paper, explain why it is wrong.

> Loud, wild rock music is ruining the morals of today's young people. For example, my nephew, Eddie, stole a car right after attending a rock concert. Even more shocking is the fact that since the introduction of rock music to the United States, the juvenile crime rate has risen steadily each year. It is clear, then, that if rock music is not banned in this country, the young people will eventually destroy the American way of life.

III As you read the following paragraph about cigarette smoking, pay close attention to the reasoning used to build the argument:

> Cigarette smoking is certainly not harmful to health. My grandfather began smoking cigarettes when he was eleven, and he lived to be ninety-five. My Uncle Jim, who smokes four packs of cigarettes a day, is a healthy seventy-two. In addition, Mike Marvel, the ace baseball player, says that Puffo Cigarettes make him feel relaxed and refreshed before a big game. Besides, everybody smokes cigarettes so it can't be wrong.

ANALYSIS: The writer of this paragraph uses two examples to try to prove that cigarette smoking is not harmful to health. These illustrations may help to clarify the argument, but they are **inadequate evidence** because they do not prove the writer's case. Two men are not representative of the millions of people who smoke. A reputable research study using a much larger sampling would be adequate evidence to convince the reader.

The writer then makes the mistake of citing a baseball player's comment as added proof. Whenever an authority is used, one must decide if the person is an authority on the subject of the essay. Mike Marvel may know a good deal about baseball, but he does not know any more about cigarette smoking than anyone else. One might also wonder if the authority had any hidden motives for making his statement. In this case, the baseball player endorsed Puffo Cigarettes because he was being paid. Therefore, he certainly was an **inappropriate authority.**

The writer ends his argument with yet another poor attempt at proving his opinion. Although a good many people do smoke cigarettes, it is a ridiculous generalization to claim that everybody does. It is more accurate to limit the statement by saying that many people smoke cigarettes. In the same way, strong words such as "never" and "always" usually have to be reduced to "sometimes" and "often." It is important to limit an **unqualified statement** to make it more accurate.

Even it it were true that everybody smokes cigarettes, this still does not prove that smoking is not harmful to health. One hundred fifty years ago many people believed that slavery was a good thing, but that did not mean it was. The **everyone-is-doing-it argument** does not prove anything, for even the majority can be wrong.

 *Try It Out*

The following paragraph is built on some of the same confused thinking that has just been discussed. Find the errors and label each with its appropriate name. On separate paper, explain why it is wrong.

> Television programs have never been as good as they are today. "The Eaton and Chilada Show," the popular cooking program, and "Branches," the drama series based on a family tree, have both won Peabody Awards for excellence. Also, Anne Tenna, the program director of the United Broadcasting Network, announced that the quality of today's television programs is much higher than it used to be. This must be true since everybody watches so much television nowadays.

IV As you read the following paragraph about flying saucers, pay close attention to the reasoning used to build the argument:

> If flying saucers do exist, they might be dangerous to our society. Thus, we should be afraid of flying saucers, if there are such things, because they could do a good deal of harm to the people of earth. Peter, my next door neighbor, claims that he doesn't consider flying saucers dangerous. In fact, he says that he would enjoy riding in a flying saucer from another planet because he loves to ride in airplanes. Personally, I do not think that flying saucers are a danger because I do not think they even exist; after all, I have never seen one.

ANALYSIS: The writer begins by presenting the logical statement that flying saucers might be dangerous if they really exist. But instead of immediately trying to prove his statement, he merely uses new words to repeat the very same argument in the next sentence. Because the reader is just being led in a monotonous circle, this error is called **circular reasoning.**

Peter is also an illogical thinker. When Peter compares riding in a flying saucer with riding in an airplane, he forgets that, although the vehicles might be somewhat similar, there are probably some very big differences between the two. Things that are being compared must be similar in all major aspects or the result is a **false comparison.**

The argument falls apart completely with the concluding statement that flying saucers do not exist because the writer has never seen one. It is invalid to argue that something does not exist because one has **no personal knowledge** of it.

 *Try It Out*

The following paragraph is built on some of the same confused thinking that has just been discussed. Find the errors and label each with its appropriate name. On separate paper, explain why it is wrong.

> All dangerous criminals should be locked up in prison for life to prevent them from doing more harm to society. Because innocent citizens must be safeguarded, thieves, murderers, and rapists should never be released from prison. We should not put these violent criminals back on the streets only to commit more outrageous crimes. I have certainly never heard nor read about an ex-convict who did not eventually commit another serious theft or assault and end up back in prison. Indeed, dangerous criminals, like other dangerous animals, should be kept in cages forever.

EXERCISE L1: Analyze each of the following statements for its soundness of reasoning. Use your own paper for this assignment.

1. Life is just a bowl of cherries.
2. If we hired many more police officers, they would catch all of the criminals and put a complete end to crime in the United States.
3. Young people today cannot think clearly because they all take drugs.
4. Never leave a job undone.
5. The grapefruit diet really works! I ate nothing but grapefruit for two weeks and lost ten pounds.
6. Watch the continuing adventures of Superman, defender of truth, justice, and the American way.
7. Because Tom likes to tell old stories, he should be an excellent teacher.
8. Mass transportation must be greatly improved in the United States so that many more people would leave their cars at home, saving valuable gasoline. Motorists would not drive as much and thus would reduce their use of costly fuel if bus and train service were considerably improved.
9. I don't intend to ever get married because I don't know anyone who is happily married.
10. Warren G. Harding could not have been a very good President because during his marriage he had a love affair with a young woman who bore him an illegitimate child.
11. Jogging is good for the heart. My 89-year-old grandfather has been jogging regularly since he was a young man, and he has never had any heart trouble. In addition, five of my friends and I have been jogging every morning for the last five years, and we are all in the best of health.
12. Rod Steele, the famous movie actor, says in his television commercial that Jumpin' Java is the best coffee on the market today.
13. Everybody smokes marijuana these days, so why shouldn't I?
14. The government must force manufacturers to stop using man-made chemicals in the preparation of foods. Otherwise, everyone will eventually die of cancer.
15. Joe must be a good date because his father is very rich.

 Name: ______________________ *Date:* ______________

APPENDIX II: COMMON PREFIXES AND SUFFIXES

A *prefix* is a syllable which, when added to the beginning of a word, affects its meaning.

A *suffix* is a syllable which, when added to the end of a word, affects its meaning.

Being familiar with the most common prefixes and suffixes can help you to increase your vocabulary and improve your spelling.

Common Prefixes

meaning	AGAINST
anti-	antiballistic
contra-	contrary

meaning	MORE THAN
extra-	extraordinary
hyper-	hypersensitive
super-	superpatriotic
ultra-	ultraconservative

meaning	THE NEGATIVE
dis-	disagree
il-	illegal
im-	immoral
in-	inadequate
ir-	irresponsible
mis-	mistake
non-	noninvolvement
un-	unhappy

concerning numbers: meaning . . .

HALF:	semi-	semicircle
ONE:	uni-	uniform
ONE:	mono-	monologue
MANY:	poly-	polysyllable

concerning place: meaning . . .

BEFORE:	ante	anteroom
BEFORE:	pre-	predate
AFTER:	post-	postscript
BACK:	re-	return
BACK:	retro-	retrofire
UNDER:	sub-	submarine
ACROSS:	trans-	transplant
BETWEEN:	inter-	interpersonal
INSIDE:	intra-	intravenous

meaning SELF:

auto-	automobile

meaning POOR:

mal-	malnutrition

Common Suffixes

noun meaning ACT OF

-tion	segregation

noun meaning STATE OF

-hood	adulthood
-ment	estrangement
-ness	kindness
-ship	friendship
-tude	solitude
-dom	freedom

adjective meaning ABLE TO BE

-able	comfortable
-ible	compatible

adjective meaning FULL OF

-ate	fortunate
-ful	tactful
-ous	pompous
-y	gloomy

adjective meaning NONE

-less	penniless

verb meaning TO MAKE, TO PERFORM

-ate	integrate
-ify	unify
-ize	computerize

EXERCISE PS1: To determine the correct prefix for a word, you will often have to consult the dictionary. In this exercise, however, the correct prefix is supplied. Form the following words:

	Using the prefix:	*Form:*	
1.	un	not happy	1. ____________
2.	il	not legal	2. ____________
3.	semi	half sweet	3. ____________
4.	post	after being a graduate	4. ____________
5.	non	not absorbent	5. ____________
6.	in	not decent	6. ____________
7.	anti	against labor	7. ____________
8.	uni	one sex	8. ____________
9.	im	not patient	9. ____________
10.	dis	not organized	10. ____________
11.	hyper	excessively tense	11. ____________

 Name: ____________ *Date:* ____________

12.	sub	below standard	12. ______________
13.	ir	not resistible	13. ______________
14.	mal	poorly adjusted	14. ______________
15.	mis	not behaved	15. ______________

EXERCISE PS2: For each word given, give a general definition. (If you are unsure of a meaning, consult your dictionary.) Next, briefly explain how the prefix influences the word's meaning.

1. automatic: ______________
2. retroactive: ______________
3. supersonic: ______________
4. premature: ______________
5. transport: ______________
6. monorail: ______________
7. polyrhythm: ______________
8. reconstruct: ______________
9. ultramodern: ______________
10. intramural (games): ______________
11. international: ______________
12. extracurricular: ______________
13. contraindicated: ______________
14. antedate: ______________

EXERCISE PS3: Construct each word by referring to the list of common suffixes and, if necessary, the dictionary.

1. noun: state of being sad — 1. ____________
2. noun: act of starving — 2. ____________
3. noun: state of being false — 3. ____________
4. adjective: full of compassion — 4. ____________
5. adjective: able to profit — 5. ____________
6. adjective: having no fault — 6. ____________
7. verb: to make liquid — 7. ____________
8. verb: to make liberal — 8. ____________
9. noun: state of being a kin — 9. ____________
10. noun: state of being refined — 10. ____________
11. adjective: full of room — 11. ____________
12. adjective: able to be resisted — 12. ____________
13. noun: state of being grateful — 13. ____________
14. noun: state of being wise — 14. ____________
15. adjective: full of fancy — 15. ____________
16. adjective: full of anxiety — 16. ____________
17. verb: to make a nominee — 17. ____________

 Name: ____________ Date: ____________

A PREFIX-SUFFIX SPELLING NOTE. Are you ever unsure of whether to use one or two *l*'s in *generally* or one or two *s*'s in *misspell*? The following principle concerning prefixes and suffixes will help you to avoid this type of confusion.

When the prefix ends with the same letter that begins the main part of the word, be sure to include both letters.

When the suffix begins with the same letter that ends the main part of the word, be sure to include both letters.

 *Try It Out*

Create a new word by joining each prefix or suffix with its main word.

careful + ly = ______________ clean + ness = ______________

re + elect = ______________ inter + relationship = ______________

un + noticed = ______________ dis + service = ______________

Here are some examples:

dis + satisfied = di*ss*atisfied im + moral = i*mm*oral
inter + racial = inte*rr*acial ir + relevant = i*rr*elevant
mis + state = mi*ss*tate il + logical = i*ll*ogical

 *Try It Out*

Create a new word by joining each prefix or suffix with its main word.

over + rule = ______________ mis + inform = ______________

dis + appear = ______________ ir + rational = ______________

im + mature = ______________ il + literate = ______________

Name: ______________ *Date:* ______________

EXERCISE PS4: Fill in the missing letters in each word using either one or two of the letters indicated. If necessary, refer back to the list of common prefixes and suffixes.

1. *e* r__valuate
2. *l* i__egal
3. *b* su__asement
4. *n* i__appropriate
5. *m* i__ortal
6. *r* ove__ipe
7. *n* u__ecessary
8. *l* coo__y
9. *n* plai__ess
10. *r* inte__eaction
11. *s* mi__interpret
12. *s* di__approve
13. *l* idea__y
14. *r* inte__act
15. *n* outspoke__ess
16. *l* i__egible
17. *r* i__egular
18. *e* r__xamine
19. *s* mi__pelling
20. *s* di__imilar

 Name: ____________________ Date: ____________________

APPENDIX III: TOPICS FOR WRITING

Here is a list of places in this book where you can find many topics for writing. For help in writing a topic sentence, see the Pointers on page 24. For help in writing a paragraph, see the Pointers on page 31. For help in writing an essay, see the Pointers on page 35.

PARAGRAPH TOPICS

ESSAY TOPICS

APPENDIX IV: STUDY AIDS

Writing Progress

Directions: Each time your instructor returns a piece of your writing, record his or her comments in the appropriate spaces below. In this way, you will be able to keep track of your progress and concentrate on those writing skills that still need improvement.

DATE AND TITLE OF WRITING	STRONG POINTS OF WRITING	SKILLS NEEDING IMPROVEMENT	INSTRUCTOR'S OTHER COMMENTS

 Name: ______________________ Date: ______________________

DATE AND TITLE OF WRITING	STRONG POINTS OF WRITING	SKILLS NEEDING IMPROVEMENT	INSTRUCTOR'S OTHER COMMENTS

Name: ______________________ Date: ______________________

DATE AND TITLE OF WRITING	STRONG POINTS OF WRITING	SKILLS NEEDING IMPROVEMENT	INSTRUCTOR'S OTHER COMMENTS

 Name: ______________________ *Date:* ______________

Individualized Spelling List

Directions: On this chart list every word that you misspell, following the directions in each column. After you have listed fifteen or more words, try to discover the pattern of your errors. If you have trouble finding a clear pattern, ask your instructor for some help. Most important, be sure to study the words on your list until you know how to spell them correctly. For several useful suggestions, see the Methods to Improve Your Spelling, in Chapter One.

WORD (spelled correctly)	WORD (spelled correctly with trouble spot circled)	PATTERN OF ERROR

Name: ____________________ Date: ____________________

WORD (spelled correctly)	WORD (spelled correctly with trouble spot circled)	PATTERN OF ERROR

 Name: ______________________ Date: ______________

WORD (spelled correctly)	WORD (spelled correctly with trouble spot circled)	PATTERN OF ERROR

Name: ______________________ Date: ______________________

Conferences with Instructor

DATE	MATERIAL COVERED	SUGGESTIONS	ASSIGNMENT (if any)

DATE	MATERIAL COVERED	SUGGESTIONS	ASSIGNMENT (if any)

Name: ______________________ Date: ______________________

DATE	MATERIAL COVERED	SUGGESTIONS	ASSIGNMENT (if any)

 Name: ______________________ *Date:* ______________

APPENDIX V: INDIVIDUALIZED STUDY PROGRAM

Grammar and Mechanics

Directions: On this chart you can keep a record of your work on grammar and mechanics exercises. You may work on your own, or you may work according to the assignments given by your teacher in class or in a writing laboratory.

For your convenience, the list of topics is in alphabetical order. Terminology is that used in the book. If an exercise number has an asterisk (*) following it, that exercise deals with more than one topic. In addition to the work listed below, brief "Try It Out" exercises occur frequently throughout the instructional material in this book.

TOPIC	EXERCISE	NUMBER OF ANSWERS	SCORE	COMMENTS, if any
apostrophe	8c	70		
capitalization	5c	95		
	8h*	may vary		
changing *y* to *i*	3c	20		
comma	8e	126–134		
	8f	may vary		
comma-splice sentences	3g*	20		
	3h*	10		
commonly confused words	6c	46		
	6d	27		
coordination	4e	10		
	4f	10		
	4g	7		
	4h	10		
	4l*	10		
(sentence combining)	4o*	15		
(sentence combining)	4p*	15		
doubling (spelling)	12c	20		
dropping the final *e*	11c	20		

Name: ______________________ Date: ______________________

TOPIC	EXERCISE	NUMBER OF ANSWERS	SCORE	COMMENTS, if any
-ed endings on verbs	5l	29		
	5m	10		
	5n	10		
	5o	20		
	5p	67		
ie and *ei* (spelling)	7c	20		
informal language	10h	15		
	10i	30		
irregular verbs	5i	44		
	5j	10		
	5k	10		
logical relationship between "set-off" section and main sentence	11j	10		
logical word placement for precise meaning	11h	may vary		
	11i	10		
parallelism	11e	10		
	11f	10		
	11g	20		
plurals	9c	20		
	9d	25		
	9e	74		
pronoun agreement	6j	23		
	6k*	17		
pronoun choice	6g	44		
	6h	25		
	6i	20		
pronoun reference and consistency	6l	25		
	6m	27		
	6n	20		
punctuation (all except the comma)	8g	may vary		
	8h*	may vary		

 Name: ____________________ Date: ____________________

TOPIC	EXERCISE	NUMBER OF ANSWERS	SCORE	COMMENTS, if any
run-on sentences	3g*	20		
	3h*	10		
-s endings on verbs	5e	15		
	5f	20		
	6k	17		
sentence fragments	3e	20		
	3f	10		
sound-alikes (homonyms)	2c	33		
subject-verb agreement	5g	20		
	5h	20		
	6k*	17		
subordination	4i	10		
	4j	5		
	4k	10		
	4l*	10		
	4m	5		
(a special case of)	4n	10		
(sentence combining)	4o*	15		
(sentence combining)	4p*	15		
to split or not to split	10c	40		
using the right word (diction)	10e	15		
	10f	20		
	10g	18		

Rhetoric

Directions: On this chart you can keep a record of your work on rhetoric exercises. You may work on your own, or you may work according to the assignments given by your teacher in class or in a writing laboratory.

For your convenience, the list of topics is in alphabetical order. Terminology is that used in the book. If an exercise number has an asterisk (*) following it, that exercise deals with more than one topic. In addition to the work listed below, brief "Try It Out" exercises occur frequently throughout the instructional material in this book.

TOPIC	EXERCISE	SCORE OR GRADE	COMMENTS (if any)
concluding paragraph	7h*		
	7h*		
essay forms: arguing an opinion	12i		
	12j		
constructing a definition	12g		
	12h		
explaining a process	12e		
	12f*		
introductory paragraph	7h*		
	7i*		
	12f*		
key words—deliberate repetition	9j		
	9k		
	9l		
	9m		
main body idea patterns	7e		
	7f		
ordering of details in a paragraph: chronological	2l		
	2m		
importance	2j		
	2k		
location	2n		
	2o		

Name: ______________________ Date: ______________________

TOPIC	EXERCISE	SCORE OR GRADE	COMMENTS (if any)
paragraph development by: comparison and contrast	2f		
definition	2e		
examples	1l		
facts	1k		
incident, anecdote or story	1m		
S-N-S	2g		
topic sentence	1e		
	1f		
	1g		
	1h		
	1i		
	1j		
words of transition	9g		
	9h		
	9i		

Name: ______________________ Date: ______________________

GENERAL INDEX

d

e

f

g

h

i

j

k

l

m

n

o

p

q

r

s

t

u

v

w

y